DEVELOPING PROGRAMS FOR THE EDUCATIONALLY DISADVANTAGED

A. Harry Passow, editor

Teachers College Press
Teachers College, Columbia University
New York, New York

Manufactured in the United States of America

CONTRIBUTORS

VIRGINIA F. ALLEN is Lecturer in Languages and Literature at Teachers College, Columbia University.

HARRY BEILIN is Professor of Education and Psychology at Brooklyn College of the City University of New York.

DAN W. DODSON is the Director of the Center for Human Relations at New York University.

ELIZABETH M. EDDY is Director of the Urban Study Bureau at the University of Florida at Gainesville.

DAVID L. ELLIOTT is Assistant Professor of Education, School of Education, University of California at Berkeley.

DEBORAH ELKINS is Associate Professor of Education at Queens College of the City University of New York.

MARIO FANTINI is Program Associate at the Ford Foundation and the Fund for the Advancement of Education.

JOHN H. FISCHER is President of Teachers College, Columbia University.

REGINA GOFF is Assistant Commissioner, Office of the Disadvantaged and Handicapped, U. S. Office of Education.

MIRIAM L. GOLDBERG is Professor of Psychology and Education and Director of the Urban Education Project at Teachers College, Columbia University.

ALBERT J. HARRIS is Professor of Education and Director of the Office of Research and Evaluation in the Division of Teacher Education of the City University of New York.

ROBERT D. HESS is Associate Professor, Committee on Human Development and Project Director of the Urban Child Study Center at the University of Chicago.

EDWARD J. MEADE, JR. is a Program Associate at the Ford Foundation and the Fund for the Advancement of Education.

A. HARRY PASSOW is Professor of Education and Chairman of the Committee on Urban Education, Teachers College, Columbia University.

FRANK RIESSMAN is Professor of Educational Sociology at New York University.

VIRGINIA C. SHIPMAN is Assistant Professor, Committee on Human Development and Research Associate of the Urban Child Study Center at the University of Chicago.

MILDRED BEATTY SMITH is Coordinator of Curriculum Services in the Flint Community Schools, Flint, Michigan.

ABRAHAM J. TANNENBAUM is Professor of Education, Teachers College, Columbia University.

GERALD WEINSTEIN is Consultant for the Fund for the Advancement of Education.

CONTENTS

TEACHING THE DISADVANTAGED: A FOREWORD

A. Harry Passow

A good many educational writings use the launching of Sputnik as the baseline event which either triggered or accelerated the current wave of educational reform and the reassessment of talent development practices. That baseline date was only a decade ago. Even more recent is the concern with the plight of the disadvantaged and with the overall quality of education in depressed areas. It has been less than a half dozen years since energies were mobilized on many fronts toward achieving the long-voiced goal of "providing equality of opportunity for all."

At the conclusion of a conference in 1962, it was observed:

> Educationally, the gaps are awesome in our understanding of the factors whose total is cultural deprivation and its consequences. What are the effects of various social and psychological factors on the attitudes of different groups toward the schools and toward education? The importance of looking at the problem in terms of its educational, sociological, psychological, economic, political, health, welfare and housing dimensions is increasingly clear. (Passow, 1963, p. 351)

In the intervening years, despite considerable expenditure of effort and money, an honest appraisal must reach the conclusion that progress has been limited and much remains to be done. Program development, research, and experimentation have mushroomed, spurred on by federal legislation and support for the war on poverty and the attainment of civil rights. Some of the comprehensive planning and cooperative efforts of school and nonschool agencies are beginning to pay off. Significantly, the intensity of the search for simplistic solutions is beginning to wane, although scapegoats are still being sought. There can be little question that research has provided a good many insights into the complex dimensions of the problem as well as leads to solutions. We know far more than we did a few years ago about the nature of the disadvantaged and the educational dilemmas that we face, even though we have not yet fully applied this knowledge, nor do we find it adequate.

There have been a number of important federal acts containing provisions for direct or indirect aid to those who are economically impoverished or discriminated against because of race or ethnic origins, beginning with the Vocational Education Act of 1963, which was designed to strengthen and extend all aspects of vocational and technical education, with specific attention to certain disadvantaged groups. The Civil Rights Act of 1964 provided subsidies to school personnel for evolving and implementing plans for desegregation and finding ways to cope with emergent problems. The Economic Opportunity Act of 1964 promoted a Job Corps, work-study programs, urban and rural community action programs, and adult basic education. In addition, the Act made funds available for remedial programs, preschool and day care centers, tutoring, materials production, and teacher education. The 1965 revision of the National Defense Education Act provided for strengthening instruction, extending guidance, using newer media more effectively, developing vocational education, and training teachers for working with the educationally disadvantaged. Several parts of the Higher Education Act of 1965 deal with teacher education for classroom and supervisory personnel in disadvantaged area schools.

The most important piece of federal legislation, insofar as the schools are concerned, has been the Elementary and Secondary Education Act of 1964. Title I of ESEA was specifically concerned with the disadvantaged, and declared it to be "the policy of the United States to provide financial assistance . . . to local educational agencies serving areas with concentrations of children from low-income families. . . ." Other sections of ESEA are applicable to programs designed to "contribute particularly to meeting the special educational needs of the educationally deprived children." Thus, perhaps more than any other agency, the schools have been called on to play an increasingly aggressive leadership role in overcoming poverty and providing for civil rights for all. While such a role is clearly "on the side of the angels," experiences over the past few years have indicated that there are major issues to be resolved and problems to be overcome. Good will is needed, but it is not enough.

Compensatory and Remedial Education

A proliferation of programs has occurred in the past few years, ranging from Project Head Start for preschool children to Upward Bound for precollege students. The summer 1965 Project Head Start involved more than a half-million children in more than 13,000 centers located in 2500 communities across the nation. These programs were of varied quality – some merely baby-sitting, but others well designed to overcome cognitive and experiential deficits.

One survey (Gordon and Wilkerson, 1966) turned up compensatory education programs in 108 communities. For those programs for which beginning dates were available, 95 per cent had been initiated since 1960 and 43 (almost 40 per cent) since the school year 1963–64. Gordon and Wilkerson noted that "data subsequently received have doubled the number of cities participating and have generally related to programs of more recent vintage. Moreover, the pace is accelerating . . ." (Gordon and Wilkerson, 1966, pp. 31–32). They observe in their critique of compensatory programs that the majority of such programs could be described as "successful" if the criterion for judgment is the enthusiasm of those initiating such efforts. But, Gordon and Wilkerson argue, something more than enthusiasm is needed, and valid assessment studies are all too scarce. Evaluative studies that have been conducted tend "to show ambiguous outcomes affecting unknown or amorphous educational and social variables." As a consequence, most of the critical questions about how to provide educationally for the disadvantaged not only remain unanswered but, for the most part, have not even been asked. While enthusiasm and good will continue to grow, we are just beginning to apply theoretical analyses, research findings, and practical field experiences – most of them not having been evaluated – to the development of suitable educational programs.

Racial Imbalance and Isolation

A major component of the forces affecting the educational attainments of the disadvantaged has been segregation and racial imbalance. The Civil Rights Act of 1964 required the U.S. Commissioner of Education to conduct a survey and report to the President of the United States concerning the "lack of availability of equal educational opportunities for individuals by reason of race, color, religion, or national origin . . . ." The study addressed itself to four significant questions: (1) the extent to which the racial and ethnic groups are segregated in the public schools; (2) the extent to which the schools offer equal educational opportunities to the various groups; (3) student attainment, as measured by performance on standardized achievement tests, in the various schools; and (4) the relationships between student achievement and the kinds of schools they attend. The study provides data of a nature, on a scale, seldom seen before. The findings and the conclusions reported in *Equality of Educational Opportunity* (the so-called Coleman Report, 1966) provide educators, behavioral and social scientists, politicians, and the general public with considerable grist for each of their mills. Racial isolation is widespread, the survey found:

> The great majority of American children attend schools that are largely segregated – that is, where almost all of their fellow students are of the same racial background as they are. Among minority groups, Negroes are by far the most segregated. Taking all groups, however, white children are most segregated. Almost 80 percent of all white pupils in 1st grade and 12th grade attend schools that are from 90 to 100 percent white. And 97 percent at grade 1, and 99 percent at grade 12, attend schools that are 50 percent or more white. (U.S. Office of Education, 1966, p. 3)

Other data establish the same high degree of isolation with respect to teachers and other professional staff members. As for academic achievement, the findings indicate that the minority pupil suffers most from schools of low quality: "Whites and, to a lesser extent, oriental Americans are less affected one way or the other by the quality of schools than are minority pupils." "The extent to which a pupil feels he has some control over his own destiny" appeared to have a stronger relationship to achievement than all other school factors put together. For Negroes, this factor seemed related to the proportion of whites in the schools—Negroes in schools with a higher proportion of whites had a greater sense of control.

Hard on the heels of the Coleman Report came the U.S. Commission on Civil Rights report entitled *Racial Isolation in the Public Schools* (1967). Focusing on the Negroes as constituting the largest minority group, the report reviews the consequences of racial isolation on disparaties in educational attainment between Negro and white students. Rejecting "years of school completed" as a valid measure of educational attainment, the Commission found that, while Negro and white pupils begin at about the same point with respect to verbal ability and reading achievement in first grade, there is an ever-widening gap as they go through school.

> By the time twelfth grade is reached, the average white student performs at or slightly below the twelfth grade level, but the average Negro student performs below the ninth grade level. Thus, years of school completed has an *entirely different meaning for Negroes than whites.* (U.S. Commission on Civil Rights, 1967, p. 14, editor's emphasis)

Moreover, the differences in educational achievement between Negro and white Americans, the Commission pointed out, has been accompanied by increasing social and economic disparities between the two groups—not that there have not been significant improvements for the Negro in the past two decades, but that the relative situation has not been drastically altered—"the closer the promise of equality seems to come, the further it slips away."

The Commission concedes that the causes of racial isolation are complex and that isolation is self-perpetuating. It is intense in cities throughout the nation, large or small, north or south, regardless of the ratio of whites to nonwhites. The Commission finds that racial imbalance has been increasing, whether in the rural south, the central city, or even the suburbs.

The assessment of the outcomes of compensatory education programs in schools isolated by social class or race leads the Commission to conclude that such programs have not been very effective.

> The evidence indicates that Negro children attending desegregated schools that do not have compensatory education programs

perform better than Negro children in racially isolated schools with such programs. . . . Compensatory educational programs have been of limited effectiveness because they have attempted to solve problems that stem, in large part, from racial and social isolation in schools which themselves are isolated by racial and social class. (U.S. Commission on Civil Rights, 1967, p. 205)

While not rejecting remedial techniques completely, the Commission seems convinced that compensatory education programs are very unlikely to improve the educational attainments of Negro students in isolated schools. Their recommendations are for strong federal action to eliminate racial isolation (1) by establishing uniform standards of balance; (2) by providing states with financial and technical assistance and encouraging flexibility in developing remedies; (3) by assisting with new construction of facilities and upgrading the quality of education in all schools; and (4) by preventing discrimination in housing and urban renewal programs.

The two reports have raised as many questions as they have answered. Some critics have quarreled with the data collection, the research designs, or the interpretations of the findings. Others have accepted the findings as reported but reject the solutions proposed as inappropriate and unworkable. There is general agreement that both reports provide the researcher, the practitioner, and the legislator with empirical data never before available. The analyses make possible increased understanding of the relationship between educational outcomes and a variety of social and psychological factors within the classroom, the school, the family, and the community. It is quite clear that the school cannot develop an educational program without resolving, or at least dealing with, problems of segregation and imbalance—racial and economic, de facto and de jure. It is equally clear that problems of housing, employment opportunities, family life, and community organization have a direct bearing on the school's basic instructional functions.

Toward Better Educational Planning

In Education in Depressed Areas (1963, p. 66), Wayland questioned the use of the concept of "cultural deprivation," suggesting that "more careful analysis is needed to sort out those features which are functions of class position and of immigrant status from those which are uniquely a function of the Negro subculture." He saw new standards arising from past successes, yielding higher aspirations. Wayland summarized these new standards as follows:

Start the child in school earlier; keep him in school more and more months of the year; retain all who start to school for twelve to fourteen years; expect him to learn more and more during this period, in wider and wider areas of human experience, under the guidance of a teacher, who has had more and more training, and who is assisted by more and more specialists, who provide an ever-expanding range of services, with access to more and more detailed personal records, based on more and more carefully validated tests. (Wayland, 1963, p. 67)

Thus, by retaining larger numbers of students for more years, the heterogeneity of the student population has increased, with the learning disabilities and adjustment problems of some students becoming more sharply visible. While program modifications tend to fall into a limited number of patterns, we appear to be moving in the healthy direction of inquiring, testing, and refining, rather than seeking the panacea or doctrinaire proposal. While improved reading scores by disadvantaged youth are certainly desirable, such a goal is too limited. What is needed is an educational program which would open the doors for continuing learning. As Gordon and Wilkerson point out:

> Even though we do not know how best to educate socially disadvantaged children, we cannot afford to wait for better answers to come. The presence of these children in our schools, the demands of increasingly impatient communities, and the requirements of an increasingly complex society demand that we apply the best that is currently available even as we seem to improve. (Gordon and Wilkerson, 1966, p. 179)

Teaching the Disadvantaged

The seventeen papers which follow are designed to provide some better insights into the problems of teaching the disadvantaged. The papers are of several kinds: some analytical, some descriptive, and some propositional. They are grouped as follows, in the six parts of the book.

Part I consists of three papers. A. Harry Passow and David L. Elliott provide the setting, with a discussion of the nature and needs of the disadvantaged. Mario Fantini and Gerald Weinstein set forth a curriculum model aimed at guiding the selection of content for an education relevant for the disadvantaged. Miriam L. Goldberg explores the difficulties in evaluating compensatory educational programs, urging that assessment procedures be built into planning from the start, in order to extend our knowledge of what constitutes effective curricular modifications and procedures.

Part II includes three papers describing compensatory programs from different vantage points. Frank Riessman provides some additional thoughts on a necessary revolution in education, suggesting some techniques which might be included in a synthesis of promising practices. Regina Goff looks back on the first year operation of Title I of the Elementary and Secondary Education Act and sees much of the promise of this legislation coming to fruition. Mildred Beatty Smith describes one school system's efforts to bring home and school resources together to upgrade the attainment of disadvantaged children.

Part III consists of three papers that relate research to necessary changes in practice. Robert B. Hess and Virginia C. Shipman tie maternal attitudes toward school and schooling to the "educability" of disadvantaged children, proposing some techniques for altering mothers' views as a means of socializing the child and preparing him for the formal school experience. Harry Beilin bases curriculum development for the disadvantaged pupil on an understanding of the cognitive strengths and weaknesses which the disadvantaged child may bring with him to the classroom. Deborah Elkins explores teaching strategies which cast the teacher in the role of mediator of learning.

Part IV includes a paper by Albert J. Harris, in which he discusses reading instruction for the disadvantaged and reports on the CRAFT project, where approaches to beginning reading were compared. Virginia F. Allèn, stressing the importance of standard English for occupational and social mobility, discusses techniques and procedures for teaching English as a second dialect, or even a second language. Elizabeth Eddy analyzes the way beginning teachers are inducted into the inner-city school and proposes changes in preservice teacher preparation as well as the first years of active service.

In Part V, Edward J. Meade, Jr. criticizes present programs for vocational and technical education and argues for major changes in the so-called general curriculum as a step toward improvement in this area. Abraham J. Tannenbaum discusses the phenomenon of the school dropout, reviewing a half-century of research and questioning the basic assumptions which underlie school procedures presently aimed at pupil retention. In a second article, Tannenbaum describes the educational programs of Mobilization for Youth, Inc., one of the forerunners of present-day antipoverty programs.

Part VI consists of two articles related to segregation and racial imbalance. John H. Fischer analyzes the issues related to racial balance, especially in the de facto segregated schools of the large urban school system. In the final article, Dan W. Dodson sets forth his views on power and powerlessness as an issue at the heart of education, employability, and social mobility.

One cannot argue with the flat conclusion of the Panel on Educational Research and Development that "by all known criteria, the majority of urban and rural slum schools are failures." In terms of conventional means of assessing scholastic attainment and the traditional goals of public education, we are just beginning to provide adequately for the disadvantaged. These papers call attention to some of the significant dimensions of the school's role in providing equal educational opportunities for all children. They remind us that "doing more of the same harder" is not likely to provide the educational breakthroughs now needed. They remind us also that we need not start from scratch but that a considerable body of research and experience already exists which needs to be synthesized, interpreted, and applied.

New concepts of educational programs are demanded, new policies, arrangements of resources, modifications of the curriculum, and—above all—a new relationship of the school to the community, family, and neighborhood. No longer can the school remain aloof and isolated, dealing only with its intramural problems. Nor can the school, out of its feeling of guilt, wage a unilateral campaign against all the problems of society. The school alone can hardly solve the problems of poverty and misery, of strife and tension, of apathy and alienation—even though some call on it to do so. But, the school can rescue the disadvantaged child from hopelessness by opening unexplored opportunities for him. This is a role which is beyond dispute for the public school—it is its life work.

A. HARRY PASSOW
Professor of Education

Teachers College, Columbia University
May, 1967

DEVELOPING PROGRAMS FOR THE EDUCATIONALLY DISADVANTAGED

A. Harry Passow and David P. Elliott suggest that in the new lexicon converging around the population they call the "disadvantaged" no one term really describes these many groups and individuals. They summarize the characteristics of the disadvantaged as a group, cautioning the reader that exceptions abound, since a composite portrait seldom fits any individual. Other writers have argued that any label leads to a stereotyping, which can be only harmful. However, the authors believe that labels in and of themselves neither create conditions nor alleviate them, nor dissolve them.

The argument is advanced that there is a substantial population experiencing severe academic retardation despite an apparently normal range of scholastic aptitude. The fact of such academic retardation is no longer questioned; the reason for its existence and the basis for its progressive nature are at issue. Two viewpoints are current: the "educational deprivation" argument (a prejudiced school system deliberately creates "programed retardation"), as opposed to the "social deprivation" explanation (early experiential and environmental forces sharply curtail development).

THE NATURE AND NEEDS OF THE EDUCATIONALLY DISADVANTAGED

A. Harry Passow
David P. Elliott

While tending to side with the environmentalist viewpoint, Passow and Elliott do not deny the existence of conditions within some schools which do stunt the growth of the students and extend the vicious cycle of poverty and insufficient education.

The writers approve of the admonition against confusing difference with defect, pointing to cultural and socioeconomic differences that represent strengths of significant value in educational planning. To understand the specific disabilities as well as the strengths in the disadvantaged population, Passow and Elliott propose a refinement of diagnostic tools. Beyond the platitude of "meeting each child's needs," they urge the development of procedures which will take children from where they are to where they ought to be — if they are to participate effectively

1

in today's society. A five-part framework for research and development is proposed, which stresses strength rather than weakness, and success rather than disability.

Finally, through exploring some of the dimensions of the instructional process — curriculum, content, materials, teaching strategies, and staff deployment — they acknowledge that the school is one of many forces which affect the lives and future of the disadvantaged population. Admitting that it is not all-powerful does not justify abandoning the school's central role as catalyst in the fight against poverty, segregation, and alienation. As in the past, the school is the strongest and most visible force for overcoming "the spiral of futility" and for introducing children into society's mainstream. For this generation's poor, the school must become the hope that it was for generations of immigrants before. However, the school cannot serve the new poor precisely as it did earlier generations, but must adapt itself to new conditions and new counterforces.

We must open the doors of opportunity. We must equip our people to walk through these doors.

President Lyndon B. Johnson

December 10, 1964

THE NATURE AND NEEDS OF THE EDUCATIONALLY DISADVANTAGED

A. Harry Passow
and
David L. Elliott*

The term *disadvantaged* is one of a number of labels being pinned to a population suffering from a cultural and economic deprivation that does not "attune them to the demands and opportunities of modern life" (Educational Policies Commission, 1965, p. 2). Other terms in a new lexicon include: *culturally deprived, socially disadvantaged, inner-city child, slum dweller, minority pupil, ghetto youth, educationally deficient, in-migrant, undereducated,* and *underachiever.* None of these terms is widely accepted. Each word operationally indicates a population for whom current planning efforts—educational, legislative, social, economic—are being made. Implicit in each term is a hint of those factors that may contribute to the individual's disadvantage. The ethnic and racial composition tends to reflect the minority groups—especially Negro, Puerto Rican, Mexican, American Indian, and mountain white—but the disadvantaged may belong to the majority in society. Nor is the population confined to the inner-city slum. The problem spills out beyond the central city to the suburban environs and marginal rural areas as well. Most of the disadvantaged are United States born and, with a few exceptions, are English-speaking, although some expose severe regional dialect problems. Many disadvantaged are recent migrants from rural areas to metropolitan centers. Probably the common denominator of the heterogeneous disadvantaged population is poverty—economic poverty with its related social, cultural, psychological concomitants. Misleading are such terms as *culturally deprived* and *culturally disadvantaged,* since both imply a value judgment: if a group departs from the majority pattern, has it, then, *no* culture?

The problems of the disadvantaged stem from poverty and unemployment; segregation, discrimination, and lack of opportunity in housing and employment, as well as in education; discontinuities with the "dominant" culture, rising out of differences in life style, child-rearing practices, and skills for urban living; and inadequate educational attainment essential for participation in a technical society. The Baltimore Area Health and Welfare Council (1962, p. 3) describes its disadvantaged as follows:

Many do not understand, or are not in contact with, modern urban living.

---

*This chapter was prepared for the Sixty-Sixth Yearbook, Part I, of the National Society for the Study of Education, published by the Society, 1967.

Many are participants in subcultures, the values and customs of which are different from urban middle-class values and experiences.

Many, particularly children and youth, suffer from the disorganizing impact of mobility, transiency, and minority group status.

Many have educational and cultural handicaps arising from backgrounds of deprivation.

Many are members of families with many problems: divorced, deserted, unemployed, chronically sick, mentally ill, retarded, delinquent.

Many lack motivation or capacity to cope with their problem or to improve their situations.

Most lack opportunities or motivation to become responsible citizens for the maintenance or improvement of their neighborhood or community.

From the school's viewpoint, this is the population whose children exhibit the most severe scholastic retardation, the highest dropout rate (exceeding 50 per cent), the least participation in higher education (probably under 5 per cent). Schools in the inner city, where the disadvantaged are concentrated, are usually described as a pulsing tangle characterized by academic retardation, pupil and staff transiency, racial imbalance, alienation, personnel and staff shortages, overcrowding, and general inadequacy of appropriate resources. It is this population, still not clearly defined except in terms of socioeconomic and minority group status, that has again forced schools to face the question posed by the Educational Policies Commission (1965, p. 2) as to whether they are up to the "weighty task of giving life to the great ideal of educational opportunity for the varied children of a heterogeneous people."

Scholastic retardation results from various handicaps, many of them recognized years ago. However, scholastic retardation and academic failure may hobble children who do not show any of the "standard" handicaps and neurological impairments. These may gain no benefit from special provisions such as those existing for the mentally retarded. Despite an apparently normal range of scholastic aptitude, the disadvantaged group does not achieve at normal levels. Coming most often from poverty-stricken homes, living in depressed-area ghettos of cities large and small, this segment of the population constitutes the disadvantaged group of concern to the schools. These are the pupils who are straining school programs, especially those of the city systems. In this population, as the children grow older, academic retardation mounts, becoming more and more difficult to reverse; early school withdrawal is common, with youngsters emerging unprepared for our changing technical society.

The inferior educational attainment of disadvantaged pupils has been documented relatively well; the *why* of retardation is still at issue. Educational deprivation as opposed to social deprivation is a current controversy. Proponents of the former explanation blame inept teachers and guidance counselors for academic retardation in depressed areas. The latter explanation attributes underachievement to experiential deficits in early childhood. The resolution of this issue, or at least one's attitude toward it, determines how the nature and needs of the disadvantaged are perceived. Kenneth Clark, for example, rejects the concept that cultural deprivation leads to cognitive deficits. He advises school staffs to look to their own prejudices to track down the learning difficulties of pupils. He asks:

> To what extent are the contemporary social deprivation theories merely substituting notions of environmental immutability and fatalism for earlier notions of biologically determined educational unmodifiability? To what extent do these theories obscure more basic reasons for the educational retardation of lower-status children? To what extent do they offer acceptable and desired alibis for the educational default: the fact that these children by and large, do not learn because those who are charged with the responsibility of teaching them do not believe they can learn, do not expect that they can learn, and do not act toward them in ways which help them to learn? (Clark, 1965a, p. 31)

While recognizing and deploring the impoverished conditions and pathologies of ghetto life, supporters of the educational deprivation theory explain inferior scholastic performance not in terms of any deficits pupils might bring into the classroom setting, but rather in terms of ineffective and inefficient teaching by a rejecting staff. As a consequence, they perceive the inner-city schools as a scene of educational atrophy and class struggle. Clark concludes:

> The evidence so far very strongly suggests that these children will learn if they are taught and they will not learn if they are approached as if they cannot learn. . . . if children, poor children or Negro children or immigrant children are taught, accepted, respected and approached as if they are human beings, the average performance of these children may approach, and eventually reach the norm performance of other human beings who are so taught. (Clark, 1965b, pp. 41–42)

Different interpretation has been provided by other researchers and practitioners. Martin Deutsch, for instance, sees minority group and class status hurting the lower-class child, since he comes to the school poorly prepared to produce what the school requires, with the result that initial failures are almost inevitable, and the experience becomes negatively rather than positively reinforced. Deutsch depicts as crucial unequal

5

experiences between lower- and middle-class children and calls teachers poorly trained to understand and cope with cultural variations.

> School is an experience which for children in the experimental group [primarily Negro, lower-class children] is discontinuous with the value, preparation, and experiences they receive from their homes and particular community; it represents society's demands that they bridge social class orientations for a few hours a day, five days a week. No catalyst is provided for this transition, and few plans have been made to facilitate the child's daily journey across the chasm. (Deutsch, 1960, p. 3)

While not minimizing or ignoring the importance of effective teaching, spokesmen for the cultural assault argue that the educator must comprehend the nature of the disadvantaged child as a complex phenomenon shaped by impoverished environments. Youngsters and their parents lead marginal economic existences, which leave parents little time for stimulating their children's intellectual growth, worrying about their educational future, or providing experiences to nurture language skills and prepare the way for the school's demands. From the school's viewpoint, limited language development, with the attendant consequences for intellectual development, marks the disadvantaged child. Other school behavior traits —including apathy and withdrawal or hostility and alienation—are seen as related to language and intellectual retardation.

This experiential deprivation, according to Ausubel (1964, p. 24), means that

> . . . when new concepts and transactional terms are acquired verbally, i.e., by definition and context from speech and reading, rather than by abstraction from direct experience, he suffers from the paucity of abstractions in the everyday vocabulary of his elders, from the rarity of stimulating conversation in the home, from the relative absence of books, magazines and newspapers, and from the lack of example of a reading adult in the family setting.

The most serious effect of the disadvantaged child's language disability is the painful, dragging transition from concrete to abstract modes of thought and understanding. Ausubel (1964, p. 25) observes:

> Because concrete thought operations are necessarily more time-consuming than their abstract-verbal counterparts, and also because of his distractibility, unfamiliarity with formal language, impaired self-confidence, and unresponsiveness to time pressures, the culturally deprived child typically works more slowly than the middle-class child in the academic setting.

The effects of early experiential deprivation and the lessened ability to abstract are not limited to language learning alone. They influence mathematics attainment as well. As Leiderman (1964, pp. 53–54) has indicated:

> If the child has not learned the necessary operations and symbolic cues during the course of his pre-school development, through a variety of stimulation leading to both finer discriminations of relationships between things and broadening categorizations, then a school program predicated on this basic development will not be successful.

The disadvantaged are also characterized by negative self-images that mirror discrimination and segregation. The psychological impact of impoverishment and ghettoization on the ego development, motivation, and personality traits of minority group children has been documented. Scholastic performance suffers from the lower self-esteem, sense of personal worth, and aspiration level of many disadvantaged children. Writing particularly about the largest segment of the disadvantaged, the Ausubels contend that certain distinctive aspects of the Negro minority status impinge directly and crucially on self-image.

> Negro children live in a predominantly lower-class subculture that is further characterized by a unique type of family structure, by specially circumscribed opportunities for acquiring status, by varying degrees of segregation from the dominant white majority, and, above all, by a fixed and apparently immutable denigration of their social value, standing, and dignity as human beings because of their skin color. (Ausubel and Ausubel, 1963, p. 109)

Increasingly educators are beginning to understand the meaning of this background, which the Negro child (and, with some variations, his counterpart in every other minority group) brings with him into the classroom from the time he enters. Fully aware of racial differences long before he enters school, the minority group child often finds that much of what goes on in the classroom reinforces his feelings of inferiority. The effects of school desegregation (that is, contact with white children and teachers, perhaps for the first time) does not, in and of itself, raise the pupils' self-concept. In fact, as has been reported by Katz (1964, p. 381–399), anxieties may be raised that, in turn, may lower the child's self-concept, unless the school acts to increase understanding and acceptance of cultural differences.

The disadvantaged child often enters the classroom having been exposed to child-rearing practices quite different from those of the middle-class. The impact of parent-child interaction on intellectual development has been studied by Wolf (1965, pp. 93–106). He correlated intelligence with thirteen variables in the home environment, classified under three headings: (1) press for achievement (intellectual expectations and aspirations for the child, information concerning the child's intellectual development, and rewards for intellectual development); (2) press for language development (emphasis on language use in varied situations, opportunities for enlarging vocabulary, stress on correctness of language usage, and quality of available language models); and (3) provision for general learning (opportunities provided for learning in home and neighborhood, availability of books and other learning supplies, nature and amount of help provided to facilitate learning in different situations). Wolf's finding of a multiple correlation of +.76 between his ratings of environment and Henmon-Nelson IQ scores of 60 fifth-graders is far higher than correlations generally found with such usual measures of socioeconomic status as parental occupation and education. The findings emphasize the significance of parental expectations and their push for intellectual attainment, as well as specific aid to help the child do well in school.

Child-parent interactions affect language and cognitive development, as well as the general learning set. Strodtbeck (1964, pp. 15–31) has described the instruction middle-class mothers provide their children almost from birth and, to some extent, intuitively, as the "hidden curriculum." Different training and disciplining techniques are used. Bernstein (1961, pp. 163–176) has observed that lower-class parents discipline their children by exercising arbitrary authority and making categorical demands, without providing explanations or permitting questioning. Thus, children have little or no experience in exploring alternative behaviors verbally and are limited in the building of a repertoire of conceptualization and reasoning. Strodtbeck found that mothers receiving funds under the Aid to Dependent Children program disciplined their children less in terms of language symbols, reasoning, or provision of positive models, but instead relied more on physical punishment. As a consequence, the children received less help in understanding the relationship between what they did and the probable adult response, nor did they learn to consider alternative behavior.

Further, Strodtbeck found these mothers spending considerable energy warning their children to be "good." He points out that in the overcrowded, cramped living quarters, "being good" means being "physically inactive, verbally nonparticipative and nonobservant." Children are taught to be cautious and fearful by mothers who, because they are extremely vulnerable to serious and unpredictable threats themselves, convey this attitude to their offspring. In the classroom, to be "good" for the lower-class child may mean to stay out of trouble with school authorities. For the middle-class child, the stress on being good means far more than avoidance of disciplinary problems; it represents pressure for achieving and, especially in the beginning, learning how to read. These differing expectations between the home and the school with regard to values, attentivity, and general child-adult interactions and relationships affect the pupil's functioning in the structured environment of the school classroom.

In summary, the disadvantaged are a group characterized by: (1) language inadequacies, including limited vocabulary and poor syntactical structure, inability to use abstract symbols and complex language forms to interpret and communicate, difficulty in developing and maintaining verbal thought sequences, restricted verbal comprehension, unfamiliarity with formal speech patterns, and greater reliance on nonverbal communication means; (2) perceptual deficiencies and problems of visual and auditory discrimination and spatial organization; (3) a mode of expression more motorial and concrete than conceptual and idea-symbol focused; (4) an orientation of life that seeks immediate gratification in the here-and-now, rather than delaying for future advantage; (5) a poor self-image, denigrating the self's potential as person and learner; (6) aspirations and motivation too modest to achieve academic goals; (7) apathy and detachment from formal educational goals and processes; and (8) limited role-behavior skills and inadequate or inappropriate adult models. As a group, the disadvantaged reveal inability and unreadiness to cope with the demands and expectations of the school program and personnel, a cumulative academic retardation and progressively deteriorating achievement pattern, and a high incidence of early school withdrawal. For many, a cycle is created that Whiteman describes as follows:

> With early failure of difficulty in academic tasks, the child's self-confidence may be impaired so that learning becomes more difficult and unrewarding. The lowered achievement level may even feed back on the slower development of the originally lowered cognitive skills. A series of interactions between underlying abilities, overt achievement, and inward self-confidence may take place — lowered abilities producing lowered achievements, lowered achievements inducing diminished self-confidence, which in turn feeds back upon the achievements, and so on. If one adds the devaluations brought about by race-prejudice superimposed on poverty-prejudice, these processes may be accelerated. (Whiteman, 1965, p. 56)

Although the inner-city child often lacks sufficient verbal and experiential stimulation to form the learning sets essential for successful academic performance, he enters school having learned a great many other things. He has acquired insights, ways of coping, a set of values, and a life style that fit him to his particular culture, one that differs markedly from the cultural mainstream, especially in the school setting.

In looking at the nature of the educationally disadvantaged, it is important, as Eisenberg has put it, to avoid "confusing difference with defect." He maintains that the inner-city child has strengths, significant ones, that should be capitalized on in educational planning. These include

9

a degree of cooperation and mutual aid that extends further beyond the nuclear family than is typical in the middle class; collective group values rather than individualistic ones; more genuinely egalitarian values and less susceptibility to status and prestige; freedom from family over-protection and greater readiness to accept responsibility for family chores; superior physical coordination and skill—"a kind of body language and grace, a style that is physical rather than verbal;" an orientation to the environment more physical and visual than auditory; out-reach rather than introspection; concrete thought rather than abstract thought; and a cognitive style that "tends to be slow, careful, and patient as opposed to clever and facile" (Eisenberg, 1963–64, pp. 10–16).

Similarly, Riessman has urged positive reinterpretation of certain aspects of the disadvantaged child's style that strike many observers today as negative. He includes, as aspects of the style:

> The cooperativeness and mutual aid that mark the extended family; the avoidance of the strain accompanying competitiveness and individualism; the egalitarianism, informality and humor; the freedom from self-blame and parental overprotection; the children's security found in the extended family and a traditional outlook; the enjoyment of music, games, sports, and cars; the ability to express anger; the freedom from being word-bound; and, finally, the physical style involved in learning. (Riessman, 1963, p. 9)

While an adequate description of the nature of the disadvantaged child is still being formulated, numerous proposals and programs — some simple, others not — have emerged for coping with the educational problems he poses. Some aim directly at the teaching-learning process, others at altering school-family-community relationships. The schools that house the disadvantaged have been depicted in grim terms. The most dilapidated, old, and inadequate buildings house staffs of teachers from the middle class or aspiring to it. Most of these teachers resist assignment to these "difficult" schools, have little faith in their pupils' ability to learn, and are unable to manage pupil behavior and provide discipline. Overly large classes in crowded, unappealing rooms reflect administrators' unwillingness or inability to provide supervisory leadership and assistance to the staff and to relate to the community. They fail in their responsibility to the student body (racially or ethnically segregated or, at best, imbalanced), using meager instructional material of poor quality or inappropriate nature; after school hours, involvement gives way to aloofness from the community's life.

While such a description may read like a caricature, it is not, to judge from current writings. On the other hand, educational success is not guaranteed by brand-new buildings, staffed by professionals who have volunteered for such assignments, located in such a way as to improve racial balance, and provided with all kinds of supplementary materials and resource personnel. "New" staff, plant, and resources can show only limited success, just as strikingly exciting programs that succeed in educating the disadvantaged can be found in ancient plants in slum neighborhoods. What makes the difference? The need cannot be minimized for better pupil-teacher ratios, improved school facilities, better prepared and selectively screened staff, a rich supply of instructional materials, expanded personnel services, and an extended school day and school year. However, most important are good programs of curriculum development and teacher education.

Still needed are better diagnostic tools for pinpointing the individual child's particular learning disabilities as well as his strengths. To say that some students do not do well in school because they are deprived or underprivileged is to narrow sharply the scope of research and development related to their problems. This diagnosis of general unreadiness because of inadequate preschool experience leads either to the obvious prescription of compensatory instruction or to a prediction of low aspirations and achievement. School-created compensatory experiences prior to the primary grades or remedial work after a child enters these grades are considered necessary to bring pupils into the mainstream of school life; without one or the other, the child is marked for low attainment and failure.

It has been common for many years to speak of "meeting children's needs" and of "starting with children where they are," bringing them along in carefully planned or at least "emerging" steps. Such an overall strategy is particularly appropriate for disadvantaged students (Ausubel, 1964, pp. 16–17), but the underlying assumption involves rephrasing; the aim is to bring children from where they are to *where they ought to be* if they are to satisfy demands of the school program at whatever grade or instructional level they may be. It is assumed that the "standard" program is what the children "need"; compensatory or remedial work is supposed to prepare them to receive it. Inadequate attention has been given to alternative strategies for teaching what is to be taught. However, it is certain that there are unexplored approaches to promoting desirable development, quite different from the ones customarily employed.

The analysis by Bloom (1964, p. 218) of the stability and variability in the development of certain characteristics from infancy to maturity — physical factors, intelligence, scholastic achievement, interests, attitudes, and personality — underscores the crucial influence of early experiences and the effects of early environment on the child's growth and development. He speculates that "very powerful environmental and/or therapeutic forces may overcome and alter the most stable of characteristics — this is yet to be demonstrated." Ausubel (1964, p. 24) is somewhat more optimistic, concluding that the "critical period hypothesis" may not be applicable to the educationally disadvantaged. Nor is all lost if such children are

11

not reached before they enter the first grade. He does see "irreparable loss of years of opportunity when reasonably economical learning could have occurred." In comparison with equally endowed peers, each year of delay leads disadvantaged students to incur a learning deficit that limits their current and future rate of intellectual development. Ausubel concludes that it "is evident that the possibility for complete reversibility of environmentally induced retardation and verbal intelligence decreases as children advance in age." However, intervention programs of various kinds are testing the idea that relatively stable characteristics can be modified. How lasting the gains are that follow even intensive compensatory programs, such as preschool experiences, is unproven still.

What is wanted is a comprehensive framework for research and development that stresses the learner's successes rather than his failures, his individual strengths rather than his disabilities. It has been suggested that researchers should concentrate on locating the means for releasing further potentialities (Murphy, 1961; Schachtel, 1959). For example, it should be possible to construct a general, multidimensional framework within which to view the direction and possibilities of perceptual-language-cognitive development and its affective concomitants. Such a framework should encompass not only the general stages of development but a wide variety of individual ways for fulfilling those stages. It should facilitate the preparation of more useful evaluative and diagnostic procedures and of better ways for recording individual progress. A comprehensive framework could provide fruitful leads to research on the nature of instruction and its relationship to various kinds of learning and development tasks. In addition, it could help in arriving at more useful operational meanings for common terminology.

Part of a framework for viewing human intellectual development and relating it to instructional experience has already emerged from past research, especially that of the past several decades. Although a thorough review of the research literature cannot be included here, five underlying assumptions for "theories of success" are stated below.

(1) Human intellectual functioning is not genetically fixed at birth and does not develop in a predetermined manner, regardless of the kind of environment in which the individual grows up. Rather, the as yet unmeasurable intellectual potential an individual possesses at birth requires stimulation and nurture through an identifiable variety of experiences. In his synthesis of the work of Piaget and other investigators, Hunt (1961) maintains that the area of early childhood learning offers potential clues to the major etiological differences between successful and not-so-successful pupils. Herein lies the rationale for nursery and prekindergarten programs of compensatory education as well as proposals for early intervention through parent training (Hunt, 1964, pp. 209–248).

(2) Although intellectual development takes place in the "whole" child, there are distinct dimensions of growth and development that can

12

be identified, described, and explained. Individuals exhibit differing profiles of strengths and weaknesses, regardless of socioeconomic, ethnic, or racial status. Moreover, each developmental dimension may be susceptible to a unique type of instruction. These dimensions may be identified as those of: *perception,* including auditory and visual discrimination skills (Deutsch, 1964); *oral language,* including vocabulary and the concepts signified (Bernstein, 1961; Thomas, 1962); *syntax* and the *cognitive operations* that are mediated or reflected (John and Goldstein, 1964; Loban, 1963; Luria, 1961; Vygotsky, 1962); *concept formation ability* and preferred style of classification or categorization (Braun, 1963; Osler and Fivel, 1961); *learning set* and other aspects of "learning how to learn" (Whiteman, 1964).

(3) Perceptual-language-cognitive development is assumed to be hierarchical, following distinct stages of growth, as in the enactive-iconic-symbolic of Bruner (1964), or the preoperational-concrete-abstract hierarchy of Piaget (Inhelder and Piaget, 1958). It has been shown that children differ in the chronological age at which they move from one stage to the next as well in the degree to which they are able to consolidate a particular stage (Almy, Chittenden, and Miller, 1966).

(4) Optimum intellectual development is influenced by certain affective or motivational factors, such as the student's self-concept, the influence of his peers, his attitudes toward himself as a learner and toward school, and parallel attitudes in his teacher (Ausubel and Ausubel, 1963, pp. 217–235). Home environment factors are related to variations in intellectual development and academic achievement as well (Bloom, 1964; Wolf, 1965).

(5) Adequate cognitive development rests on the stimulation and channeling of experience by good instruction, and the eventual interpretation of experience. This essential instruction occurs in many aspects of any child's life, both in and out of school. Types of teaching relevant to the developmental dimensions can be identified, described, and (eventually) explained. Pupils come to school having absorbed "instruction" from other sources—home, mass media, peers—as well as the classroom. Studies of the effect of instruction on aspects of development at different levels may result in the invention of teaching strategies that really reach children.

Understanding the nature of the disadvantaged child, the culture from which he comes, and the demands and the promise of a changing society, it is inappropriate to consider his educational goals limited to the currently practical and utilitarian. The secondary school is still terminal for most disadvantaged youngsters. However, for many, a successful school curriculum would open up a channel into the stream of continuing life-long education, an essential in today's world. Basic literacy is step one—but it is too lowly an ultimate objective for the inner-city child. Besides literacy and mathematics concepts, he needs understanding of his own and other cultures; attitudes of citizenship; sound personal health habits; a feeling of the place of adolescents in society; an understanding of ethical concepts of American society; an appreciation of the potential worth to American society of varied ethnic and racial groups, immigrant and in-migrant alike; an understanding of the world of work and the requirements for finding and retaining a job, the meaning of mobility, and the dependence of employment on continuing education, both formal and informal; an orientation to the leisure resources of the urban community.

School programs must take into account improving conditions of life and work that are in accord with our national middle-class and humanitarian aspirations. The basic skills, insights, and achievements that constitute a general and common education — the "cultural imperatives" — are as valid for the disadvantaged child as for the middle-class youngster. The perimeter of curriculum must be extended to include understandings, processes, concepts, attitudes, norms, values, and feelings. The disadvantaged student needs help in developing not only basic learning skills and whatever special talents he may have, but also essential personal qualities, including responsibility and self-discipline. His program should include exploration, preparation for further training, knowledge of educational and vocational opportunities in a changing occupational structure. Thus, a curriculum for disadvantaged youth will embody the essential elements of an appropriate general education, remediation in the basic areas as required, exploratory work experience, use of leisure time, and skills in home and family living.

The unique intellectual and cognitive abilities of specific children must be understood. Educators must be adept at the strategies for directly teaching certain skills, attitudes and behaviors, and they need the professionalism to select content to ensure the "proper match" (in Hunt's term) between the child's developmental level and materials and activities provided.

One type of instructional content is basically *compensatory,* in the sense of overcoming deficits in experience and knowledge. Here, activities and experiences are furnished in such areas as visual and auditory discrimination, concept formation, ego-development, motivation, and general urban acculturation and orientation. A second kind of instructional content is *developmental* in the sense that it incorporates the basic skills that everyone needs as part of a general education. A third class of content derives from today's urban world — its vast and complex problems as well as its opulent resources. While educators still tend to be gun-shy of anything that might resemble "life adjustment education," the fact is, as Edgar Dale (1963) reminds us, that

> . . . the critical choices of individuals are *not* chiefly mathematical, linguistic, scientific, or historical. Rather, they are choices of values, of the use of time, energy and money, choices of friends or of a mate, choices in receiving and expressing ideas.

14

The curriculum must help all students—not only the disadvantaged—learn to live effectively in a complex, changing society: an understanding of urbanization, automation, mass communication and all of the interrelated problems that are part of modern living is as crucial for the advantaged as for the disadvantaged. However, these needs are less apparent in privileged children in more favored schools than in the disadvantaged. In the more advantaged homes, experiences happen, resources accumulate, motivation and support are provided. "Reversing the spiral of futility," overcoming a deprecatory self-image, and implanting hope where there is hopelessness: in these tasks the school must try to succeed where families have failed.

Analyses of learners' needs are the prerequisite to developing and applying strategies for upgrading scholastic attainment. Real understanding of the world from which the disadvantaged child comes, the specific kinds of deficiencies he brings with him, and the dissonances between self-expectations and school tasks is essential. The particular teaching strategies and methods that reach the disadvantaged are probably not strikingly different from those normally used—only their application differs. Sometimes they are developmental strategies, other times remedial. To a large extent, they are really the continual striving toward understanding and improving know-how in individualizing instruction—working with numbers of learners with a wide range of abilities, attainments, and aspirations in such a way that each is reached at his own level.

In the last few years, there has been an outpouring of instructional materials aimed at the disadvantaged population in our schools. For the first time, in many cases, the existence of minority groups is recognized—through content as well as illustrations. Slowly, even the basal readers where, as Klineberg (1963) once put it, "life in general is fun, filled almost exclusively with friendly, smiling people, including gentle and understanding parents, doting grandparents, generous and cooperative neighbors, even warm-hearted strangers"—even these are changing. But much remains to be done to capture the richness of urban life and the expressiveness of the disadvantaged child in the content of reading materials. The materials flood also includes self-instructional, remedial, and enrichment materials. Of equal significance in development of appropriate resources for disadvantaged pupils are teacher-prepared materials. Time must be found and support given for teachers to locate and develop materials for their own classrooms, specifically adapted to their own populations.

Teachers and administrators in depressed-area schools are often depicted as blinded by their middle-class orientation; prejudiced toward pupils from lower-class, racial, and ethnic minority groups; culturally shocked and either immobilized or punitive in the classroom; and groping for safer berths where success, in terms of their pupils' academic achievement, is more likely. Some—not all—teachers are hostile, vindictive, inept, or neurotic, but many more are compassionate and skillful. The

15

task is to recruit, train, encourage, support, and retain the dedicated and competent personnel: The great difference between the successful and the unsuccessful depressed area school is staff. Staff creates the overall climate of the classroom and the school, that powerful influence on what is learned and how. Teacher and staff preparation must create understanding and acceptance of various subcultures among the disadvantaged. Teachers must learn to recognize strengths and positive aspects on which to build, as well as deficiencies for which to compensate.

The needs of the disadvantaged include a teaching staff, an administrative organization, and special resource personnel who have acquired the insights and understanding of the different and diverse cultures from which the disadvantaged children come; who are able to cope with the frustrations which come from slow and minimal academic achievement and nonconforming classroom behavior; who are flexible in adapting procedures and resources to the particular populations within the school; who are idealistic and committed without being overly sentimental and vacuous; who understand their own biases and their impact on the pupils and their parents. Above all, the disadvantaged need a professional staff who fully comprehend the demands gripping the school in the current social, economic, and political turmoil, the better to plan and act in terms of these realities. Organizationally, administrators are revising staff deployment to spur more opportunities for much-needed one-to-one relationships between pupil and teacher. Schools are finding ways of using professionals differently and involving nonprofessionals more effectively. But, perhaps more important have been the efforts to develop better insights, attitudes, and competencies on the part of staff.

The school is called on to become the child's haven from the problems of depressed-area living, a reception center for the talents and hopes and frictions and despairs of a lower-class minority group culture. The school can and should secure many essential social-welfare benefits, but it must balance these against the demands for intellectual development. It can be the setting for integration, while providing for differentiating learning experiences. These demands cannot be met simply with a show of good will. At times, courses of action seem to be contradictory or at least divergent. The riddle is one of educating the inner-city child out of his subculture into society's mainstream—while preserving and developing his own individuality, as well as the divergency and other positive elements of his culture.

The school cannot look away, dealing only with intramural problems, nor, from a sense of guilt, wage a unilateral campaign against the ills and problems of society. The conscience of the American educator must fight a blurring of the school's role as a counterforce against poverty, segregation, and alienation. The school alone can hardly solve these problems, even though it is called upon by some to do so. But the school can rescue

16

disadvantaged children from hopelessness by opening unexplored opportunities.

References

Almy, Millie; Edward Chittenden and Paula Miller, *Young Children's Thinking: Studies of Some Aspects of Piaget's Thinking.* New York: Teachers College Press, Columbia University, 1966.

Ausubel, David P. "How Reversible Are the Cognitive and Motivational Effects of Cultural Deprivation? Implications for Teaching the Culturally Deprived Child," *Urban Education*, 1 (Summer 1964), 16–38.

_____. "A Teaching Strategy for Culturally Deprived Pupils: Cognitive and Motivational Considerations," *School Review*, 71 (Winter 1963), 454–463.

_____ and Pearl Ausubel. "Ego Development among Segregated Negro Children," in *Education in Depressed Areas*, ed. A. Harry Passow. New York: Teachers College Press, Columbia University, 1963.

Bernstein, Basil. "Social Structure, Language and Learning," *Educational Research*, 3 (June 1961), 163–176.

_____. "Social Class and Linguistic Development: A Theory of Social Learning," in *Education, Economy and Society.* New York: The Free Press, 1961.

Bloom, Benjamin S. *Stability and Change in Human Characteristics.* New York: John Wiley and Sons, 1964.

Braun, Jean S. "Relationship between Concept Formation Ability and Reading Achievement at Three Developmental Levels," *Child Development*, 34 (September 1963), 675–682.

Bruner, Jerome S. "The Course of Cognitive Growth," *American Psychologist*, 9 (January 1964), 1–15.

Clark, Kenneth B. *Dark Ghetto: Dilemmas of Social Power.* New York: Harper and Row, 1965.

_____. "The Cult of Cultural Deprivation: A Complex Social Psychological Phenomenon," in *Environmental Deprivation and Enrichment.* New York: Ferkhauf Graduate School of Education, Yeshiva University, 1965.

Dale, Edgar, "Life Management Curriculum," *The Newsletter*, 29 (November 1963), 1–4.

Deutsch, Cynthia P. "Auditory Discrimination and Learning: Social Factors," *Merrill-Palmer Quarterly*, 10 (July 1964), 277–296.

Deutsch, Martin. *Minority Group and Class Status as Related to Social and Personality Factors in Scholastic Achievement.* Ithaca, N.Y.: The Society for Applied Anthropology, 1960.

Educational Policies Commission. *American Education and the Search for Equal Opportunity.* Washington, D.C.: National Education Association, 1965.

Eisenberg, Leon. "Strengths of the Inner-City Child," *Baltimore Bulletin of Education*, 41 (1963–64), 10–16.

Health and Welfare Council of the Baltimore Area, Inc. *A Letter to Ourselves: A Master Plan for Human Redevelopment*. Baltimore, Md.: The Council, 1962. Mimeographed.

Hunt, J. McVicker. *Intelligence and Experience*. New York: Ronald Press, 1961.

———. "The Psychological Basis for Using Preschool Enrichment as an Antidote for Cultural Deprivation," *Merrill-Palmer Quarterly*, 10 (July 1964), 209–248.

Inhelder, Barbel and Jean Piaget. *The Growth of Logical Thinking from Childhood to Adolescence*. New York: Basic Books, 1958.

John, Vera P. and Leo S. Goldstein. "The Social Context of Language Acquisition," *Merrill-Palmer Quarterly*, 10 (July 1964), 265–276.

Katz, Irwin. "Review of Evidence Relating to the Effects of Desegregation on the Intellectual Performance of Negroes," *American Psychologist*, 19 (June 1964), 381–399.

Klineberg, Otto. "Life is Fun in a Smiling, Fair-Skinned World," *Saturday Review* (February 16, 1963), 77.

Leiderman, Gloria. "Mental Development and Learning of Mathematics in Slow-Learning Children," in *Conference on Mathematics Education for Below-Average Achievers*. Stanford, Palo Alto, Calif., School Mathematics Study Group, 1964.

Loban, Walter D. *The Language of Elementary School Children*. Champaign, Ill.: National Council of Teachers of English, 1963.

Luria, A. R. *The Role of Speech in the Regulation of Normal and Abnormal Behavior*. New York: Liveright Publishing Corp., 1961.

Murphy, Gardner. *Freeing Intelligence through Teaching*. New York: Harper and Row, 1961.

Osler, Sonio F. and Myran W. Fivel. "Concept Attainment: I. The Role of Age and Intelligence in Concept Attainment by Induction," *Journal of Experimental Psychology*, 62 (July 1961), 14–23.

Riessman, Frank. "The Culturally Deprived Child: A New View," in *Programs for the Educationally Disadvantaged*. Washington, D.C.: U.S. Government Printing Office, 1963.

Schactel, Ernest. *Metamorphosis*. New York: Basic Books, 1959.

Strodtbeck, Fred L. "The Hidden Curriculum of the Middle-Class Home," in *Urban Education and Cultural Deprivation*, ed. C. W. Hunnicutt. Syracuse: Syracuse University Press, 1964.

Thomas, Dominic R. *Oral Language Sentence Structure and Vocabulary of Children Living in Low Socioeconomic Urban Areas*. Detroit, Mich.: Wayne State University, 1962. Doctoral dissertation, unpublished.

Whiteman, Martin. "Developmental Theory and Enrichment Programs," in *Environmental Deprivation and Enrichment*. New York: Ferkhauf Graduate School of Education, Yeshiva University, 1965.

_____. "Intelligence and Learning," *Merrill-Palmer Quarterly*, 10 (July 1964), 297–309.

Wilson, Alan B. "Social Stratification and Academic Achievement," in *Education in Depressed Areas*, ed. A. Harry Passow. New York: Teachers College Press, Columbia University, 1963.

Wolf, Richard M. "The Measurement of Environments," in *Proceedings of the 1964 Invitational Conference on Testing Problems*. Princeton, N.J.: Educational Testing Service, 1965.

Vygotsky, L. S. *Thought and Language*. Cambridge, Mass.: M.I.T. Press, 1962.

Mario Fantini and Gerald Weinstein tackle the complicated question of "relevant content for the disadvantaged" in a model proposing to establish effective guidelines for instructional programs, criteria for the dimensions of relevance, and new practices for the classroom teacher.

To Fantini and Weinstein, concern with the disadvantaged is symptomatic of a more complex and basic problem—the inability of our schools to educate suitably the diverse population found in classrooms. However, like other thoughtful educators, they view this preoccupation as a solid base for innovations that will win a response from all learners. Their concentration here is on the development of "prescriptive technology functionally linked to descriptive theory," a term for matching strategies and content to the numerous descriptions of the disadvantaged learner. They are critical of present efforts at "reform" which seem inapplicable to the disadvantaged.

The traditional question of the relationship between the affective and cognitive dimensions of learning is the focus of their notion of curriculum relevance. Their fundamental premise is that institutionalized content basically re-

A MODEL FOR DEVELOPING RELEVANT CONTENT

Mario Fantini
Gerald Weinstein

quires linking the cognitive aspects of learning with the affective dimensions—and in that crucial order. Underlying this insistence is their belief that "cognition is not only functionally linked to affect, it 'serves' affect." In developing their model, the authors discuss the centrality of affective concerns as the basis for real motivation on the part of the learner. They argue that the school is concerned primarily with altering behavior, and since affect is more closely linked to behavior than cognition, the school could achieve far greater impact if it dealt with the learner's affective content as a force for motivation and learning.

The model that Fantini and Weinstein present is intended to guide discussion and study by teachers and other educational planners in tailoring curricula to the group of learners called "the educationally disadvantaged."

A MODEL FOR DEVELOPING RELEVANT CONTENT

Mario D. Fantini
Gerald Weinstein

The current preoccupation with the disadvantaged has served to revive Herbert Spencer's classic question, "What knowledge is of most worth?" The "in" word which is being utilized presently to answer the Spencerian query is *relevance*. Thus, knowledge which is relevant is of most worth. Unfortunately the substitution of terms does little to illuminate the basic question. The problem now becomes "What knowledge is most relevant?" —and if the focus happens to be on one particular group of learners (for example, the disadvantaged), relevance is applied to them.

It should be clear by now that our present confrontation with the disadvantaged is symptomatic of a more basic problem—the inability of our present educational institutions to educate fully a total diverse population. Consequently, our "crisis" with the disadvantaged offers educators unusual opportunities to consider basic educational questions and to introduce needed innovation and reform that is now demanded for the sake of all learners.

Most of what we say is based primarily on our own direct experience with so-called disadvantaged learners and our observations of others throughout the country dealing with similar populations. We present our thesis, then, as involved observers who have accumulated a series of clinical hunches that seem to be pointed in a particular instructional direction. Much of what we say is based on our involvement in the Elementary School Teaching Project supported by the Fund for the Advancement of Education.

Our experience indeed supports the contention that most teachers and administrators who work with disadvantaged learners want answers to the question, "How can we make education more relevant for our children?" These same schoolmen, hungry for answers, flock to the many workshops and institutes recently made available by federal legislation. At these special sessions, teachers learn a great deal about the nature of the "culturally deprived child," that is, they learn more about the disadvantaged learner descriptively. As one teacher explained to us, "I understand my children better now, but I still don't know what to do with them." When we probed further, this same teacher said, "Well, I learned, for example, that one-third of my children probably come from broken homes and that this poses severe problems for the growing child. Now that I know this fact, what do I do to teach them better? I still must go back in September and teach them social studies, math, science, and the rest."

Unfortunately, descriptions about the nature of the disadvantaged learner are well ahead of instructional prescriptions that are appropriate. Our concern is with the development of such prescriptive technology functionally linked to descriptive theory. (We realize that such leaps are fraught with hazards, but, being action-oriented, we do not hesitate to take the plunge.)

The term "prescriptive technology" refers to the engineering or applied sectors of teaching and learning. After *diagnosis* is made, *prescriptions* are advocated. Presently, any specialized technology that does exist for the disadvantaged is rudimentary and takes the form of isolated practices which appear promising, for example, role playing, using "hip" language, simulation, and so forth. The teacher exposed to such practices may find them exciting and try them. But soon she uses up her specialized practices and is left to search for other isolated practices that may work. Between practices, she is left with the standard content and methodology that she knows is not making contact with the learner.

Attempts to beef up this standard content such as the Biological Sciences Curriculum Study, the Physical Science Study Committee, the Educational Services Incorporated, and other packaged products of the so-called curriculum reform movement similarly appear to lack contact capability with the disadvantaged. The problem appears to be one of developing an analytic instructional model from which teachers can generate a whole order of relevant content and appropriate pedagogic strategies and procedures. Such a model could become a tool for a prescriptive technology. Our leap will be in attempting to suggest such a model.

However, before we consider the model itself, let us turn our attention to its rationale. The ground rules are quite simple: We want to link description with prescription, relating the central concepts of each to the institutional reality of the school. Concepts that are defined outside the reality dynamic lose their utility as analytic tools and their transfer value is severely restricted.

For the authors, the focus on the disadvantaged has resulted in a reexamination of a classical pedagogic issue — the relationship between affective and cognitive dimensions of learning and teaching. In light of this, our fundamental premise is this: Institutionalized content or curriculum relevance is largely a problem of relating the cognitive dimensions of learning with those that are affective. This is not as simple as it

24

sounds. We could just as easily say, "The problem is one of relating the affective dimensions to those that are cognitive." The direction that we suggest—from cognition to affect—is crucial. That is, while attempts have been made to make the affective instrumental to the cognitive, attempts might be made, now, to make the cognitive instrumental to the affective. We accept an affective theory of learning.

What do the terms "cognitive" and "affect" mean? We realize that cognition as an abstract concept concerns the act of processing perceived information and developing higher orders of abstraction and conceptualization. Affect refers to feeling or the emotional aspects of consciousness. We are also cognizant that a dichotomy between these two may not exist.

However, such definitions reveal little about the relationship these terms have to motivation and learning. To us, affect is feeling or emotion, but it is also an expression of the innate instinctual drives of the child. It is related to his psychic energy, to his unconscious need to move in a particular direction in order that his inner needs be satisfied. In essence, we are starting with the established notions of basic drives, both physiological and psychological. Affect appears to be close to the natural biological drives that direct and control behavior. These drives respond to certain basic needs. The physiological needs are apparent. Despite our awareness of psychological needs, the school continues to view them superficially. The focus on the minority group has made salient certain of these inner needs, such as self-concept, power, and connectedness. These are the affectively disposed intrinsic drives that motivate behavior.

Much of our descriptive concepts contain elements central to both Freud and Dewey. Our perspective, however, is the school as an institution, and the concepts employed are defined to "fit" this reality. Although our orientation is toward an affective theory of learning, this is not to say that it is a Freudian psychoanalytic theory of learning.

It is Freud's search for underlying motivation—psychological and personal linked to the shaping social forces—that interests us and that offers certain insight for instructional strategy. The marriage of psychological with the sociological is quite important. Viewing our instructional problem from the perspective of one discipline only, that is, psychology, would be restrictive. Keniston, author of The Uncommitted, pinpoints this limitation: ". . . put simply, the psychologist often misses the shaping social context of individual lives; the sociologist may not attend to the depth and richness of human experience . . ." (Keniston, 1965, p. 10).

Cognition appears to be a natural way of equipping the organism with more capability for dealing with his basic drives. The more analytic the organism, the more alternatives are available for satisfying these inner needs. Consequently, the cognitive machinery links innate drives to the environment and provides the organism with constraints for coping with the requirements of the environment. In other words, cognition is not

25

only functionally linked to affect, it "serves" affect. Moreover, cognitive development cannot be viewed as independent of affective development.

An affective theory of learning, however, does not minimize the role of cognition. On the contrary, cognition is given greater potency because of its instrumental relationship to affect. Although educators have been hinting at such a unity, most proceed to emphasize one or the other. The functional linkage is seldom made. This is particularly true today at the height of the cognitive period in education.

So-called normative cognitive development schema (those of Piaget, for example) do not explain fully the consequences of affective drive interaction with differential social environments, such as lower class, subculture, and caste. Moreover, the present-day diagnoses of the effects of deprivation on cognitive development (especially with the early childhood or preschool movement) assume that affective drives must be satisfied if cognitive maturation is to be facilitated. These diagnoses, while admitting a linkage of cognition with affect, do not make clear just how these affective drives are to be satisfied in an institutional setting such as the school. They suggest that a stronger cognitive organism will be better equipped to satisfy his affective drives.

This cognitive emphasis is actually serving to reinforce the predominantly cognitive orientation of education.[1] The standard educational process equalizes cognitive development with mastery of a body of institutionally prescribed content, with "understanding" or "knowing about" a variety of academic subjects. The entire machinery of the school, including its reward system — grades, promotion, recognition and so forth — reflects this stance. In fact, the operational definition of learning used in the school is cognitive, that is, the classical notions of learning as a "change in behavior" in school actually could be taken to mean "a change in cognitive behavior" measured by paper and pencil tests and verbalization. Thus, the institution assumes that a learner who gets straight "A's" in, for example, "Principles of Democracy," possesses the cognitive understanding to behave or perform democratically. It is obvious that understanding about something cognitively is not a guarantee for behaving in terms of the understanding. We need only mention the performance of most citizens with regard to social justice to suggest that this cognitive road to learning, as presently conceived and implemented by our schools, may not be affecting behavior centrally. Studies attempting to determine the relationships between academic achievement and performance in real-life situations point to the same conclusion. As Holland and Richards summarize this in their own study:

The present study lends strong support to earlier studies which obtained similar results but generally used a narrow range of

---

[1]The crucial definitions of "affect" and "cognition" are not theoretical but operational, i.e., how these concepts are being translated by the institution.

talent. For example, the studies by Thorndike and Hagen (1959), Getzels and Jackson (1962), MacKinnon (1960), Richards, Taylor and Price (1962), Torrance (1962), Gough, Hall, and Harris (1963), Holland and Nichols (1964), and Astin (1962), all suggest that the relationships between measures of aptitude or academic potential and various measures of real life achievement or originality are typically small. Our study strongly implies that these earlier findings hold for broad ranges of talent, and that attempts by critics to attribute all these earlier findings to methodological and statistical defects — restriction of range and unreliability of predictors or criteria — are no longer plausible. Taken together, these studies of academic and nonacademic potential and achievement have little relationship to other kinds of nonacademic potential and socially important performance. (Holland and Richards, 1965, p. 20)

Cognition allows the organism to reconstruct reality symbolically, abstractly. In this sense it is removed from the real, and is disconnected from the feeling level of learning. For example, there certainly is a difference between knowing that three-fifths of the world population is starving and actually seeing three out of five people starving.

To "learn from experience" is to make a backward and forward connection between what we do to things and what we enjoy or suffer from things in consequence. Under such conditions, doing becomes a trying; an experiment with the world to find out what it is like; the undergoing becomes instruction — discovery of the connection of things. . . . Experience is primarily an active-passive affair; it is not primarily cognitive. (Dewey, 1961, p. 140)

Our hunch is that strongly cognitive knowledge (if effective) can lead to behavior that is cold, objective, detached, and uncommitted. Why? Perhaps the type of cognitive content advocated by present educational institutions, divorced from the affective bonds of motivation, is tantamount to computer-like information stored in the brain to be recalled upon request in an examination.

The institution defines "affect" primarily in terms of readiness, play, interests, classroom climate, teacher-pupil interaction, and motivation, which are utilized to encourage the learner to accept prescribed content. A young child is not pushed into a structured reading program if he appears not to be ready emotionally. In such cases a reading readiness program is utilized, or teachers capitalize on the interests of learners as a way of forging a link from the child to the content.

Early childhood programs use play as the vehicle for introducing content. Play and interests represent the basic "hooks" for linking "outside" content to "inside" natural dispositions. This hookup is more than a problem of "the match" as psychologist McVicker Hunt calls it. The problem

27

also involves the direction or flow of the match. The conventional orientation is to utilize affectively disposed areas, like interests, as the instrumentality for getting to institutionalized cognitive content, or subject matter. All instructional roads seem to lead to cognition. This direction represents to us a reversal in the natural biological flow of cognition as an instrument serving affect. In one sense, this reversal (affect as an instrument serving cognition) represents a switching in motivational direction from the intrinsic (affective) to the extrinsic (cognitive). It appears to us that the wants, interests, concerns, fears, anxieties, joys, and other emotions contain in them the seeds of intrinsic motivation and are content in their own right. Why? Because they are manifestations of the innate feelings of the learner as his basic physiological and psychological drives seek expression and satisfaction. All individuals possess the same innate needs, and these, as such, are potent motivational energies, central to learning — the key aim of the school.

Our hypothesis is that relevance becomes a matter of linking extrinsic, or institutional, content to these basic drives. It is not surprising, for example, that when a *sex* unit is covered at school, the motivation of students is quite obviously higher. Similarly, religious content relates to the basic concern for identity ("Who am I? What am I?") and subsequently may affect behavior very directly and deeply.

What we are suggesting is that school content linked to the more affective drives of the learner will have greater learning payoff. The intrinsic nature of the motivation makes the potential for learning more powerful. Content so linked will not be unrelated or phony, for the connection of content will be with the learner's real concerns, the very basis of his motivation.

Affect thus becomes the basic reality content for the learner. It is the closest reality to the learner's cognitive mechanism, but the content least tapped for instruction. Instead, we ask the learner to give up this inner content in favor of the other content, or academic content. This adjustment, although made, appears at best an exercise to be tolerated.

The direction, then, from those aspects of institutionally defined content (cognitive) to the learner's intrinsic concerns (affective) represents a reversal in the normative instructional strategy found in education. To implement the reversal involves not only the reorientation of schoolmen, but the introduction of new resources, such as psychiatry, pediatrics, anthropology, sociology, and clinical psychology into the mainstream of instruction. We must make quite clear that we are not suggesting that the classroom become a place for solving individual emotional problems. What we are searching for are more *general* patterns that stem from a psychosocial base.

Our observations force us to conclude that the school is a cognitively oriented institution that assumes that learners will be motivated to adjust to an extrinsic body of content, called curriculum, if enough pressure is placed on the learner to do so. In one respect, the present pressure to succeed imposed on learners (especially by parents) is creating emotional tension which is affectively negative but which, nonetheless, drives the student to learn. The problem with this negative affect is that learning is forced and unnatural.

It must be emphasized that we are suggesting more than a return to the child-centered notions of the progressive era. The cliche of the progressive era—"needs and interests of girls and boys"—was never really made explicit. More attention was focused on interests than needs, because interests could be adapted more easily as a vehicle for leading the learner to institutional content, for example, by starting with animals as means for moving to farm products. What interests a child, however, may not be what really concerns him. As important as the interest linkage was, and is, we are probing more in the direction of "needs," that is, what a child *has a need to know.* What he has a need to know is motivated by his affective content and becomes signaled through his *concerns.* On the other hand, what he *needs to know* is what the institution feels that all learners need to possess—good citizenship, reading, writing, and so forth. It is extremely crucial at this point to understand that we are *not* suggesting that what the child has a need to know is what he needs to know. What we *are* hypothesizing is that what he needs to learn, as institutionally defined, will have greater learning payoff and more relevance if a means can be devised to link it to what we perceive to be the real motivational force— his affective concerns. Presently we are suggesting the concept of concern as a "new" bridge to the affective. Concerns convey the notion of an inner uneasiness which seeks cognitive assistance. "Concerns" carries a heavy, permanent connotation. "Interests" connotes lighter, more temporary items. What we are suggesting is that we need much more powerful motivators, with more long-range impact. Therefore, to the extent that the learner can utilize institutional content as a tool to probe his basic concerns, we are suggesting that a more relevant educational linkage will be possible.

What then, is the purpose of teaching skills, concepts, and subject matter? Are they not tools to be utilized for some reason? Educators have been trying to prove to the learner that reading, writing, and social studies are important tools. What we are suggesting is that they become tools that have a functional relationship to the concerns of the organism.

Finally, we must distinguish two types of content that the learner brings to school. One we are calling "affective content," based on his natural feelings and concerns as a growing organism. He is concerned with his identity ("Who am I? What am I? Where am I going?"), with feelings of power and powerlessness, with feelings of belonging and alienation, connectedness and disconnectedness. These are manifest as concerns for status, prestige, recognition, commitment, and so forth.

The second content area is based on what he learns from experiences provided by his life space, or the social context in which he lives. This we label the learner's "cognitive content." It may or may not be related to the affective content. For example, he may learn how to take care of his younger brothers and sisters, or how to use the streets as a playground. He may learn the characteristics of a gang leader, the names of the disc jockeys, the latest rock-and-roll tunes, "hip" language, that a policeman cannot be trusted, and so forth. The migrant worker's child may learn characteristics of a good worker, a good boss, crop rotation, and so forth.

When the child comes to the school, these two content areas usually form the basis for making contact with him. At the present time, some linkage is beginning between institutional content and the child's experiential cognitive content. For example, if the child understands and uses hip language, the institution may utilize this language in the classroom through the use of "hiptionaries" and reading poetry in hip language. This strategy, however, is always aimed at getting the learner to accept institutional cognitive content. Moreover, if affective concerns are considered at all, they provide a vehicle for making contact with the learner. For example, fear of doctors may be used as the basis for developing a unit on "Our Community Friends," the doctor, the dentist, and the nurse. Thus, the fear itself is not viewed as content worthy of attention. Rather, fear is a means of inducing the student to learn more about institutionally prescribed content.

At this point a diagram might be helpful in synthesizing the main points of the rationale.

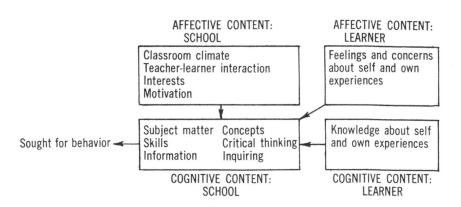

In Chart I both the institutional (school) content and the learner's content are viewed as being both cognitive and affective. It is clear from the direction of the arrows that the institution gives cognitive content the highest priority. This priority is reflected in the deliberate attempt to view other content areas as instruments for getting to the cognitive. This assumes that once the cognitive content is mastered, the individual has learned those behaviors appropriate for performing in the greater society as a mature school product. The fundamental question is: Has such an assumption given us the product we express the desire for? Our review of such products leads us to serious doubts.

Pedagogic strategies to date have been considered relevant if they relate other content areas to institutional cognitive content. Thus, when a system is created for linking institutional affective content with institutional cognitive content, the school is considered to be excellent. If the learner's cognitive content can be linked also, then the school can claim to "start where the child is."

Moreover, if the learner's affective content is tapped too, then all roads could be said to lead truly to cognition. However, it is the learner who is expected to adjust to the institution, not the institution to the learner, and if the learner's affective content is tapped at all, for example, fear of hospitals, it is used to induce the learner to study about the prescribed content—hospitals, doctors, nurses, and so forth. To us, the above chart depicts what is presently considered relevant content.

Our proposal is literally to reverse the direction of this orientation.

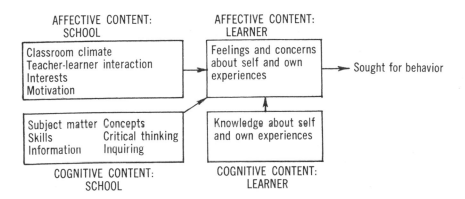

From our point of view, the more natural flow, as shown in Chart II, would be for "all roads" to lead to the learner's affective content, for the other content areas to serve as channels for this realm. It is this realm that we feel contains the real intrinsic forces for motivation and that, consequently, may have greater impact on behavior.

Put simply, our view is that the relationship between cognition and behavior is weaker than the relationship between affect and behavior, in other words, that affect is more closely linked to behavior. Since the school is in business to change behavior (learning), then this alternative deserves consideration.

Now for the model itself. It is hoped that such a model can be used: (1) *as an organizer*, to help sort out those components that could provide effective guidelines for a school's instructional program; (2) *as an aid to establishing criteria for relevance*, to help explore the dimensions of relevance; (3) *as a generator of new practices*, to help the teacher relate a given practice to the totality of the components identified, and thereby initiate further developments, or extensions, or newly conceived procedures. Let us examine the model in terms of its purposes.

The Model as an Organizer

How do we handle the tremendous input of information concerning education and the disadvantaged? We need a pigeonholing system that would not only contain the various pieces of information, but also establish some kind of relationship among them.

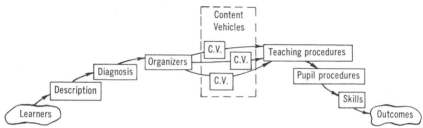

There is a great deal of discussion about "the disadvantaged," as though they were a general group with common characteristics, when at the same time, various separate groups can be identified within the disadvantaged group—the urban lower-class Negroes, the urban lower-class Spanish-speaking children, the migrant workers, including Negroes, Spanish-Americans, and Indians, differing from tribe to tribe. Many of these categories are overlapping and yet distinct, so the first block in the model identifies the group of learners who are being discussed.

The second block in the model handles the description of this group of learners, containing life experiences, styles, conditions, cognitive processes, feelings, attitudes, needs, concerns, language, and perceptions.

The third block isolates *explanations* of the descriptions that occur in Block 2, analyzing psychological, social, physical conditions as well as other causative factors which contribute to the descriptions.

The description now comprises the *what*, the diagnosis, the *why*.

The fourth block was stimulated by newer curriculum developments, the attempts to examine the structure of the various disciplines, and to communicate that structure in the form of ideas, generalizations or concepts. These, it is hoped, would serve as the new organizers around which curriculum content could be developed.

We have noted that many excellent lessons developed by teachers stop short at the conclusion of the lesson, and have no way of moving from that point to another level of instruction. In some cases, teachers "open up" children and get them to "express" themselves but fail to utilize the outcome to further some aspect of learning with the children. Teachers say, "I just had one of the best lessons I've had in a long time. I really got the children to pour out their souls. It was great." When asked, "What do you think the children learned as a result of this outpouring?" the teacher is generally stymied.

All of this suggests the need for some ordering hooks for the teacher so that she might have a clearer idea of how to organize the variety of experiences she provides for children. These organizers might assist in more effectively feeding back the children's responses into the educational process. The organizers, then, would be the most generative and transferable items in the educational process, especially those that cut across discipline lines. Concepts such as "Man *learns* to judge his worthwhileness on the basis of certain cultural factors that may or may not be rational or accurate," are more inclusive than the fact that "The largest city in the world is New York," or the concept in mathematics, "There are many ways of naming numbers." We realize that we may be referring to generalizations rather than concepts, but one of the problems in this area is that we still have not adopted a common language for referring to these categories of ideas. Be that as it may, however, we have labeled part of the model as containing systems of organizing concepts or generalizations around which curriculum might be developed.

In the model, the fifth block (of circles) is a pigeonhole for the variety of content that is being developed by curriculum projects. In order to keep it as inclusive as possible, we say that anything from a field trip to a book, a film, an incident in class, a unit, a topic, a subject area such as science, history, language, can be regarded as "a content vehicle."

The sixth block in the model deals with the teaching act—the methods, strategies, or the interacting procedures that the teacher utilizes in the attempt to instruct.

The seventh block houses materials that describe general procedures children must master in order to become more adept at learning—in other words, the "learning how to learn" procedures: rational processes, inquiry, critical thinking, analytic problem-solving, evaluating, hypothesizing, planning, predicting outcomes, and generating alternatives.

The eighth box contains materials and ideas concerned with the basic skills, the "fundamentals" such as numerical and language-art skills. It also contains diagnostic procedures for determining how well the learners have mastered these skills.

Finally, the ninth block handles all statements related to the outcomes of educational goals, whether they are general ("An educated man should be . . .") or more specific statements of behavioral changes that we would like to see occur in the learner.

Now that some of the data has been categorized, we shall examine it for clues determining the dimensions of relevance.

The Model as Used in Establishing Criteria for Relevance

It appears that there were at least three main ingredients in situations contributing to relevance for the learner: the learner's concerns, his reality, and his learning style. Learning is relevant: (1) when the *teaching procedures* match the *learning style* of the youngster; (2) when the *content vehicles* are related to or coincident with the *learner's reality* or *learner's content;* and (3) when the *content vehicles* and *teaching procedures* deal in some way with the *affective concerns* of the learner.

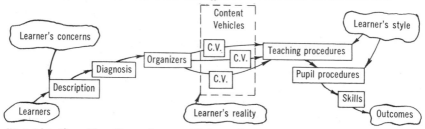

Matching Teaching Procedures with Learning Style

This was the focus during the first year of the Elementary School Training Project (Harmin and Simon, 1965). Characteristic learning styles of the disadvantaged were outlined, and teachers were sought whose procedures matched those learning styles.

However, as a logical extension, if the telephone directory were the prescribed content vehicle of a school system and a teacher were teaching it while matching her procedures to the learning style of a particular group of pupils, this would have to be regarded as an effective teaching procedure.

Obviously this first conception is too limited. To many disadvantaged youngsters, much of the conventional content is no more relevant than the telephone directory. (In fact, in some instances, the directory would be more relevant.)

Content Vehicles and Learner Reality

There are some movements across the nation to develop materials that deal with life more as the child knows and experiences it, for example, urbanized basal readers about children having a variety of socio-economic backgrounds and racial origins. Other efforts are made by teachers who attempt to utilize content familiar to the child. The popular music of the learner, for example, is used to introduce him to poetry. Thus starting with the child's content and matching teaching procedure to learning style becomes a way of increasing relevance.

However, even so, we notice that while we frequently awaken interest via the child's content (popular music), we tend to lose the child's interest when we move solely to the subject (poetry). What seems to occur, then, is a temporary situation of motivation that lacks real sustaining power. To express it more succinctly, the child's reality is being used to connect him with other content that may lack intrinsic meaning. Where else, then, can we look for cues as to how we might sustain relevance?

As a beginning house-cleaning task, we will look again at some of the material from Block 2 – the description.

First, any descriptive material dealing with "cognitive discrepancies," that is, language difficulties, reading problems, analytical processes, we will include under pupil procedures and skills (Blocks 7 and 8).

Next, any descriptive material dealing with the way in which the child has been taught, or the way in which he has learned to learn, will be placed under the teaching procedures, Block 6, or pupil procedures, Block 7. This is what we refer to when we talk about "learning style."

We transfer, next, descriptions of the children's content – what they bring to school, or what they might be able to teach the teacher. This would be put under the content vehicle, Block 5.

The Affective Concerns of the Learner

What remains in Block 1 is largely that portion of the descriptive material related to how children in particular groups feel about themselves. These feelings are communicated in a variety of ways. We find reports in the professional literature on their alienation, self-rejection, passivity, and rebellion, their kind of motivation and self-concept. We know these feelings through their own words – the things these learners say about themselves, their lives, and their relationship with the world. These descriptions and statements are evidence of profound emotional presses. It is in the emotional domain that the key to relevance lies.

Most of what we read about the disadvantaged lies within the emotional domain. Ironically, when the school finally begins to program for the youngster, its point of departure is usually the cognitive domain. "Where is the child academically? What skills does he need? What are his language difficulties?" These are all typical of the questions raised. Somehow the emotional domain is avoided, and the program concerns itself with "plugging" the cognitive deficits. If the emotional domain or the *affect* of the learner is considered at all, it is used as a tool for connecting the learner with something that bears little or no intrinsic relationship to his persistent emotional condition.

But what is an alternative? Is there another way of thinking about affect so that it becomes more than a motivating tool for cognitively inspired material?

From time to time we come across statements made by disadvantaged children that seem at the core of what we term "relevance."

From a child, after his teacher had taken a group of youngsters on a bus tour of the community, through the "better neighborhoods": "Why do I live in the slums?"[2]

---

[2]Observed at Project Apex, New York University, New York.

Or, from a high-school graduate, who was given a college scholarship, to his college teacher:

"Listen, see if this is right. I'm here to get educated right. You're educated—so it's like you're telling me I've got to be like you. Now, if I've got to become like you it means that what I am now, isn't too good. So what I want to know is, how much of me do I have to give up to become educated?"[3]

Or, these statements:

"Whenever I leave Harlem, I feel like I'm a fish out of water!"[4]

"I think about what I should do when I get out of school, and I just don't know. The people in my neighborhood, in Harlem, or downtown, they're all doing it wrong. And if one tries to get out, the rest laughs. Like they say that they tried and couldn't do it, so you're not going to do it either. And this guy feels, 'Well, maybe I can't do it,' and he comes back into the slum. You figure, you know, they failed, man, I might as well give up. . . .

"And that's the thing that gives a feeling of inferior. It tells a person that no matter how hard they try, they can't get out. That's the whole thing right there." (Mayerson, 1965, p. 104)

Why are these statements so significant? For us, they are questions that the youngster is grappling with that are rooted in the core of his being, questions that all humans face but that for the disadvantaged child have been so compounded that they have become the essence of his disadvantage. They are evidence of what we shall call his *affective concerns*. To label them "emotional needs" isn't adequate, because such a term doesn't imply the frustration or anxiety that *concerns* does. We call them "affective concerns" because they project what the disadvantaged youngster *feels* most uneasy or anxious about.

When these children confront a curriculum that continually ignores such concerns, the problem of relevance becomes clear. In order to show that merely calling upon children's interests may be limited, it becomes important to distinguish between interests and concerns.

Interests and Concerns. As we have said before, much of the progressive education movement was dedicated to building curriculum around the "interests" of students. Teachers attributed their difficulty motivating the learners to the learners' not being really *interested* in what was being taught. Therefore, it was thought if we could assess those interests and build programs from them, we would no longer encounter the problem of motivation. If children were interested in space exploration, that's what they studied. If they were interested in animals, they studied

---

[3]Observed at Project APEX.
[4]Observed at Project APEX.

animals. The concept of curriculum building based wholly on "interests," however, is limited. We don't always know what we are or could be interested in, and, secondly, what we say we are interested in may not really be the thing that concerns us. A teacher told us, for example, that her class had an almost compulsive interest in science. "What aspect of science?" she was asked. "Evaporation—the children seem utterly intrigued by evaporating water." After a further investigation, however, we found that it wasn't so much *evaporation* as such that intrigued the class as it was a concern about change, permanence, and absence, for, as they phrased it, "If water can disappear, can we?"[5]

Boys who express an interest in "strong men" may be really concerned with power and potency. Girls who express an interest in "dating" may be concerned about sex and popularity and their role in society. Therefore, it is *concern* rather than interest that we are recommending as containing more durable relevance.

To summarize, concerns are feelings of uneasiness. A person may have interests and yet not be concerned, or, on the other hand, interests may reflect concerns. What are the cues to concerns?

Cues to Concerns. A teacher may ask, "By what cues can I recognize these concerns?" The professional literature is one such source, given the fact that the disadvantaged have been described and evaluated by a great variety of professional observers in a number of fields. However, these areas are the least direct and most general. Another source of cues to concerns lies in the normal give-and-take discussion among colleagues within the school, particularly in the descriptions of incidents as they occur. A third source, clearly, is one's own direct observation. Obviously the same cues observed by different people will lead to a variety of interpretations; what is needed are ways to refine the particular concerns that a cue stand for. This we intend to pursue.

Should concerns become a more intrinsic part of the school's programing? According to our hypothesis, the more relevant teaching is, the better the chance for making contact with the disadvantaged learner and the greater the potential for learning to become consonant with action and feeling. So oriented, we will now explore the use of our model in generating an instructional program from the concerns of youngsters.

The Model as a Generator of More Relevant Curriculum

Let us show the use of the model in a specific situation.

Who is the learning group?

Developmentally—(12-year-olds, 13-year-olds, 14-year-olds)
Economically—(poor, middle-class, upper-class)

---

[5]Reported by Judy Gutman, Bank Street College of Education, New York City.

37

Geographically — (rural, urban)

Culturally, racially, ethnically — (Negro, Indian, Mexican-American)

We now will restrict our inquiry to an urban disadvantaged minority group.

What cues indicate patterns of affective concern in this group?

An examination of observations and reports showed these general affective concerns among the urban disadvantaged minority groups: *self-rejection*, reflecting concern for a more positive self-concept; *disconnectedness*, reflecting concern for establishing connections with others and with society at large; *powerlessness*, reflecting concern for greater control over what is happening.

The following are groupings of children's statements under the various cues just mentioned. Several of these statements imply a combination of concerns.

Self-rejection

"Why do I live in the slums?"

"I may be brown, but I'm not black!"

"How can you like me when I don't like myself?"

"We're the dumb-class special!"

While the last two statements could easily occur across socioeconomic lines, the first two imply the variables of class and caste.[6]

Disconnectedness

"Whenever I leave Harlem I feel like a fish out of water."[7]

"Why should I listen to my parents? Look at the way they live!"[8]

"In order for me to get educated, I gotta be like you? What about me?"[9]

"You can't trust nobody, white or Negro."[10]

Powerlessness

"It's no use trying — there's nothing you can do."[11]

"I'm Hercules — I can do anything."[12]

"What the hell can I do? This is the attitude: that we can do nothing, so leave it alone. People think you're always going to be under pressure from the white man, and he owns and runs everything, and we are so dependent on him that there's nothing I can do. This is the general impression I've gotten from most of the adults in Harlem" (Harlem Youth Opportunities Unlimited, Inc., 1964, p. 344).

---

[6]All these statements from Observations at the Urban Teacher Preparation Program (UTPP), Syracuse, New York.

[7]Observed at APEX.

[8]Observed at Pima Indian Reservation, Tempe, Arizona.

[9]Observed at APEX.

[10]Observed at UTPP.

[11]Observed at UTPP.

[12]Reported by Joan Fiori, Philadelphia, Pa.

How and why have the distinctive manifestations of concern patterns emerged for the identified learning group?

While the pattern of self-rejection-disconnectedness-powerlessness may be common to most members of our society, their manifestations may be due to different forces characteristically operating on particular groups within the society. While a disadvantaged child is struggling for greater control because he had very little support from his social milieu, an advantaged child may be struggling for greater control because he has been given too much protection.

To cue us to his concern for power the disadvantaged child says, "So what if I graduate from high school—I won't get a good job anyway," whereas the advantaged child might say, "Sure I'm glad I finally got my own car. When I'm winging along in it I feel free as a bird. It's the only time I'm really in control."

Once we diagnose the reasons for the feelings of powerlessness among the disadvantaged, we can begin to consider desired outcomes.

What would we like to see in the learner's behavior that would be different from what we observe now?

If feelings of powerlessness are evident, it is not enough to state as an objective that we would like to have the learner feel more powerful. We must go on to ask, "What would a child *do* if he felt more powerful that he isn't doing now?"

A person who feels potent is able to develop a variety of strategies for overcoming obstacles. He can tap, reorganize, and manipulate a variety of power sources to get things done. He shows this by *trying* to do things, persisting through alternate routes, and making statements such as, "Let's try it this way," or "Let's figure out how to do it," rather than "It's no use, nobody can do anything." He is able to be realistic as to what he can achieve alone or with groups.

It is important to note here that we do not attempt to change concerns but *cues*. Concerns are only labels and do not describe behavior.

Thus far we have identified the learner and some significant cues, their diagnosis, and the outcomes. Now let us move to a consideration of the school program.

What organizers can be used to integrate the concerns, the desired outcomes, and the instructional program?

There are at least three types of organizers that are useful.

Generalizations. Having made a diagnosis and stated our outcomes, what ideas are there, whatever their source, that would be most relevant in explaining the concern cues we are dealing with?

To find these ideas is to reverse the traditional approach, in which the subject-matter discipline dictates what ideas are most important. We propose that certain generalizations be given priority and that this priority be determined by the diagnosis of the learners.

This is a situation in which a teacher sets in motion a variety of learning situations that lead the child to the attainment of the generalization.

Procedural Organizers. In this situation, the learners acquire a set of procedures to help them control the problem situations in which the original cues were manifested. They may acquire new ways of thinking about and acting upon these situations. Examples of some procedural organizers might be:

Analyzing a problem to find out what it is and what its possible causes are.

Learning how to negotiate with someone with a different point of view.

Generating alternatives to a situation, trying them, and evaluating the outcomes.

Procedural organizers used without accompanying generalizations may not aid the learners in understanding these situations any better, but they offer a more instrumental kind of help in developing new strategies and experimenting with new behaviors.

Questions. A series of questions that facilitate inquiry for both the teacher and the learners into the concern can serve as a third way of organizing instructional experiences.

Regardless of which organizers are used—and whether they are used alone or in combination—some relevant organizer is essential for sustaining an instructional program.

What content vehicles can provide the learning situations that we have just discussed?

A content vehicle can be anything that serves as a starting point for instruction. Not only does it include the conventional subject areas of the school's curriculum such as English, social studies, math, and science, or prescribed units such as "Colonial Times," "Our Community," "Matter and Energy," and "Communication," but also the following:

Other subject disciplines, such as psychology, sociology, anthropology, philosophy, or education.

Media, such as films, books, pictures, or trips.

Classroom incidents and problems.

Pupils' experience—in and out of school.

The children themselves.

The concept of content has been purposely broadened so as to give the teacher a greater range of choices for content that is most appropriate to achieve the stated outcomes.

In the discussion of relevance it was previously stated that the content that is most closely connected to the learner's reality will have the best possibility for engaging the learner — especially the disadvantaged learner. Therefore, we suggest that the initial series of content vehicles selected be close to the learners themselves — *their* content.

What content does the child bring to school? What does he already know? What can he teach the teacher? What does he talk about when no one is structuring his talk? The answers to these questions may lead to the initial content vehicle.

What teaching procedures, strategies, or methods are most appropriate to the learners' style and to the desired outcomes?

It is possible that even if one did match teaching and learning styles, the methods used might not enhance the desired outcomes and in fact might even contradict them. For example, if the desired outcomes were related to having the learners feel greater potency and the teaching procedures were such that the learners were in dependent learning roles, it is difficult to see how the outcomes would be achieved. It is one thing to talk about power, but perhaps even more essential to experience power with its responsibilities and problems. Therefore, teaching procedures should allow for this kind of experience.

Some excellent procedures that allow the learners to experiment with power roles have been recorded. Cross-age teaching is one, giving older children responsibility for teaching younger pupils.[13]

Here again, describing the learning patterns of the disadvantaged comes into play. The kinds of criteria for effectiveness of teaching procedures used in the first year of the Elementary School Teaching Project can now be reviewed in a more significant context.

Helping teachers to give the learner emotional support and feelings of worth is important here. Much of the work on changing teachers' attitudes involved developing a climate of mutual respect.

What procedures, ways of thinking, examining, behaving would the learners need to acquire in order to attain the desired outcomes?

Again, if power were the central issue, procedures involving the generation of real alternatives to action, planning change steps or mapping out of strategies, experimenting with new behaviors, and evaluating outcomes become the most crucial.

What skills does the learner have and/or need in order to expand his base of resources for attaining the concepts, procedures, and outcomes?

The acquisition of a great many of the pupil procedures depends on the skills the learner possesses, especially language skills. It would be hard to imagine pupils engaging in an analysis of their experience without at the same time developing greater mastery of speaking, listening, reading, and perhaps writing skills.

---

[13]The work of Ron and Peggy Lippitt, University of Michigan, is a good example.

41

We by no means intend to suggest that all skill development could or should be connected with all of the components of the model. This would be stretching a point. However, it is possible that more direct relationships can now be made.

Evaluation: To what extent were the desired outcomes attained?

In which areas did the programing seem weak or strong — the diagnosis, the content, the procedures? To what extent were the outcomes achieved? Where do we move from here? If behaviors were changed, what new strategies or content are suggested? Is there evident a different learner reality, learning style, or learning readiness? How much more intensively do we want the learner to deal with concerns? How much time do we have to spend?

Such questions lead to a movement through the model again — in ever increasing spheres of complexity and elaboration.

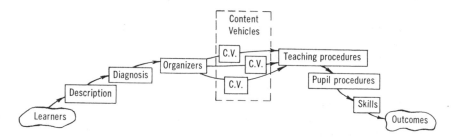

We close with an appropriate quote from the paper of J. Clayton Lafferty (1963) entitled "Values That Defeat Learning."

> The great purpose to be served by the schools, teachers, and students rests in the development of the capable individual. This, of necessity, involves [the behaviors] ideas, beliefs, values, and the clarity and consistency with which they are taught and demonstrated. The task of a free society is appropriate education for all, a task no other nation in the world has attempted and consequently a task which no other nation does as well. A free and responsible citizen is not produced by failure but by success, not by rejection, isolation, and prejudice but by feeling as if he belonged, by a belief in the possibility of altering his own life pattern, by an expectancy that he can succeed, and by the belief in his own intrinsic worth.

> It is to these feelings and beliefs all school roads must lead.

References

Dewey, John. *Democracy and Education*. New York: Macmillan Co., 1961.

Harlem Youth Opportunities Unlimited, Inc. *Youth in the Ghetto: A Study of the Consequences of Powerlessness and a Blueprint for Change*. New York: HARYOU, 1964.

Harmin, Merrill and Sidney B. Simon. "The Year the Schools Began Teaching the Telephone Directory," *Harvard Educational Review*, (Summer 1965), 326–331.

Holland, John L. and James M. Richards, Jr. "Academic and Nonacademic Accomplishment: Correlated or Uncorrelated?" *ACT Research Reports*, 2 (April 1965), 20.

Keniston, Kenneth. *The Uncommitted: Alienated Youth in American Society*. New York: Harcourt, Brace and World, 1965.

Lafferty, J. Clayton. "Values That Defeat Learning," in *Proceedings, Eighth Interinstitutional Seminar in Child Development, 1962*. Dearborn, Mich.: The Edison Institute, 1963.

Mayerson, Charlotte L. (ed.). *Two Blocks Apart: Juan Gonzales and Peter Quinn*. New York: Holt, Rinehart and Winston, 1965.

Miriam L. Goldberg urges the design of tools for the evaluation of compensatory programs for the disadvantaged in terms of their real and sustained effects on intellectual and scholastic performance.

Dr. Goldberg details some of the many problems in sound evaluation and the many blocks which must be removed if educators are to collect the data needed to justify expenditures on programs for the disadvantaged. Efforts on behalf of the disadvantaged continue to be hampered by a fundamental lack of insight into what works and what does not work, for which particular children, under what circumstances.

Seven problems are discussed: (1) the pressure for "solutions" which threatens careful, objective evaluation; (2) evaluation performed as an afterthought without prior criteria and valid pre- and post-data; (3) fuzziness in formulating objectives and determining significant content; (4) the failure to design assessment procedures which discriminate among programs and strategies fit for varying populations; (5) the unwillingness of educators to combine populations and programs in developing the larger research design needed for cross-community evaluation; (6) the reluctance to distinguish between short-term and long-term outcomes; (7) the failure to develop and implement longitudinal programs, and to support the need for such programs.

Recognizing the interaction among these problems, Dr. Goldberg urges the initiation of carefully designed experimental programs to assess alternative theoretical positions. Cooperation among school systems will be necessary to provide populations adequate for sound appraisal. Dr. Goldberg is especially adamant in advising program planners and proposal developers to think of evaluation and assessment from the start. To treat evaluation as an appendage to an ongoing activity is to jeopardize its value and its validity.

PROBLEMS IN THE EVALUATION OF COMPENSATORY PROGRAMS

Miriam L. Goldberg

45

PROBLEMS IN THE EVALUATION OF COMPENSATORY PROGRAMS

Miriam L. Goldberg*

Recently, in a discussion of the reading retardation and consequent academic difficulties which consistently beset children from depressed areas, a colleague asked, "Is this a new problem, or has it been with us all along?" Implied in the question, though unstated, was, "Why all this fuss today?"

The answer, of course, is that the problem is not new. What is new is the overt recognition of its existence and the growing sense of urgency about its solution. If, as a nation, we were not in the past goaded by moral outrage to rectify the social and educational conditions that allowed a segment of our population to remain semiliterate, barred from access to any but the most menial work and poorest living conditions, we have now been forced by the shifting economy, the civil rights movement, and the vision of "social dynamite" accumulating in our great cities to attack the problem.

It is not the spirit of the old do-gooders that characterizes present efforts; it is, rather, a spirit of giving people their due, of affording them the education and the power to enter and share fully in the benefits of an affluent society. The effort is massive, backed by billions in public funds, resembling big business in its dimensions if not its efficiency. Unlike the individual service or philanthropic effort of earlier days, which found its rewards in the act of giving and in the personal gratification which came from "uplifting" even a single individual, the present approach is not only impersonal on the part of the funders, but like any good business, it will demand an accounting of returns for money spent. And the accounting will be in terms of such measurable factors as decreases in the rate of delinquency and crime, increases in employability, and a rise in the holding power of the schools and in the educational attainment of the students.

Such an accounting may place demands upon the educational and social service establishments that were never confronted before. Demonstration of effort through the provision of special services, increased personnel, or improved facilities will no longer be enough. Nor will verbal assertions of significant effects on the part of participants (either the servers or the served) suffice. Hard money will call for hard facts.

---

*Reprinted by permission from the Journal of School Psychology.

But there is an even more compelling need for tight and careful evaluation of special programs for the disadvantaged that grows out of moral and educational commitments rather than fiscal ones. If, as educators, we are committed to the thesis that much of the learning difficulty (and consequent social and economic problems) of disadvantaged young people results from poor preparation and motivation for learning at home and ineffective teaching at school, then compensatory programs must be developed which demonstrate real and lasting gains in intellectual and academic performance. Any program that fails to accomplish these ends must be modified or replaced until effective procedures are evolved.

To date, the various educational intervention programs for disadvantaged pupils introduced over the last half-dozen years have provided little definitive evidence on their effects, although each has had its vociferous proponents and many glowing descriptions appear in the literature. Thus, the total effort remains handicapped by a lack of knowledge of what works and what doesn't work for which children.

What follows is an attempt to delineate some of the problems that interfere with sound evaluation. The list is by no means exhaustive, nor is it ordered in terms of importance or sequence. The various problems not only overlap, but, in some instances actually grow out of each other. The reader should proceed with these caveats in mind.

Urgency, Action, and Commitment

Perhaps the most serious deterrent to effective evaluation derives from the compelling nature of the problems that the compensatory programs set out to tackle. There are hundreds of thousands of children who aren't acquiring the level of literacy necessary to function adequately in our increasingly technical, reading-dependent society. Thousands are dropping out of school and flooding the labor market without any salable skills and often without the basic preparation to benefit from on-the-job training. Teachers are frustrated in their attempts to teach and are clamoring for help; parent and community pressures beset the school authorities. Something must be done! Under the press and clamor for action, it is difficult, indeed, for the school to countenance the aloof stance of the researcher or even to attend to the pleas of those who want to postpone broad-scale introduction of procedures whose worth remains untested. Schools attend, instead, to those who have an action plan. Some of these plans are predicated on the belief that any innovative action is better than no action and that a new procedure, especially if based on some theoretical rationale, will certainly be no worse than what it replaces and may even do some good. Other plans are proposed by proselytizers who are committed to a specific solution, know all the answers, and convince the school to put their ideas into practice on a large scale. In both instances, a considerable investment of effort and money goes into the new programs, and schools become committed to their continuation and expansion. There is neither time nor perceived need for careful, objective evaluation. The program is a success—the laudatory statements of teachers, students, and parents testify to the fact. As one administrator said, "I'm not going to let any evidence stand in the way of my program."

Evaluation—An Afterthought

In many instances, however, evaluation of special programs is deemed desirable and consultants are called to help in the assessment. Unfortunately, they are invited after the program is already in full swing. They generally find that no information had been collected on the pupils before the program began; all eligible pupils have been involved and provided with a great array of special services, so that no one procedure can be assessed independently for any group of children. Small wonder that the research consultant is frustrated by the task and supports the school in soliciting testimonials or making gross comparisons with pupils of previous years "to prove" the effectiveness of the program.

Input Unspecified or Confounded

Perhaps more critical than the methodological problems of *how* to evaluate a program are the substantive ones of knowing *what* is being evaluated. Most of the compensatory programs have been based either on apparently logical action corollaries derived from theoretical formulations or upon the expanded use of procedures that had proved effective in other contexts.

The most recent example of programs based on theoretically derived action is Head Start. The theory (supported by a considerable body of evidence) asserts that intelligence is developed through experience, that the impoverished cognitive and language environment of the disadvantaged child prevents the development of his full intellectual capacities and consequently retards his academic progress. The action corollary is to provide early, compensatory experiences, to give the disadvantaged three- or four-year-old in school the enriching experiences that the middle-class child normally receives in his home, in short, to develop compensatory prekindergarten programs.

On the other hand, the Great Cities Projects, for example, are built around multiple services such as increased personal guidance, extended remedial teaching, smaller classes, extended school day, and so forth (Research Council of the Great Cities Program for School Improvement, 1964). They assume that since such services were effective with slow learners from middle-class backgrounds, they will, of necessity, be effective with disadvantaged pupils, and if one service is good, two are better. This is the "massive-attack" approach.

Unfortunately, both kinds of programs as now constituted preclude effective evaluation. The massive-attack approach, in which many special services are used conjunctively, does not allow for assessing the effects

49

of any one nor the interaction of any cluster. As a result, programs that appear to affect gains in their pilot stages (where all services are intensive and heavily funded, and where a strong Hawthorne effect operates) turn out to have little if any effects when they are disseminated to many schools on a curtailed budget. Since there is no way of identifying which services or combinations were responsible for the positive effect, nor the money to achieve in a hundred schools (without benefit of the Hawthorne effect), the full impact possible in the pilot school, the expanded programs, as in the case of Higher Horizons in New York City, turn out to be ineffectual.[1]

What is far more serious than the waste of money and effort is the failure of five or six years' work to increase our knowledge of what works and what doesn't. The only ones served by such failures are those who use them as confirmation of their belief in the basic inferiority of disadvantaged children.

Apparently, the rapidly expanding prekindergarten programs are heading into the same difficulties but for somewhat different reasons. The hypothesis that the disadvantaged child's intellectual, language, and social development and, consequently, his later school learning can be enhanced by enriched experience before grade school is derived from sound theoretical formulations. But it remains a hypothesis to be tested. Thus far, however, there is no agreement on the kind of program that will most effectively "enrich" the child. Some see the standard nursery-school model with its emphasis on free play, creative expression, and socialization as appropriate. At the other extreme, there is the "prep school" model which provides short periods of intensive instruction in the areas of deficit-language, reading preparation, number concepts.[2] Between these two extremes are the Montessori programs (Standing, 1962), the semistructured enrichment programs that introduce specially designed teaching exercises as well as utilize the children's play activities as vehicles for language and concept development (Institute for Developmental Studies, 1965), the programs that stress interpersonal relations and the provision of a warm and affectional climate, and, finally, those that are, perforce, eclectic, since they have no specific rationale.

Nor is there any consistency in the amount of time spent in the program. Some schools operate four days a week, two hours per day; others have the children every day of the week for anywhere from two to eight hours per day. Some are summer programs of four to eight weeks' duration; others are all-year programs; some extend over a two-year period.

Teacher qualifications vary considerably. In some cases a teacher must hold certification in preschool education; in others, a primary school

---

[1]For the effects of the pilot program in a single junior high school see New York Board of Education (1960). For the final evaluation of the Higher Horizons program, which grew out of the P.S. 43 pilot study, see Wrightstone (1964).
[2]The best example of a highly structured, instruction-oriented program for four-year-olds is described by Carl Bereiter (1965).

certificate suffices, and in some instances any teacher is eligible. The exposure to a six-day special training course (as was the case for Head Start teachers last summer) can do little to bring a common orientation to the teachers and even less to provide them with needed skills. To ask of this amorphous mass whether it improves the school performance of the children is to ask whether medication will cure infection. It is an unanswerable question until both the nature of the infection and the medication have been specified.

Yet, such a question is even now being asked and, in the near future, will be asked even more insistently. To attempt to evaluate all of the varied, discrepant, and unspecified prekindergarten programs as if they represented a single common intervention procedure can only be justified by those who hold the position that just *any* supervised group experience for young disadvantaged children will upgrade their later academic attainment, a position that is hardly tenable in the face of the evidence (Swift, 1964). What is more, the varied rationales (where there is any rationale at all) lead to different diagnoses of the problem, and to different concepts of what constitutes appropriate education for young children as well as to differences in the degree to which the program can be specified.

Whether any one approach is more effective than another in achieving the end goals of improved school learning, whether some programs that achieve better academic results jeopardize the emotional development of the child *en route*, so to speak, whether the amount of time given to the program or the kind of preparation the teachers have really makes a difference still remain to be discovered. To answer these questions requires, before anything else, precise operational descriptions of the various programs as they exist in practice so that it becomes clear, in each instance, *what* is actually being done. Only then will the evaluator be in a position to make statements with some confidence regarding the effects of what was done at the prekindergarten level on what happens in the later school years.

What Works for Whom

Not only is the content of the programs often left unspecified, but the varying characteristics of the children involved usually remain unidentified. At the grade-school level, there is generally some initial test information available against which to measure gains attributable to the special programs. At the prekindergarten level, not even such limited information is available. There is a tacit assumption that children from homes where the income is at poverty level are all more or less alike in their educational needs and any group is, generally, representative of all poor children. In actual fact, however, this is not the case. In the first place, most of the participants in the prekindergarten programs are volunteers, children of parents who are willing to make the special effort necessary to get their children to school. Are these children similar in their developmental status to those who are not sent? Does the very fact of sending a

51

three- or four-year-old child to school reflect an attitude in the home which affects the child's development? To generalize from the volunteer group to all disadvantaged children is hardly appropriate. To discover how representative the voluntary participants are of the total population requires finding ways to involve children whose parents do not voluntarily bring them to school.

Similarly, there is a tendency to ignore characteristics related to the ethnic background or to the structure and life style of the families from which the children come. But it is more serious to allow the fact of common poverty to mask individual differences among the children. Disadvantaged children vary not only in general learning ability but in particular areas of development. Some may be mature, independent, and feel totally accepted at home; others may be dependent, rejected, or neglected. Some children may be bold, willing to take risks, and try new things. Others may be timid, frightened of anything unknown, and unwilling to participate in school activities. Some children may have serious perceptual difficulties due to neurological impairment or developmental retardation; others may exhibit difficulties in language, listening ability, or attention span. Thus, both adaptations of programs and the valid evaluation of their effects depend upon procuring initial information on the unique characteristics of the children to be served. This requires the use of assessment measures that effectively discriminate among young disadvantaged children. Unfortunately, standardized objective measures valid for a disadvantaged population are presently unavailable. Although individual intelligence tests do provide some valuable information, they do not give a sufficiently clear or complete picture of the learning potential of the disadvantaged child. If we are to understand the effects of specific compensatory activities on the amelioration of the variety and range of disadvantages presented by poor children, the development of appropriate techniques of assessment becomes crucial.

The Myth of Localism

Inadequate evaluation is often a function of the size of the population. In many communities there are not enough "disadvantaged" children to allow for appropriate control groups and certainly too few to make comparative studies of various approaches possible. Yet, many such small communities could participate in cooperative studies (such as the multisystem study of prekindergarten programs now being conducted under New York State Education Department auspices) and, thus, make up for the small numbers in each separate district. But, too often, the traditional belief that somehow each community is substantially different from all others leads to the assertion that a meaningful program must be tailored to the local situation, and, thus, must be locally developed. Such attitudes not only preclude joint cross-district enterprises, but also make it difficult to duplicate previously tested programs.

How influential are local differences on the performance of children from the same ethnic groups and the same low socioeconomic status? How different, for example, are the needs of poor Negro children who live in the suburbs of New York rather than in the suburbs of Chicago, or, for that matter, in one New York suburb as against another? Does it really matter whether rural Appalachian children have moved to Cincinnati or to St. Louis? The sacred cow of localism leads to rejection of nationally developed or even state-developed programs and thus precludes effective evaluation of any coherent, common approach. As more adequate assessment instruments become available it may be possible to demonstrate that individual differences within the disadvantaged population in any one locale are greater than those due to differences among relatively similar districts (suburban, urban, rural, regional). Until school districts recognize that their children differ more among themselves than they differ, as a group, from the children of the neighboring town or small city, there will be a proliferation of minor variations in programs, which, while of little consequence in their efforts on the pupils, make cross-community evaluation programs impossible.

Short-Term Outcomes and Long-Term Goals

Human effort wants its recompense. And even middle-class educators, with their ostensible ability to defer gratification, are impatient for some tangible signs that their work has borne fruit. But to understand this need is not to condone the confusion that develops when signs of progress in the ongoing situation become the basis for determining a program's ultimate success.

Any compensatory program has both intermediate and end goals. In fact, some of the intermediate goals are set because they are considered to be instrumental to the achievement of the long-range objectives. For example, one city has greatly increased personnel and services in a group of pilot schools in slum areas in the belief that more intensive work with individual children, closer, more personal relations between teacher and pupils made possible by smaller classes, more opportunities for social and academic interaction among the pupils, will lead to improved academic performance. Such programs, of course, fall into the trap of the multi-attack strategy discussed before. But here they are considered for another reason. Despite the fact that the evidence on achievement gains is far from definitive (Public Schools of New York City, 1965), the program is to be extended to other schools next year. The data reported make no mention of control groups, but instead show greater achievement for the 8-month period than was previously noted. No consideration is given to the probability that May gains are lost by September. Nor was any attempt made to control for the Hawthorne effect. The decision was therefore based on an assessment of the situation in progress. In most of the pilot schools pupils appeared more motivated, more engaged. Teachers were more satisfied. There was more remedial work, more time spent helping individual children. The climate in the school was more relaxed, there were less disciplinary difficulties, and a businesslike atmosphere prevailed. Desirable as these phenomena may be, and they are certainly inherently worthwhile, they do not insure that the end goal—retention of gains in academic performance—will be reached. It is difficult to question the apparent logic that a more benign school climate, increased individual attention, and enhanced teacher and pupil satisfaction will automatically lead to academic improvement. But logically derived hypotheses are not evidence, as witness the achievement outcomes of the Higher Horizons Program or the All-Day Neighborhood School Program in New York City, both of which were predicated on sound logic (Sexton, 1965).

The problem of confusing short- and long-term gains is most clearly seen in the prekindergarten programs. Nursery school education can provide the young child of any social class with valuable experiences. It helps him learn to cope with himself, his peers, and the demands of a social situation. There is little need to evaluate nursery school education in any terms other than those which derive from its effects on the child *while he is in the school.*

We do not expect that the middle-class child who has had nursery school experience will necessarily do better in grade school than one who hasn't. In fact, the evidence on middle-class children seems to indicate that by the end of first grade, equally bright children with or without nursery or kindergarten experience are hardly distinguishable from each other (Swift, 1964). Under normal circumstances, nursery education is not viewed as a "head start" for school but rather is appropriate to the young child's present developmental level.

But for disadvantaged children, the expectations from nursery level education are far greater; perhaps unreasonably so. What underlies the current support of prekindergarten programs is the hope that the children will develop the necessary skills and attitudes to *cope more effectively with school learning.* This is the end goal. And until there is evidence that such programs do, indeed, foster improved academic performance, one cannot judge them successful, regardless of other desirable outcomes that may emerge. If the end goal implicit in the present Head Start movement—for such it has become—is improved intellectual and academic functioning, then the formal evaluation must wait at least until the end of second grade at which point academic performance becomes reliably predictive of later school achievement.[3] Studies must, therefore, be longitudinal, covering a span of at least four years. The practitioners and eval-

---

[3]An unpublished series of studies recently completed by Joseph M. Breen, Director of Reading for the Farmington, Connecticut Public Schools, found correlations of .75 to .80 between reading scores at Grades 2 and 5 and even higher correlations between second-grade reading and fifth-grade composite achievement test scores.

uators need patience and forebearance and, while satisfying their own needs for effort rewarded by looking at evidence of short-term improvement, must hold in abeyance the final judgment on the effectiveness of specified early enrichment programs until the achievement data are in.

The One-Shot Fallacy

From the few experimental studies done here and abroad on the effects of early compensatory education, it would appear that many of the cognitive gains made in prekindergarten years tend to level off and disappear after a year or two in the normal school situation.[4] This finding may result from the nature of the intervention programs: they may have had too little structure or too much; they may have focused on experiences not sufficiently relevant to school demands, or they may have started too late. These problems can and should be investigated experimentally. But an equally tenable hypothesis — again to be studied experimentally — is that no one dose of compensatory experience is enough. Whatever limitations the child's environment imposes on his early development may well continue to limit his later school learning. For the middle-class child, the home and the community remain active teaching agents throughout childhood and adolescence, and the teaching generally enhances the work of the school. Thus, even if the nursery experience succeeds in raising the perceptual, cognitive, and language development of the disadvantaged preschool child to a level commensurate with his more advantaged peers, is it logical to assume that beyond that point the child whose home or community provides little school-related learning or motivation will do as well as the middle-class child continuously taught and motivated by home and community?

What needs study is not only the nature of the compensatory experiences that are most effective at the nursery level, but also how long such special intervention must continue. If nursery school gains are to insure improved academic work in the grades, what kinds of "enrichment" experiences need to be carried over to the following years? What parts of the current primary curriculum need to be postponed or changed? What kinds of special services need to be introduced?

At this stage of our ignorance it would be tragic, indeed, if we abandoned support of the Head Start approach because, by itself, it fails to improve later learning or if we continued it for its inherent values and failed to study the effects of combined nursery and primary compensatory efforts.

---

[4]The several reports evaluating nursery enrichment programs generally show little effect on grade-school performance (Klaus and Gray, 1962; Weikart, et al., 1964; Ypsilanti Public Schools, 1964; Alpern, 1965). A verbal communication recently received indicated that the substantial gains in IQ found at the end of a two-year intensive compensatory enrichment program for children from four to six almost disappeared by the end of first grade.

The Need for Planned Experimentation

It is quite apparent that the several problems treated separately in this paper are, in reality, interdependent. To gain dependable knowledge of what constitutes effective compensatory education or what curricular modifications result in the greatest improvement in the school achievement of disadvantaged children requires that all of the problems be considered simultaneously.

Unfortunately, it is difficult to impose all the necessary strictures on programs now in progress. The lack of specificity of input and population, the multiservice approach, the professional as well as emotional investment already committed to ongoing programs make changes necessitated by effective evaluation difficult to make. Instead of counting on the evaluation of ongoing programs for the needed knowledge, it may be wiser to develop carefully designed experimental programs based on various current theoretical positions and invite the cooperation of many, varied school systems. Such a procedure could obviate many of the problems that now hamper effective evaluation: they would be free of prior commitment to any given approach on the part of the researcher but could capitalize on the varied convictions and commitments of teachers, thereby minimizing the Hawthorne effect. They could be highly specific as to input and pupil populations, use adequate sampling procedures and appropriate measurement instruments, allow for short- and long-term assessment, build in necessary longitudinal variations and, above all, provide clarity of desired outcomes. Multiple approaches tested under a single experimental design could provide some dependable knowledge of what kinds of compensatory programs really make a difference in the development and achievement of disadvantaged children at different ages. Only then will we be in a position to make optimum use of the growing funds becoming available for compensatory programs and to face both the fiscal and moral day of reckoning with confidence.

References

Alpern, Gerald D. *The Failure of a Nursery School Enrichment Program for Culturally Disadvantaged Children.* Indianapolis: Indiana University Medical School, 1965. Mimeographed.

Bereiter, Carl and S. Engelmann. *Teaching Disadvantaged Children in the Preschool.* Englewood Cliffs, N.J.: Prentice-Hall, Inc., 1966.

Institute for Developmental Studies. *Annual Report, 1965.* New York: New York Medical College, 1965.

Klaus, Rupert A. and Susan W. Gray. *Early Training Project: Interim Report, November, 1962.* Nashville, Tenn.: George Peabody College, 1962. Mimeographed.

New York City Board of Education. *Demonstration Guidance Project, Junior High School 43 Manhattan and George Washington High*

School. Fourth Annual Progress Report, 1959–1960. New York: The Board, 1960.

————. *"Encouraging Progress"* in the More Effective Schools. Staff Bulletin No. 4. New York: The Board, 1965.

Research Council of the Great Cities Program for School Improvement. *Promising Practices from the Project for the Culturally Deprived.* Chicago: The Council, 1964.

Sexton, Pátricia C. *An Assessment of the All-Day Neighborhood School Program for Culturally Deprived Children.* Cooperative Research Project No. 1527. New York: New York University, 1965. Mimeographed.

Standing, E. M. *The Montessori Method. A Revolution in Education.* Fresno, Calif.: E. M. Standing, 1962.

Swift, Joan M. "Effects of Early Group Experience: The Nursery School and Day Nursery" in *Child Development Research*, Vol. I, eds. Martin L. and Lois Wlades Hoffman. New York: Russell Sage Foundation, 1964.

Weikart, David P., *et al. Perry Preschool Project Progress Report.* Ypsilanti, Mich.: Ypsilanti Public Schools, 1964. Mimeographed.

Wrightstone, J. Wayne, *et al. Evaluation of the Higher Horizons Program for Underprivileged Children.* Cooperative Research Project No. 1124. New York: Bureau of Educational Research, New York City Board of Education, 1964.

Frank Riessman was one of the first to alert the educational community to the plight of the disadvantaged. The Culturally Deprived Child (1962) spearheaded the flood of literature of the past few years. Here, Riessman presents some additional ideas he has had in the intervening period. Successes have been limited, he declares, for at least three reasons: the lack of an integrated theory; an emphasis on deficits rather than on the utilization of strengths; and minimal efforts to equip the classroom teacher, who has not been perceived as a strategic change agent.

What is needed, the author declares, is a revolution in education which would not only cope with the disjointed hodgepodge of compensatory programs but would select and blend those approaches which seem — to professional analysts — to have worked. Riessman would recruit a large number of nonprofessionals from the ranks of the poor to aid the teacher. Instead of simply seeking to produce "a carbon copy of the middle-class child," teachers are advised to capitalize on the strengths of the inner-city child in emerging programs.

FURTHER THOUGHTS ON EDUCATING THE DISADVANTAGED

Frank Riessman

Several promising techniques are spelled out by Riessman. He illustrates several of them, including a "dialect game," which builds on the youngsters' "hip" language, the utilization of students as "peer teachers," and role playing — a particularly congenial means of cultivating verbal skills among the disadvantaged.

The author concludes his paper by urging an educational commitment on the scale of our current investment in a "moon shot." Measures short of such a commitment are bound to fail.

FURTHER THOUGHTS ON EDUCATING THE DISADVANTAGED

Frank Riessman

In the past several years, enormous interest has been expressed concerning the education of the disadvantaged, inner-city child. Programs developing in various cities throughout the United States have met with varying success. Among the most promising events:

> Negro Assistant Superintendent of Schools Sam Shephard has quickly brought youngsters up to grade level in St. Louis with special motivational appeals to parents and youngsters and a new "listening" approach to teachers.

> Special teacher preparation developed at Hunter College in New York appears to aid teachers in slum areas.

> New approaches have overcome illiteracy in adults with surprising speed in the Army.

> Programed learning has had some marked effects on dropouts in New York and prisoners in Alabama whose level of intellectual functioning was quite low.[1]

> Montessori techniques have achieved results in Los Angeles and Mount Vernon; imaginative "hip" lessons combined with role playing have proved exciting in Syracuse; team teaching has worked in Pittsburgh; new readers have improved reading levels of educationally deprived youngsters in Detroit.

Despite these encouraging reports, large-scale improvements in the learning of disadvantaged youngsters have not been achieved, for at least three reasons.

> The efforts have been piecemeal and unintegrated. One technique is used here, and another there, but there has been no theoretically directed integrated approach.

> The major emphasis has been on deficits and "compensatory" efforts directed toward overcoming them; there has been little understanding of how to use the strengths of disadvantaged youngsters, if, indeed, it is recognized that those strengths exist at all.

---

[1] Nongraded classes, multiple periods, use of imaginative gamelike techniques, to name just a few other approaches, have also shown considerable potential.

61

There has been no concerted effort to meet the felt needs of the teachers — for lower student-teacher ratios, techniques that work, a voice in decisions that affect them, and so forth. The classroom teacher has not typically been perceived as the strategic agent for massive improvement in the learning of the poor.[2] (Instead, much stress has been placed on parents, preschools, teaching machines, psychological guidance, and special services.)

The present period combines the strong demands of the Civil Rights movement for *quality* integrated education with tremendous financial support from the Federal Government and a "Great Education President." In this climate, it would seem that a revolutionary breakthrough in the education of the poor can now be planned, as a first step in revitalizing our public schools and winning back the middle classes who have fled to the private schools. It is truly time to aim for the moon and not accept improvement up to grade level.

What, then, should be the ingredients of our projected revolution in education? Should we combine all the various features that have worked, in a kind of potpourri, or should we rather selectively choose approaches based on an analysis that offers an explanation in a coherent fashion of why they have worked? The latter is not only theoretically more meaningful, but probably less expensive.[3]

We would now like to propose the outlines of such a program.

The New Manpower

Perhaps the major complaint in the schools today is the large classes that each teacher must manage. The ratio of students to teachers is frequently greater than thirty to one. New manpower to assist the badly overworked teacher is the paramount need of the day. Where can it be found? The utilization of large numbers of people drawn from the ranks of the poor themselves, so called nonprofessionals, to serve as teacher assistants, teacher aides, parent-teacher coordinators, and the like may be the answer.

Currently in the classroom there is but one designated role — teacher. Incorporated in that role are a great number of diverse functions — the teacher is an educator, but he is also a clerk, a custodian, an operator of audio-visual equipment, and an audio-version of a printed book. In many slum schools the impression gained is that the teacher is part lion-tamer and part warehouseman. The latter roles must be eliminated, and many of the others can be assumed by less qualified personnel.

---

[2]The current concern for a national Teacher Corps and special teacher training programs sponsored by NDEA, etc. is in the right direction.

[3]The program could be placed within the framework of the developing educational parks or educational complexes that would allow for economic utilization of a great variety of new techniques and facilities (educational TV, programed learning, team teaching, and so forth) under one roof, but that is not necessary for our "moonshot."

The use of this kind of nonprofessional manpower would serve a number of functions.

(1) It would free teachers from the many nonprofessional tasks they now perform, for example, taking attendance, helping children on with their boots, tying children's shoelaces, running moving-picture projectors, and taking youngsters on trips. The new teacher aides would take over many of these tasks, freeing teachers for their basic professional assignment, teaching and teaching creatively.

(2) Nonprofessionals (especially males) drawn from the ranks of the poor would serve as excellent role models for the disadvantaged youngsters in the schools; the youngsters would see that it is possible for people like themselves, drawn from their own neighborhood, to "make it" in the system. Communication between the trained nonprofessional and the disadvantaged youngster would probably be good because the nonprofessional drawn from the neighborhood speaks the language of the poor and understands his peers. Many of the advantages of peer learning or learning from people at the same level would be utilized.

(3) The atmosphere of the school would be quite different and many of the management problems that are anticipated in the urban, newly integrated schools might be dissipated. The tremendous shortage of school personnel predicted for the next decade might be drastically reduced through the employment of one million nonprofessionals in the schools.[4]

It goes without saying that the use of aides would not be imposed upon teachers. In fact, teachers' associations and unions should participate in the entire planning for the use of nonprofessionals, and guarantees should be introduced to insure that no aide infringes on professional domain by engaging in actual teaching or other professional functions.

Probably the best way to introduce nonprofessionals into the system is to ask teachers to volunteer to accept an aide to assist them. The teachers who make the selections can then define the tasks on which they would like nonprofessional assistance. (They may also receive consultation on this from the program planners.) It is quite likely that if the aides are really helpful, the program will contagiously spread, and other teachers will request nonprofessional assistants for their classrooms. In this way the idea can be institutionalized with the full cooperation of the professional staff and the new professional-nonprofessional team can be built on a solid foundation.

Teachers not only need new manpower to assist them in the classroom; they need a new approach as well.

---

[4] Pearl and Riessman (1965) have provided a more detailed description of how nonprofessionals could serve the school.

Too often nowadays, teachers are being asked to act like psychologists —and understand the underlying emotional conflicts of the child; like sociologists—and appreciate the environment and culture of the deprived; like prison guards—and keep order and prevent violence; like substitute parents—and love the children; like ministers—and impart the right values.

It is time that teachers concentrated on teaching, developing and applying that art and science to the utmost. It is toward this objective that the following techniques are directed.

But before turning to the techniques themselves, a word about basic classroom strategy: Everything the teacher says and does in the classroom should be related to learning. He should repeat over and over and over again: "I am here to teach and you are here to learn." This should be expressed in the teacher's every action and should be related to every rule and value.

Thus all rules related to punctuality, aggression, and so forth, should be strictly oriented toward their usefulness in relation to learning. The teacher says: "We can't conduct a class if children fight, or come late, or walk around. . . ." This is not a minister informing children about values— that fighting is "bad." Rather, it is a teacher conducting a class.

Techniques and Goals

The emphasis on teaching technology in the entire effort is very important. Teachers cannot be expected to become sociologists or psychologists and acquire an intensive understanding of the psychology and culture of the poor. Rather, they must come to understand something about the relation of their techniques to the style and strength of the poor, but the emphasis must be on the techniques themselves. As teachers successfully utilize these techniques, their confidence will improve and their motivation will be enhanced. Our accent, therefore, is on giving teachers what they want, namely know-how.

The techniques to be employed should be based fundamentally on the goals one is striving for with the disadvantaged. I do not have the goal of simply producing a carbon copy of the middle-class child.[5]

To aim for this middle-class replica is not only inappropriate in principle but actually not easily achievable in practice. The disadvantaged child will probably resist this objective, and to the extent that he acquieses, he will become a poor edition of the middle-class youngster—a very faded

[5]The real question, for those who want to "middle-classize" the disadvantaged child, is "Which middle class—the professional upper middle class? The anti-intellectual lower middle class? The new "hip" class that has adopted much of the speech and some of the manners of various disadvantaged subcultures? The progressive student left?" Furthermore, isn't it possible that the disadvantaged youngster will selectively choose those middle-class characteristics that at least articulate with some of his own traditions and feelings?

carbon copy. My objective, therefore, is to build on the strengths of the inner-city child, not to deny them or suppress them, but rather to utilize them as the key to developing, for example, language and interest in language. But my concern for building on the strengths of the disadvantaged child is not simply so that he can be more efficiently brought into the mainstream of American life; rather, I want also to have him bring into this mainstream some of his characteristics: his style, his pep, his vitality, his demand that the school not be boring and dull, his rich feeling for metaphor and colorful language.

One group of disadvantaged people in America, the Negro people, have made an enormous contribution to the mainstream of American life through their articulate, noncompromising demands for integration "now." These people have brought a new morality to American life as a whole. To the extent that we are beginning to hold our heads up high and feel again like democratic, ethical, human Americans. In education, likewise, the mainstream of American life can profit from what the various groups among the poor can bring to the school system both in terms of the demands made upon the system that it be peppier, livelier, more vital, more down-to-earth, more real, and more in touch with the style and interests brought to the school. This style will enable the school to become far less bookish and will enable it to utilize a far greater variety of styles—an action style, a physical style, a visual style—than the over-utilized and over-emphasized reading-lecture styles traditionally in vogue.

The techniques that I will discuss are uniquely related to these goals and to the belief that there is a positive style in the disadvantaged that can be utilized to the great benefit of all classes. But if this goal is not accepted, the techniques can still be utilized with varying degrees of effectiveness. Thus the reader can go on even if he does not accept the overall objective.

The Dialect Game

The best way to illustrate the relationship of the teaching technology I am advocating and the goals being put forth is to take a look at one very simple technique that I learned from a teacher, who evolved it out of her own practice. I call it the *dialect game.*

One day a youngster said to this teacher, "Do you hear that boid outside the window?" and the teacher responded, "That's not a boid, it's a bird." Following the old joke, the youngster replied, "He choips just like a boid." It is fairly clear that this way of teaching the youngster the standard pronunciations of words can be not only unsuccessful in its avowed objective, but can, in addition, produce cognitive confusion about the object itself.

The teacher thereupon decided that it could be very easy to teach youngsters the standard pronunciations if they were not required to reject their own dialects, their slang, their "hip" language. So she decided to play a game by taking any word at random and asking the youngsters how

65

it would be said in their language, then how it should be said in the standard language. The youngsters, as well as the teacher, found this game very exciting and both learned a great deal. They now were learning the standard words as they might learn a foreign language, and they were discovering that their own language was perfectly acceptable and merely had to be used in the proper circumstances — in their discussions with friends and family, and on the street — while for formal purposes, another language was appropriate and was being taught in the school. But something else happened in this situation. The youngsters began to become very much interested in language as such, so that in discussing the hip word "cool," for instance, indirectly, language nuances were beginning to be taught. Youngsters began to understand why we use certain foreign words that are not completely translatable, like "coup d'etat," because they have special connotations in their original language that our language cannot duplicate.

They learned something else, too. They learned that their own language was not something negative to be denied or suppressed, but that actually many of their words had nuances and meanings which had not been fully acquired in the standard language and that therefore the slang and hip words had been adopted by the larger culture, so that today, "jazz," "cooling it," "copping out," and many, many other rich colorful words are accepted usage in English. This is building on their positives, not rejecting them, and bringing their strengths and interests into the mainstream of our life.

There are a number of other simple adaptations of this dialect game. Recently in tutoring a disadvantaged high school student in English, I employed a "hiptionary" in a completely systematic and formal fashion. The first and rather immediate result was that the student learned a great many new English word definitions for the hip words with which she was long familiar, namely:

Hip Word[6]	Definition
bug	to disturb, bother, annoy
cop out	to avoid conflict by running away (in a manner not considered admirable or honorably accepted)
cool it	to be quiet, peaceful, tranquil
far out	not comprehensible
weak	inadequate, inappropriate

[6]The words in this list were taken from an unpublished hiptionary entitled **The Other Language** developed by Anthony Romeo (1962) at Mobilization for Youth, New York.

Words such as "tranquil" and "inappropriate" were not known by this youngster, but through use of the hip word game she quickly became familiar with them and derived great pleasure from a new found use of various "big" words.

Another interesting illustration is furnished by the problem of teaching English to Puerto Rican and Mexican children entering our school systems in New York, California, and other parts of the country. The typical tendency is to force these youngsters not to speak any of their mother tongue, namely Spanish, but rather to insist that they speak only English, on the supposition that this would be the best way of their acquiring the English language. While this may be a perfectly acceptable way of teaching language to an adult in certain contexts, when it is associated in the child with rejection of his minority culture (something he experiences quite frequently), he is not likely to be an apt pupil in the new language. Furthermore, he is constantly in the inferior position of having to acquire this language while the remainder of the youngsters in the class already know it. The dialect game can be utilized beautifully to reverse the whole procedure. Instead of emphasizing the need for the Spanish-speaking children to learn English, the situation can be reversed for part of the day, and the Spanish-speaking children can be instructed to teach Spanish to the English-speaking children. In other words, both languages become important in the class. The English-speaking children have an opportunity to learn a foreign language (presumably a positive benefit when that language is French or Latin), and the Spanish-speaking children can be placed temporarily in the position of some superiority through helping others. In addition, of course, in order for the Puerto Rican youngster to teach Spanish to the American child, the Puerto Rican child must be able to communicate to some extent in English, and in the very process of teaching the foreign language, he must acquire more English in order to communicate (unless *he* arbitrarily insists that only Spanish be spoken when he is instructing!).

Thus the dialect game, which can be utilized by anyone as a "gimmick" or an auxiliary technique in teaching, takes on considerable depth when seen in the context of two cultures, two languages functioning alongside of each other, both being respected, both affecting each other with no condescension toward the minority culture.

The Helper Principle: Learning Through Teaching.

Another fascinating approach to the expansion of classroom learning. is to be found in Lippitt's intriguing "peer learning" experiments, which demonstrate that youngsters in the sixth grade can be helpful in teaching younger children — and can benefit themselves from playing the teacher role (Lippitt, 1965, p. 29).

At the recent White House Conference on Education, Professor Jerrold Zaccharias proposed that as a major avenue for improving their own learning, we have students *teach*. Montessorians have long had children help other children learn in the classroom.

Mobilization for Youth has used homework helpers with a fair amount of success, in that the recipients of the help showed some measurable academic improvement. It may be that even more significant changes are taking place in the high-school youngsters who are being used as tutors. Not only is it possible that their school performance is improving, but as a result of their new role these youngsters may begin to perceive the possibility of embarking on a teaching career.

A connected issue worthy of mention is that in the new situations in the schools, where (hopefully) integration will be taking place, youngsters coming from segregated backgrounds will need help in catching up, in terms of reading skills and the like. It is generally argued that the white middle-class children who do not need this extra assistance will suffer. Their parents want these youngsters to be in a class with other advanced pupils, and do not want them to be "held back" by youngsters who are behind.

However, in terms of the helper principle, it may very well be that the more advanced youngsters can benefit in new ways from playing a teaching role. Not all fast, bright youngsters like to be in a class with similar children. We have been led to believe that if one is fast and bright he will want to be with others who are fast and bright and that this will act as a stimulus to his growth. It does for some people, but for others it most certainly does not. Some people find they do better in a group in which there is a great range of ability, in which they can stand out more, and, finally — and this is the point of the helper principle — in situations in which they can help other youngsters in the classroom. In other words, some children develop intellectually not by being challenged by someone ahead of them, but by helping somebody behind them, by being put into the tutor-helper role.

As any teacher can report, there is nothing like learning through teaching. By having to explain something to someone else, one's attention is focused more sharply.

The helper principle may be especially valuable for disadvantaged youngsters because in their informal out-of-school learning they tend to learn much more from each other, from their brothers and sisters, than from having their parents read them a book or answer their questions. They are essentially peer learners by style and experience.

Capturing the Action Style through Role Playing

Role playing can be used to teach arithmetic and economics by "playing store," to teach history by acting out George Washington signing the Constitution, even to teach language by acting out words — in fact, the game "In the Manner of the Adverb" consists of "doing" the adverb, walking *quickly,* writing *quickly,* and so forth.

Role playing has long been popular with disadvantaged youngsters (Lippitt, Lippitt, and Fox, 1964; Riessmann, 1967). This appears to be so because the technique is very congenial with their style: physical, down-to-earth, concrete, group-centered, problem-directed. Their style is externally oriented rather than introspective, game-like rather than test-oriented; it is easy, informal in tempo. In essence, disadvantaged youngsters tend to work out mental problems best when they can do things physically, whether it be through role playing, dancing, or taking a trip.

A Route to Verbalization. In role playing sessions, it has been observed that the verbal performance of deprived children is markedly improved in the discussion period following the session. When talking about some action they have seen, deprived children are apparently able to verbalize much more fully. Typically, they do not verbalize well their response to words alone. They express themselves more readily when reacting to things they can see and do. Words as stimuli are not sufficient for them as a rule. Ask a youngster who comes from a disadvantaged background what he doesn't like about school or the teacher, and you will get an abbreviated, inarticulate reply. But have a group of these youngsters act out a school scene in which someone plays the teacher, and you will discover a stream of verbal consciousness that is almost impossible to shut off.[7]

We cannot give here all the various techniques and approaches that might be utilized in our "moon-directed" program of education for the poor. *Scope* magazine presents a great variety of games and approaches suited to the action style of these youngsters.

Any of the following might be important "extras" to be added, depending upon the *style, interests,* and *abilities* of the teachers involved in the program.

The "organics" approach of Sylvia Ashton-Warner (in *Teacher,* 1963). This should be especially valuable in utilizing the interests and strengths of the youngsters, and guard against their being "acted upon" (the current trend in many of the compensatory programs designed for disadvantaged who are supposedly deficit-ridden.

The modified curriculum developed by Gail Donovan in Boston, which vastly stimulated interest in literature among poor youngsters.

---

[7]Role playing has been utilized to some extent in the schools, but there has been little awareness of its special potential for connecting with the style of the disadvantaged and as a crucial avenue for developing their verbalization. Its use may serve a very different function for middle-class children; it may force them to be more concrete and reduce some of their tendencies to over-intellectualize. Teachers should be aware of these potential uses of role playing.

Use of the dance as a method for developing concepts and language, as developed by Claire Schmais in Washington, D.C.

Techniques for developing "verbal mediators" (silent speech, so to speak) in problem solving (Jensen, 1966).

Blueprint for a Revolution

Piecemeal approaches to the improvement of the education of the poor have provided many exciting experiments and some definite gains in learning. The time is now ripe for an all-out attack, integrating our best knowledge in an effort to produce truly great, enduring improvements in the learning of disadvantaged youngsters *at all ages*. This requires leadership, new techniques, and new manpower.

In order to "aim for the moon" in educating the poor, the following have been proposed.

The use of nonprofessional teacher aides who are recruited from among the poor themselves, to assist teachers more fully in their professional roles. The use of this auxiliary manpower to provide excellent male role models for educationally deprived youngsters.

The training of young teachers in newly developed techniques such as the dialect game, the helper principle, and role playing — techniques all attuned to the styles and strengths of disadvantaged children. Correcting limitations in reading, school know-how, language skills, and so forth in terms of the positives of these children. Positive teacher expectations built on an understanding of why he is using the exciting new technologies.

In addition, educators of the disadvantaged are urged to consider the following:

The use of trained master teachers in the new inservice teacher institutes to introduce knowledge and techniques related to immediate classroom problems. The attempt to have teachers use techniques that fit not only the style of the children, but their own style and interests as well.

Full participation of the trainees with regard to formulating their needs and their suggestions for meeting these problems — perhaps in small teacher meetings organized for discussion and role-playing ways of meeting classroom difficulties. A group or team approach in the training with a strong emphasis on building *esprit de corps*.

Experimental basal readers, such as those that have been developed in Detroit by the Follett Publishing Company and in

New York by Bank Street College and Macmillan, incorporating a more representative view of urban life.[8]

The use of the new literacy program, *Words in Color*, published by the Encyclopedia Britannica, and Woolman's *Progressive Accelerated Technique* with nonliterate adults.

The use of new administrative arrangements such as team teaching, multiple periods, nongraded classes, educational parks, and intensive extra-school programs during summers, weekends, and after school hours. Introducing specialists into the school, such as artists, dancers, musicians to develop the artistic talents of the youngsters. Planning programed learning and educational TV.

The use of special parent-teacher groups, led by nonprofessional parent-education coordinators, directed toward developing full, genuine *two-way communication* between the parents and the schools. The use of parents as important supportive elements in the program to back up the role of a school that really wants to teach the child. These parents should be listened to attentively by the school and by the nonprofessional parent-education coordinators who mediate between them and the school. They should not be asked, however, to read to the children or to do homework with them or to do any tasks that they find essentially uncongenial. They can check up on homework, as Sheppard has had them do in St. Louis, and work in a unified way with the school, encouraging the child to learn, to attend punctually, to do his homework, and so forth.

What is needed most for our "moonshot" is an astronaut—an exciting, committed educational leader. Fortunately there are a number of such qualified individuals potentially available: George Brain, who did such a fine job in the Baltimore school system; Daniel Schreiber, whose charismatic leadership first brought Higher Horizons to national attention; Samuel Shephard, whose experiment in St. Louis has been perhaps the most outstanding in the United States—just to name a few possibilities. This type of leader will "expect more," and he will get more. He must be flexible enough to permit and encourage the needed innovation.

Conclusion

Large-scale improvements in the learning of disadvantaged youngsters have not been achieved in the past because most of the previous programs were unrelated to each other, accented deficits, and failed to focus on the teacher as the key to the revolution in education.

---

[8]The research in Detroit indicates that all youngsters read better with these readers, not only disadvantaged children—that they laugh more and feel that the stories are more interesting and lively.

The "moonshot" we have proposed is directed toward meeting the felt needs of teachers. Teachers want smaller classes, new materials, and methods to aid them in teaching, a voice in decisions that affect them, a reduction of discipline problems, a feeling of importance and respect.

The program is intended to meet these objectives to varying degrees. It attempts to provide nonprofessional assistance for teachers in the classroom; it introduces new methods for teaching the children; it encourages the participation of teachers with regard to the use of the new manpower and the new techniques; it does not impose new methods on the teachers but rather stimulates them to select and develop methods appropriate to their styles and interests; it leaves entirely to the individual teachers the decision as to whether they will select nonprofessional aides to be used in their own classes; it endeavors, through the use of added personnel, to meet the discipline problems within the classroom, in the lunch period, and in the corridors; it brings new importance to the teacher by focusing on him as the significant change agent. And it raises the position of the teacher in the school hierarchy.

The program endeavors to help the student by building on his positives and expanding them. It aims to do this by helping the teachers to develop and utilize approaches especially suited to the styles and strengths of disadvantaged youngsters, but *applicable to all youngsters.* The program, in essence, endeavors to overcome the difficulties in the student's learning by concentrating on his positives. It hopes to build bridges from his strengths that will enable him to overcome deficits.

The approach is directed toward convincing the disadvantaged student that he *can* learn and become educated without necessarily becoming a middle-class stereotype – that he can retain his own identity. The keynote is in the following words of Ralph Ellison:

> If you can show me how I can cling to that which is real to me, while teaching me a way into a larger society, then I will drop my defenses and my hostility, but I will sing your praises and I will help you to make the desert bear fruit.

References

Ashton-Warner, Sylvia, *Teacher.* New York: Simon and Schuster, 1963.

Hawkinshire, Frank B. W., "Training Needs for Offenders Working in Community Treatment Programs," in *Experiment in Culture Expansion.* Sacramento, Calif.: State of California Department of Corrections, 1963.

Jensen, Arthur R., "Cumulative Deficits in Compensatory Education," *Journal of School Psychology,* 4 (1966), 37–47.

Lippitt, Ronald, "The 'Helper' Therapy Principle," *Social Work,* 10 (April 1965).

————; Peggy Lippitt and Robert Fox, "Children Look at Their Own Behavior," *N.E.A. Journal*, (1964), 14–16.

Lippitt, Rosemary and Anne Hubbell, "Role Playing for Personnel and Guidance Workers," *Group Psychotherapy*, 9 (1956), 89–114.

Pearl, Arthur and Frank Riessman, *New Careers for the Poor*. New York: Free Press, 1965, Chapter 4.

Riessman, Frank, "Role Playing in the School and the Community – What It Is and How To Do It," Union, N.J.: Scientific Resources, Inc. Mimeographed.

Schmais, Claire, article in *Helping the Disadvantaged Pupil to Learn More Easily*, ed. Frank Riessman. Englewood Cliffs, N.J.: Prentice-Hall (1966).

Regina Goff focuses on the fulfillment of the promise of Title I of the Elementary and Secondary Education Act of 1965. EASEA, as it has become known, is one of the most significant pieces of legislation affecting education ever to be passed by Congress, with Title I directly aimed at the development of educational programs to overcome the debilitating effects of poverty.

The introductory section of Title I, as quoted here, places the Federal government forcefully and directly on record as follows:

Sec. 201. In recognition of the special educational needs of children of low-income families and the impact that concentrations of low-income families have on the ability of local educational agencies to support adequate educational programs, the Congress hereby declares it to be the policy of the United States to provide financial assistance (as set forth in this title) to local educational agencies serving areas with concentrations of children from low-income families to expand and improve their educational programs by various means (including pre-school programs)

TITLE I PROMISES FULFILLED
Regina Goff

which contribute particularly to meeting the special educational needs of educationally deprived children.

As Assistant Commissioner in charge of Title I programs, Dr. Goff describes the scope and diversity of programs during the first year of operation of the act. Title I support has activated preschool projects; nongraded programs; new positions for personnel such as speech therapists; increased use of instructional materials, especially the audio-visual; summer programs of many kinds; field trips; and curriculum adaptations at all levels and of many kinds. Teacher inservice training related to working with the disadvantaged has flourished.

An unusual feature of Title I is the built-in evaluation feature: each program proposal must carry with it an evaluation design. However, the snags that have developed in the evaluation of Title I projects indicate a need for a great deal more sophistication, research-based confidence, and general know-how than most school systems are able to provide. While the problem of designing and implementing valid assessment programs persists (see the paper by Miriam L. Goldberg), the built-in requirement represents a long step forward in federal legislation. Looking back at the end of the first year, Dr. Goff sees the tremendous promise of the act already fulfilled.

TITLE I
PROMISES
FULFILLED
Regina Goff

"Just nothin! I don't want to be nothin when I grow up!" was the retort of eight-year-old Gwen to a well-meaning query about her ambitions—an answer sharpened by her companion, who volunteered, "You're that already!" These statements by implication were based not on what society believes, but on what it actually does in terms of the attainment of the good life for all.

The world of Gwen prepares her for "nothingness"—a world perceived in terms of what is most immediately imitative, what is most subtley or overtly suggestive, a world that is too frequently an ill-proportioned caricature of what might have been. Too many Gwens succumb to the pains of aloneness and forced denials, faced as they are with the constant mobility of their families among impersonal, decaying neighborhoods and the lack of sufficient warmth and attention in homes that inadvertently protect weaknesses, since they are unable to make viable any latent strengths of the adults in the family. Their aspirations and enthusiams for "becoming" collapse aborning. Their mental and emotional energies are dissipated in techniques of hostile defense. Many of these children become cold, suspicious adults, unloving and unlovable.

But there are also those like Larry—children eager and responsive, yet failing in tasks assigned by the greater society, which their world has failed to define. Larry's movements are periodic sharp darts followed by no movement at all, then a dash in another direction. When asked is he looking for something, and can he be helped, he spurts out, "My teacher told me to come out here and get a breath, but I can't find it!" Until there is a meaningful substance for Larry, he will continue to chase shadows.

New Attitudes, Translated into Action Programs

Fortunately, the stereotyped and emotionalized attitudes that distract us from the realities of the disadvantaged today are being displaced by attitudes that reflect social and emotional reconditioning—the intelligent understanding of the basic factors that perpetuate physical, social, and emotional ills. Convictions no longer accommodate themselves to the slow pace of national thought. Current critical thinking on social issues has become not only vocal, but functional.

Federal legislation and subsequent programs attest to this concern. Action programs transcend maxims and exhortations to provide concrete examples of the salvaging of human potentialities. Young children are helped to realize themselves through school experiences that offer them success and motivate them to continue their achievement. These programs give support to a "self" that otherwise might easily be suppressed, to a promise of the full-blown individuality that may emerge. The Title I program concentrates specifically on the education of children of low-income families. Arthur Harris, Associate Commissioner, Bureau of Elementary and Secondary Education, who administers the act, has said that it is designed to "feed the few children starving, not to give a lollipop to every child in class."

Title I funds are paid directly from the federal treasury to the state education agencies. The amount each eligible local school district gets is determined by a formula based on two major factors: the amount of money it spends per pupil, and the number of school-age children from low-income families it has. Each school district is obliged to furnish to its state education agency a comprehensive plan of what it hopes to accomplish.

Basically, then, local communities are going to shape results. The initiative comes from local people, and it is the quality of the programs carried on by the local schools that will determine the success of Title I. With this emphasis on local thinking, planning, and judgment, a wide latitude of program action is encouraged. Different problems call for different remedies. Plans frequently include health and welfare services as well as purely educational measures: a hot lunch, a pair of shoes, or eyeglasses for an impoverished child; a reading specialist, a counselor, a qualified chemistry teacher, or inservice teacher training to bolster a weak school staff.

Early Reports of Title I Programs

Congress has asked that the Office of Education keep the American people informed of the progress made under Title I programs, and thus communities are encouraged to learn from one another. The Office of Education does this by requesting reports from the states. These began to reach Washington late last fall. The first hundred received by the Office of Education provide an interesting cross-section of the projects being undertaken:

> The total cost of the projects underway in these districts is $18,501,805, and 347,047 children are participating, including 60,141 children enrolled in private schools.
>
> Remedial classes in reading, speech, or mathematics are being undertaken by 31 of the districts. Fifteen have introduced guidance, counseling, and testing of underprivileged youngsters. Eleven of the districts are providing food for the children. Other projects include health and recreational services, classes for handicapped children, cultural classes, vocational training classes, special tutoring, and courses in English as a second language.

More than 124,000 adults are involved in the first hundred projects. These include educators, volunteers, and parents. Some of the parents serve as teacher aides.

The reports have come from such widely separated geographic areas as Alton, Maine, and Hatch Valley, New Mexico. Both rural and urban districts are included. Youngsters in Detroit's fifteen elementary schools in low-income areas are getting help in reading. One Detroit project is a demonstration experimental program in methods of teaching basic reading. Another project is a regional reading center serving public and private school children.

The most remote school district heard from was that of Kayenta, Arizona, an isolated settlement populated mostly by Navajo sheep herders. One project there is helping teachers find new ways to teach English to elementary school pupils who hear only the Navajo tongue spoken in their homes. The project is aimed at closing the gap between the Indian and the middle-class American culture.

The various programs discussed here are examples of both Title I projects and other programs that have proved valuable over the past few years in helping the disadvantaged child. They are all described in the hope that they will provide a rough guide to help schools and school districts take full advantage of this historic legislation.

Experimental Preschool Programs

Some communities may wish to use the opportunity provided by these funds to conduct special programs for children of preschool age. (A third of the first hundred school districts were using at least a part of their Title I funds for preschool projects.) The general emphasis of such programs is on providing the child with ordinary experiences. Children of the poor often display an appalling lack of everyday knowledge. They frequently are unable to distinguish colors. No one at home has ever taught them that a lemon is yellow and a tomato is red. They may never even have seen a tomato or a lemon. They often do not recognize common objects. Shapes, sizes, distance, and time mean little to them. They are unskilled in communication. Unlike most preschoolers, these children are unpracticed in curiosity: They do not wonder why.

Teachers in preschool programs for the disadvantaged fill this vacuum in a variety of ways. They bombard the children with chatter. They encourage speech. They introduce ideas. They take children on trips to museums, stores, and construction projects.

Mothers are encouraged to learn how to provide more stimulating experiences at home. Many preschool centers require (as a "tuition fee" for the child) that the mother attend weekly classes in the physical and mental development of children. Both mothers and fathers attend eagerly, seeking other ways to contribute.

79

In a Michigan preschool, teachers visit the home of one student each afternoon, ostensibly to report to parents on a child's progress. But the visit is mostly taken up with engaging the mother, the preschool pupil, and perhaps half a dozen brothers and sisters in games, story reading, and work with crayons and paper, thus encouraging the mother to become a preschool teacher herself in her own home.

Efforts in the Early Grades

Preschool programs have been overwhelmingly successful in preparing youngsters for first grade. But the preparation is in vain if efforts are not sustained throughout the remaining school years. For this reason, many preschool specialists recommend intensified activities for children during the early grades. In the first hundred programs submitted, the greatest concentration of effort was in the first four grades.

Some experts suggest the value of a nongraded system of classes that allows children to progress at individual rates for at least three years. They urge that the level of a child's lessons be dictated by what he individually needs to learn next, without reference to time, the progress of his schoolmates, or the national averages. They want him to be taught—and promoted—in terms of his own ability, instead of by comparison with others.

Some communities are using Title I projects to establish just such nongraded classes and explore possible variations on the nongraded idea. Whatever the particular needs of a community for its own early schooling program, Title I affords a wealth of alternatives. Many schools, for example, are using Title I to concentrate on reading and the development of language skills. These, as every teacher knows, are the chief foundations of knowledge.

One rural school in the South has originated a project employing a speech therapist to test children for language skills and selective attention. Children who lack sufficient development are given special training in the two chief aspects of oral communication, listening and production of speech. Classroom teachers and the speech therapist then cooperate in providing experiences in hearing—and naming with specific words—common environmental sounds: "horn," "bell," "scratch," "squeak." The sounds of words and the objects they identify are also emphasized: "pen" and "pencil," "hat" and "head." In this way, the children learn to discriminate among a variety of sounds. They learn the subtle differences among speech syllables, voice inflections, and rhythms; they receive training in auditory memory and, most useful of all, in vocabulary building. Stories are told, conversation is made, and "experience trips" of various sorts are scheduled to reinforce their new experiences.

Teachers in the second and third grades frequently find great value in using tape recorders in their work with disadvantaged children. The children listen to tapes (easily prepared by teachers) that illustrate basic sounds and differences between sounds. They are asked to coordinate listening with written exercises. Many children show remarkable improvement in speech development after the exciting experience of hearing their own voices.

Middle-Grade Programs

Grades four to six are perhaps the most difficult years when it comes to setting up special programs for the disadvantaged. Children in these grades are nine to eleven years old and are difficult to cope with. The scope of curiosity and "doing" enlarges. A boy of this age takes the alarm clock apart. He empties his father's shaving cream in the sink to see how the aerosol bomb works. He is no longer interested in storybook pictures of fish but wants to see a real electric eel in an aquarium. He not only worships Willie Mays but works to imitate the finest nuances of the way he swings a bat and leaps for a ball.

In his school classes, the normally advantaged fourth-to-sixth grader begins to organize the basic learning of the early grades — simple reading, simple arithmetic, relatively simple play — into new, complex patterns as he reaches forward toward his new conception of adulthood. The disadvantaged child is driven by the same impulses. But lacking the opportunity to inquire and having insufficient mastery of his early school experience, he must find other ways to feed his drive toward growth. If he can't find his excitement in school work, he will find it elsewhere — in the streets, in clandestine — sometimes destructive — play, in rebellion.

If the disadvantaged child of this age has failed to master early-grade fundamentals, his catch-up work must be based on new forms. If he is to learn reading of simple words, he needs emotionally charged stories to make them worth learning. Arithmetic, more than ever, must have real-life meaning. Simple science, if the wonder of cause and effect is visible, is dramatic and right down his alley — even more so, if he is permitted to perform the wonder with his own hands. He especially wants physical tasks: building things, disassembling things, mixing things, doing things. Frequently, teaching machines are found helpful in providing remedial experience in his class work.

Some of the most successful efforts with children in the middle years place learning tasks in an out-of-school or camp atmosphere, or in programs Saturday or after school. While summer programs are the most ambitious, and probably the most fruitful undertaking, these activities, in the main, can be duplicated in after-school projects. Either type may be developed with the aid of Title I funds.

A typical example of a summer camp for disadvantaged children is one recently held by the schools of a southern city. "Doing" activities of shop, homemaking, and arts and crafts were emphasized. A special effort was made to relate reading, writing, and figuring with the "doing" tasks. Field trips introduced pupils to places of interesting adult work. Camping trips were held to emphasize natural science observation. Physical fitness activities stressed action and organized games. Similarly, a city-wide antipoverty group in New England concentrated on a remedial reading program for a group of boys at camp. The youngsters' motivation and interests improved noticeably as a result of the experience. In another eastern community, a summer school program offered academic courses in remedial reading and mathematics.

Field trips, when imaginatively conceived, lead to exploration of books and ideas far beyond the immediate topic, particularly if the pupils engage actively in planning.

One Midwestern school system includes in its middle-years social studies courses, a program allowing children of low-income families to become acquainted with people of other backgrounds. Children visit other neighborhoods and meet people from different backgrounds, racially, culturally, and economically, and learn of the different jobs people have. After becoming pen pals with such children, they meet face-to-face on exchange visits.

Efforts at the High-School Level

At the high-school level, the most publicized efforts on behalf of the children of poverty have been special "dropout" programs. There is by now convincing and inspiring evidence that the lives of seemingly hopeless, hostile high school failures can be redirected. Promising programs have been developed in both rural and urban areas giving emphasis to new kinds of educational activity. The world of work which surrounds the school has been tested through direct work experience by teenagers and through introducing workers having various skills and talents into the classroom. Guidance that prepares students for making realistic job choices is proving successful. New courses to develop specialized competencies are being taught. College orientation programs are now underway for students who would normally never aspire to college.

An experimental junior high school has been set up in downtown Minneapolis in an effort to reach youngsters who are likely to drop out of school. A store-front building was selected because it puts students in closer touch with the realities of the vocational life of the community. The greater informality of a school-away-from-school was also a consideration. The students go to a standard junior high school for certain courses, however, such as physical education, music, and typing. The entire faculty takes part in home visits and student-parent conferences.

Substantial experience has been piled up on other projects that are serving the needs of children from low-income families. There is, for example, a remarkable program for disadvantaged high school students that a small Illinois city now operates after having first carried out a youth motivation study for eleven years. It combines bold innovation in the academic classroom, practical job training, and parent involvement. The classroom portion of the program has three chief goals: improving communication skills, developing consumer and family skills, and updating job information. Teachers of the various subject specialties coordinate classwork closely, working as a team. Students use instructional materials having strong motivational content and proceed at their own rate. They receive individual attention in arithmetic, speaking, and listening.

In this program, consumer education involves practical projects. Store visits are arranged to simulate purchasing. Extensive practice is scheduled in the use of mail-order catalogs. Mathematics instruction is directed at household budgeting. Both know-how and motivation are instilled by driving students around to "shop" for the purchase of a house, emphasizing such factors as size, neighborhood, and price. In the classroom, students calculate mortgage payments and the down payment required for their home "purchase" and estimate the personal income needed to make the purchase a reality. This study is followed by "furnishing" the house and pitting the cost of furnishings against other possible purchases within the student's projected income. Needless to say, many students have an eye-opening experience when confronting such budget realities.

Introduction to the world of work involves four elements: classroom study, "make work" practice within the school, real work experience at the project's training school, and employment for pay in an outside job with school credit.

The parent-involvement program consists of letters, home visits by a family counselor and teachers, and group meetings of parents and teachers to reinforce their understanding of the program. Mothers and fathers are invited on many field trips and are encouraged to speak to classes about their work experience. One father, occupationally unskilled but very expressive and community-minded, was hired to serve as a liaison between the school and neighborhood in promoting parental involvement. His door-to-door "sales effort" achieved a high degree of cooperation.

Prospects for the Graduate

In coping with the problems of disadvantaged students, most of an educator's effort is directed toward preparing a maximum number of students for employment after leaving high school. This effort should not obscure the recent advances in preparing youngsters of low-income families for college. The individual enrichment and personal attention they require may be expensive, but few would question the worth of the program. Colleges today stand more ready than ever to make every reasonable effort in opening the way for disadvantaged high school graduates. Liberal scholarships are available from many sources, as is federal assistance under the Higher Education Act of 1965. This legislation provides grants to college students with exceptional financial needs and loans to students of middle- or upper-income background.

Programs to prepare young people to take advantage of these opportunities may be carried out with Title I funds. A pilot program to aid bright but undermotivated students from disadvantaged areas, for example, is being conducted by one city school in cooperation with a technology institute. The program includes two summer sessions of six weeks each plus Saturday classes during the regular school year. During the summer, selected tenth-grade boys and girls receive instruction in mathematics, English, and biology on the institute campus. A public school teacher and college professor are in charge of each classroom. Students live and take meals on the campus, participating in academic, cultural, and social activities.

In rural areas, educational deprivation is often devastating to the individual. A rural school that is largely dependent upon the low taxes of submarginal farms gets caught in a downward cycle, its plight perpetually worsening.

A school board member from such a downward-spiraling town in the Ozarks, himself the father of two children, explains the seemingly insoluble problem of the migration from the farm:

> With the young parents and teenagers around here gone looking for work in the cities, fewer kids get born, so state aid to schools keeps going down. We're too small to keep teachers for specialized subjects. A couple of years ago our school had to drop music and industrial arts. Before that we lost our science teacher. The state law requires the teaching of science, so our kids had to take it by correspondence course.

The agricultural world needs trained people. Great companies serving the modern farmer — makers of animal foods, chemical fertilizers, farm machines — are pleading for trained workers and professionals, yet good paying jobs go begging every year. Even with the prospect of promising opportunities in rural areas for well-educated young people, the huge population flow toward the city will undoubtedly continue. Rural young people with meager educational and economic backgrounds arrive in the cities at a great disadvantage. They are unable to compete for jobs and are socially in a strange world.

A farm community knew it was losing its high school graduates to a sizable city about 60 miles away. The school board faced a painful truth: job opportunities at home were almost nonexistent. It decided to take an

84

unusual step: prepare students for city life. The board established a course intended mainly for high school seniors but open to other students also and to out-of-school youngsters in the community. The following aspects were covered: kinds of jobs, application for a job, use of city transportation, communications, city services, and a place to live.

A distressing number of the children of poverty suffer physical and mental as well as educational and cultural handicaps. Programs designed to help the physically handicapped are often expensive, requiring special teachers and special equipment. In Phoenix, Arizona, a new special education department has been set up with Title I funds to given instruction to handicapped children. The speech-handicapped, visually impaired, hearing-impaired, emotionally disturbed, and the educable mentally retarded are getting some of the help they need. Staff for the project includes a speech therapist, social workers, a psychologist, two art teachers, and five specialists in teaching children who are mentally retarded.

In setting up programs under Title I, local communities must take care to include deprived children enrolled in private schools and youth who are out of school, as well as children enrolled in public institutions. Dual enrollment (or shared time), educational radio and television, educational media centers, and mobile educational services and equipment are used in fulfilling this requirement.

The programs mentioned above may be thought of as a series of experimental procedures. After hardly a year of operation, no exhaustive analysis has been made to determine which set of conditions among alternative possibilities are most influential determinants of behavioral change. Programs may have different results for different children, for deficits are not uniform in children. Variations in program emphasis may result in positive influence on some constituent factors in intelligence and growth and not on others. End results among the many programs therefore may not be comparable. Nevertheless, already observable are positive consequences from the serious attack being made on the composite of those maladaptive traits inconsistent with academic and social demands. Improvements have been noted in areas of motivation, cognitive development, communication skills, and self-appreciation. Such improvement may be considered progression in a continuum toward eventually more discernible behavioral change.

The Office of Education Research Center, in cooperation with the Bureau of Elementary and Secondary Education, looks forward with anticipation to forthcoming major evaluative studies of these programs.

Mildred Beatty Smith describes the program undertaken in the Flint (Michigan) Community Schools to lift the achievement level of children from low-income families. In an effort to link home and school, the program focused on the children's "significant others," and worked deliberately to raise their expectations of achievement by the children. The rationale for the program was that the family has a major responsibility for teaching the child, and that, in discharging this responsibility, family pride increases. In addition, the program aimed to join the parent and the teacher as partners in the teaching-learning process. Dr. Smith, stressing the importance of home and school on the achievement and motivation of children, argues that under-achievement can be overcome in both areas by improving the home conditions that contribute to poor attitudes toward school achievement and low motivation, and by creating school conditions to raise teacher morale and reduce turnover. Unless the two situations —home and school—are improved simultaneously, she believes the problem will get worse.

SCHOOL AND HOME:
FOCUS ON ACHIEVEMENT

Mildred Beatty Smith

Dr. Smith reports on the design and operation of the experimental program. Although the original idea came from the school, parents and teachers did considerable planning together. There was little time spent in making the usual general abstractions; the emphasis was on many specific techniques that the parents could implement in the home situation. Not only did the parent give the child direct assistance and support with home study and school work, but the school-child-parent relationships were strengthened. Special materials were designed and distributed to the parents. In addition, new materials and services were provided to the teachers as well. To raise levels of aspiration of the intermediate-grade child, the school featured occupational information in social studies programs at that level. The considerable gap between aspirations and expectations called for many approaches and enrichment programs.

The results of the evaluation were generally positive. Children in two experimental schools were compared with pupils in a matched control school. On most standardized measures of reading, vocabulary, and comprehension, the experimental group did significantly better than the control group. The parents and teachers appear to be enthusiastic about the program and its consequences.

Dr. Smith contends that it is an error to believe that parents of low-income children are not interested in their children's education. Flint's program has demonstrated that parents who are helped to work with their children respond quite favorably. (See also the following paper by Hess and Shipman, which discusses research with mothers of preschoolers.) While some parents are resistant or difficult to involve, the extra effort, Dr. Smith believes, is repaid by the gains for the child. The techniques used were, of course, applicable not only to disadvantaged children. In fact, Dr. Smith believes that we can well afford to develop from these experimental findings innovations valuable for all children.

SCHOOL AND HOME: FOCUS ON ACHIEVEMENT

Mildred Beatty Smith

A major challenge to society, including its schools, is that of helping its economically and educationally disadvantaged citizens become fully functioning and therefore self-sustaining members of the group. The question that baffles many individuals is, "How to interrupt this vicious cycle and bring about the desired changes?"

The contributions that can be made by society's institutions, such as the home, the school, and the church, are limited by the scope of their responsibilities as defined by society. The schools, however, have a unique role because their chief goal is that of augmenting and supplementing the family's child-training responsibility and transmitting the cultural heritage to the young.

A program, directed by this writer, was undertaken in the Flint Community Schools to improve underachieving children's chances of succeeding in school. Since it was felt that basic habits and attitudes are developed early in the lives of children, the program was begun as early as possible.[1] It focused teacher and parent attention on the achievement of each child. Together, they worked to implement an experimental program. This paper is an account of their efforts.

The Experimental Program

The Experimental Schools

"School and Home: Focus on Achievement" was an experimental program designed to raise the academic achievement and goals of underachieving elementary school children. The experiment was undertaken in two public elementary schools during the 1961–62 academic year. It involved approximately 1,000 children enrolled in kindergarten through grade six. The program was later expanded to other elementary schools in the inner city.

Most of the children in the experimental schools were Negroes, primarily from low-income families living in the industrial city of Flint, Michigan. With few exceptions, parents of these children had come from the rural South to seek employment in local industrial plants. The educa-

---

[1]Children enter school in Flint, Michigan, at the kindergarten level. Preschool children were included in "Read-To-Me," and other home related activities.

tional backgrounds of many parents were, therefore, quite limited, although they wished the best for their children. Elementary school children with similar socioeconomic backgrounds, who were enrolled in another public school in Flint, were selected to be a control group for this experiment.

The Theoretical Frame of Reference

The theoretical frame of reference for this focus on achievement was based on the action theorist's postulations that the group in which the individual is socialized influences his motivation to achieve in school. It seemed obvious, then, that a program designed to raise the achievement level of children who lacked the necessary motivation to achieve adequately must involve working with these children's "significant others" for the purpose of getting them to expect more of these children.

After the above generalization was made, the remaining question that needed answering was "Who are the 'significant others' for these children?" An assumption was made that parents and teachers are significant others for elementary children insofar as the academic achievement is concerned. It was further assumed that parents relate in a more significant way to children than do teachers because young children learn their interests and values from parents.

Teachers have always been identified as an important influence on children's school achievement. This program tapped another, and possibly more significant, source of influence upon the child's school learning—the parent.

The program that is based on the theoretical framework described earlier is theoretically justifiable for three reasons. First, it restores to the family its rightful responsibility for teaching the child. Second, it gives the family pride in being the teacher. Third, it brings together the child's "significant others"—the parent and the teacher—as *partners*, not competitors or strangers, in the child's learning process. Neither can do this job in opposition to the other or in isolation.

A description of some of the characteristics and problems of the underachieving child is presented below. This description is followed by a resumé of the experimental program and the methods used to bring the child's significant others, teachers and parents, together as partners to improve the child's achievement. This program is appropriately entitled "School and Home: Focus on Achievement."

The Underachieving Child—His Characteristics and Problems

The typical underachieving child has some characteristics that can be identified by observation. When one visits a classroom, one can informally determine whether individual children are high, average, or low achievers by observing their work habits and the attitudes they exhibit toward their school tasks. The underachiever displays a poor attitude toward his school work, and he exhibits poor work habits. If one asks the typical underachiever to open his notebook, one finds that it contains torn and rumpled papers that lack organization. An examination of his desk reveals a jumbled assortment of wrappers from bubble gum, candy, and the like. He is frequently without pencil and paper. If he has a pencil, it is usually short and unsharpened; if he is asked to take a sheet of paper from his notebook, he will jerk or tear it from the notebook rings rather than open the rings to remove the paper intact. What do these observations tell us about the underachiever? They tell us that he is not interested in his school assignment: it is not important to him, and, therefore, he cannot see any reason for working at it.

An examination of the notebook of a typical high achiever reveals good organization. Notebook dividers will separate papers for the various subjects that he studies. He has a supply of unused paper in his notebook. He has two sharpened pencils (a spare one ready for emergency use). His desk is organized—pencils and erasers in one section and books in the other section. The high achiever invariably has a library book in his desk which he keeps handy for reading when he completes his work earlier than many of his classmates. One of the reasons he finishes early is simply because he works harder than others do. The high achiever wants to do good work in school. It is very important to him; therefore, if he can, he consistently achieves at a high level.

The student who works with one eye on the teacher and the other eye on his paper, who talks and pokes others when the teacher turns her back on him to write on the board, who is interested in playing with gadgets kept in his pockets and desk, and who occupies a large portion of his time with eating bits of candy, pretzels, and potato chips, will not achieve as much as the child who exhibits interest in school work by listening to assignments and directives, by working at a task until completed, by studying his vocabulary and spelling words. This student is not satisfied with a job until it is done well. The latter student is motivated from within himself to do good work in school. He has determination, drive, desire, and the ambition to achieve. These qualities contribute as much to school success as native ability. In many instances, therefore, the major difference between the underachiever and the high achiever can be expressed as "the will to do."

The problem of getting the underachiever to do better in school rests with the ability to develop in him a desire to do good work and to learn his school subjects. In order to accomplish this goal, one must first examine reasons why the underachiever does not possess a desire to achieve in school.

Each individual's values and goals are learned from those people who are most important to him. This learning occurs, in most instances, in an incidental manner. A young child begins to imitate the behavior of those significant others at a very early age. These significant people are, first of all, his parents. At a later time, when the child enters school, the teacher becomes one of them. How important or influential the teacher is to most children has not been determined. The teacher's degree of effective importance to children varies with circumstances; but in most instances, it is secondary to that of the parents. Exceptions probably occur when children deprived of parental affection are forced to seek a surrogate.

Since the home and the school influence children's school achievement, the home and the school must be the focus for helping the underachiever improve his achievement. A brief discussion of the problem faced by the home and the school follows.

The Importance of the Home Environment in School Achievement

The values and attitudes that parents possess provide the pattern by which the child's values and attitudes are shaped. Much of what a child learns from his parents is learned indirectly. For example, if a father takes pride in his car and washes and polishes it frequently, his son will observe this and will value it. Likewise, if a father reads books frequently for enjoyment, his son will observe this and will be more likely to read books for enjoyment. If parents have routines in the home—certain chores which must be done at a certain time and done well—the child will develop the habit of doing a job on time and doing it well. It is the example set for the child that determines what the child's attitudes and values will be. A child who comes from a home devoid of books, magazines, newspapers, and dictionaries will not see these items as important in his daily living and, therefore, will not value them. What is said to a child is not important unless this talk is supported by example. The proverb, "What you do speaks so loudly that I cannot hear what you are saying," applies here.

The child has a good chance for success in school who comes to school from a home in which he is required to do a job on time and is rewarded for doing it well, in which he sees his parents reading books and magazines as leisure-time activities, and in which his parents show an interest in his school work by asking question of him. A child with comparable native ability has much less chance for success in school when he comes from a home in which there is little or no routine, in which his parents seldom if ever read anything for enjoyment—except to manifest loving care for automobiles, pets, furniture, or sports equipment, in which his parents show no interest in what he is doing in school, and in which no one appears to care whether he does a job well and at a particular time.

These reasons why some children achieve at a low level show that the solution to this problem rests heavily upon changing the behavior and

92

attitudes of parents. There is real hope for solution, because, basically, almost all parents wish the best for their children. Nevertheless, many of them are unaware that what they do has this kind of impact on their children's school work. In the case of the underachiever it is what parents are *not* doing that is the salient influence. If they are tactfully informed how to help their children they are most grateful.

The Importance of the School Environment on School Achievement

A second phase of the problem rests with the school itself. The vast majority of underachievers are known to come from homes that have a climate not conducive to developing in the child the attitudes and values needed to achieve in school, although many other desirable attitudes and values are stressed. Teachers of these children are confronted with some additional problems which make their jobs more difficult. All the escape mechanisms employed by children who are not interested in school place teachers in the role of policemen; the children then become even further alienated and the teachers themselves are further deprived of the reward of having their children succeed academically.

Teachers who do not receive such rewards become depressed and lose enthusiasm. They can request a transfer to another school by saying, "The other school is closer to my home and I am getting older and do not like driving that distance," and claim snow and ice as an insurmountable driving hazard. A perceptive personnel director will try to accommodate a good teacher who has given years of service to the school system by helping her out in her "snow and ice" problem. A second course of action that can be taken by teachers who have lost enthusiasm is to stay at the school but assume that they are in a hopeless situation. They adjust to the situation by thinking, "What's the use?" or "These children can't learn any way." Neither course of action improves the situation. Some teachers with missionary zeal remain in these schools, however, and continue to try.

Many teachers need help in understanding that the problem of the underachiever is not necessarily one of insufficient capacity or ability, but is frequently one of inadequate environmental support or motivation. Moreover, high staff turnover undermines the instructional program of the school. Teachers who transfer may not order an adequate supply of materials for the new teachers because of pending grade assignment changes. All of these problems—teacher turnover, inexperience, problems of maintaining good discipline—may mean that teacher's time as well as materials may not be used as advantageously as is possible under more favorable circumstances.

Many new teachers in a building create a supervision load for the principal and the consultants. The principal is further burdened by family welfare problems which are known to exist in some of the homes of many

93

underachieving children. In addition, much of the principal's time is consumed in attempts to identify an individual who started an argument or a fight en route to or from school. Such problems are compounded when there is a high principal turnover—a characteristic of many inner-city schools.

These above conditions, intensified by those which children bring with them to school, further undermine the achievement of underachieving children.

Solutions to the problem of underachievement, therefore, are as follows: (1) improving home situations that cause children to develop poor attitudes toward school achievement, and (2) creating a more desirable situation in the school to raise teacher morale and reduce teacher turnover. Both problems must be attacked together, since one problem complements the other; otherwise, the vicious cycle cannot be broken.

Objectives of the Program

The purpose of the program was to raise the achievement level of children who were achieving at a lower level than they should have been. This program required that *parents and teachers work together* to improve children's basic attitudes toward academic work and to improve their work habits in school. The objectives of this program were carried out by helping academically uninterested parents develop or raise their expectations of their children by providing a climate at home that is conducive to study. Parents were expected to:

Provide a quiet period in the home each day for reading and study assigned by the teacher. They were informed by the teacher that: "This period is to be at a regular time so that it becomes a part of the life of the child. . . . Remind the child of his assignment. . . . Young children will forget."

Listen to their children read.

Read regularly themselves, in the presence of their children.

Read aloud regularly to their children, including preschool-age children.

Show interest in their children's work by asking questions, giving praise and encouragement when needed and deserved.

Prevent the school-age child's work from being damaged or destroyed by preschool children.

See that the child has pencils and paper at school and at home so that he has the tools necessary for doing a good job.

Get the child to bed at a regular time each night so that he gets the proper sleep and rest.

Get the child up each morning with adequate time for a good breakfast.

Remind the child of work papers and books that should be returned to school. Young children need this assistance.

Have the child leave home with the attitude of going to school for the purpose of learning.

The program was further implemented by helping teachers to understand underlying causes of underachievement, particularly among children who lack motivation from parents, by helping teachers realize the significance of the impact of their behavior on children, and by helping teachers update teaching materials and teaching techniques so that they can be utilized most effectively.

Description of the Program

Teacher-parent planning. After teachers had developed the program, meetings of parents were scheduled for the purpose of explaining it to them and asking them to participate. The objectives of the program were outlined to parents. This responsibility was shared by teachers in their respective buildings. A bulletin[2] was provided each parent who attended. This bulletin contained items outlined in the list of objectives described above, as well as related details. The parents were made to understand that without being aware of it, they were not setting the kind of example that brings about desirable attitudes and habits toward school work.

PTA meetings were held in the evening and also during the day to accommodate those parents working the evening shift. The prepared bulletin was handed each parent at the beginning of the meeting and its contents were thoroughly discussed with them. Parents then took the booklet home for further reference. Extra time and effort was undertaken to make the bulletins as neat and attractive as possible, communicating to the parents that the schoolpeople had confidence in their abilities to cooperate, and—most important—respected them and considered them important. The goal was to enhance the self-concepts of parents so that they could, in the same way, enhance their children's self-concepts.

A record was kept of each parent in attendance at each meeting. Homeroom mothers utilized this record to contact parents not in attendance and to schedule them for meetings.

A question frequently raised was "How did you get these people to come to your meetings?" Several techniques were used. On one occasion, a group of thirty interested mothers assigned blocks in their school district to themselves, and each made a personal call on every family in her assigned block(s), inviting parents to a planned program to "learn what they could do to help their children achieve better in school." A single-

---

[2] A printed bulletin was provided parents at all information-giving meetings. Parents who had difficulty reading, received the information verbally. Such parents were not embarrassed, therefore. At no time did their identities become known. Parents who could read benefited from verbal elaborations that were made.

sheet bulletin on colorful paper containing the time, place, and objective of the meeting was left at each home just in case parents forgot.[3]

In other instances, homeroom mothers telephoned every parent in the school. Other successful techniques involved a trophy, which was "loaned" to the class with the highest percentage of parents in attendance at a meeting. Other classes competed to get the trophy away from the last winner. Children enjoyed the competition, and more and more parents were in attendance at these meetings.

The home study assignment. Each family was asked to set aside a quiet time in the home each day so that children could do homework assignments. These daily assignments, given by teachers, consisted primarily of studying vocabulary, reading from supplementary materials, studying spelling words, and reading trade books. Assignments in the content areas included practice work in numbers, for example, or viewing a science-related television program.

Parents were asked to "manage" the quiet time and to give support and encouragement to children. They understood that they were not expected to "teach," since all assigned work could be done independently by the children. They were, however, encouraged to schedule the quiet time at the same time each day so that the habit of doing something constructively became an integral part of each child's *daily* routine. Parents discussed this situation with their children and planned it together.

This quiet time was not scheduled during favorite TV programs, because the goal was to get children to value school achievement and to enjoy the experience of being successful in academic type situations. A denial of some other activity that a child enjoyed would bring about an adverse affect on the primary goal: getting these underachievers to value school achievement and to want to be successful in school.

Teachers worked together and established a nine-point set of criteria regarding their assignments. Included were such stipulations as:

The homework activity should not be used as punishment.

It should require no teaching by the parent.

It should involve only materials on which the child can work independently and complete within a short period of time.

---

[3]We learned that these parents, like their children, frequently forget to follow through with commitments although they have good intentions, at the time, of following through. Although the lack of regard for punctuality appears to be a "pattern of behaving" which is prevalent among low income people, it should be noted that the many severe problems and pressures that they face cause them to relegate middle class expectations to a secondary level. This occurrence is frequently misinterpreted as "lack of interest." This writer suggests that critics of this behavioral characteristic might behave in a similar manner if confronted with the same set of social and economic problems.

Teachers agreed to limit assignments to a maximum of 30 minutes for later elementary children and around 15 minutes for primary children. Teachers felt that lengthy, laborious tasks would influence children to dislike school, thereby defeating the goal of the program.

Parents also discussed the situation with the parents of their children's friends and planned together so that this activity would be held at the same time each day, thus providing group support for this effort. This planning also provided that "Johnny" would not have to leave the game when it was his turn at bat or at the time when it was his turn to shoot at the "purey." These children were learning that academic pursuits would not deny them other kinds of activities that they enjoyed.

During the quiet time, televisions and radios were turned off so that there was no competition for the children's attention. Parents managed the quiet period so that there was no talking on the telephone either. A caller would be asked please to call back. Parents read to their preschool-age children in a nearby room or gave the children items such as crayons and paper so that they were constructively occupied; thus, the parents were preventing the preschoolers from being destroyers of books, papers, and other essential materials. Again, mothers were informed that it was their responsibility to protect older children's school property so that it did not become mutilated or defaced by younger children.[4]

Every morning, each child reported to his teacher. Teachers kept a large wall chart and noted on it whether or not the child had completed the assignment. This became as routine as the taking of attendance. The child was always checked on whether or not he completed the task rather than on how well it was completed. Every child could, therefore, be successful, provided that his parents were giving the needed support at home. If a child frequently failed to complete a task, the parent was sought for a conference. The parent, therefore, became the problem. This record-keeping by teachers assured each child that the two people concerned with his academic achievement were in constant communication with each other.

Children sometimes reported verbally to the teacher about an assigned task, particularly when it was a reading assignment. This type of reporting required that the child's word become the only evidence of the completed task. Teachers accepted this evidence and checked the child's name on the chart. This told the child that his teacher trusted him. For some children, it was the first time they had been trusted by an adult in a position of authority. This was a valuable learning experience for them.

In addition to the educational value that the child derived from home reading, practice work, and vocabulary study, the overriding values were

---

[4]This frequently is a serious problem for older children, overlooked by parents and underestimated by teachers. Many children are reluctant to take library books home because they are afraid of returning a damaged book to the teacher. This anxiety about the care of books may inhibit the enjoyment of books.

(1) the support given by parents, which communicated by *example* that his educational achievement was important to his parents; (2) the establishment, early, of the habit of following through with an assigned task and completing it on time, so that it would, hopefully, carry into adulthood; (3) the young child's learning, through the expectations of his "significant others," parents and teachers, that he could achieve and that he could like school; and (4) the development of positive academic self-concepts by these children.

A dictionary for each family. A child's dictionary was made available to each family with a child in grades four through six. This dictionary was used for word study at home. For the majority of the families, this was the first dictionary the child had ever owned. Each family was asked to pay a dollar for it, and the additional cost was underwritten. In a few instances, the dictionary was provided without cost, although families were encouraged to pay some small initial fee (in some cases ten cents) so that they had invested something in it.

Families were encouraged to write their names on the inside cover page to emphasize the satisfaction of *owning* a dictionary. Teachers gave children many word-study tasks, since test results showed them to need this especially.[5] This dictionary, therefore, became a valuable learning aid.

Other techniques were utilized to improve vocabulary development. A metal file box and file cards were provided each child in grades one through six, enabling them to keep a record of difficult words and to study them at home and at school. This technique improved knowledge of word meanings as well as word recognition. Teachers reported this as being one of the most helpful reading innovations for these children, because cultural speech patterns create unusual difficulties with the regular phonics approach to word recognition. Furthermore, their meaning vocabularies are limited by the environment.

The "Word for the Day" was initiated in order to broaden vocabularies and to encourage children to use words with more precise definitions.[6] A pocket chart, appropriately labeled, was displayed in each classroom. Each morning, a new word was placed in the pocket and remained visible during the entire academic day. This word might be taken from test materials, but it was frequently taken from current news items. For example, the words "apogee" and "perigee" were frequently seen in pocket charts when astronauts were orbiting the earth.

Children were encouraged not only to learn to pronounce the word and to learn its meaning(s), but to use it in conversation during the school

---

[5] Reading test results show that most children of families with limited formal education are likewise limited in vocabulary development. This is influenced by the limited language facility of parents and peers.

[6] It should be noted that although vocabularies are restricted, these children can be fluent speakers. The limitation is in the quantity of words in their speaking vocabularies. This use of "implied" rather than "specific" vocabulary, however, handicaps the child on IQ tests since specificity is valued more highly.

day, thus enlarging their speaking vocabularies. Teachers were, of course, listening for this and called attention to it, giving immediate reinforcement to children. One teacher related that on an occasion when she was reading poetry to the class, a child interrupted, saying, "We should be getting a new word from this poem." This activity caused children to become word-conscious.

Children were taught how to study their vocabulary effectively by following prescribed study steps. Since this is a major problem for under-achievers, the parents of these children were taught the study steps in order to support the child in his study effort. A bulletin was prepared and explained to parents at one of the parent meetings. This bulletin contained the study steps and the parents' role in the study process.

The "Read-To-Me" Program. Parents were asked to read aloud to their children each day for the purpose of stimulating interest in reading and showing the children that reading is important to their parents. A booklet giving suggestions to parents about reading aloud was prepared and discussed with them at a parent meeting. Our group developed a "Parent's Pledge" that they recited in unison at meetings. This pledge, to read daily to their children, was written by one of the mothers in the neighborhood.

Fathers, too, were encouraged to take turns reading to their children, thus demonstrating, particularly to boys, that men also value reading. Fathers were encouraged to take turns with library duties and to serve as "male storytellers"—assuring boys that books and masculinity are compatible.

Parents were made to understand that all of them, including non-readers, could motivate their child to want to learn to read. Such a parent was encouraged to look at picture books with his child, discussing the pictures with him, thereby telling the story to the child. The fact that a parent takes time with a book shows that he values reading and wants the child to read. The child likewise values reading and wants to learn to read.

Kindergarten children took a book home for their parents to read to them. On the days that kindergarten and primary children took books home for parents to read to them, they wore tags on their lapels that read: "Please read to me." Older children were given book markers imprinted: "May I read to you?" They took turns reading to the family, thereby providing appropriate models for the younger children.

Summer activities to focus on achievement. After the program was underway, toward the conclusion of the academic year, parents became concerned about what they could do informally during the summer to broaden their children's experiences. A bulletin entitled "Summer Activities to Focus on Achievement" was prepared by the teachers. It contained such suggestions as:

Encourage your child to begin some kind of hobby.

Encourage your child to listen to the radio for news.

See that your children visit the library frequently.

Take trips that provide learning opportunities by encouraging children to observe carefully and to discuss their observations.

This bulletin was discussed with parents at a PTA meeting during the last month of the academic year and then was given out to be taken home for reference.

Materials provided for teachers and pupils. Every effort was made to provide new materials and services for teachers and children. New materials improve children's learning, as well as motivate teachers and raise their morale.

Stories in typical basal readers lack appeal to disadvantaged children because the illustrations and story content depict life experiences unfamiliar to them. The reading program therefore was augmented with multilevel, individualized, self-help materials. Teachers reported that the children were enthusiastic about these materials. They not only enjoyed the story content, but appreciated the opportunity to check their work and correct their mistakes. When asked to evaluate these materials, one respondent replied: "I like them because they put me on my own more, and I don't have to depend on the teacher so much." This child, who had experienced frequent failures, punctuated by teacher criticism, was delighted to be able to find and correct her own mistakes rather than to have some other person always find them.

Teachers reported that children were able to work at individual instructional levels "without the feeling of having 'low' or 'high' reading groups in the classroom." This adjustment of materials to instructional needs also provided each child with successful experiences. Undoubtedly, the highest tribute paid these materials was the vote of the student council to purchase with money from its own fund additional sets for use in the building. A sixth-grade teacher summarized her children's attitudes as follows: "The children said, 'They are marvelous and lots of fun!'"

The program was also enriched with supplementary materials: trade books, literary collections, word games, listening skill building materials, "Bookworm Club" materials,[7] and individual stories reconstructed by the mothers from outdated reading books that provided children with the satisfaction of reading several "books."

Underachievement in disadvantaged children is generally manifested in all subject areas. When the program was initiated, emphasis was placed on work habits and attitudes toward academic work which would be re-

---

[7] In the program referred to as the "Bookworm Club," children in grades two through six were given tally sheets on which they placed stickers on the fifteen segments of the "bookworm"—one for each book read. This program allowed them to earn a "bookworm" lapel button when six segments were covered and a "diploma" when all fifteen were covered.

flected in all subject areas. Reading, however, was designated as a most crucial subject, since the mastery of reading greatly influences success in other subjects. Attention was given to mathematics because test results indicated that the skills of these children in numerical computation were particularly inadequate: they did not know their number facts. They knew the processes of multiplication and division, but when they computed, got wrong answers.

Learning the number facts, though not difficult, requires a certain amount of disciplined study. These poorly motivated underachievers had not developed discipline, and time was not available during the academic day for the supervised study of the number facts. Homeroom mothers made sets of number fact cards for all children for individual study.

These mothers made 40,000 fact cards so that each child could have a set to take home for study. When mothers took the time to do this, the children knew they cared about their success in mathematics.

Occupational information provided. Lack of motivation for these children is synonymous with lack of hope. A questionnaire was administered to all fourth, fifth, and sixth graders in one of the experimental schools to ascertain their occupational and educational aspirations and expectations. The majority indicated that they expected to hold blue-collar jobs in adult life, and that few expected to graduate from college. Any white-collar jobs expected were limited exclusively to the professions — such as teaching, medicine, social work, or the ministry. It is interesting to note that none of the respondents *expected* to hold jobs in the skilled trades, which require less than a college or professional education, but require specialized training, including mathematics and science courses in high school — even though many such skilled workers are employed in the area.

These children expected to hold the types of jobs held by their parents or their parents' friends. Since many of them had had contacts with Negroes holding professional jobs, such as teacher, doctor, social worker, and minister, some assumed, therefore, that they could likewise hold such jobs.

As a result of this survey, a decision was made to integrate occupational information into social studies programs for all fourth, fifth, and sixth graders. This was done not only to broaden occupational horizons but also to help them understand, early in the school career, that such subjects as mathematics and science, taken at the time, had relevance for future occupations. It was hoped that their motivation in these subjects would be enhanced.

An educational director from a local factory visited the schools and showed slides of people performing varied skilled jobs. He explained the advanced high-school courses required for eligibility in his training programs and reminded the children that competence in science, reading, spelling, and mathematics would make them eligible for those courses.

Negroes in the area who held skilled jobs visited classrooms, explained their jobs, and told how their elementary school subjects had been important to them later in their lives.

Clerical assistance provided teachers. Co-op business students typed and duplicated teacher-made materials and provided other such services, freeing teachers to give more personal attention to children. This was one of the greatest morale-boosters for teachers that the program provided. Typewriters with large-size print were made available for producing materials for primary level children.

An inservice program for teachers. Workshops designed to help the teachers make more effective use of the new materials were held. These workshops were planned jointly with the teachers. They became involved in evaluating their behavior so that it would be a more positive and encouraging influence, since they knew that children's behavior is influenced by teacher expectation and that IQ test results are influenced by the environment. Attention was given to the study of environmental influences on such behavior as attitudes, values, and language, and also to helping children improve their self-concepts.

Social-psychological conceptions about learning were explored. The thesis that all behavior is learned and that learning is continuous gave hope for changing poor habits and attitudes that interfere with the learning process. In this context, the role of the teacher is defined as that of a helper. She has faith in children's ability to learn, and she communicates this faith to them through a positive and supportive approach. This type of teacher is frequently heard saying: "Go on and try!" "I know you can!" "That's better!" The teacher's faith in the children increases their faith in themselves so that they come to see themselves as capable of learning.

Evaluation of the Program

Both formal and informal techniques were utilized to evaluate this program. Reading tests were administered. Parents and teachers were asked to give opinions regarding the program. In addition, a survey was undertaken to determine if parents had set aside a quiet time in the home. These findings follow.

Reading test results. Forms 1 and 2 of the Gates Revised Reading Tests were administered to all children in the two experimental schools. The same test was simultaneously administered to all second- and fifth-grade students in a third elementary school that served as the control. Children in the control school had similar backgrounds. Their reading gains were compared with gains made by second- and fifth-grade children in the two experimental schools.

The tests were administered in November 1961 and May 1962. Since the two tests were administered five months apart, the normal gains in reading can be expected to be five months.

Children in the two experimental schools showed overall gains of 5.3 months in reading during this 5-month period. Children in the control school showed overall gains of 2.8 months in reading during this period. Gains made by one experimental school (School C) were generally greater than those made by the other school (School B). A factor that may have contributed to this finding is that Experimental School B entered the program somewhat later than did Experimental School C, and there were some problems in involving the staff completely in this school. Children in all schools showed greater gains in acquiring reading vocabulary than in developing reading comprehension. Since reading comprehension is broader-based than vocabulary, equivalent gains in comprehension would be expected as time passes.

Vocabulary and comprehension gains made by second-grade children. Tables 1 and 2 on the following page compare gains of second-grade children in the two experimental schools with those of children in the control school. The gains made by the children in the experimental schools were significantly greater. Experimental School C made slightly greater gains in comprehension than School B.

Vocabulary and comprehension gains made by fifth-grade children. Tables 4 and 5 on the following page compare gains of fifth-grade children in the two experimental schools with those of children in the control school. An examination of Table 4 shows that children in the two experimental schools made significantly greater gains in vocabulary than did children in the control school. An examination of Table 5 shows that the gains made in comprehension are moderately significantly greater for children in Experimental School C but not significantly greater for children in Experimental School B.

Gains made by second-grade children when vocabulary and comprehension are combined. A comparison of gains in vocabulary and comprehension combined shows that children in the two experimental schools made significantly greater progress than did children in the control school (see Table 3 on the following page).

Gains made by fifth-grade children when vocabulary and comprehension are combined. The comparison of gains in vocabulary and comprehension combined in Table 6 does not show significant differences for children in Experimental School B when compared with the control school (School A). The differences for these children are at a low positive but not quite significant level. Highly significant differences are disclosed, however, for children in Experimental School C.

TABLE 1. Second-Grade Children's Mean Gains in Vocabulary.

		Scores in Months		Significance of Differences	
Schools	Number of Children	Mean Gains	Standard Deviation	Z— Scores	Probability
Control A	66	3.6	3.6		
Experimental B	82	5.5	4.9	2.71	.01*
Experimental C	71	5.8	3.9	3.44	.01*

TABLE 2. Second-Grade Children's Mean Gains in Comprehension.

		Scores in Months		Significance of Differences	
Schools	Number of Children	Mean Gains	Standard Deviation	Z— Scores	Probability
Control A	68	4.1	4.6		
Experimental B	82	4.9	5.3	.99	N.S.
Experimental C	71	7.1	4.9	3.70	.01*

TABLE 3. Second-Grade Children's Gains for Vocabulary and Comprehension Combined.

		Scores in Months		Significance of Differences	
Schools	Number of Children	Mean Gains	Standard Deviation	Z— Scores	Probability
Control A	63	3.9	3.2		
Experimental B	82	5.1	4.2	1.97	.05†
Experimental C	71	6.4	3.1	4.63	.01*

---

*Such a low probability that the difference occurred by chance may be interpreted as highly significant.
†This probability may be interpreted as moderately significant.

TABLE 4. Fifth-Grade Children's Mean Gains in Vocabulary.

Schools	Number of Children	Scores in Months		Significance of Differences	
		Mean Gains	Standard Deviation	Z— Scores	Probability
Control A	63	1.4	8.9		
Experimental B	70	6.4	7.9	3.42	.01*
Experimental C	54	6.1	8.1	3.01	.01*

TABLE 5. Fifth-Grade Children's Mean Gains in Comprehension.

Schools	Number of Children	Scores in Months		Significance of Differences	
		Mean Gains	Standard Deviation	Z— Scores	Probability
Control A	63	1.8	9.0		
Experimental B	70	1.3	9.7	.31	N.S.
Experimental C	54	5.7	10.3	2.17	.05†

TABLE 6. Fifth-Grade Children's Gains for Vocabulary and Comprehension Combined.

Schools	Number of Children	Scores in Months		Significance of Differences	
		Mean Gains	Standard Deviation	Z— Scores	Probability
Control A	60	1.7	6.4		
Experimental B	70	3.7	6.2	1.80	N.S.
Experimental C	53	6.0	6.4	3.55	.01*

---

*Highly significant.
†Moderately significant.

Parent opinion questionnaire results. One questionnaire was sent to each family in the two experimental schools to ascertain what opinion parents held about this program. The questionnaire contained three multiple-choice questions and three open-ended questions. Parents indicated that they felt the program helped the children with school work, that they would like to have the program continued and that it helped them improve their own skills.

TABLE 7. Parent's Responses to the Three Multiple-Choice Questions About the Program.

Question		Experimental School B	Experimental School C
1. Was home study helpful?	Yes	146	153
	No	0	1
2. Was "Read to Me" helpful?	Yes	147	148
	No	1	0
3. Should program be continued?	Yes	148	158
	No	1	0

Home study survey results. A survey was undertaken in the two experimental school communities to determine if parents had set aside a quiet time in the home for study and for reading. A secondary purpose of the survey was maintaining contact with parents to help sustain their interest. Although all the children reported to the teacher each day, the researcher wanted to know if parents had established a routine period for these activities. Parents indicated the daily study time on the questionnaire, and they signed the questionnaire. Approximately 90 per cent of the children in the two schools returned completed questionnaires.

Teachers' observations. The multilevel self-help materials were considered especially beneficial by the teachers. Support from home brought about an improved social-psychological climate in the classroom. Teachers noted improvement in the children's work habits and in their attitudes toward school work. Children were more eager to learn. The work of the teachers, therefore, became more rewarding and satisfying.

Summary and Observations

Parents were eager to participate in the program. The contention that these parents were not interested in their children was not, therefore, supported; in fact, it was overwhelmingly refuted. This finding suggests that appropriate techniques are an important factor in involving parents with limited educational backgrounds in improving the academic achievement of their children. With few exceptions, parents followed through with the suggestions made in the program. The few exceptions included parents too burdened with emotional and psychological problems to effectively follow through with any organized efforts.

Some parents were more difficult to involve than others, but more effort was exerted in order to involve them. This effort was justified on the basis that the child's academic welfare is of a paramount importance and that each child must be helped to become all that he is capable of.

In any experiment, improvements may be expected during the experimental phase. However, after the experimental phase is ended, those innovations that brought about the improvement must become a part of the ongoing program if the pace of learning is to be sustained.

It should be noted that innovations in this program were beneficial for all the children. Procedures beneficial to the severely academically retarded child were equally beneficial to academically able children. It is this writer's opinion, therefore, that some of the best teaching innovations for *all* children will be derived from experimental programs for the educationally disadvantaged child.

In this situation, the role of the school was not to assume parental responsibility. First of all, the school, as organized in our society, cannot assume such control over the child; secondly, no outside agency, school or otherwise, should assume the appropriate role of the parent.

The rightful role for educators is seen rather to be that of teaching parents to assume their appropriate responsibilities and assist them in this task. The relationship sought is the cooperative sharing of responsibilities by the parents and the schools, working together to bridge the educational gap with purposeful educational programing and planning.

Robert D. Hess and Virginia C. Shipman report on their studies of the relationship between maternal attitudes toward the school and the "educability" of the child—"educability" being their term for "orientations, skills, and motivations that prepare the child to learn in a formal school situation." The study focuses on the discrepancies between the behavior and values of families of low socio-economic status and the requirements for social and academic performance set by the schools. While admitting that the children of these families are not prepared to operate effectively in the schools, they attribute this failure not to low intelligence, but to disorientation to the school and its processes, from which the children suffer, for the youngsters' preschool experiences are constantly being reinforced by the home and community environment. This paper shows how cultural experience of these children affects their cognitive behavior and, eventually, their academic achievement.

MATERNAL ATTITUDES TOWARD THE SCHOOL AND THE ROLE OF PUPIL: SOME SOCIAL CLASS COMPARISONS

Robert D. Hess
Virginia C. Shipman

Hess and Shipman see the disadvantaged child as presenting a "problem in acculturation." Patterns developed before formal schooling begins can either impede or facilitate the child's success in the academic setting. From the viewpoint of these authors, the cognitive development of children can best be understood in terms of mother-child interaction, which transactions are modified by the family's position in the social structure of the community. The mother's behavior influences the learning, or information-processing, strategies in the child. The child's early experiences with authority and cognitive activity affect his later behavior in the formal learning setting of the schools. To reveal the significant aspects of the mother's behavior, Hess and Shipman studied 163 mothers and their four-year-old children. Their data reflect the mother's role in socializing her child and preparing him for life as a pupil. Four areas are examined: (1) the mother's image of the school as an institution and of the teacher as an authority figure representing the school; (2) the kinds of

109

behavior the mothers believe appropriate for their children in a classroom setting and the way they define these expectations; (3) the mother's aspirations for the children; and (4) the relationships between the attitudes and practices of mothers and the school-relevant performance of their children.

The researchers have data to support the assumption that even at age four the early maternal attitudes are transmitted to the child and affect his cognition and other maturities. They find a cause-effect relationship between the mother's attitude toward school and the child's I.Q., as well as his behavior in the testing situation. They conclude that mothers of children who achieve relatively poorly do not lack respect for the school as an institution nor do they believe the educational process is ineffective; rather, these mothers regard the school, the teachers, and the administrative staff as comprising a "formidable institution with which they have very little interaction or over which they exercise very little control."

Consequently, the authors propose a variety of procedures to help mothers change their own views of the school. The initiative must come from the school itself. They believe their study has important implications for parent education, particularly for the reorientation in attitudes or so-called "acculturation" or mothers of young children from lower-class homes.

MATERNAL ATTITUDES TOWARD THE SCHOOL AND THE ROLE OF PUPIL: SOME SOCIAL CLASS COMPARISONS

Robert D. Hess
Virginia C. Shipman*

This paper is concerned with the origins and antecedents of educability in young children whose families live in economically and socially depressed urban areas. Educability, as we use the term, refers to a mingling of orientations, skills, and motivations that prepare the child to learn in a formal school situation. Educability includes at least three components: first, a cluster of *cognitive skills* (language, visual and auditory discrimination, conceptual ability, adeptness with logical operations, and so forth), a degree of *motivation to learn* and to achieve in a school and classroom setting (curiosity, interest in inquiry, need for achievement, and so forth), and *acceptance of the role of pupil* (orientation toward authority of teacher and school, acceptance of rules of the classroom and school, an understanding of the central purpose of the school, and so forth). Although we are interested in the various influences that create or retard the development of educability, this paper is focused upon the role of the mother in the emergence of this complex set of orientations and response patterns.

The development of an ability to learn in school settings has traditionally been of widespread professional concern only in special cases involving children with mental retardation or defects of some kind, or in cases involving children with emotional blocks to learning. The contemporary focus upon the educational problems of the poor has raised a number of questions about the discrepancy between the behavior and values of children from low socioeconomic groups and the expectations for social and academic performance under which the public schools operate. It is frequently observed that children from the lower working-class sectors of American society are not prepared to operate effectively in the schools. One of the assertions we will make in this paper is that this lack of preparation is not merely a matter of intelligence but represents orientations to authority, the school, and the learning process that have come from the

*The research in this paper was supported by Research Grant #R34 from the Children's Bureau, Social Security Administration, Department of Health, Education and Welfare; by the Ford Foundation Fund for the Advancement of Learning; and by grants-in-aid from the Social Science Research Committee of the Division of Social Sciences, University of Chicago.

child's preschool experience and are constantly reinforced by his home and community environment.

The concepts and results we are reporting in this paper are part of a larger study, begun over four years ago, which was designed to assess the cognitive environments of urban preschool Negro children and the impact of these environments upon the cognitive behavior and motivation of young children. In attempting to identify and study those variables in the environment of the preschool child that appear to facilitate or interfere with subsequent cognitive growth, we have focused upon the role of the mother as a socializing agent in areas of behavior usually associated with success in school.

The Background for the Study

The general problem to which the project addressed itself was understanding how cultural experience is translated into cognitive behavior and academic achievement. This question, however, developed out of a concern for understanding what is meant by "cultural deprivation" or "cultural disadvantage." There has been considerable documentation of the depressing effect of social and cultural disadvantage upon academic ability. The more basic problem, however, is to understand the mechanisms of exchange that mediate between the individual and his environment. In focusing on the input features of the socializing process, we hope to be able to conceptualize social class as a discrete array of experiences and patterns of experience that can be examined in relation to their effects upon the emerging cognitive equipment of the young child. The study was not intended to demonstrate or examine social class differences as such. Rather, the interest in social class divergencies is a starting point from which to understand the specifics of mother-child interaction having cognitive consequences for the child.

This conceptual approach represents a view of the educationally disadvantaged child as presenting a problem in acculturation. He comes to the school not only deficient in language skills and in ability to discriminate auditory and visual input but with a pattern of behavior that is not readily adaptable to the school. Typically, he is from a part of the society that has not been permitted to learn the routine daily social and occupational behavior of the dominant sectors of the society. It is, of course, these sectors of society that have developed the schools, the curriculum, and the teachers with whom he must interact. The alienation he feels from the mainstream of society has begun before he reaches school, and his modes of adapting to this fact have created behaviorial tendencies that must be changed if he is to succeed in school. In this regard, the school must serve as a *resocializing* as well as a socializing unit. The importance of this fact is not generally recognized, and its profound implications for early education and for teacher training have not been adequately explored. The social and cultural distance between the home and the school is sometimes taken to indicate a lack of effort on the part of teachers or a lack of motivation on the part of parents. It seems more likely that neither of these is true, that an attempt to fix the blame upon either the school or the home evades more fundamental problems in the structure of the society.

It is evident from the preceding comments that we regard the early years as especially significant in the development of educability. This is not so much because of any existing assumptions about the critical nature of early experience, but because of the implications that early patterns of learning have for later experience in the school. These patterns are developed before formal schooling begins and necessarily impede or facilitate the transition of the child to academic success. We view early experience as a time when the child begins to learn ways of sorting and ordering the mass of information that his input modalities bring to him, developing techniques for selecting or ignoring the stimuli that reach him from internal and external sources. Part of the role of a socializing adult in this early experience is to give the child catagories of thought and ways of dealing with information. These modes of dealing with stimuli may be regarded as information-processing strategies that enable the child to make some sense out of the incredibly large number of pieces of information with which he must cope. These strategies are learned in interaction with the total environment, especially in the interaction with other persons. In this early learning process the mother plays a central, perhaps dominant, part.

In our view, many of the differences in mental ability and cognitive styles that appear among different cultural and socioeconomic groups in the United States can best be understood in terms of the transmission of information-processing strategies from parents to children. It is also our contention that the position of the family in the social structure of the community is related to the techniques used by the children to deal with their information and to the range of alternatives for action and thought that are available to them. A family in an urban ghetto has few choices to make with respect to such basic things as residence, occupation, and condition of housing, or on the minor things that come with adequate discretionary income. A family with few opportunities to make choices among events that affect it is not likely to encourage the children to think of life as offering a wide range of behavioral options among which they must learn to discriminate.

To recapitulate, it is our argument (1) that social-class and cultural effects upon cognitive development of children can best be understood in terms of the specific interactional transactions between the mother and her young child, (2) that the nature of these exchanges is influenced by the family's position in the social structure of the community and the number of its alternatives, (3) that maternal behavior induces complementary

113

learning or information-processing strategies in the child, and (4) that the child's early orientation to authority and cognitive activity facilitates or retards his ability to adopt the role of pupil when he encounters formal learning stiuations in the public schools.[1]

There are five aspects of maternal behavior that were important in the study under consideration. The first of these was the mother's techniques for regulating and controlling the behavior of her child. These techniques may be *imperative-normative*, relying on appeals to formal rules or authority or social norms of conduct, and making a relatively low demand on the cognitive resources of the child. They may be *subjective-personal*, relying on appeals to inner states, to feelings, moods, personal preferences, and approval of others. These techniques encourage the child to see himself from another's point of view and to be sensitive to the perspectives of surrounding peers and adults. These techniques may also be *cognitive-rational*, relying on an appeal to long-term consequences and related to the task to be accomplished rather than to feelings and established rules.

The second of these aspects was maternal teaching techniques, or the ability of the mother to organize and give meaning to the information that reaches the child or to help him make sense of new information in terms of knowledge he already possesses. These techniques were studied in teaching sessions that we asked the mothers to take part in with their four-year-old children and included: the mother's tendency to be specific, to orient the child to the task, and to present material and ideas in sequences that give the child some experience in following a chain of ideas and in working toward clear goals set for him. These techniques are described in greater detail in other papers (Brophy, Hess, and Shipman, 1966; Hess and Shipman, 1966).

The third of these aspects, maternal language, was another point of special focus in the study. Scales for analyzing maternal language were developed by Ellis Olim, and the relation of maternal language to the cognitive behavior of the child was investigated. These have been reported in detail elsewhere (Olim, 1965; Olim, Hess, and Shipman, 1965) and will not be discussed in this paper.

Obviously, maternal cognitive skills, the fourth aspect of behavior studied, are viewed as part of the cognitive environment. The level and style of mothers' cognitive activity were assessed by several techniques including the WAIS and the Sigel Sorting Task. Along with the mother's behavior in socializing the child into the role of pupil, the fifth aspect studied, this feature of maternal behavior will be described in more detail in this paper.

---

[1] The concepts utilized to analyze mother-child interaction draw significantly from the formulations in Basil Bernstein's published and unpublished writings on social learning, linguistic codes, and family control strategies (Bernstein, 1961, 1962).

Although these maternal patterns of behavior have some interest in themselves, the purpose of this study is to examine the effect they have upon the cognitive behavior and educability of the child. Cognitive behavior is especially difficult to assess at age four, and our tests of cognitive performance are very limited. We are following up the research group and are concentrating upon obtaining more complex and varied data on cognitive abilities during the early years of school. The measures we had at this time for children at age four are: verbal ability, as reflected in the capacity to use labels and respond on measures of performance with verbal answers; performance on the Stanford Binet; performance during the maternal teaching sessions; and conceptual style as indicated by the Sigel Sorting Task.

Research Plan

A research group of 163 mothers and their four-year-old children was selected to provide variation along four dimensions: socioeconomic background, type of housing, economic dependency status, and intactness of family. All the subjects were Negroes, nonworking mothers, free from any obvious mental or physical disabilities. The research group includes only Negro mothers and children because of the special, historically based educational problems confronting the Negro sector of our population. It is a racially homogeneous group for methodological reasons. The criteria for selection of subgroups were these: Group A was selected from the college-educated, at the professional, executive, and managerial occupational levels; Group B was selected from those with not more than high school education, at the skilled blue-collar occupational level; Group C came from those at the unskilled or semiskilled occupational levels having predominantly elementary school education. Group D differed from Group C in the fact that the children's fathers were absent and the families were supported by public assistance. Groups were similar with respect to the sexes of the children and except for Group A, with respect to the number living in private as opposed to public housing. Typical social class differences in intelligence test scores appeared among the group (Table 1).

TABLE 1. I.Q. Scores of Mothers and Children (Means)

| Test | Social Status Groups | | | |
	A (N–40)	B (N–42)	C (N–40)	D (N–41)
WAIS Verbal I.Q.	109.4	91.8	82.5	82.4
Stanford-Binet I.Q. (Form LM)	109.4	98.6	96.3	94.5
Difference	0.0	6.8	13.8	12.1

115

The mothers were interviewed in their homes about their activities with the child, their daily schedules, the availability of cognitive and intellectual stimulation, and other features of the home environment thought to be related to cognitive development. The mother-child pairs were then brought to the university for testing and for an interaction session that required the mother to teach the child three simple tasks that she had been taught by a project staff member. One of these tasks was to sort or group a number of plastic toys (cars, spoons, and chairs that were red, yellow, and green) by color and by function. A second task was to sort eight blocks that differed in color, size, shape, and mark by two characteristics simultaneously. The third task required the mother and child to work together to copy five designs on a toy called an Etch-A-Sketch.

In this paper we will present data relevant to several questions about the mother's role in socializing her child into the behavior expected of pupils in a major city educational system. These questions are:

What are the elements of the images the mothers of our research group have of the school as an institution and of the teacher as a figure representing the school?

What kinds of behavior do mothers of our group believe to be appropriate for pupils in a classroom setting? How do they define the expectations of the school and the complementary role of pupil for their young children?

What are the mothers' aspirations for their children?

What relationships appear between the attitudes and practices of the mothers and the cognitive and school-relevant performance of their children?

By *role of pupil* we mean a set of behaviors, nonacademic in nature, that structure interaction between the child and the teacher, the tasks and materials of learning, the institutional rules, and the peer group. The process of socialization into this role is not learned directly; the child's definition of his role as a pupil, his expectations of the behaviors to be demanded of him by the school system, are attained through indirect learning.

Attitudes toward learning, toward institutions such as the school, toward persons of authority such as the teacher, and toward his own abilities and limitations as a member of the public school complex, are conveyed to the child during the preschool years by older persons in the home environment. More specifically, in her everyday behavior and through the close mother-child interaction obtaining during those early years, the mother acts as the primary socializing agent of the child into the role of pupil.

The poorly prepared child is not uneducable because he has learned nothing during the preschool years, but because he has learned the wrong things. Successful socialization should result in a set of behaviors conducive to learning: the child is capable of establishing a good working relationship with his teacher; he is prepared to deal with her both as an authority and as a source of information; and he has confidence in his abilities to manipulate materials and to attempt challenging tasks. Unsuccessful socialization is expected to lead to poor teacher-child relationships, resulting in the blocking of information transmittal, and leading to a set of behaviors disruptive to the learning situation. The child who has learned to be compliant and submissive, to regard himself as ineffective in dealing with authority and inadequate in problem-solving, comes to school unready to meet the demands that are made upon him. This is seen as a potential explanatory model for the lower-class child's inability to meet successfully the role demands of the public school system.

Mothers' Attitudes toward the School

The primary instrument for assessing the images the mothers of the research group held of the school was composed of rating scales developed through interviews, pilot administrations, and item analyses. The final instrument used in the project included 27 items, each of which was to be rated on a five-point scale from "strongly agree" to "strongly disagree." A factor analysis of the responses yielded six factors accounting for all items: each item was heavily loaded with only one factor.

Scores reflecting each factor were obtained for subjects by summing responses (on a five-point scale) to the individual items comprising each factor; a high score, then, represents disagreement with the individual item contained in the factor. Mean scores for each of the four socioeconomic status groups, on each of the six factors, are reported in Table 2.

TABLE 2. Mothers' Attitudes toward Education (Means)

Attitude*	Social Status Group				
	A (N-40)	B (N-42)	C (N-40)	D (N-41)	Range of Possible Scores
Powerlessness	18.0	17.0	15.0	14.3	5–25
Conservatism	19.0	17.6	18.0	16.7	5–25
Resignation	14.7	12.7	11.3	11.7	6–30
Importance of Education	11.2	11.0	9.4	10.2	4–20
Importance of Nonacademic goals	8.5	9.2	10.0	9.7	3–15
Defense of Schools	8.4	8.4	8.0	8.4	4–20

*Low scores indicate presence of the attitude in question.

T tests were computed for differences between mean scores of each group contrasted with each other group; those reported here as significant reached a probability level of .05 or better.

The central themes in factor one, "powerlessness," were feelings of frustration, futility, and the uselessness of attempting to change either the system or the unruliness of children. Middle- and upper working-class mothers tended to disagree with the statements loaded heavily with this factor, while mothers in the two lower-class groups tended to agree with them. All differences between classes were significant except that between Groups C and D.

The central themes in factor two, "conservatism," were attitudes that discourage fun in life and complain about the "waste of time" in extracurricular activities provided by the school. Although social class differences are not so great as they are with respect to the first factor, middle-class mothers tend to disagree with the central theme, and mothers in the public assistance group to agree. The middle-class group differed significantly from both Groups B and D.

The central themes in factor three are pessimism (as opposed to optimism) and resignation to one's lot. The factor is composed of negatively loaded items, in which "yes" answers represent optimistic feelings of reliance on education for bettering one's lot. Lower-class mothers tended to agree with these negatively stated items. All cross-class comparisons were significant, except that between Groups C and D.

The themes in factor four, "importance of education," are concerned with positive attitudes toward the school system and getting a formal education. Middle- and lower upper-class mothers tended to disagree with the statements; lower-class mothers to endorse such statements. All social class differences were significant except that between Groups A and B.

Factor five deals with the issue of whether success in formal education is the most important goal in life. Mothers from middle-class backgrounds feel that other things are also to be highly valued; mothers from Groups C and D emphasize the overriding value of an education.

In their attitudes toward education, then, mothers from middle-class backgrounds rejected themes of powerlessness vis-à-vis the authority of school, denied a conservatism which dictates more work and less play, denied an optimism which says that formal schooling is the only means to a better life, and agreed with the notion that there are other goals in life as important as education.

Group B mothers showed less intense feeling on these factors, but they tended to agree with Group A mothers in denying that they are powerless and that education is the central hope for bettering one's lot in life.

Mothers in both Groups C and D agreed with statements of the futility of attempting to use one's power against the school system, but they also tended to agree with the notion that a good education is an important means to improving one's status. In addition, mothers in these groups tended to express or endorse a conservative attitude, a rigidity about working and not wasting time on play.

A second, less direct opportunity to describe the school was provided by a task requiring mothers to describe what they believed was happening in a photograph of a mother and a teacher seated at a large desk in a school classroom. The mother was given the following instructions: "Here is a picture of a teacher and mother together in a school classroom. Can you tell a story about why the mother came to school and what they're talking about here in the classroom? We would like to know what is happening in the picture and what will happen as the result of their conversation."

The first distinction to be made was whether the meeting between mother and teacher was perceived as a problem-oriented session. Although in each group more mothers described the meeting as problem-oriented than did not, the difference was less for the middle-class group (67 per cent) than for the other groups (95, 76, and 74 per cent respectively). Among those mothers describing the meeting as problem-oriented, there were no clear trends as to differences in the type of problem described.

Mothers were also given an opportunity to reveal their views and feelings about the school in the interview in response to this question: "If you had the power to do as you wished about education in the school, what would you do?" Mothers' responses to this question were grouped into categories: (1) those suggesting no change; (2) those suggesting changes that are commonly held to be within the domain of an educational system— changes in curriculum or other academic aspects in the physical plant, or in the school's mechanical and administrative functions, reflected in responses concerned with the need for more schools and teachers or for special facilities, discipline of children, and improvements in the training of teachers or in their motivation and dedication; and (3) those arguing for changes in the school as a social-political institution or as an instrument of social policy—responses dealing with integration and school-community and parent-teacher relationships.

Although more than one type of response was possible to this open-ended question, the majority of mothers gave short replies containing only one suggestion; suggestions in more than one area were made by 16 mothers in Group A, 7 in Group B, 3 in Group C, and only 1 in Group D.

Because the number responding in any one of the nine specific categories was very small, the response types were grouped into the three main categories described above. When chi-square values were computed for each of the three response groups (use vs. nonuse), social class differences were significant (p < .01) for each. Twice as many mothers in Groups C and D as in Groups A and B had no suggestions; the majority made vague references to improving the schools, said they had never thought about it, or did not know what they could do. And twice as many Group A and B as Group C and D mothers made concrete suggestions for changes

119

in curriculum, in physical and administrative aspects of running the schools, in discipline, or in training of teachers. Finally, more middle-class mothers discussed issues involving the school in a wider social and political system than mothers in all other groups combined (Table 3).

TABLE 3. Mothers' Suggestions for Improving the Schools (Percentage of Mothers Recommending Changes)

Type of Change Recommended	Status Groups			
	A	B	C	D
Essentially none	12.5	26.2	48.7	51.2
Educational	70.0	66.7	38.5	43.9
Political, social	35.0	11.9	17.9	4.9

Mothers' Interaction with the School

A mother's feelings about herself and her relationship to the school system may set the pattern for her child's belief about the typical relationships of the individual to the institution. How does a mother describe her role in interaction with the school and with its main individual representative, the teacher?

Statements of mothers' feelings about their relationship to the school and its representatives come from their description of the relationship between the mother and teacher in the photograph. Responses for mother-teacher relationship were scored on the relative status positions ascribed to the two women and the affective tone or mood of the described interaction. A third consideration, especially if there was a problem being discussed, was whether the outcome was good, hopeful, or poor. The proportion of mothers utilizing each scoring category is reported in Table 4.

Although the differences among groups were not statistically significant, there were some apparent differences in patterns of response. The greatest proportion of respondents described the relationships as a working together of the two women to reach a solution or agreement, with neither dominating and with no friction between them. This response was more typical, however, of the Group A and B mothers than of mothers in Groups C and D; the latter tended to describe the mother as a passive figure seeking information and advice from the authoritative teacher.

A response describing the relationship as one of equality, in which the affect was explicitly positive and both parties were exchanging information and gaining insight, was found more often among middle-class mothers than among mothers in any of the other groups. Lack of information about the relationship or its affective tone was far more typical of Groups C and D than of Groups A and B.

120

TABLE 4. Mothers' Perception of the Nature of the
Mother-Teacher Relationship
(Percentage of Mothers Having This Perception)

Relationship	Social Status Group			
	A (N–39)	B (N–38)	C (N–37)	D (N–38)
Positive: Cooperation of equals or working together	59.0	42.1	21.6	31.6
Conflict	23.1	28.9	24.3	31.6
Passivity	10.3	23.7	40.5	23.7
No information or vague	7.7	5.3	16.2	13.2

Middle-class mothers, then, saw their role in interaction with the school and its representatives as one of equality; the mother's meeting with the teacher was typically seen as a friendly visit between equals who were interested in gaining insight into the child's behavior.

Mothers of Group C, while they did not emphasize positive affect and equality to the extent that middle-class mothers did, tended to describe the mother-teacher relationships as a working together of the two to reach some common goal.

Mothers in both C and D groups tended to describe the mother's role in the conference as a passive one: mother went to the school to ask the teacher what to do, or she went to "get satisfaction" from the teacher for something that had been done to her child, and the conference was characterized by friction between the two which might not be resolved. Group C and D mothers were also more likely than Group A and B mothers to ignore or to describe only vaguely the affective relationship between the mother and teacher.

Mothers' Definition of the Role of the Pupil

How a mother defines the school indicates which aspects of the new situation (that is, new to the child) are important to her. Until he has entered and actually experienced this new realm, the preschool child's notions about school are likely to be hazy and inaccurate. He can, however, anticipate it, especially if his mother prepares him, drawing his attention to those aspects she deems most important. If she does not tell her child what she thinks of school nor describe the daily round of a classroom, she will often express her attitudes and expectations indirectly, guiding her child in developing attitudes and behavior she believes will be necessary for his success in school.

121

To obtain the mothers' definitions and perceptions of school, they were asked to imagine that it was the first day of school: "Your child is going to school for the first time. What will you do? What will you tell him?"

Responses to this question were scored for six categories. The "obedience" category includes responses in which the mother defined the classroom as a place where the child would have to behave in a socially accepted and obedient manner toward the teacher and/or his peers; to conform to classroom routine; to follow a set of rules pertaining to health, safety, and property rights; or simply to behave or be nice. For example, a mother in the public assistance group said that she would tell her little girl:

> "Obey the teacher. Do what the teacher asks her to do and that's all to do or say. Just tell her to sit quiet and listen at the teacher and do whatever the teacher tells her to do and get her lessons."

Another, less concerned with school itself than with getting there and home safely, said:

> "I would tell him to be aware of cars, you know, don't step out in front of a car is something that is dangerous. And don't pick up different things that don't concern him. Go straight to school and come straight home from school."

A somewhat less explicit statement of the importance of obedience was given by a Group C mother:

> "Well, the first time I would tell him to be nice and learn to listen to the teachers and do what they tell him to do and mind . . .",

while a Group B mother listed a group of behaviors she expects her child to remember when he goes to school for the first time:

> "I'd tell him to go straight to school and stop at the patrol lady . . . don't cross, because she tells you to. Mind your teacher; be nice; raise your hand, and when you have to go to the bathroom, ask her, you know, and don't talk in school, don't eat any candy or chew any gum. Be nice."

Mothers of middle-class background tended to elaborate more and to suggest rather than to demand obedience:

> "I will tell (her) that she is beginning her education. And here she will learn to play with other children. She will learn to listen to the teacher and how to act properly in a control situation such as not talking out any time she wants to . . . and I will tell her to be

very cooperative and do whatever the teacher wants her to do. And try to be friendly and get along with the children."

The following middle-class mother drew an analogy between obedience at home and at school:

"The only thing I will definitely stress to her is authority, that the teacher becomes the authority head. Mother and Daddy are the authorities at home, and that she has to respect and obey the teacher and likewise the teacher will respect and obey her wishes, and I think this is mainly what I will tell her about it; that there is authority outside of the home and this is it, you are just going into it, your teacher will be your main center of authority at school, and you must obey her as I want you to obey me."

A second response category defines school as an opportunity to attain increasing levels of achievement in academic skills. A mother might say, as did one in the public assistance group, "She's going there for to learn things which will help her for whatever she might want to be when she grows up"; a Group C mother said, "I'd tell him that I want him to go to school so that he can prepare himself how to work or help him get a good job."

In addition to defining school as an authority system or as an educational system, some mothers were concerned with the beginning school as an emotional or affective experience. These mothers anticipated their children's fears of the new and strange experience and stressed the adventurous aspects of meeting new people and the change in status from baby to "big boy." One middle-class mother, concerned with affect, spoke only in positive tones:

"First of all, I would take (him) to see his new school. We would talk about the building, and after seeing the school I would tell him that he would meet new children who would be his friends, he would work and play with them. I would explain to him that the teacher would be his friend, would help him and guide him in school, and that he should do as she tells him to. That will be his mother while he is away from home."

A public assistance mother was more explicit about the potential negative feelings:

"Well, by her being kind of bashful, the first thing I think I'll have to go with her. And tell her that she only have to stay here for a few hours and play with the kids. And everything's going to be fine. And she'll be able to come home. I'll come and pick her up when school is out."

123

An eloquent statement of mixed emotions was given by a Group C mother:

"I know he gonna be ner-frightened, you know, to stay there by himself, uh with the teacha. I just don't know what I would tell him. I try, I'd tell him that, uh, that he gonna have a lot of fun, you know, with the drawin' and everthin', and uh, playin' with the rest of the kids. Lots of kids there to play with — the rest of the children. And I'll tell him that I'll be back for him, and uh, it's fun, it's a lot of fun to go to school, cause he looks forward to goin' to school, but I know that first day, I know how it is that first day, when your mother leave you, you just don't know what to do."

Responses to this open-ended question often constituted or included statements that did not directly answer the question. Mothers mentioned actual experiences the child had had that they felt were helpful in preparing him for school, such as visiting the school or playing and talking about school with older siblings and friends, or actual skills that she had attempted to teach him herself, such as tying his shoes, or learning his ABC's. A Group B mother related that she would tell her daughter "how to undress and pull off her shoes and rubbers and how to go to the washroom, and hang her coat and hat and things like that." Concern for the academic aspect of school was expressed in preparation by a public assistance mother: "I would help her with her ABC's, things like that. I would help her learn to count, you know, and do as much as I could to help her."

The coding system devised for responses to this question defines a unit as a completed thought, usually a subject-and-predicate clause. For each respondent the number of units devoted to each scoring category of response can be expressed as the percentage of the total number of units contained in her response. It is for this reason that vague and irrelevant response-units were included in the total score. Table 5 reports the average per cent of usage for each category obtained within each of the four socioeconomic status groups.

The overall level of response (that is, the number of total message units) did not vary much among the four groups, although a slight trend was seen for both total length and variety of response to be greater at the upper socioeconomic levels.

It is clear, though, that the total response is partitioned differently in the different groups of mothers, with an especially marked difference in the use of obedience and affect categories by the middle-class mothers as contrasted with the other three groups. Middle-class mothers are apparently more concerned with the emotional aspects of the new situation, with its meaning to the child, than with his displaying good behavior; they are perhaps more aware of the emotional aspect than are the mothers in the other groups.

As a group, in responding to this question, mothers paid only slight attention to academic achievement and formal preparation for school, although middle-class mothers did show a greater tendency to relate rele-

**TABLE 5. Mothers' Relative Use of Different Response
Categories on the First Day Technique
(Mean Percentage of Mothers Giving this Type of Response)**

| Type of Response | Social Status Groups | | | |
	A (N–39)	B (N–40)	C (N–38)	D (N–40)
School-Relevant Instruction:				
Obedience	21.3	49.1	44.2	46.7
Achievement	2.2	1.4	2.9	3.2
Noninstructive Orientation:				
Affect	31.2	14.3	14.5	21.5
Preparation	8.6	3.9	1.1	1.3
Other:				
Vague	16.4	13.7	23.4	17.5
Irrelevant	19.6	15.2	13.2	12.8
Sum	99.3	97.6	99.3	103.0

vant incidents, either coincidental or purposeful, to which their children had been exposed. Vague and irrelevant statements made up more than a third of the total response in all groups. It is interesting to note that in the A and B groups irrelevant statements were more common, whereas in Groups C and D, vague responses predominated. Responses labeled "irrelevant" generally took the form of ramblings about unique, personal qualities of the child or his anxious anticipation of the beginning of school.

It seems, then, that middle-class mothers were aware of the emotional implications of the beginning of school experience for children and were sensitive to the need for reassurance which would make this exciting adventure less strange. They tended not to define a mother-teacher meeting as a discussion of specific problems with a child, but as a friendly exchange. They made specific suggestions for changes in the school system which indicated awareness of the various functions of the school, and of the role of the school system in relationship to the larger society.

The Group B mothers stressed both obedience to a new authority, the teacher, and general good deportment in the child's behavior on beginning school; they defined school as a place in which the child is expected to conform to a new routine. More than mothers in any other group, they described a mother-teacher meeting as a problem-oriented session, the topic being the child's grades or a combination of grades and conduct. They made concrete suggestions for changing the school, specifically in its physical-administrative functions and in the quality of its teachers.

The Group C mothers, too, defined the school as a situation calling for conformity and obedience to authority. They saw a mother-teacher

125

meeting as a conference oriented toward some problem; although relatively unspecific as to its nature, it was likely to involve the child's school work and perhaps also his behavior. Given the opportunity to make suggestions for changes in the school, they agreed that there was need for improvement but did not know what they should or could do.

The mothers on public assistance (Group D) were very similar to the Group C mothers in their definition of school; it is a system of authority to which children must conform. A mother-teacher meeting was viewed as a session oriented toward solving a specific problem with a child's grades, behavior, or some complaint about something the teacher had done to the child. These mothers, too, may have stated that the schools needed improving, but did not make specific suggestions and, more than mothers in any other group, responded, "Don't know," or some other indication that they had not really thought about it, or that they did not think they could accomplish anything.

The Mothers' Aspirations for the Child

It has already been noted that working-class mothers feel a powerlessness and a lack of personal effectiveness against the authority of the school system, although they have great respect for education as an important tool for achieving a better status in life. They express a belief in the importance of good behavior on the part of their children. The frustration that appears to accompany these attitudes and beliefs was strikingly illustrated when mothers were asked about their aspirations and expectations for their children's educational achievement (Figure 1). The majority of mothers in all social class groups said that they would like their children to finish college. The majority of mothers in the working-class groups, however, when asked how far in school they thought their child would actually go, were less hopeful. Group B mothers' aspirations and expectations were more diverse, but the majority of those who aspired to a college education for their children also expected that their children would finish

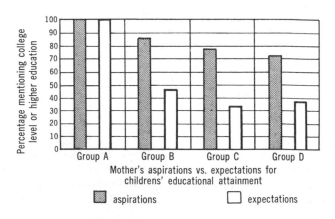

Mother's aspirations vs. expectations for childrens' educational attainment

▓ aspirations   ☐ expectations

college. Discrepancies between expressed aspirations and expectations among middle-class mothers barely existed; they wanted their children to finish college, and they believed that they would.

Discussion and Summary

In this paper we have described some of the significant aspects of the attitudes that mothers of young children hold toward the public school and toward education. We have also examined the degree to which the mothers' attitudes and behavior are reflected in the child's performance in various tasks and tests in our study. These are only rough estimates of what will happen when the child eventually arrives in school. We are now in the midst of a follow-up study that will determine in a more adequate manner how these early maternal attitudes will be translated into children's behavior in kindergarten and first grade. It seems important, however, that even at age four these attitudes toward the school are associated with certain cognitive and other behaviors of the child. Although these relationships have been reported in some detail in other papers (Bear, Hess, and Shipman, 1966), it may be appropriate to summarize them here. The mother's attitude toward the school as reflected in the Educational Attitude Survey is significantly related to the child's IQ and to the child's behavior in the Stanford-Binet testing situation. The two factors that appear most frequently in these two sets of data are factors one and six. Factor one (feeling of power or powerlessness) is particularly important. It is negatively related to the child's tendency to engage in initiatory behavior in the Stanford-Binet testing situation, to his quickness of response, social confidence, and comfortableness with an adult examiner. Thus the mother's attitude toward the school, which is apparently part of a larger cluster of attitudes toward herself and toward achievement in areas related to education, already has a discernible influence on her child's ability to deal with adults in formal testing situations and his ability to perform on cognitive tasks.

The images that these mothers hold of the school and that are probably transmitted to the young child in some form are particularly relevant for early education and the child's success in the school. The mothers' attitudes indicate that the problem is not due to a lack of respect for the school or to the belief that it is ineffective; it is due to the fact that the mothers regard it as a distant and formidable institution with which they have very little interaction and over which they exercise very little control. This leads to the kind of injunctions and preparation indicated in responses to our "first day" techniques, where the mothers from working-class areas typically talk in imperatives, presenting the school as a place in which one must obey the teacher and follow the rules rather than have opportunity for interaction and learning. Thus the initial relationship between the

127

child and the teacher is posed in terms of authority rather than interaction and in terms of rules of obedience rather than inquiry and exploration. This early attitude supports and reinforces the passivity of many working-class children who come into contact with middle-class institutions. It represents an orientation toward authority and toward learning that has indeed been taught by the mother and by the community environment and which needs to be modified through experience with teachers who interact on a basis other than authority and obedience. We have explored this issue in more detail in the paper discussing the relationship between maternal control and authority and the developing cognitive processes of the child (Hess and Shipman, 1966).

If the general picture that has been sketched here applies, it would seem to have implications for parent education, particularly as regards interaction between the school and the parent. It suggests, for example, that engaging parents in the activities of the school in some meaningful way may indeed assist the child in developing more adequate and useful images of the school, of the teacher, and of the role of pupil. More interaction between the home and the school, particularly in cases where the children are coming into the first grade or kindergarten, might make the initial orientation smoother and easier and provide an initial setting for the child in his first contact with the school that would make the task of resocialization somewhat simpler.

References

Ausubel, D. "A Teaching Strategy for Culturally Deprived Pupils: Cognitive and Motivational Considerations," *School Review* (1963), 454–463.

Bear, Roberta M.; R. D. Hess and Virginia Shipman. "Social Class Differences in Maternal Attitudes toward School and the Consequences for Cognitive Development in the Young Child." Paper presented at the American Educational Research Association meetings. Chicago, Illinois, February 19, 1966.

Bernstein, B. "Social Class and Linguistic Development," in *Society, Economy, and Education*, eds. A. H. Halsey, J. Floud, and A. Anderson. New York: Free Press, 1961.

———. "Linguistic Codes, Hesitation Phenomena, and Intelligence," *Language and Speech*, 5 (1962), 31.

Brophy, J.; R. D. Hess and Virginia Shipman. "Teaching Behavior of Mothers in Structured Interaction with Their Four-Year-Old Children: A Study in Frustration." Paper presented at the 38th Annual Meeting, Midwestern Psychological Association. Chicago, Illinois, May 5, 1966.

Davis, A. *Social Class Influences upon Learning*. Cambridge, Mass.: Harvard University Press, 1948.

Gray, Susan and Rupert A. Klaus. "An Experimental Preschool Program for Culturally Deprived Children," *Child Development*, 36 (1965), 887–898.

Hess, R. D. and Virginia Shipman. "Early Experience and the Socialization of Cognitive Modes in Children," *Child Development*, 36 (1965), 869–886.

————. "Cognitive Elements in Maternal Behavior." Presented at the First Annual Symposium on Child Psychology, Minnesota, May 20, 1966.

———— and D. J. Jackson. "Some New Dimensions in Providing Equal Educational Opportunity," *Journal of Negro Education*, 34 (1965), 220–231.

Harry Beilin explores the cognitive base for curriculum development in terms of findings from developmental and educational psychology. He sees the principal task of the teacher as that of identifying the nature of the events that the child is to experience, whether these be facts, concepts, persons or institutions, and determining the sequence by which these events are to be experienced in terms of some rational criteria and organization, and in consideration of the nature of the child who is to experience them. This is what he means by "curriculum." His conception entrusts teachers with control over the structure of knowledge, which is then programed for a particular child.

He maintains that the data clearly show that disadvantaged children start with fewer cognitive resources than their middle-class counterparts, and that the gap progressively widens. The lacks of the lower-class child can be inferred from comparable differences in capacities and functions, and most of the compensatory programs have, as a consequence, been oriented to reconstruct cognitive resources.

A COGNITIVE STRATEGY FOR CURRICULUM DEVELOPMENT

Harry Beilin

Most of this paper devotes itself to the characteristics of a cognitive curriculum strategy, with the several illustrations concerned with mathematical concepts. The characteristics of such a strategy involve (1) the schematization of knowledge in terms of concepts, one efficient way of organizing discrete events; (2) the recognition of the cognitive resources of the particular learner; (3) the articulation of schematized knowledge with a curriculum organization that reflects the cognitive resources of the learner. The author denies that the disadvantaged child needs to practice the processes of learning; rather, he needs experience in successful school-related problem-solving. He needs to develop adequate conceptual frameworks within which problem-solving can occur and within which knowledge can take on meaning. Within this strategy, the disadvantaged has the chance to attain valid educational objectives.

131

A COGNITIVE STRATEGY FOR CURRICULUM DEVELOPMENT
Harry Beilin*

Every curriculum theory or model is an interpretation of how the school should fulfill its purpose. Even a simple attempt to describe the activities represented by the term "curriculum" is bound to reflect decisions dictated by already available conceptual systems or models. At the same time, the curriculum is never simply what one is willing to make it. The conception of curriculum is determined in part by the reality of what occurs in the school and the community. Although providing an adequate definition of curriculum may be difficult, redefining the term would be more difficult. It takes conceptual revolutions of major and minor proportions to create new ways of looking at the world, and the world of the school is no exception. However, a revolution of sorts is presently under way, in which a formerly discredited way of conceptualizing about education is being revitalized and reconstructed. This view of curriculum is based upon an updated structuralism and results in part from a new look in general, developmental, and educational psychology.

The Cognitive Base

In recent times the term "curriculum" has lost much of its meaning in being extended to refer to the entire school program, encompassing all the activities taking place in the school. This defeat of a good word has come about through the fallacy of thinking that since almost everything that occurs in a school has an effect upon curriculum that, therefore, curriculum *is* everything that goes on in the school.

To make clear what is meant by "curriculum" requires as a starting point a characterization of reality and of how that reality comes to be known. The world is not quite the "blooming, buzzing confusion" to the infant that William James thought it to be, although in contrast to the world the adult knows, it certainly would seem so. Nor does this world, full of light, sound, odor, and pressure, inscribe itself on the *tabula rasa* that Locke ostensibly conceived the mind of the child to be. Even from birth, the child's nervous system is programed to respond to stimuli in

*The author is grateful to Dr. Francis Palmer, Director, Division of Child Learning and Development, Center for Urban Education, for making bibliographic reviewing services available during the preparation of this paper.

some highly sterotyped ways. This programing, which is the product of species-specific genetic coding, accounts for the fact that as human beings we are so much more alike than different.

Human behavior, of course, is the product of more than just fixed behavior patterns, and the world as experienced by the child does affect him in many ways. But consider how vast and complex that world is. The child's mother is not just one or two sources of stimulation, she is many. Her physical presence is a visual array of considerable detail and complexity. If her characteristics are to be distinguished from those of others, how shall this be achieved? Which details will act as distinguishing features so as to make her easily identifiable? How does the child come to the realization that she still exists even though not seen? These are not simple or easy achievements, and it takes months and years to acquire the ability to treat the world in such fashion as to discriminate its features, recognize complex activities, and realize that objects and even qualities remain invariant when perceptual conditions change. This world is far too complex to be dealt with in its entirety, either by the child or the adult. Unselected attention to multiple stimuli can lead to personal disaster when driving an automobile—and even a kiddy-car. What one attends to and how one attends to it is of particular importance, first, in coming to know the world, and then, in performing within it.

The world is not a closed system in either a phenomenal or a real sense, particularly to an infant. This open system with a constant stream of stimulation requires continual adaptation to novelty. The adult city-dweller may shut out or otherwise control this stimulation after a life of overstimulation, but the child has the challenge and excitement of establishing order and organization within it, eagerly seeking and responding to the novel without elaborate scheduling by adults.

Control Systems: Genetic Structures

From birth, then, the child progressively develops a system of perceiving and responding to reality that represents increased control of received stimulation as well as increased control of his response to it. Control is achieved through the development of a monitoring, transforming, and activating system that is identified by students of the problem in different ways. It is variously characterized "cognitive structure, strategies, plans, schemata, rules," or in other ways. Generally, these concepts are included in the term "cognition." An interesting feature of this development, as already indicated, is that stimulus and response control is present from birth. The child is born with a control system in some ways very sophisticated, in others very primitive; more elaborated physiologically, less so behaviorally. But even behaviorally the child responds with some identifiable regularity and consistency. Early control is mediated primarily through genetic control. The molecular organization of the nucleic acids of the gene represents a complex code by which the structural and behavioral properties of the organism are in part determined. Control through genetic determination remains with the organism throughout his life. Although the coding mechanism does not spell out the development of an intelligent adult, it enables such a development to occur.

The genetically determined organization of infant receptor and response systems influences the manner in which the world is experienced. This is illustrated in Fantz's studies of infant perception, in which it was shown that consistent discriminating responses were made within hours after birth (Fantz, 1961). The mechanisms that give the child control over the environment change, however. Not too much is known of how these mechanisms of control undergo change, although it is a very lively subject of interest at the moment. Some models of this change have been presented, of which Piaget's is probably the most notable (Flavell, 1963).

Control Systems: Event Structures—A Transactional View

In addition to genetic control, control is achieved through organismic changes that are exclusively the consequence of experience or external events acting upon the organism. The classes of such events are likely to be small, just as the examples of genetic determinants untouched by experience are likely to be small. There are few events whose effects are completely independent of the nature and state of the organism, the state of the organism at any time being a result of prior learning and prior maturation. The more usual case is one in which control is achieved through the interaction of external events acting upon what is already genetically programed and previously learned, with the organism actively taking part in the selection of the events that affect it. An organism just does not have experience. It selects in good measure what it perceives, even though this selection may not be mediated by conscious control. At the same time, hardly a behavioral system remains unaffected by external events.

Formal and Informal Agents of Change

For the young child, the home acts as the principal source of stimulation and serves as his principal educational institution. It is a setting in which learning takes place, although it is not necessarily a place in which there is instruction. Where instruction occurs, it is more likely to be in a middle-class home. Middle-class parents come closer to having the characteristics possessed by professional teachers than do lower-class parents. There is also a qualitative difference between the informal instructional program of the middle-class home and that of the lower-class home (Hess, 1964).

The learning that occurs in the home is largely informal. It is at the same time a kind of planned informality. As some of Basil Bernstein's recent research shows,[1] the middle-class parent's selection of toys, gifts,

---

[1] Personal communication.

135

and play objects are often made with an educational objective and an awareness that even informal activities such as play offer an opportunity for learning. The lower-class parent's choice of toys and gifts are not programed in the same fashion nor to the same degree. But whether instruction is formal or informal the child nevertheless acquires a repertoire of knowledge and skill that permits adaptation to his particular environment.

It is not necessarily to be assumed that either formal or informal means of instruction is superior to the other. At different ages, apparently, the effects are differential. Formal methods of instruction in the life of the infant or even the three-year-old may be much less effective than informal methods. Although very little is known of the consequences of such influence, there is evidence that experience itself is of crucial significance. This has given impetus to the idea that infants should be provided with sensorially interesting surroundings both in physical and human emotional terms. Other than putting colorful and musical mobiles within sight or hearing of the infant (and providing him with a warm loving mother), however, little is done at this age to foster perceptual learning in a manner that is thought possible with somewhat older children. Some kinds of cognitive learning are achieved better informally. This is the case with conservation abilities so strikingly described by Piaget. Conservation reflects the development of a physical concept by which the child recognizes a property invariant in spite of a variety of physical transformations. If two lengths of cord are placed side by side and it is established that a child recognizes these to be the same in length, then if the shape of one of the cords is altered, the nonconserving child will insist that the *lengths* are now changed. The conserving child on the other hand, thinks you are daft to be asking him so silly a question, to which the correct answer is so obvious. A number of investigators have been spending a great deal of time and effort recently trying through various experimental and formal instructional methods to train nonconserving children to become conservers. One fact which emerged out of my own attempts at this (Beilin, 1965) was that kindergarten children who achieved, through nonformal means, one kind of conservation, such as length conservation, were much more likely to conserve with area and number than children who learned to conserve through experimental training procedures. The latter children, if they are able to learn at all, could conserve only on what they had been taught and not on all types of conservation. It is possible to explain results such as these simply on the basis that "natural" conservers perform because maturational phenomena put them into a position to do so. True generalization could occur, then, only when some kind of maturational process permitted structural achievement. Although I believe that this is in part true, it is equally likely that there is something in natural experience that is not captured in some of the formal training procedures. It is equally possible that at early ages learning is achieved much more efficiently through informal active participation in the world than through methods that require concentrated attention and symbolic capacities. At generally appropriate times, these formal procedures, however, do become more efficient.

Formal Instruction: Progressive Control

When school days begin, whether these be in nursery school, kindergarten, or the first grade, a dramatic change in instruction occurs. The change is largely one of programing. Almost all school settings involve some kind of instructional control, and even the child-centered nursery is highly programed. It is programed in at least two ways. First, it is designed to be as much an analog to a home (a middle-class home, of course) as is possible. The playground space is organized with areas: the house area (with simulated kitchen, etc.), the free play area, the group activity area, etc. The school day is likewise programed so that it may start with free play, followed by story telling and a variety of other activities. Particular toys or utensils are chosen, either to be available for "free use" or used in more systematic and organized ways as in Montessori-like programs. As the child progresses in school he encounters even greater programing of this sort. It is usually thought that this control over material selection and ordered activity reaches a maximum in high school and diminishes in college as the student hopefully does his own programing to an increasing extent.

The role of the school in this is threefold. First, physical facilities and personnel management are organized to fulfill school objectives. These are usually identified as the functions of administration.

Second, the goals of the school are achieved through the programing of the knowledge taught and skills and attitudes learned. These functions are identified with curriculum.

Third is the organized manner by which conditions are created for the acquisition of knowledge, skills, and attitudes. These functions are identified with instruction.

Many a treatise has been written about educational objectives, but no matter how they have changed or been influenced by social, economic, and cultural conditions, the purpose still remains, as most teachers see it, to facilitate learning (Beilin, 1959). What is to be learned and how that learning is to be achieved is a matter of less agreement. But more precisely, the principal task of the teacher in the school is that of identifying the nature of the events the child is to experience whether these be facts, concepts, persons, or institutions, and determining the sequence by which these events are to be experienced in terms of some rational criteria of organization, and in consideration of the nature of the child who is to experience them. This is generally what we mean by curriculum, and in essence it represents the achievement of rational control by school per-

137

sonnel over the structure of knowledge, programed for presentation or experience in an order appropriate to the learner.

Curriculum in this sense is affected and determined by at least three categories of influence: the values and goals of the community, the state of educational technology, and the state of knowledge—both of the child as a learner and of the disciplines from which knowledge derives.

Curriculum Organization and Structure

The key proposition in this conception of curriculum is of organization. It is based upon a conception of reality as capable of organization, and of knowledge and experience as well as human thought and response as equally capable of organization. I refer to these as "capable of organization" rather than as *being* organized, in recognition of the hypothetical status of the term "organization." Organization is only a construct that aids in the interpretation of the data of experience. We would like to think that our conceptions are in accord with reality, but evidence on this score is sometimes tenuous. Nevertheless, even on a common-sense level, it is clear that even if the world were not itself as ordered as we think, it is nevertheless helpful and even necessary that it be approached in ordered ways. Survival, in rural or urban settings, is closely associated with order and organization in spite of the fact we would like to believe the contrary and take joy in the thought that our cities are not organized like beehives and ant hills. The person who learns to adapt to this world is required to approach it with due respect for its structure; even lower-class life requires it. School learning, not surprisingly, is therefore oriented to provide the sequences by which the child acquires the structured capacities to adapt to it. These capacities involve organization much more complex than that of cities. Providing the best ways to achieve this organization in the child is one of the objectives of both curriculum development and instructional technology.

Curricula for the Disadvantaged

The concern of those who work with the economically disadvantaged is to provide such children with the cognitive resources equal to those of other children in dealing with the rather complex realities of urban life. The data clearly show that disadvantaged children are not the equivalent of middle-class children in these resources by the time they enter the school (even at the nursery level) and that the disadvantages in some respects increase progressively. This condition has led to the development of a number of strategies for dealing with the problem, including the type of program associated with the term "compensatory education." This program is designed to do what it says—compensate for resources never developed through a kind of education ostensibly never received. What the lower-class child lacks is inferred from differences in capacities and functions from middle-class children. One finds the catalogue of such characteristics dominated by differences in language, conceptual thinking, and "learning sets" listed among the intellectual resources, and differences in impulsivity (lack of ego control) and value orientation listed among the personality and social characteristics. It is no wonder then that many of these compensatory programs have been oriented as much as they have to the construction or reconstruction of cognitive resources.

A Cognitively Oriented Curriculum Strategy

To say that the objective of a program of education is to develop such cognitive resources does not provide a curriculum with a strategy for doing it, and not a cognitive strategy at that. I will attempt to specify, even if only programatically, what some of the characteristics of a cognitive curriculum strategy might be, with illustrations taken mainly from elementary mathematics instruction.

The Schematization of Knowledge

It would be difficult to find a human endeavor that is not organized or integrated in some fashion, whether it be a physical activity such as a sport, an aural activity such as music, a response to one's experiences as in poetry, or a statement about causality, as in physics. If there is to be thought, communication, and efficient learning, the multitude of facts to be comprehended and manipulated requires some organization. The key to this organization is the concept. A concept is an efficient way of organizing discrete events. Each concept is a class with certain defined properties that differ from the defined properties of any other class. Instead of dealing with the few or many of members of the class, we are able to deal instead with a single abstract entity. The ways in which concepts are related vary. They are related in our natural language through the rules of syntax, and in special languages through sets of rules which function as a syntax. Mathematics, whose concepts are represented by different symbolic systems, has a syntax in the form of operations that relate the terms of these languages. The same general language model, in which there are concepts identified by symbolic terms and related through a syntax, is found in all intellectual disciplines as diverse as physics and music. This model is not without its difficulties, however, since it is not always possible to find adequate class terms that identify the common dimensions of some elements or events. This is true for aesthetic and emotional as well as intellectual categories. In addition, practically every event is capable of multiple classification, and it may be difficult if not impossible to know whether a particular conceptual identification is the best or most appropriate to a need. The virtues of conceptualization, on the other hand, are, first, that great amounts of information can be reduced to manageable proportions without too much loss of information. Second, although con-

139

cepts are developed through a thought process, once produced, they may facilitate thought. Certain kinds of problem-solving are possible only because of such conceptual achievements. This is especially the case with problems of the greatest generality, as seen in the theoretically advanced sciences as well as in the humanities. Third, on a more fundamental level, the ability to retain information is facilitated by concept formation represented in linguistic symbols or symbols in other forms. It is much easier in many instances (although not exclusively so) to solve a problem concerning a particular type of triangle if one can remember the appropriate operations in the form of a statement such as $a^2 + b^2 = c^2$ than if one were to reconstruct a pragmatic solution to the problem each time one encounters another form of the problem. The recollection of a circuit diagram is usually easier than remembering individual connections made in the circuit, just as a map will help one get around the subways of New York, Paris, or London more efficiently than from recollection of individual subway stops or even from a verbal description. It is not by accident that we have the slogan, "A picture is worth a thousand words." Yet the representation of the skill in riding a bicycle is more efficiently represented in muscles and nerves than it possibly can be by verbal or pictorial representation.

In general, then, the form of representation of reality provides the means for thinking, remembering, and communicating efficiently. Since representation is so intimately associated with these functions, the act of curriculum making is likewise bound to be associated with the examination, organization, and representation of events and ideas.

Discovery and Algorithmic Methods of Learning

A major controversy in curriculum and instruction has been concerned with whether the organization of knowledge should be made by the teacher or by the student. The structuralists in education propose that the material presented for learning should be presented with some relationship to the "natural" or logical structure of an area of knowledge. Such knowledge is seen either to have an inherent structure, or it is conceived that such organization can be imposed upon knowledge. An additional contention is that such organization, as already indicated, facilitates learning and further thought.

The alternative view is that if there is organization in reality it should be discovered and that education is essentially interested not in the end product (that is, things discovered), but in the act of discovery itself. The structuralist response to this is that the characterization of the end product, the things learned or discovered, are in fact many different "kinds" of things. As a rule, "discovery" advocates are concerned with the learning of facts (and particularly by rote methods). An obsessive collection of facts is desirable mostly for information clerks at railroad and airlines terminals and is certainly not an objective for all learners. At the same time, practically no adult thinking goes on without information. The more important objective is structured and organized knowledge because structures and organizations lend themselves to generalization. No child or adult has enough hours in his day to discover all the known concepts, generalizations, and rules. Even discovery of the most simple concept represents a formidable human achievement.

Additionally, what are called discovery methods by most educators are not discovery methods at all (Ausubel, 1964; Cronbach, 1965). They represent fairly well-organized and structured sequences of learning, in which the teacher programs the learning situation in such fashion that the order of presentation and the juxtaposition of facts leads to "discovery." As Cronbach puts it, "No teacher is truly teaching unless he is either arranging the conditions for discovery to occur or explaining." These methods are coming to be more adequately identified now as "guided" discovery. Discovery is, of course, a highly desirable end in itself, and it should be an objective of learning, but it has to be recognized that discovery in every type of intellectual and artistic endeavor takes place within a system that already has some organization.

A specific example in which the argument over discovery learning has raged is in relation to the learning of algorithms in mathematics. An algorithm is a rule for the procedure to solve a problem. In finding the area of a triangle, for example, there are various methods for finding the solution. Giving the formula $S = 1/2 \ a \ h$ does not provide, in itself, the way of solving the problem. One procedural rule is to take the base, multiply it by the altitude, and then multiply the product so obtained by 1/2. Another procedure is to multiply the base by 1/2 then multiply the result by the altitude. Each such procedural rule is an algorithm. The reason, in this case, that these alternative algorithms can be used is that the commutative principle for multiplication applies, as well as the associate and distributive principles. Although the question of whether one algorithm is better to use than another may not seem important, in this particular case there has been a great deal of controversy in elementary mathematics education over the algorithms used in addition. More significantly, however, the entire use of algorithms in mathematics education has been under attack for many years in ways parallel to the general attack on verbal learning and rule learning. The arguments against the algorithmic method may be summarized as follows (Landa, 1963):

(1) The use of algorithms rigidifies the way of solving a problem. The child is given the impression that there is only one kind of solution.

(2) Learning an algorithm masks understanding of the logical and mental activity that enters into solution.

(3) Many problems are not algorithmically solvable.

(4) As a description of a problem, a formula is a better description of the functional relations than an algorithm.

(5) Algorithms are used primarily for computational purposes.

141

(6) Algorithms are applicable only to the specific problem and yield less transfer than other methods.

The response to these criticisms reflects the general defense of rule learning, verbal learning, and nondiscovery methods.

(1) The learning of a rule of procedure in problem solutions is rigidifying only if a single rule is learned. No such requirement exists; in fact, such an approach would be highly undesirable.

(2) For every formula, a number of algorithms may exist that reflect different conceptual issues. Learning more than one procedural rule provides the means for learning about the conceptual nature of the problem. Algorithms can be used to expose the logic of a problem rather than mask it. An example will help to illustrate these two points.

Understanding of the multiplication of whole numbers can be illustrated in terms of addition so that 3×6 means $6 + 6 + 6$, although multiplication as repeated addition has its limitations, in that it cannot be extended in a general way to sets of numbers other than whole numbers (Lowry, 1965). It is possible to arrive at the same notion through the technique of finding the number of objects in a rectangular array, or from finding the number of pairings that can be made between the elements of two sets of objects.

It can also be shown to the child that writing the example 23×3 in the form $(20 + 3) + (20 + 3) + (20 + 3)$ allows one to proceed to $3 \times (20 + 3)$ and from this to $(3 \times 20) + (3 \times 3)$, reasoning from the addition above. This provides the learner with a pattern of applying the distributive principle of multiplication that can be arrived at intuitively, even if he is not able to verbalize the rule itself.

The associative principle for addition as it applies to the problem $(20 + 6) \times 3 = 60 + 18$ can be shown by the following steps: $60 + 18 = (60 + 10) + 8 = 70 + 8 = 78$.

Although in each of these examples there is an algorithm to provide a computation model, the algorithms can be utilized to reveal the arithmetic principles at work in the examples.

(3) It is true that there are many problems that are not algorithmically solvable. It is also true that it is not advisable to teach an algorithm for every problem. One must in fact discover those situations for which they are apt. By the same token there is no instructional method that is applicable to all learning.

(4) It is true that algorithmic methods have been replaced by formulas as methods of description of mathematical relations. But the abstract identification of a relation such as $S = 1/2\ a\ h$ does not provide its own means of solution, even though the means for solution are implicit in the formula. The important thing for education is that the relation between formulas and algorithms be learned, that is, that the child learn how to proceed from formula to algorithm and to see the various algorithms im-

plicit in the formula. In this sense, every algorithm represents a rule that "follows from a theoretical proposition and the latter can be inferred from the rule" (Landa, 1963).

(5) Although algorithms are used a great deal for computational purposes in mathematics, algorithms also provide models for the solution of problems beyond mathematics. The logic of an algorithm may be the kind of logical strategy that can apply to one or many sets of problems within mathematics itself but also to problems in physical, biological, and even psychological sciences. The computer, which operates through the development of such algorithms, has shown how the solution of problems in one area provides models for the solution of problems in others.

(6) A crucial question is by what means transfer occurs and whether it is facilitated more by discovery learning or by algorithmic methods. Years of research on this problem yield such a mixed picture of results that no simple judgment is possible. It is no doubt true that under certain circumstances and for certain problems transfer is greatest through the application of algorithms and under other circumstances, with other kinds of problems, it is discovery and other methods that are superior. At the same time one must recognize that there are different levels of abstraction and generalization among algorithms and that the higher the level of the inferred theoretical proposition represented by the algorithm, the more the algorithm permits of generalization to different operative systems (Landa, 1963).

In considering a curriculum for the disadvantaged, one must recognize that the same considerations apply to this curriculum as to curricula in general, although with some different emphasis. First, discovery methods of learning, even guided discovery methods, presuppose a fund of information and skills available to a child, most crucially, problem-solving skills. It is these skills that disadvantaged children lack. If there is to be problem-solving and discovery learning with disadvantaged children, as there should be, it has to be conducted within a plan that provides more information than is usually given, with a juxtaposition of elements that would make the development of concepts and inferences more likely.

With disadvantaged children, two contrary propositions have to be considered. First, discovery is most important at an early developmental level when a manipulative encounter with the world is necessary to gaining knowledge of it, as Piaget has shown. Second, beyond this early developmental level discovery methods are relatively unnecessary for the teaching of subject contents. At levels where abstract learning is possible, didactic teaching methods can proceed directly to abstract understanding (Ausubel, 1964). The difficulty for many of the disadvantaged is that they are chronologically at an age when they should be able to think abstractly, but are developmentally at an age where a manipulative encounter is often necessary to achieve understanding. A way out of this dilemma will be suggested later.

Generally, the emphasis in curriculum development for the disadvantaged learner should be on the organization of material or experience, since the learning sequence must more closely approximate the capacities of the child than is true for the child with greater cognitive resources.

Cognitive Structure in the Child

A cognitive curriculum strategy, in addition to concerning itself with the schematization of knowledge, is based upon recognition of the cognitive resources of the learner. It starts with the proposition that the infant's reception of stimuli takes place in an organized fashion, although there is much random searching and random response. Starting with a small repertoire of organized responses, the interaction of genetically given systems with the consequences of experience results in the development of a cognitive system that progresses in complexity and integration with the growth and experience of the individual. Piaget's work has been most illuminating in describing this development as well as in providing an explanation of it (Flavell, 1964). He traces a developmental pattern that focuses on the way new experience is adapted to existing structures (schemata), and existing schemata are integrated and brought to bear upon the solution of new problems. With change in age, there is a change in the general types of structure that are developed—from those that are sensorimotor, wherein the actions of the child are seen to obey a set of logical rules, to those that represent what Piaget calls concrete operations, that is, intellectual operations involving certain logical processes that are carried out through the manipulation of concrete materials, to the development of formal logical processes of a hypothetical-deductive type that can be utilized independently of external reality. Bruner (1964) has interpreted the same development by emphasizing the different techniques of information-processing developed in the child. The Geneva group, while also concerned with information selection, storage, and retrieval, consider the transformation of information and its integration to be of greater significance (Inhelder *et al.*, 1966).

Transitions. Out of these conceptions of cognitive development come relevant principles for curriculum development. First is the recognition that cognitive development involves the transition from one stage, or state, of thought to another qualitatively different stage. The mode of intellectual activity characteristic of a four-year-old, for example, is different in kind from that of a eight-year-old and from that of a fourteen-year-old. Piaget proposes a theory to account for the transition from one stage to the next, but it is too early to say how much confirming evidence there is for this theory. The theory, very Deweyite in flavor, conceives of schemata or operations as arising out of the conflict which results from the discrepancy between the child's anticipations of reality and the reality. In Piaget's view, cognitive development takes place principally through "natural" conflict. Piaget is somewhat skeptical of experimental

144

and educational efforts to facilitate early acquisition of cognitive operations. His position is based upon the evolutionist view that periods of development, whether gestation periods or periods of cognitive development, are species-specific characteristics, and the attempt to foster earlier acquisition for processes under some genetic control are likely to fail. At the same time, he recognizes considerable variability in the development of cognitive operations and structures both within cultures and across cultures. There is evidence, for example, that conservation is achieved later in lower-class children than in middle-class children (Almy, 1966; Beilin, 1964A), and also later in some societies than others (Piaget, 1964). Why and how social influences affect certain logical thought processes is still an open question.

Cognitive conflict. The Piaget conflict theory has been subjected to some experimental testing, particularly in regard to the acquisition of the operations of conservation (e.g., Smedslund, 1961; Wallach and Sprott, 1964; Beilin, 1965), but it is not clear whether the introduction of conflict necessarily creates the schemata needed to the solution of conservation tasks. However, when schemata are already available to the child, the introduction of conflict does lead to solution (Beilin, 1966B).

The question remains as to what is a necessary condition for cognitive change if conflict is not. A number of solutions are offered, not the least of which is that language independently or in concert with conflict may induce change. In one study, the acquisition of conservation was most effectively achieved by conservation solution failure followed by verbally formulated rule instruction related to the cause of failure. In this circumstance, the achievement of conservation was more effective than conflict alone and superior to the equivalent of an experimental discovery approach (Beilin, 1965). Language approaches have likewise been effective in other circumstances as well (Bruner, 1964; Ervin, 1960). At the same time verbal rule instruction has not been as effective as perceptual confirmation training when the task involved the visual representation of horizontality and verticality, in the form of water level representation (Beilin, Kagan, and Rabinowitz, 1966A).

The role of language in cognitive development and performance is highly debated. It is interesting to see that in this controversy Piaget stands with the discovery group, even though they part on other issues. The position they take is that cognitive changes occur through nonverbal activity and that language merely provides for the representation of these achievements. Those who place greater reliance on the role of verbal learning in cognitive change are of at least two views. They hold either that verbal learning can be effective at all ages after the child has acquired language skill, or, as Ausubel does (1964), recognize that manipulative learning may be more significant early in development and that intellectual achievements can take place more efficiently through language once the child is capable of abstract thought. Piaget would probably not

145

argue with the latter point, since he does recognize that some advanced intellectual efforts are possible only with language. The point at issue, then, is over the role of language in early concept development, and, as is evident, the issue is still under much discussion.

Curriculum transitions. The recognition of the importance of stages in development and learning is not new. It has long been a tenet of educational practice that if learning is to take place efficiently in young children, ideas must be achieved through the manipulation of concrete materials, whereas at older ages ideas can be developed conceptually and abstractly. What is new, as a consequence of the Piaget influence, is the recognition that the crucial problem in development is the transition from one stage or state to the next. The implication for curriculum of this conception is that a major concern in curriculum development should be the question of how to program the transition.

When one is concerned with educational practice, particularly with the problems of learning among the disadvantaged, the matter of transition takes on particular importance. The ordering of learning experiences and the determination of the nature of the experiences themselves should have some relation to the phenomena that lead to the acquisition of relevant problem solving and reasoning skills. Very little has as yet been done, even in the context of cognitively oriented curricula, toward this end. Most curricula for the disadvantaged may in fact be placing emphasis upon the wrong kinds of learning. Almost all preschool educational programs for the disadvantaged place primary emphasis upon language learning, since the most evident deficits are language deficits. But from the Piaget view, the most critical deficits are not language deficits but conceptual deficits, and there is evidence from Piaget's co-workers (Inhelder *et al.*, 1966), as well as others, that simply introducing language whether natural or special into the child's learning will not in itself ensure successful problem-solving. The acquisition of language is dependent upon the existence of a conceptual base that makes language "meaningful." Language itself is not necessarily meaningful to a child. Prior conceptual acquisitions, sometimes achieved through activity with objects and persons or through pictorial and schematic representation, may have to precede linguistically mediated problem-solving.

Curriculum translations. This suggests the second curriculum generalization to come out of this work, namely, that the curriculum requires planning and preparation for the appropriate translation of concept attainment from one type of information-processing to another. In essence, this involves the translation of concepts arrived at through manipulative and figural or schematic representation to linguistic or other symbolic modes of concept representation. If a disadvantaged child or any poor learner has difficulty with linguistic conceptualization, then problem representation and problem solution may have to be introduced in other than language and symbolic terms. In theoretical mathematics, where difficult problem solution may not come easily when functions are expressed in the typical algebraic symbolic form, a solution may often be achieved by carrying out the appropriate operations using a schematic or geometric model instead of the more usual algebraic model. This may not be the method of choice for àll mathematicians, but enough mathematicians utilize such techniques to suggest that forcing problem-solving and thinking solely into a linguistic mode may straightjacket thinking for adults and may inhibit it in the young and disadvantaged.

Some recent approaches to mathematics instruction are attempting to provide systematic means of making the transition from problem-solving in the mode of manipulative and figural representation to reasoning in the typical symbolic and linguistic notational systems of mathematics. Some important features of the present reform in elementary mathematics make it easier to establish such conceptual translations. One such source is the extensive introduction of geometry into the elementary and pre-elementary curriculum (Robinson, 1966). The emphasis is on nonmetric geometry, which deals in part with the defining characteristics of various classes of geometric and topological figures such as rectangles, squares, and closed spaces, but even more significantly reflects an interest in mathematical operations and relations. The opportunity is provided for the use of "many and varied manipulative and pictorial materials" and it is also suggested that these "should precede the use of symbolic notation" (Mastain and Nossoff, 1966). The emphasis in some of these programs is simply on concept attainment and rule learning as such, through the use of manipulative and pictorial materials. There is a lack of recognition that these materials and their use may provide translational links between thinking manipulatively and thinking linguistically. Some mathematicians who are concerned with elementary instruction, however, do define this type of translation as their goal (Dienes, 1963, 1964).

Dienes (1963), for example, who has collaborated with Bruner and has been affected by the work of Piaget, places great emphasis upon the use of play as a vehicle for making these translations. He delineates three types of play: manipulative, representational and rule-bound (somewhat analogous to the motoric, iconic and symbolic modes of representation suggested by Bruner, 1964). He proposes that the goal in mathematics instruction should be to program the transition from one type of play and its means of creating conceptual understanding to the next, leading ultimately to the ability to use mathematical symbolism in mathematical problem-solving. The relations among these conceptual modes is made clear in the statement:

It is possible to use symbolism sometimes for developing an idea further, provided that the corresponding mathematical imagery is developed. The mental manipulation of imagery re-

147

places the physical manipulation of an actual concrete situation. Conversely, if the imagery is not well developed, it may be necessary to develop it by concrete experiences isomorphic to the structures being learned before the symbolism can be used as an adequate language by whose means further learning can take place. (Dienes, 1963, p. 137.)

He provides an example of these "isomorphisms" (or translations, in our terms) through the demonstrated equivalences of the quadratic expression $X^2 + 2X + 1$ with the geometric arrays representing $X(X+2) + 1$ and $(X+1) X + X + 1$. He also demonstrates quadratic equivalences with operations on a balance. His Multibased Arithmetic Blocks, the balance, and a variety of other materials to facilitate the translations and transitions from one mode of conceptual achievement to another.[3]

An interesting aspect of these developments in elementary mathematics instruction is that not only can equivalences be shown between representations, but equivalences can be demonstrated between one type of mathematics and another. In measurement, a geometric model can be useful to an understanding of the number system, as is shown in the relations between continuous and discrete (discontinuous) quantities. The measurement of discrete quantity requires counting or knowledge of one-to-one correspondence, and physical models are often used with children to demonstrate their character. If one wishes to study continuous quantities, the obvious model to use is a geometric one, utilizing lines, curves, and points. But it is also possible to use the geometric model for discrete quantities and sets, and for some relations a geometric model is even more desirable. Using geometric models makes it possible to demonstrate in elementary terms that we measure the lengths of curves, measure subsets of the plane interior to closed curves, measure solids and measure subsets of space interior to solids, and show that the terms "perimeter," "area," "surface area," and "volume" are names applied to the measurement of such connected sets (Robinson, 1966).

The properties of natural numbers are likewise demonstrable in geometric terms. Geometrically, a natural number greater than one can be arranged in rectangular form, unless it is prime (not divisible by any other whole number but itself and 1). The number 12 can be arrayed as 6 twos, for example, or 3 fours.

A variety of other number characteristics can be demonstrated through such arrays such as the commutative principle of multiplication which is shown by placing objects into rectangular arrays in two ways (as above).

The properties of order in the natural numbers can also be represented geometrically. The number line is useful for this purpose, as well as to

---

[3]Dienes, Z., **An experimental study of mathematics learning** (1963) is particularly recommended to those interested in the description of an excellent series of techniques which can be used in pre-elementary and elementary mathematics instruction for all children.

demonstrate arithmetic operations such as $2 + 3 = 5$ as connected sets as
follows.

The number line has the virtue also of making it possible to interpret
$(+2) + (−3)$, which is difficult to do in terms of the union of two discrete
sets, the instructional method in many "new" mathematics programs.

These developments, which introduce geometric models to preschoolers, parallel the evidence provided by Piaget (1941, 1948) of the
child's capacity to acquire conceptions of space and number at early ages.
These developments also offer the theoretical (both mathematical and
psychological) basis for ensuring the availability of models of translation,
particularly for disadvantaged learners.

Structural Articulation

A cognitively oriented curriculum strategy requires that the schematization of knowledge be adequately articulated with a curriculum organization that reflects the cognitive resources of the learner. There have been
a number of demonstrations of the facilitating effects of material organization upon learning. There is also a body of literature on the need for the
learner to be in a particular state to receive information. Research that
involves the manipulation of both variables has been minimal, although
the relationship has been recognized (Hunt, 1961). Ausubel, for example,
has shown that providing the learner with "advanced organizers" such as
labels, frames of reference, or rules for processing information lead to
more effective learning than takes place when these are not provided
(Ausubel, 1960). It is implicitly assumed that only a subject who can
process the organizers will be able to profit from their provision. There is
a consistent body of research evidence reflected in the "mediational deficiency hypothesis" (Reese, 1962), which shows, however, that providing
the children, particularly the young, with verbal labels or rules will not
of necessity lead to improved learning or to use of verbal material.

Cognitive Efficiency. Another feature of the relationship between
information and the learner is reflected in the phenomenon of "cognitive
efficiency." A child who is given a difficult task to perform invokes a more
powerful cognitive strategy than when he is faced with a simpler task.
The demand of the task brings forth the appropriate technique for solution
so long as the child has both strategies available to him. There is less
tendency to use powerful cognitive resources with situations that don't
demand them. At the same time there is evidence that under some circumstances, because of the operation of sets, some strategies will be inappro-
priately applied to new situations, and inappropriate sets will prevent the
introduction of appropriate strategies. This may occur even though the
subject may have the means for solving a problem. The interaction be-

149

tween the stimulus and the child's cognitive resources is sometimes quite subtle. We have found that although Piaget is fundamentally correct in conceiving the child as cognitively active rather than passive, his activity is not independent of the stimulus. For example, a stimulus in motion gives a kind of information different from a static stimulus. Under static conditions, there are greater demands placed upon the organism to act to provide itself with information. This is demonstrated in the phenomenon of quasiconservation. A child who is required to recognize that two areas are the same even though their patterns differ, will find this a more difficult task when the patterns are static than when a transformation is made from one pattern arrangement to another before the eyes of the child. In the Piaget conservation experiments, contrary to common belief, the transformation of stimuli does not in itself create difficulty for the child (except the nonconserving child). In fact, it provides the basis for the conserving child's ability to make the correct response by providing the information that leads him to question his incorrect inferences (Beilin, 1966B). What these facts suggest is that the nature of the stimulus — its complexity, activity and dimensionality, generally its organization — is to be considered in relation to the cognitive resources of the learner. For the disadvantaged learner, the so called "match" between the stimulus domain and the child's cognitive domain demands some approximation. As is clear, however, this does not mean that all knowledge must be keyed to the interests and absolute level of understanding of the child. It suggests rather, that the level that needs to be approximated is the general level of cognitive structure available for the use, not the understanding, of particular ideas. Secondly, greater cognitive demands than the learner's actual understanding suggests may be made, so long as the capacity for such functioning is present.

Dynamic Structure. The child's cognitive structures undergo constant change and development. From Piaget's view, the change, in its major dimensions, is ordered and sequential. In like fashion, the choice of materials for learning may be organized differently depending upon the cognitive state of the organism. The kind of material or ideational organization that is inappropriate at one time or stage of development may be appropriate at another stage. The conception of the spiral curriculum is based upon an organization of subject matter in these terms, although beyond general organization the techniques of instruction may involve discovery, guided discovery, or algorithmic methods. It is sometimes thought that knowledge has to be communicated in a pure, correct, and elegant form to be considered honest instruction. Often, however, before a child can conceptualize a problem in these terms, intuitive and less rational types of presentation of a problem may be more appropriate. This is so even in mathematics instruction, usually considered the purest and most rational of disciplines. It is closer to the truth to recognize that much instruction and deviation from formalization exist in problem-solving, and

150

it does no violence to a cognitive position to accept the fact that less perfect cognitive procedures can lead to more adequate ones. This is illustrated in the algorithms of multiplication, where it might be efficacious to start such instruction with algorithms that are laborious and inefficient, leading to more elegant and efficient procedures (Lowry, 1965).

Modes of Information Transmission. As already discussed, the manner in which knowledge is communicated to the learner is important to curriculum development. When information is transmitted from a sending to a receiving unit, some efficient means must exist for the transmission to occur. As a rule, the nature of perceived reality and the information contained within it cannot be processed in its original form. This is true, for example, of stimulus information carried to the individual in the form of light, or sound, or pressure. Transmitting information so received by the central nervous system requires that the information be reprocessed into a form more manageable and appropriate to the receiving unit. For sensory experience, this is achieved through imposed variation in the state of electrical activity in the nervous system at the point of input at the sensory receptors (or analyzers). A second condition that holds in information transmission is that too much information is usually presented to the organism at any one time to be processed efficiently. Providing an efficient means of reducing information is usually achieved through a code or coding system. All information in living things is subject to some such coding. The one that has received the most attention of late is the genetic code. An enormous amount of the information is coded into the relatively simple molecular structure of the nucleic acids which in effect program the structures of the organism to be produced and provide the "rules" for their production. These internal biological codes are paralleled by external communication codes in which individuals within a species relay complex information to one another by very simple means. The dancing pattern of the bee represents such a code in which information of the location of food is transmitted to other bees. The expressive movements of primates reflect another such code, and the spoken and written languages of humans represent still another. These languages are efficient coding devices for transmitting information to others and to oneself. A great deal of information from various stimulus sources can be translated into messages in these codes. Learning the natural language code and the rules for producing statements in the code can be achieved by children between the ages of three and four, although the ability to produce or even decode messages of some conceptual difficulty is achievable only at later ages. As B. Bernstein has suggested (Bernstein, 1960, 1962), the various social classes learn different variations of the natural language code. One variant of the code is used extensively in school contexts, and those who are reared in the middle class learn this code as part of their socialization. Lower-class children learn a code too that serves reasonably well for their environment, and in this sense it is cognitively efficient, but it is not particularly adaptive to school requirements or to special work environments. Special language codes such as those used in mathematics are difficult to learn, even for many middle-class children, and they are less likely to be learned easily by lower-class children. At the same time it is not really known whether lower-class children might move directly into learning mathematical languages without first learning the elaborated natural language code common to the middle class. If it were possible, it could greatly facilitate mathematics learning.

In all learning, including the learning of mathematics, acquiring knowledge of a code does not of necessity ensure thinking in the code. The communication function of language, whether it be the natural (verbal) language or a schematic code is not the same as the thought function associated with language. Language in this sense is the vehicle of thought; it is not thought itself. Concepts and rules may be expressed in these languages, and a code may have a particular structure, but the structure is the outcome of some thought process, although there is a school that holds to the reverse (Whorf, 1956). Consequently, although we should rightly pay considerable attention to the learning of languages, natural and special, the fundamental concern should be with the processes involved in discrimination learning, concept development, and problem-solving to provide the conceptual basis for the acquisition of language. Once some facility for handling language in conceptual contexts is acquired, then the development of rules, codes or other types of structures will provide the means through which further information can be stored, recalled, and processed.

The Set to Learn. Increasing activity and increasing organization lead to even greater learning achievement. This is a case of the cognitively rich getting richer, and the cognitively poor getting poorer. The more one actively learns, the more he acquires of the techniques for learning as well as the organization to which the products of learning refer. Research in learning sets supports this view although it is evidence for more than just practice. In the research of Harlow (1958), there is evidence that when an organism solves a particular kind of problem over a period of time his performance keeps improving, not because he has acquired more knowledge of the problem but because he has learned more about how to solve the problem. This phenomenon has also been referred to as "learning to learn." The full ramifications of this phenomenon are not known, but they suggest that acquisitions under these conditions are not simply a matter of the learner developing motor skills (although this may sometimes be the case), or acquiring the ability to attend (although this is also an important feature), or that he learns what to avoid (although again, this may be true), but it involves fundamentally the opportunity to develop an organized view of the problem and a systematic way of approaching learning. It is often suggested that learning is more effectively achieved when unfamiliar material is related to the familiar. The reason for this is probably that the familiar receives its familiarity from the organized body of knowledge of which it is a part. Relating the unfamiliar to an organized body of knowledge is the key to this kind of instructional strategy.

Disadvantaged learners are characterized both by the lack of the learning sets necessary for achievement—having had too little experience in successful school related problem-solving, and by the lack of adequate conceptual frameworks in which problem-solving can occur and from which knowledge can take on meaning. Disadvantaged children do not lack the processes of learning as such. They are able on the whole to *learn* as well as other children (Beilin, Kagan, and Rabinowitz, 1966A), but when the deficits they start with are very considerable, then it is difficult to compensate for what has been lost.

Coda. A cognitively oriented curriculum strategy, then, involves (1) the schematization of knowledge, (2) a selection and organization of curriculum contents consistent with the cognitive resources of the learner, and (3) the programing of experience in relation to the learner's ability to profit from the experience, as well as the preparation of the learner's conceptual resources to foster maximal utilization of experience.

Although the examples given of how such a strategy might be developed have been derived principally from elementary mathematics, this strategy may be applied to all aspects of the curriculum in the areas of the humanities, social science, science, the arts, and even those areas of school experience associated with personality and character development.

References

Almy, M. *Young Children's Thinking.* New York: Teachers College Press, Columbia University, 1966.

Ausubel, D. P. "The Use of Advance Organizers in the Learning and Retention of Meaningful Verbal Material. *J. of Educational Psychology,* 51 (1960), 267–272.

———. Some Psychological and Educational Limitations of Learning by Discovery. *Arithmetic Teacher,* 11 (1964), 290–302.

Beilin, H. "Teachers' and Clinicians' Attitudes toward the Behavior Problems of Children: A Reappraisal," *Child Development,* 30 (1959), 9–25.

———. "Perceptual Cognitive Conflict in the Development of an Invariant Area Concept," *J. of Experimental Child Psychology,* 1 (1964), 208–226.

———. "Learning and Operational Convergence in Logical Thought Development," *J. Experimental Child Development,* 2 (1965A), 317–339.

——— and L. Gotkin. "Psychological Issues in the Development of

153

Mathematics Curricula for Disadvantaged Children." Presented at Conference on Mathematics for Underachievers, School Mathematics Study Group, 1964B.

————; J. Kagan and R. Rabinowitz. "Effects of Verbal and Perceptual Training on Water Level Representation," *Child Development*, 37 (1966A), 317–329.

Beilin, H. "Feedback and Infralogical Strategies in Invariant Area Conceptualization," *J. Experimental Child Psychology*, 3 (1966B), 267–278.

Bernstein, B. "Language and Social Class," *Brit. J. Sociology*, 11 (1960), 271–276.

————. "Social Class, Linguistic Codes, and Grammatical Elements," *Lang. and Speech*, 5 (1962).

Bruner, J. S. "Some Theorems of Instruction Illustrated with Reference to Mathematics," in *Theories of Learning and Instruction*, ed. E. R. Hilgard. Yearbook, N.S.S.E., Part 1. Chicago: University of Chicago Press, 1964.

————. "The Course of Cognitive Growth," *American Psychologist*, 19 (1964), 1–16.

Cronbach, L. J. "Issues Current in Educational Psychology," in *Mathematical Learning*, eds. L. N. Morrisett and J. Vinsonhaler. *Monogr. Soc. for Research in Child Development*, 30 (1965), 109–125.

Dienes, Z. P. *The Power of Mathematics*. London: Hutchinson Educational, 1964.

————. *An Experimental Study of Mathematics Learning*. London: Hutchinson and Co., Ltd., 1963.

Ervin, S. M. "Transfer Effects of Learning a Verbal Generalization," *Child Development*, 31 (1960), 537–554.

Fantz, R. L. "The Origin of Form Perception," *Scientific American*, 204 (1961), 66–72.

Flavell, J. *The Developmental Psychology of Jean Piaget*. New York: Van Nostrand, Inc., 1963.

Harlow, H. F. "The Evolution of Learning," in *Behavior and Evolution*, eds. A. Roe and G. G. Simpson. New Haven: Yale University Press, 1958.

Hess, R. D. "*Educability and Rehabilitation: The Future of the Welfare Class.*" Report of the Committee on Human Development, Chicago: University of Chicago, 1964. Mimeographed. ·

Hunt, J. McV. *Intelligence and Experience*. New York: Ronald Press, 1961.

Inhelder, B., et al. "Comment: On Cognitive Development." *American Psychologist*, 21 (1966), 160–164.

Landa, L. N. "The Algorithmic Approach to the Analysis of Teaching Methods Is Valid." *Voprosy Psikhologii*, 4 (1963), 143–152. Translated in *Office of Tech. Services Bulletin No. 63*: 41254 (JPRS: 22,075).

Lowry, W. C. "Structure and the Algorisms of Arithmetic." *The Arithmetic Teacher*, 12 (1965), 146–150.

Mastain, R. K. and B. C. Nossoff. "Mathematics in the Kindergarten," *The Arithmetic Teacher*, 13 (1966), 32–36.

Reese, H. W. "Verbal Mediation as a Function of Age Level," *Psychological Bulletin*, 59 (1962), 502–509.

Robinson, G. E. "The Role of Geometry in Elementary School Mathematics," *The Arithmetic Teacher*, 13 (1966), 3–10.

Smedslund, J. "The Acquisition of Conservation of Substance and Weight in Children: V. Practice in Conflict Situations without External Reinforcement," *Scand. J. Psychol.*, 2 (1961), 156–160.

Wallach, L. and R. L. Sprott. "Inducing Number Conservation in Children," *Child Development*, 35 (1964), 1057–1071.

Whorf, B. L. *Language, Thought and Reality* (J. B. Carroll, ed.). Cambridge, Mass.: M. I. T. Press, 1956.

Deborah Elkins recommends fundamental changes in teaching and learning strategies for the disadvantaged child, particularly in junior high school. Noting how social changes and their psychological consequences have affected the school, Dr. Elkins sees little hope of learning improvement until teachers deepen their understanding of the learning process, the meaning of intelligence, and the assault of environmental deprivation upon both learning and intelligence. Changes in the role of the school, she warns, must begin at the foundations: "No crash programs, no remedial measures will do the all-encompassing task that is essential."

Dr. Elkins views the teacher as mediator. If children are to exploit adults as sources of information, teachers must help children learn how to ask questions and to feel free in doing so. Knowing the importance of verbalization and ways of encouraging it are intrinsic to this mediating role. Analyzing the teacher's role in motivation, Dr. Elkins advises the teacher to organize the classroom and its activities in a way that allows motivational energy to spring from a feeling of belonging. By setting the stage for satisfying this need for belonging, the teacher is able to respond to the constant pressure for attention and affection.

TEACHING AND LEARNING STRATEGIES FOR DISADVANTAGED YOUTH

Deborah Elkins

Another approach to instructional strategies comes through diagnostic procedures and learning sequences, obtainable from many sources cited in the article. Learning sequences must not be superficial; children need to study topics in depth, although their attention span may be relatively short. Dr. Elkins describes in detail a unit in which youngsters began to experience control over elements in the learning situation, as they proceeded, step by step, through a particular learning sequence. Content was centered around common concepts, a technique which "allowed individualization of instruction . . . without destroying the feeling of unity in the class." The concepts *were common for all, but the details that are learned by each student were, of course, quite different.*

Dr. Elkins supports a design involving a variety of concrete objects and events from which the children learn to work toward the abstract. The emphasis is on cognitive processes. Unless schools build ability to analyze, hypothesize, discover, generalize, seek cause and effect, and distinguish similarities and differences, learning of all kinds will be hampered, for these processes strengthen motivation and provide a meaningful framework for other kinds of learning.

TEACHING AND LEARNING STRATEGIES FOR DISADVANTAGED YOUTH

Deborah Elkins

There are a number of highly complex factors that have contributed to the concerns involved in educating the disadvantaged youth of today's urban centers. These factors stem from sociological, psychological, and educational conditions that are all-encompassing. They stem, too, from widespread misunderstandings of those conditions. Because the strategies of teaching and learning must take carefully into account the existing situation, it is necessary to highlight a few of the basic elements bearing upon the education of disadvantaged children and youth.

Social Changes Affecting the School

The feverish pace of industrialization and urbanization has created a need and a drive for a more educated citizenry. The consequent growth in the school's population has increased its heterogeneity. Until recently, the academically apt pupils constituted the school population, for the most part. Thus, when school enrollment increased, any additions were, of necessity, new elements from the population at large. Since the higher socioeconomic groups were already in school, any additions had to be drawn from the less academically inclined and from the lowest social and economic ranks. This is the situation the schools are experiencing today: heterogeneity increased in a new dimension, one which the school has not yet been ready or willing to handle (Taba, 1964).

The new complex includes, too, children who are plunged into the big city from rural areas in the South, the Southwest, or Puerto Rico. They are bewildered and alienated in an urban society they cannot understand. In addition to this aspect of alienation, there is inflicted upon them another aspect, stemming from forced existence in closed and hemmed-in ghettos. Not only does their existence in encapsulated communities make it impossible for them to learn the values of the culture at large, but the school culture itself, through its unfamiliar content, pace, methods, and expectations, breeds failure. It thus intensifies the alienation they feel.

159

To strain the degree of alienation, there appears the problem of the young adult for whom there is no place in the world of work. Thousands of jobs have been eliminated from the industrial scene. One has merely to look at the statistics of unemployment to note that the jobs requiring low levels of skills are the first to disappear in all industries. Forty years ago the world of work was a satisfactory path for growth toward adulthood. Now, however, that path is disappearing at an alarming rate. Thus, when school fails to provide a safe and satisfying channel for growth to adulthood, youth is trapped: there is no place to go, no chance to *become* (Havighurst, 1961).

The hopelessness is aggravated by the fact that the "replacement cycle" now does not play a role in the integration of newcomers or new urban dwellers.

In a still-expanding economy, each newly arriving immigrant group served its apprenticeship and time of poverty, ignorance, rejection, and suffering. This period, however, was temporary. Sooner or later, with the arrival of still another wave of new immigrants, they could be absorbed into the mainstream of American society. (Hickerson, 1966, p. 64)

But the Negro, the Puerto Rican, and the Mexican-American have come to the city to find work at a time when there is no prospect of a new group to start the "replacement cycle" in motion again.

Psychological Implications

As one might expect, the result can only be a syndrome of psychological consequences stemming from the sociological factors. Alienation breeds hostility, hopelessness, low ego strength, and unsatisfied needs for identification as well as for belonging.

There is little being done to actually stem the tide. As the culturally disadvantaged continue to swell the ranks of the urban population, the proportion of students who fail to learn through the curriculum and methods currently in use in urban schools steadily increases. When the school, however unwittingly, contributes to the dismal picture of failure, of devastated self-concept, of alienation, it simultaneously adds its share to rising delinquency and to other manifestations of hostility and frustration.

This situation will continue until teachers are helped to understand the learning process, the meaning of intelligence, and the effect of environmental deprivation upon both. The literature increasingly elaborates upon the concept of intelligence as the capacity for coping with the environment or for problem-solving, a capacity that is based on past experiences (Hunt, 1961, p. 109). In discussing the development of intelligence, Hunt (1961, p. 168) cites Piaget's explanation of the necessity for a *variety* of situations requiring "accommodation" by the child. The greater the variety, the more rapid will be his intellectual development. Although the influence of heredity is by no means renounced, that of environment has taken on new significance—a result of recent and continuing research in the area of thinking and cognition. The environment must provide a variety of objects to be encountered because "the more new things a child has seen and the more he has heard, the more things he is interested in seeing and in hearing. Moreover, the more variation in reality with which he has coped, the greater is his capacity for coping" (Hunt, 1961, p. 259). Lack of appropriate and varied objects and events in early environment affects later capacity.

Here we have a crucial clue to a number of factors connected with the learning process and the manifestations of intelligence. If a child is interested in seeing and hearing, he is motivated to learn. If he is interested, he is attentive, which means curiosity becomes more highly developed. If he is made curious about a wide variety of situations, initiative unfolds; with initiative he is energized to learn.

"Clear and stable" concepts and abstractions are critical aspects of this whole process of learning and intelligence because they serve as anchors and organizers for new material. Without these, the learner is "trapped in a morass of confusion" (Ausubel, 1963, p. 80). Interestingly enough, the key to the development of abstractions often lies in the learning skills involved in observing and manipulating concrete objects. Friedlander (1965, p. 22) directs attention to the fact that the value of the Cuisenaire rods lies in the provision they make for "performance of repetitive manipulative operations in the acquisition of abstractions." He points out further that such devices are educationally useful because they require children to observe the consequences of their actions as they manipulate the objects. Bernstein notes that many interpretations and many meanings need to be given to any one object, thus increasing the area and intensity of the child's curiosity and receptiveness:

> This leads to an awareness of the formal ordering of his environment, notions of its extensions in time and space and so is the beginning of the formation of primitive interpretive concepts. (Bernstein, 1958, p. 165)

Another condition for learning and development of intelligence is the adult mediator. He is the one who gives order to the stimulants in the environment; it is he who helps the child to interpret that environment. The interpretation and order are achieved by talking over and reminding the child of a shared experience, thus helping him to "remember," to develop memory.

In the light of the concern with ordered experience, variety of objects, and adult mediation as major factors in the development of intelligence, the picture of the deprived home as a catalyst for learning is a bleak one.

161

Bare walls, uninteresting objects—even the pots, pans, and furniture as well as toys—are in sharp contrast to the rich environment that provides the stimulation needed in order for the learning process to flourish.

The sparsity of objects and lack of diversity of home artifacts which are available and meaningful to the child, in addition to the unavailability of individualized training, gives the child few opportunities to manipulate and organize the visual properties of his environment . . . . (Deutsch, 1963, p. 170)

The limitations in environment include lack of verbal expression, so necessary for energizing intellectual growth. The deprived home is not a verbally oriented one; adults do not serve adequately as mediators in explaining objects and events. They do not help children to express feelings verbally; rather, feelings tend to be communicated through nonverbal means (Bernstein, 1958, p. 168). Nor do adults talk over whatever shared experiences they may have with the child; thus he is deprived of basic training in "remembering."

Related to attentivity is memory. Here also we would postulate the dependence of the child . . . on interaction with the parent. . . . The combination of the constriction in the use of language and in shared activity results . . . in much less stimulation of the early memory function. (Deutsch, 1963, p. 171)

Nonverbal orientation does not mean quiet surroundings. There tends to be much noise in the life of the disadvantaged child, but the noises are often meaningless to him. He is forced to "tune out," to become inattentive. Early in his school experience, "inattentive" becomes a label attached to him; his capacity for tuning out has been well nourished. The consequences are serious because inattention means that the child does not use available stimuli for the development of his intelligence.

The child thus suffers from lack of the systematic interpretation of his environment that should ensue through verbal mediation of the adult. He suffers, too, from the consequent lack of development of memory and attention, as well as the absence of a variety of meaningful environmental stimulants for learning. Nor does the adult provide motivation, which, as Ausubel (1963, p. 228) points out, is needed for energizing the learning process. The child does not seek out the adult as a source of information. This is evident even from the casual observation of a teacher who asked children to interview an adult about the diseases or insects that worried them most and what they usually did about it. The children stared in utter disbelief at such an assignment: "My Ma would tell me 'go way, you crazy.'" "I wouldn't ask my Grandma nothin'! She tell me nothin' anyway. Jus' bug me."

When children do not use adults as sources of information, there are underlying reasons which may not be evident from cursory observation. For example, Kardiner (1962, pp. 309–310) points out that among Negroes in the United States "ideal formation" is virtually impossible.

The parent is a member of a despised and discriminated-against group. Hence this ideal is already spoiled because it carries with it a guarantee of external and reflected hatred. No one can embrace such an ideal.

Interviews with fifteen lower-class parents of three-year-olds in an encapsulated community revealed that *no* parent read stories to his child and that none reported the experience of having had a parent or guardian read to him. A few of them, however, remembered stories that had been told to them. Interviews that focused on the kinds of things children asked about when adults took them to the store, dressed them, bathed them, or fed them revealed either that parents were not aware of questions or that children didn't usually ask them. The conversation tended to turn to descriptions of behavior: "He don't sit still." "He cry and cry." "He splash water all over the floor." The parent does not look upon himself as a source of information any more than the child sees the parent as playing this role. Unless the school reverses some of its practices and encourages children to *ask* questions rather than to answer them on demand, the school reinforces the void created by the lack of adults as mediators or sources of clarification. Too many current school practices further alienate the child from what should be a most important educational agency.

Changes Needed in the Role of the School

Deficiencies in environment such as are experienced by disadvantaged children are crippling and cannot be counteracted in a short period of time or by any one special project. To overcome deficiencies, especially those of early childhood, requires many years of carefully planned experiences. A vicious cycle of failure has already been set in motion, and certain unused reflective schemata can wane if the environment fails to encourage their functioning (Hunt, 1961, p. 258). Knowledge and understanding of the effect of environment on intelligence leads to the undeniable conclusion that what the school is now doing is much less than adequate. As has already been demonstrated (The Bridge Project, 1965), it is within the power of the school to provide experiences that raise to a significant degree the intelligence level of the learners. Intelligence tests measure *learned* behavior. The charge of the school is clear and present: ". . . unless there is significant expansion and reorganization of his experience, the tests will predict with fair reliability how he will function academically in the future" (Goldberg, 1964, p. 169).

The changes must proceed from the very foundations. They must be thoroughgoing. No crash programs, no remedial measures will do the all-encompassing task that is essential.

The Teacher as Mediator

The most important figure in the new order is the teacher as mediator, a function that is critical in the development of intelligence. Recognizing that adults at home cannot talk over shared experiences with the child, the teacher first needs to provide *shared* experiences and then to mediate in the talking that is done about them, and in the interpretation of them. Thus he gives training in memory and in conceiving cause and effect relationships.

An example of such mediation can be cited from one event that took place in an informal workshop organized for prospective teachers and held in a disadvantaged community. The participants were thirty college students, fifteen young children, and fifteen adolescents who were labeled by their school as "slow learners" and "disturbed." The participants were arranged in teams of four: an adolescent, a young child, and two college students. One standing assignment for the adolescents was to learn to read a book, to prepare it carefully — each with the help of "his own private teacher" — so that he could read it perfectly to "his very own child." Adolescents made hypotheses about "what parts you think your child will like best" in order to discover, for the edification of all, the kinds of incidents in stories which have most appeal for young children (Elkins, 1963, pp. 18–22).

When the task was completed, the adolescents met to discuss findings and problems. College students sat beside the youths in their respective teams, and served as teachers and helpers. The role of teachers as mediators is apparent in the following excerpt.

JERRY: I read to three children.
TEACHER: *Three* children! Let's hear about that.
JERRY: Well, one was little Joey, and two was big Joey, and three was Ronnie. I read them "The Three Pigs" and .. uh ..
EDUCATION STUDENT (Jerry's "own private teacher"): (whispers) Tell about what they liked best.
JERRY: Oh, yah. We were supposed to find out which part of the book our children liked the best. Mine liked the part about the pigs' building the house. Ronnie, he liked the first pig. Joey, little Joey, he liked — he liked — the — first pig.
EDUCATION STUDENT: Oh, are you sure, Jerry? Is it the first pig that he liked?
JERRY: *No!* I was talking about big Joey. Big Joey, he liked the first one, too. Now, little Joey, the littlest Joey, liked the third one. Ronnie liked the first one. Little Joey liked the third one. He was the only one that liked the — the — little

Joey—little Joey was the one that liked the third one. I had to persuade him.

TEACHER: Why did you have to persuade him?

JERRY: Because he was the only one that liked the third one. I thought he would like the first one because that little pig didn't do no work, and he played and everybody likes to play.

TEACHER: Yes. But can you say why you tried to persuade him?

JERRY: 'Cause all of the rest wanted the first one. The third did all the work; he only worked. (Laughter from the adults.)

TEACHER: Well, now let's see. Let's all see if we can figure out what often happens to us when we try to persuade someone to our way of thinking. What happens? Jerry, can you tell us what did happen?

JERRY: Well, he didn't want to listen no more! But I didn't have to persuade the other two. But little Joey, he just liked that little pig. Big Joey liked the little pig that played and didn't do work 'cause he liked to play hisself. And Ronnie liked the one that liked to play all the time, too; but little Joey, he wanted that third one. And Big Joey and Ronnie, they liked the first one. But that little Joey, he liked the third one.

The findings were clear: two children liked pigs who played and one preferred the pig who worked. But that peeved Jerry, and he tried to exercise the authority of an older member of the family. The teacher succeeded in helping him to verbalize a consequence of his own actions to which he had given no previous thought. The feeling of frustration about Joey's stand began to change to one of puzzlement. The teacher didn't try to push the gains any further at this point. Jerry needed time to think about all that had happened. However, Jerry's own private teacher took upon herself the task of summarizing what Jerry's findings meant in terms of our knowledge of children (the topic under study). As she did this, she proudly mentioned Jerry's name as a source of this new knowledge.

In order for teachers to fulfill their function as mediators, they need to help children learn to use adults as sources of information. This means children must learn how to ask questions and to feel free in doing so. To create a situation which stimulates such questions, teachers must use concrete materials about which to verbalize and conceptualize.

In the workshop mentioned earlier, several real skulls were brought to class. Among these were a human skull, that of a turtle, and another of a bird. One fourteen-year old boy was so affected by the experience of handling them, examining them closely, comparing them and talking about them, that in a twenty minute period there poured from him alone, a veritable flood of twenty-two recorded questions including the following:

If our skull is so hard, how can the brain grow?
Why do skull bones have cracks?

Is that why they say, "You're cracked in the head?"
What makes your brain think?
A turtle has a brain in that skull, right? Then, if he grows, why
doesn't it think like us?

The answer to the second question caused a flurry of excitement. The college students were unable to answer the question. The "ball" was passed from college students to pupils and back, until the questioner became impatient and declared, "Maybe it's because if you didn't have seams in your skull you wouldn't have room for your brains to grow when you get bigger, so the seams let them grow." Not a bad cause and effect relationship for a "slow learner" to draw! The appreciation expressed by all listeners was the young man's greatest reward. His supreme success this day served as a high motivating force for his learning during the remainder of the workshop and beyond. Teachers the following year talked of the great difference in this boy's achievement from one grade to the next. He had been known as a "nonreader" and a "nonwriter" in the previous grades. The labels by no means disappeared but there was a new attitude on the boy's part and a new interest on the part of teachers.

It was not only this one type of procedure in the workshop that seemed to have made a surprisingly long-term difference in the lives of this young man and most of the other participants; it was the many varied experiences, objects, and events, and the sheer enjoyment of participation in their own learning. The questions came because there were objects and events that inspired them. The process of gathering data, planning for it, and using the findings was in itself a sharp stimulus for questions. One situation was thus created in which children could use adults as sources of information. If the work of a very few weeks can bring initial results such as these, the possibilities that a full year can hold have not yet been fathomed. The potential of the school has not yet begun to be tapped.

The fact that disadvantaged children are reared in nonverbally oriented homes yet desperately need a chance to verbalize creates an acute problem in two ways. If the verbalization on the part of the teacher is lengthy, children do not have the support of the necessary concrete materials from which *they* can do the verbalizing and conceptualizing. Without this support they cannot attend to what the teacher is trying to "put across." Inattention is the result, manifested either by "tuning out" or by discipline problems. If the teacher tries to hold a discussion with no anchor for such procedures, the result is often chaotic.

There *must* be verbalization; it is essential for development of intelligence. Teachers must learn new ways of providing a variety of stimuli — not only the verbal — as foci for the building of concepts and abstractions and therefore, as foci for verbalization. At first, the preparatory and follow-up discussions are short; the concentration is on an activity which encourages the child to deal with an object or data or event on his own terms, on his own level, and in his own style. The activities surrounding the object or event are varied. The teacher creates a situation that encourages the child to be an active participant in his own learning.

Verbalization . . . does more than just attach a symbolic handle to an idea so that one can . . . communicate it more readily. It constitutes, rather, an integral part of the very process of abstraction itself. When an individual uses language to express an idea . . . he is engaged in a process of generating a higher level of insight that transcends . . . the previously achieved stage of subverbal awareness. . . . Even the seemingly simple act of making a choice of words in developing an idea involves complex processes of categorization, differentiation, abstraction, and generalization; the rejection of alternative possibilities; and the exclusion of less precise . . . meanings. (Ausubel, 1963, p. 148)

When the teaching is almost solely verbal, with no supporting concrete objects and events, the disadvantaged child is further at a disadvantage. It is only as children make strides in verbal communication that the discussions become more lengthy and involved. They have more to talk about, more need to communicate it, and to use verbal stimuli.

The Teacher's Role in Motivation

In the previously mentioned workshop, there were many examples of how concrete activities were used to encourage abstraction and verbalization. With slight modification, the following example is as applicable to a classroom situation as it was to this particular workshop. The data-gathering process was extended to work in mathematics. Each adolescent made a hypothesis about how tall the child in his group was and learned to use both the yardstick so that he could measure the height of his child and the scale so that he could find his weight.

The data were to be studied to discover the range in the height as well as in the weight of these three- and four-year olds and to compare the range with that of adolescents. Are both of these age periods considered to be periods of growth spurts? What are the chances that a small child will remain small? What are the factors that are likely to determine this? These were some questions to consider after data were gathered.

The next day arrived and the class gathered for reporting of findings. Problems aplenty! There had been much trouble with the concept of feet and inches—which led college students to permit adolescents to bring to class the measurements in inches. Now the figures needed to be converted.

CARL: Janie was just three feet.
SEVERAL ADOLESCENTS: What!? That can't be; she'd be too small. Wattza matter with *that?*
CARL: That's what she was. Just three feet.

167

TEACHER: Can you explain how you went about measuring her?
CARL: Well, if you take this yardstick and you put it where her
head touches the wall — That's what I did.
TEACHER: Can you show us? I'll be Janie. (Laughter)
CARL: You're too big.
TEACHER: Then let's get Janie. (She is brought in from the play
room.)

Carl began by measuring Janie from her ankles up so that the yardstick figures would "come out just even!" In actuality, Janie measured three feet four inches. Carl had not known how to arrive at this result nor how to set it down.

The discussion about measurement went on for three sessions, with much talk and many questions about heredity and nourishment, as well as mathematics. The point is: There was a fact-finding problem of great interest to growing adolesecnts. There were real people around whom the data-gathering could take place. Comparisons, conclusions, and generalizations were made as a result of manipulating data. There was total participation and involvement of every learner. And there was talk. The sheer volume of it was amazing in the light of the fact that these were considered nonverbal pupils. But now there was something to talk about. They had *experienced* the content; they *knew*, and they wanted now to know more. As in an earlier instance cited above, the questions came in a veritable flood. Adolescents were concerned about their own growth, their own bodies. The college students read voraciously that night to help their charges find some of the answers and to prepare appropriate materials that were suddenly in great demand.

Through just such means do teachers nourish aspirations that must be grounded in real satisfaction and achievement. If he cannot achieve his aspirations, there is a gap between a child's potential and his "effective intelligence" (Kardiner and Ovesey, 1962, p. 322).

The teacher also has it in his power to organize the classroom and its activities in such a way as to build motivational energy through a feeling of belonging. Children who are habitually truant, children who are constantly on the move from one city to another need the motivational power of *belonging*. A sense of belonging comes with the knowledge that one is needed and wanted, with the opportunities for participating in activities that carry prestige. The participating child, the child who is deeply involved in classroom or school activities, who has the sense of belonging, is rarely a truant.

Setting the stage so that the need for belonging can be met serves another function: It relieves the teacher of the constant, insistent pressure for attention and affection. Other children assist in the task of meeting these needs. When these needs are met, there is further reinforcement of motivation. The child wants the teacher's affection. If he can get it by pleasing the teacher and if he knows that his attempts at learning bring a word of praise, a smile, this is a legitimate positive force that furnishes the fuel for the initial spark. Then, when the real success in learning, the new mastery, the new power have had a chance to come to fruition, they can take over the task of providing emotional energy. Especially in the very sensitive personal area of language development, it is important that personal warmth be the atmosphere of the classroom.

Certainly the kind of external rewards to which a middle-class child responds are not motivation for the lower-class child. Nor does the teacher provide any motivation when he exhorts the child to study because he'll "need it later" or because he'll "get a better job." As Hickerson (1966, p. 58) notes, "To be convinced that preparation today will lead to a better tomorrow, one needs to have experienced a good yesterday."

Instructional Strategies

"After all, instruction is a vehicle through which the purposes of education are executed. If the vehicle is not appropriate, these purposes will not be served . . ." (Taba and Elkins, 1966). And if the purposes of education include raising the level of cognitive functioning, building self-concepts, and developing skills, attitudes, and interests among other things, then the teaching strategies as well as the selection of content and of materials must be appropriate.

Diagnosis

No teacher can possibly know what is appropriate for any group of children until he makes a penetrating and continuous diagnosis, analyzes the data, and uses the findings to determine curriculum and instructional procedures. Without diagnosis, the teacher cannot know the degree to which students are ready for certain materials and activities, precisely what gaps in learning need to be filled, what is obstructing the learning process, and what strengths can be mustered to aid that process.

Though every contact reveals much to the insightful teacher, the teacher needs to know how to observe and what to observe as well as how to conduct such observation in a systematic manner. Achievement tests are not enough; as a matter of fact, their validity is highly questionable for disadvantaged and insecure students. Informal devices of a specific nature are much more fruitful for curriculum planning.

Systematic observation is important especially where disadvantaged children are concerned, because writing and speaking skills are so poorly developed, thus eliminating two important means of diagnosis. How does he feel about particular school activities? About peers? How does he go about a study assignment? To whom does he respond during a discussion? What books does he choose? Is the shy, withdrawn child managing to hold his own? The teacher can observe a few children systematically and record observations, or can select an aspect of behavior related to basic needs he suspects are not being met. For example, in looking for strength of self-concept, the teacher notes the following: one child overtly rebels at taking a test or simply ignores it; another disappears from the room as soon as social studies books come out; a third loses his pencil whenever the math lesson begins. Keeping records of observations helps the teacher see the relationship between teaching strategy and pupil behavior. As the teacher reviews his records, the specific relationships appear more and more clearly and can serve as important guides to instructional planning.

Excerpts from the records of one teacher give clear examples of these relationships.

9/28 Howard feels secure with facts, sticks to them, can't go beyond them. He is used to a million workbooks. He resisted the observation of pest control products. "You mean I just go into a store and *look?*"

9/30 He loves that horrible workbook! He was an angel during the twenty minutes he didn't have to think.

10/2 When the kids were raising their questions about insects, he was right there. "Do insects go to the bathroom? Do they all have feelers, or do some have eyes? Do they have families, like we do?" Didn't seem to want the workbook.

10/5 He's beginning to read his biography of Jenner, but he doesn't want me to know. He sneaks it.

10/6 We discussed people's feelings about germs and insects. Resisted. "People don't *feel* about insects." Happy with the workbook, but sneaked another peek at Jenner.

10/7 He got upset because he had categorized an insect as "good" when the specimen set said "bad." Went back to his workbook.

10/8 He went wild over the insects under the microscope. No workbook today! When I asked him to explain the expression "I'm sick—I've got a bug," he said it came from "You're bugging me." Then he kept saying, "I saw a lice," and I said "No. One is a *louse*, and that's that!" But he came back with *"Louse?* You don't say that in school!" Look who's talking! He says worse than that.

No use trying to work with that social studies text today. Howard and the others were too full of "bugs." He said, "A bedbug is so tiny, and it sucks blood! It's so tiny, and I have to move the slide around to see the whole thing. He looked like a *monster* under that microscope, and he's so small. Geez! You can't hide anything from us!" That's the first time that he's said *us*.

10/9 He was amazed by the grasshopper scene from *Let the Hurricane Roar*. He talked about it over and over, all day. "Here they came to the West—free land and everything, and all the hope.

And they had to struggle so, and the loss." That "bugged" him. (Ha!)

He drew a marvelous picture of the grasshoppers attacking. He even used the whole piece of paper.

10/12   Howard managed the microscopes for the slides on which we had let water "ferment." When he saw those "wiggly digglies" under the microscope, it was exciting — something wiggling past where he couldn't see anything before. *"That's* just a drop of water? Wigglies!" No sign of his workbook.

He finished his biography of Jenner in the open!

10/13   This is supposed to be a two-week sequence, but Howard and all the rest — me, too — are too involved. We observed the cells of a leaf. Howard said, "Hundreds and hundreds of them on that tiny piece." Then when they saw the protozoa on the leaf, Howard said, "One cell! How can he live? How can he eat? How can he go to the bathroom?" He moves. Howard can't get over that. One cell, and he moves!

10/14   Almost all the kids brought in books. Howard's had beautiful enlarged pictures. The kids crowded around his desk. First time. He kept arguing that certain insects were harmful that the books said were beneficial because they kill other insects.

Back at the books. "Look! They've made a mistake. This butterfly can't be harmful." A cabbage moth. He was so taken with the idea that a beautiful thing could be so destructive. Kids on his side against the book. Happy to be supported, but kept saying, "That terrible thing."

10/15   I couldn't generate any interest in TB. We had been going to write letters for information, because so many of the kids have TB families, but they made a big howl and fuss, so I dropped it — said I'd call instead. Howard went back and drew a really impressive picture of protozoa swimming and floating around. I picked up the clue, and all the kids made pictures. He liked that! Then I said "O.K. So you're excited about this. But what does it all mean?" He said, "That's what I'd like to know!" then, sort of mimicking me, "Is it good? Is it bad?," but really *with* me, knowing that just looking is not enough. No one knew what protozoa did to the fish. He said, "I'll find out!" I nearly collapsed. He's going to find out *why* they are there. I don't know myself.

Howard's mother is pleased that he's interested, but she said, "We're going out of our minds with his questions. How do *I* know how protozoa get into the fish tank?" I had a feeling that she'd like to know.

10/16   The film was dull. Howard couldn't have cared less. He cut up. Even though it was real — bacteria souring milk and giving cheese its flavor — it wasn't real to *them* somehow. When Howard's doing something, all is well. But not this time. (Maybe he's been an observer too long.)

171

10/19 He loves the historical sketches—reading about the Yellow Fever and the Black Plague. That wasn't even an assignment, but several kids got interested in the brief sketches I mimeographed. Howard actually came out with a wonderful paper. He mentioned *Let the Hurricane Roar* again and said, "Even people in our country have suffered."

He wrote for almost half an hour! He's always hated it. "Social Studies!" he'd say. Now he reads. He picked up a book on Schweitzer in the school library. "He liked *everyone*," he told the class.

10/20 Howard got into a brawl when groups were preparing reports on historical events. He chose to make the world map and put all the events on it, like the Black Plague and Jenner's discovery of the vaccine. But another kid was putting these on a time line. Howard went into a fit. He had chosen the map because he thought it would be the greatest thing, but Emily's time line turned out to be great, too. He tried to tell her everything was wrong, and the other kids jumped on him. They were mad, anyway, because he was supposed to check *their* choices to be put on the map, and he didn't.

Another diagnostic device is the use of open-ended questions. The fourteen-year old boy who wrote about "My Worries" gave clues to the teacher about his self-concept and about the kinds of activities that were a fundamental part of his life. Here were leads concerning what needed to be done for him, even the following excerpt by itself:

I am always getting yelled at like losing the slip to father's pants or forgetting to mark someone paid on my book or forgetting that I was supposed to do something or other or forgetting that my little sister is only four, so not to be rough.

In an encapsulated community, the topic "fear" brought a veritable outburst: fear of drunkards, of being attacked, of rats, of accidents. A thirteen-year old girl's response was typical:

When I am walking to the store and it is dark and there are only three people. I am in the middle. It is alright if someone walks in front of me, but not in back of me. I feel that they might come up and grab me. You have heard of people getting strangled. That's why I get so scared.

The greatest majority of students had little idea about how to achieve their ambitions, although most had some ideas about what they wanted for a career; some had very confused notions. In encapsulated communities they responded to the topic, "The Job I'd Like To Have," with evidence of great gaps between ambition and plans for attaining the goal. Excerpts from papers by seventh and eight graders demonstrate this:

(Girl)   After I finish high school I would like to get a typist job because I like to typ. If I do not be a typest I would like to be a secretary that has her own office. Instead of being a secretary maybe I would be a nurse that takes care of children.

They wanted jobs which would given them power or would offer them an opportunity to help the sick or poor. Though a few mentioned money as a goal, the number was surprisingly low in the light of the need.

(Girl)   . . . if I'm working for someone they will want to tell me what to do and how to do it . . . If I had my own shop I would not tell the people who is working for me what to do and how to do it.

(Boy)   I would like to be Architecture went i get out of the Navy i take up some like arcitecture in the Navy and went i get out i will get a premit job of Architecture.

(Girl)   . . . to become a Register Nurse during the future because I love helping people who are very sick.

Girls wanted to "get marry and live happy ever after," an almost inevitable concluding statement, no matter what else they chose. Sometimes, boys concluded with the same aspiration, though more often they were concerned with violence and physical protection.

(Boy)   . . . a nice job in office . . . you would have a good barin to work in office. Im going to buy me a house my on home and fine me a nice wife and live happen very after.

(Boy)   I would like to be with the police department. I would want to be a *Katrate* instructor. And hold first degree black belt *Katrate* export. And to teach *Katrate* to the policemen, women and children the act of self defense. So these people could protect their self in a night attack of a group of people.

In all groups there was high incidence of tales expressing need for affection and attention which was revealed in response to the open-ended question, "My Three Wishes."

. . . to have my mother stop working so that she wouldn't be tired at night and she could have time to listen to me, or give me a hug.

Papers on various topics have revealed frustrations at home, at school, and in peer life, as well as a total lack of belief in the possibility of any change for the better or of any power, individually or collectively, to take positive steps to bring about that change. The papers reveal little understanding of the motivations of other people, which gives an important clue to the very immature development in interpersonal relations and in communication skills that one finds.

Another fruitful diagnostic procedure is discussion of conflict in stories, which may be read up to the climax, letting the students probe solutions. Or the entire story may be read and the ensuing discussion may be guided by questions such as, "What would happen if the mother decided to tell the father?" or "Why do you think Charles was naughty in school?" or "Why do you think he didn't wave 'goodbye' to his mother?" The teacher does not put a stamp of approval or disapproval on any answer. His purpose is to discover the level of conceptual development or to diagnose some other aspect of learning. This is not to say that the teacher gives no guidance in a discussion nor that he asks nothing but open-ended questions. But the questions and the guidance must match the purpose. Diagnosis requires open-endedness. Questions that are more specific and direct come later and serve other purposes.

Sociometric testing is another extremely useful diagnostic device, for it gives clues about interpersonal relationships that hinder or encourage the learning process. Interpersonal relationships are allied to discipline problems, the willingness of the child to speak out and express himself verbally, and the ability of the child to communicate with others and therefore to have available to him the stimulation others can offer. Teachers discovered that children chose people whom they had known longer than others. This meant they needed help in including newcomers, since the rate of mobility in some disadvantaged schools exceeds 100 per cent.

Parent interviews were another source of diagnostic information. Parents cried, "*Be* somebody, *be* somebody," to their children and pleaded with the teacher to help the child *be* somebody. They begged the school to teach the child to read, to be polite, to "act good," and the cry for help was one of desperation. The basic human needs that are not met get in the way of learning. The school must meet them before the children can learn; else the school fails. "For the school to fail them is to consign them to years of growing despair and frustration . . ." (Taba and Elkins, 1966). The school dare not.

Learning Sequences

Instruction needs to be planned with a view to the fact that though the attention span is short, the children need to study topics in depth. Not "coverage," but depth of understanding is the ingredient missing in the curriculum. A few long-term topics broken into a series of short sequences is a framework that recognizes the short attention span and the simultaneous need for adequate time to gain rich understanding. *Man and His Environment* is an example of a large topic, large enough to hold a number of short sequences which, when added up, can amount to depth study. Such sequences can be: How Insects and Germs Have Affected Man's History, Animals in the Life of Man, The Sea—Friend or Foe? *The Family of*

Man is another example, with possible shorter sequences being Human Hands, Walls, and Aspirations.

These have been chosen for study in turn by different classes because they held concepts important for the students. All people everywhere strive for something; human beings have basic similarities; men learn to control nature only by working together toward this end.

The particular sequences and procedures selected depend upon the diagnosis of the children's level of intellectual, social, emotional, and physical development.

In each case, it is necessary to initiate the study with concrete topics or activities, all close to the students' experiences. Every activity that follows the initial activity builds upon the previous one and prepares for those to follow. Each topic selected must lend itself to the building of varied experiences and must permit flow from the concrete to the abstract. These criteria can be met in all the sequences mentioned above.

Initial activities can be varied and can be selected from several levels and varieties of concreteness. For example, when the "Hands" sequence was started, each child drew an outline of his own hands on paper. This unleashed a discussion about the similarity of all hands and the beauty of human hands. (Portions of this sequence are taken from Taba and Elkins, 1966, Ch. 5.) Those children who could, wrote about "Important Things My Hands Can Do." Hands can pray, take care of children, and punish; with hands you eat and drive a car and wash. As children told about what they had written, the teacher quickly recorded their offerings under two categories: *work* and *play,* thus giving children their first experience in categorizing. She did it with them, helping them to discuss the *intent* of each act because the same act could be work or play depending on what it meant to the person doing it. Then, after four or five offerings were recorded and discussed, a committee was assigned the task of tallying the ideas of the whole class with instructions to consult the author if his intent was not clear. Each child received a copy of the tally next day, because it would be needed for use that day as well as later.

Here was an initial activity including the concrete drawing of hands upon which was built the more abstract activities that followed: there was a sharing of ideas and beginnings of concept development from the very start; the students wrote about themselves because that is what the teacher was sure they knew at this point; they made a tally so that chaotic stimuli of long unwieldly lists were seen as having order and meaning. The tally also helped begin the process of differentiation. A small group of children quickly and naturally serviced the class; children's special tasks immediately had attached to them the criteria of respect for classmates' ideas and feelings (check with *them* if you don't know their intent!); and the class result of the day's work was in their hands, ready for immediate use, and for exploration of feelings about how much they had accomplished in one day.

The variety of activity that already was present is apparent: the children talked about something they knew; they wrote; they read their own creations as well as the list they made; specific beginnings were made with the building of the concept that things of an apparently chaotic nature can have order and that the deeds of hands may have intent behind them.

Now one class could move a little further away from their own experiences, but they needed *emotional* content with which to make that move. Therefore, the teacher read them a chapter from *Big Doc's Girl* (Medearis, 1942), the story of a young girl who is responsible for the care of two younger sisters and who punishes them for not returning immediately from school. One child accepts the punishment; the other cannot. The story was discussed — briefly, but with vehemence — the issue of discussion revolving around whether or not a sister has the right to use physical punishment. Here, an emotional experience led to conceptual considerations, laden with values. The class reconsidered the categorized list they made of the activities of hands, and added newly found actions from the story as they reread it for this purpose. For example, they added "drawing" (for on the wall the child draws a large picture of the longed-for mother).

The students themselves raised again the notion of intent when discussing whether "hitting" was work or play. Some felt people enjoyed striking others. Several disagreed: "It makes you too much nervous." The issue was left unresolved, with one child referring the class back to the book — the responsible adolescent in the book did not enjoy it.

Now the sequence had moved to further abstraction, somewhat away from themselves, but still with close emotional reference to themselves. This discussion already was slightly longer than that of the previous day, although the teacher had not intended to permit this. However, there was not a child who lost interest; "hitting" was too real. The punishment, the missing loved one, and the problem of intention were critical issues in their lives. During this second day the teacher had built upon the previous day's work and achieved much: the conceptualizing, the short step away from self, the attentive listening to a lengthy story, the rereading in cases where a few copies of the book were available, the analysis necessary for addition to the list of items created the previous day.

It was necessary now for children to be required to *look*. They were asked to observe for a half-hour what adults and young children do with their hands, and to record their observations. Note-taking was called for, but children had none of the required skills. Therefore, the teacher asked them to discuss what the people they would observe might be doing. They mentioned getting dinner, feeding the baby, ironing, cutting the hedges, locking the door, fighting. One child volunteered to enact what happens when teenagers sit down to do homework. She selected a friend, and, with the aid of guiding questions from the teacher, role played a scene while the class tried to take notes. At its conclusion, there was a volley of demands for "my chance." Suddenly, something new had awakened interest. The teacher realized that the children did not trust adults or adult promises such as, "Tomorrow you'll have your chance." But, to go on with the role playing now would not permit the course of events to move forward. Therefore, she assigned a date and a specific hour (10:10 A.M., and so forth) to each group of three children who were sitting together. (The seating was sociometrically arranged.) At that hour, their chance would come. The suspicion was still present but there was also an attitude of wait and see. Now, however, the class was able to proceed.

The children discussed note-taking. "How can you take notes and watch at the same time?" "How can you write so fast?" The teacher helped them understand that notes were reminders; she read her own and asked them to fill in the omitted parts to make complete ideas. There was a second scene enacted; now with the help of the teacher each child was able to record at least two items. They felt ready to tackle the assignment.

Here again, multiple learnings were taking place; not only note-taking but much needed discussion skills, role playing with its motivational impact, wary beginnings of trust in an adult, skills of observation, and knowledge of importance of pursuing stated goals despite desire for immediate gratification. The last achievement could not have been accomplished if the observation assignment had not also been an accepted and desirable goal.

When the class met again, observations were shared and tallied. This time the class made decisions about at least one category, and the teacher supplied the rest, in order not to belabor the new process of categorization but to move it along one step. Observations were written up and were duplicated so that each child could have his own copy of the booklet containing all of the class members' reports. The students corrected their work again and again, without protest; complete accuracy was necessary before any author could receive a ditto master on which to write neatly his production. Students were encouraged to receive help from their classmates in correcting their work. In such cases, it became the obligation of the helper to explain the reason for his correction. It is always amazing to teachers how much children can do collectively toward the correction of mechanical errors in writing. The teacher was there as umpire and as the final judge of such perfection. With each child's name signed to his creation on the master dittos, the task was finished until next day. Even children who ordinarily refused to set a word down on paper came through with a "story" for the booklet on the "Family of Hands."

It is important that any production like this be ready for use the very next day; tasks involving difficult skills must show results quickly. The copies were ready on time for the children to collate as the two available staplers were shared. Just as very young children need to be helped to wait their turn and share, so did these twelve to fourteen year olds. But the atmosphere already created made it possible with a minimum of frustration on the part of the teacher and students. Every child wanted the stapler first in his hurry to get on to the fun of reading what he and his classmates had wrought. But every child was also anxious that the activity *not* stop. So, the mere possibility that the staplers would be taken away at the slightest possibility of trouble offered the maximum control and the opportunity to learn to share, to wait, and to understand anew that there are adults who do keep their promise but only under conditions which permit those promises to be kept.

Each child has control over those conditions. For the first time in the lives of most of the students this was verbalized for them. *They* had power to bring about better conditions, but the power would be limited unless it could be used for the benefit of all. For the first time, they begun to experience control by a *situation*, even though the teacher was an element in that situation. If the control is merely personal on the part of the teacher — exercised without creating a situation in which all children *want* to participate — such learnings cannot take place. Disadvantaged children desperately need this experience for they usually get it nowhere else and therefore cannot internalize controls in a healthy fashion.

The booklet stimulated great excitement. To be "in print" is a sure builder of self-concept. Children who for years had crumpled up their papers and sent them sailing into the basket now were listening to their very own creation being read by others or by themselves. The teacher had plans for asking volunteers to read a few and then to use the booklet for a guided silent reading lesson. The students would have none of that; they wanted to hear everybody's. This same class would never have sat through the reading or reporting of anything by as many as three members let alone thirty. Now there was not one sign of lagging interest. Each group selected a different one of its members to read his story each time their turn came around. The teacher's task, once this routine was set, was to supply constant reassurance that everyone would have a chance.

The tally of observations that the committee had completed and duplicated constituted the summary sheet for the booklets. The class examined textbooks to decide how their book could be made like it. This was one of the first uses to which textbooks were put. A table of contents received unanimous approval; students' names would appear once more, and everyone would know the page to turn to when he wanted to read someone's story again. What this kind of activity can do for the self-image is unbelievable. It is important to note, too, that the same activity served to boost the ego of all the children at the same time, and it was not necessary for the teacher to intervene personally with each child. He had established a climate in which students could help each other.

In more academically oriented classes, a committee expanded the summary sheet to serve as an index. A second committee prepared a statement comparing the two tallies: the first one students had invented and the new one born of their observations. To add to the wonder of it all, adults at home reacted with genuine astonishment, and even a measure of awe.

Again, the very same day the new feeling of self-respect was strengthened.

Self-respect is a misnomer because initially no one can build respect into himself. It takes the other people around him to do this. And it takes much doing, daily, with even more than one act daily to rebuild a shattered self-image. It is important to remember that there is a goodly number of children for whom "interested adults" do not exist. Usually such students do not even bother to show their work to anyone outside of school. When the teacher can identify these children, he can take one of a number of steps: send students to different teachers in the building who can be relied upon to give adequate sincere praise. Or, extra copies of the work made with especially beautiful covers can be sent to the school library or to the reading room of the student's church.

To give students some perspective on their findings, the teacher read them a chapter from *Caddie Woodlawn* (Brink, 1963) which tells about Caddie being punished for doing something unbecoming a young lady. Since the story does not describe the punishment in any great detail, but concentrates rather on Caddie's reaction, the work of hands had to be inferred to some extent. Here was an opportunity to move from concrete considerations to the more abstract. The students had already discussed activities and functions of hands concretely. The consideration of people in fiction was only one step removed from real life. This served as a natural bridge to abstract thinking. In making the transition, the teacher helped them refer back to *Big Doc's Girl* for comparison. Now the class saw that punishing hands indicated the presence of anger in one case and worry in another. They tried to infer what the mother's hands were doing when she punished Caddie and by contrast what the father's were doing in his plea for Caddie's understanding. He tried to reduce the impact of the punishment and to explain that it was he who wanted her to be given a chance to "run wild" as a child, but now the time had come when life demanded new behaviors.

Wherever help was needed in making this difficult transition, the teacher described some situations involving emotions and did a solo role-play of one such situation. "I am walking down a dark alley. Suddenly I think I hear footsteps, and something looms large in front of me. What do I do?" She pantomimed, withdrawing in terror, and asked the children what her hands did. They hadn't noticed! She repeated the performance. This time they saw her hands draw closer to her body as if to protect. Several protested. "That's not what I'd do," came from one boy. When he was invited to demonstrate, he used his hands to strike out against the imagined danger. Two more demonstrations were sufficient to clinch the concept that an emotion like fear is evident in the movement of the hands, that hands can manifest an emotion.

By now, the children were involved in reading short simple paperback books and were instructed to search for an emotion expressed by what the hands are doing. One child who was reading *Blue Willow* (Gates,

1940) actually was able to express verbally the loving tenderness Janie felt for her one meaningful possession, the blue willow plate. She was able to find passages to verify her argument: Janie lifted the plate slowly, "blew an imaginary speck of dust off it," held it in two hands for fear of dropping it, and put it down slowly "her eyes still feasting on the treasure." Though most children were able to do much less than this, all but a few could find some inferences about emotions connected with the action of hands in the books they were reading individually.

It is interesting to note that long after this sequence was completed, students talked about *intent,* in connection not only with hands but with words. Children asked, "Did he intend to hurt your feelings?" Their observations of the actions of hands continued for some weeks after the conclusion of the study. The teacher knew she had had at least partial success in achieving her goals because almost invariably students related the actions to the emotions. "The baby put his whole hand in his mouth because he was so hungry." "My brother felt so bad that he walked all the way home with his hands in his pockets."

Most classes concluded the sequence at this point. Teachers feared going on any longer, even though interest was high. In some, however, new and varied activities continued the theme. Some teachers rexographed newspaper ads for jobs demanding skills that ranged from the manual to the mental, and the students described the work of the hands. The teachers knew better than to ask children at this point to find ads for themselves. In the first place, most of them did not have command of the necessary reading skills; in the second place, selection of pertinent items from the tremendous number of ads in a city newspaper required too high a level of differentiation and was too complex a task. Also, the teachers needed common materials with which to teach a new aspect of the work, and besides, they knew that newspapers were not available to the children. Each student was given a rexographed sheet of ads while the teacher passed around newspaper clippings of those ads pasted on a sheet of paper. They feared the children would believe the rexographed copies to be "fake" ads, and they knew these children were concerned about "real" things and about people telling them the truth. Again, this new activity served to move thinking of the students beyond their own immediate surroundings and to continue the development of abstractions, contrasts, and comparisons. Now they were given their first experience with comparison through rank order. They arranged the advertised jobs in rank order using the criteria of the importance of hands in the performance of the task. This triggered heated discussions. Were hands less important in the work of an architect than of an auto mechanic? Is it true that jobs requiring hands were less highly regarded than "brain jobs?" The boy who wanted to be an architect thought so. Then his classmates challenged him. "How come most people thought hands are as important in the architect's work?" This discussion demonstrated a markedly higher level of abstraction than did any of the previous ones.

Some teachers expanded this activity until it became, for all intents and purposes, a sequence within a sequence. Students read about careers, interviewed people, held heated discussions in an effort to arrive at some answer to the puzzle of discrepancy in prestige attached to jobs, and wrote personal reactions to the problems.

There were other activities that took on the nature of a sequence within a sequence. One centered around an examination of pictures. The chief purpose was to provide varied ways of moving children beyond their own little world. Teachers brought in pictures from *Life* and *Look;* the photographs in these magazines were large enough for all the class to see at a distance. The pictures were examined for story content related to the role of hands as well as to the intent behind what they do. Content of the story had to be discussed first as a transition from the concrete picture to the abstract inference. A doctor's "soothing" hand placed upon the brow of a screaming child caused some dissension. How can he be "soothing" when the kid is screaming? Fear of doctors and of illness, deep concerns about their own health and that of their families came through above and beyond the consideration of human motivation as seen through the roles of hands.

In some classes, the work with pictures was expanded. Working in pairs, children found pictures about which they wanted to write. The pictures and their stories were mounted for group consideration with the gamut of human motivations for behavior being highlighted as a consequence.

An extension of this activity came with an examination of human interest articles in newspapers. This was done almost solely with academically oriented groups because it required a very high level of abstraction to read an article, infer the role of hands from the action, and then infer the motivation behind the role. This activity again presented to children a wide range of human motivation. This time, the similarity of events selected and the great span of motivations attributed to similar acts were discovered by the children—admittedly, no mean accomplishment. It was during a period of time when fear stalked the streets of the city, and violence between races held sway. "He hates white people"; "No, white people hate him and he just wants them to leave him alone." "Police *have* to break up riots." "But they don't have to *like* pushing people around." They finally reached the conclusion that the point of view people hold depends on their own concerns. To say the least, the teacher was pleased with this manifestation of cognitive development.

Teachers found it possible for a few classes to handle another short group of activities based on historical events. They wanted children to gain historical perspective about the motives for what people do, about ways their acts affect future events, as well as the "good" and the "bad" of these acts. The textbooks could not serve the purpose. However, biographies did. There are, fortunately, many simple biographies available with format acceptable to older children. There are adequate numbers to permit children to select a book in accordance with individual interests. Children read for what people did, why they did it, and what difference it made.

With content centered around common concepts, individualization of instruction can take place without destroying a feeling of unity in the class. Warm group feeling and rapport are important for strengthening self-concepts. When teachers group children into rigid units, believing they are providing thus for heterogeneity, they tend to destroy the unity.

Such concepts as "What hands do is affected by the motivations of people," or "What we do will affect future generations," provide the focus for a wide variety of individualized activities all of which are related to group goals. For example, children make individual selection of a book based on the broad concept which the whole class is considering. The class focus remains intact while heterogeneity is permitted to enrich the learning. Each person selects a book which is of interest to him and on his own skill level. The topic is broad enough to suit many tastes and abilities. John Paul Jones, Buffalo Bill, and Kit Carson satisfy the taste for adventure, Florence Nightingale, and Narcissa Whitman for service.

The concept is the same for all, but the details that are learned by each student are different. This spread of details enriches the knowledge of all, while the concept itself provides a framework for learning those details in a meaningful and lasting way.

Other important motivating activities include the writing of "drama" for classroom enactment. Certainly this is no easy task, but children will write and revise and work persistently at the task, because the promise of fulfillment through dramatization drives them on. Once they have been driven sufficiently by such overt means, the urge to learn to know takes over. One dramatization, one booklet, one "real play" will not suffice. The deficit is too great by the time children reach the middle school. There must be immediate success and many successes. Only then will there be unearthed the pleasure inherent in the learning process itself, in the task itself, in the feeling of achievement that comes with mastery.

The design is a variety of activity, concrete objects, and events as foci for developing the power to abstract. The stress is on such cognitive processes as analyzing, hypothesizing, discovering, generalizing, questioning, relating cause and consequence, differentiating, and seeking similarities and differences.

Disadvantaged children manifest critical lacks in such cognitive processes. Unless schools build ability to perform these processes, there will be a serious deficit in all other learning. It is these processes which strengthen motivation and provide a meaningful framework in which to learn other skills.

References

Ausubel, David P. *The Psychology of Meaningful Verbal Learning.* New York: Grune and Stratton, 1963.

Bernstein, B. "Some Sociological Determinants of Perception: An Enquiry into Subcultural Differences," *The British Journal of Sociology,* 9 (1958), 159–174.

The BRIDGE Project. *The Preparation of Teachers for Schools in Culturally Deprived Neighborhoods.* Cooperative Research Project No. 935. New York: Queens College of the City University of New York, 1965.

Brookover, Wilbur B. and Thomas Shiler. "Self-Concept of Ability and School Achievement," *Sociology of Education,* 37 (1964), 271–278.

Bruner, Jerome S. "Learning and Thinking," in *Readings in the Psychology of Cognition,* eds. Richard C. Anderson and David P. Ausubel. New York: Holt, Rinehart and Winston, 1965.

Deutsch, Martin P. "The Disadvantaged Child and the Learning Process," in *Education in Depressed Areas,* ed. A. Harry Passow. New York: Teachers College Press, Columbia University, 1963.

Duncan, Carl P. "Transfer after Training with Single versus Multiple Tasks," in *Readings in the Psychology of Cognition,* eds. Richard C. Anderson and David P. Ausubel. New York: Holt, Rinehart and Winston, 1965.

Elkins, Deborah. *Reading Improvement in the Junior High School.* New York: Teachers College Press, Columbia University, 1963.

Friedlander, Bernard Z. "A Psychologist's Second Thoughts on Concepts, Curiosity and Discovery in Teaching and Learning," *Harvard Educational Review,* 35 (Winter 1965), 18–38.

Goldberg, Miriam. "Adapting Teacher Style to Pupil Difference," *Merrill Palmer Quarterly,* 10 (April 1964), 161–178.

Havighurst, Robert J. and L. J. Stiles. "National Policy for Alienated Youth," *Phi Delta Kappan,* (April 1961), 161–178.

Hickerson, Nathaniel. *Education for Alientation.* Englewood Cliffs, N. J.: Prentice-Hall, Inc., 1966.

Hunt, J. McVicker. *Intelligence and Experience.* New York: The Ronald Press, 1961.

———. "How Children Develop Intellectually," *Children,* 11 (May–June 1964), 83–91.

Kardiner, Abram and Lionel Ovesey. *The Mark of Oppression.* Cleveland: The World Publishing Co., 1962.

Taba, Hilda. "Cultural Deprivation as a Factor in School Learning," *Merrill Palmer Quarterly,* 10 (April 1964), 147–159.

——— and Deborah Elkins. *Teaching Strategies for the Culturally Disadvantaged.* Chicago: Rand McNally and Co., 1966.

Albert J. Harris reports on a study of beginning reading instruction for disadvantaged children. He traces the concern with reading disability from the early 1930's to the present, when the reading problems of the disadvantaged have begun to present themselves as a separate subject for research.

The author questions the assumption that preschool attendance in itself guarantees readiness to read. Instead, the research suggests that readiness develops best when there are carefully planned instructional programs. Intensified and extended readiness programs are worthwhile, especially for disadvantaged pupils ranked below the fiftieth percentile in reading achievement. He reviews recent first-grade studies in the United States and then sums up the CRAFT Project, which contrasted two main approaches to beginning reading. By comparing a skills-centered and a language-experience approach, along with two adaptations of each, researchers found that the teacher's use of time significantly determined reading achievements. Interestingly, the basal reader method was slightly superior to the language-experience method, not only in developing reading comprehension but also in bettering attitudes toward reading.

Eleven conclusions drawn at the end of the first year of this study are listed. The same methods that apparently work with middle-class white children enable disadvantaged Negro children to progress in learning to read in first grade. Despite certain auditory and perceptual deficiencies, restricted vocabulary, and other readiness handicaps, these youngsters do respond to superior teaching. The language-experience approach yields higher scores if supplemented by the use of audio-visual materials. If a "new way of teaching" really is to be tried, continuing inservice education is a necessity.

Noting that the findings so far are tentative and inconclusive, the author links the good showing of the basal

BEGINNING READING INSTRUCTION FOR EDUCATIONALLY DISADVANTAGED CHILDREN

Albert J. Harris

reader method to the familiarity of these materials and the confidence of the teachers in using the detailed lesson plans keyed to the basal readers. Finally, educators are cautioned against assuming that a method that works well with middle-class children will always work equally well with disadvantaged children. He recommends that each new method be tried out under carefully controlled conditions which permit assessment of immediate and long-range results.

BEGINNING READING INSTRUCTION FOR EDUCATIONALLY DISADVANTAGED CHILDREN

Albert J. Harris*

The schools of America woke up to the presence of disabled readers back in the 1930's. Those children previously considered to be just stupid or lazy were shown by intelligence tests to be of normal or even of above normal mental ability in areas other than reading. It is only during the past thirty years that we have recognized reading disability as something correctible and have introduced diagnostic testing and remedial and corrective programs to reduce the severity of the problem.

The recency of professional concern with the reading problems of the disadvantaged can be shown by inspecting the programs of the annual conventions of the International Reading Association. From 1960 through 1963, there were no papers in the I.R.A. programs that were specifically concerned with the reading problems of the disadvantaged. In the 1964 program, however, there were thirteen papers in this general area. General concern with the reading of the disadvantaged seems to have started after 1960, and to have produced printed papers and reports starting in 1963.

By the time the severely disadvantaged child reaches junior high school, his grade score in reading is likely to be two to three years below the national norms. For example, in a longitudinal study that started with beginning seventh graders in the fall of 1961, the mean grade score for all entering seventh graders was found to be 4.8 in word knowledge and reading on the *Metropolitan Achievement Test.* This was for pupils in a junior high school located in an urban Negro ghetto neighborhood in New York City (Downing, 1965). With intensive effort on the part of a devoted staff of teachers and consultants, the mean achievement of this group rose 1.9 grades by May, 1964, near the end of the ninth grade. In a control school in which the initial achievement was almost exactly equivalent, the increase in mean grade score was only 60 per cent of that in the experimental school. While determined efforts to improve the achievement of

*This paper is based in part on Projects Nos. 2677 and 3246 of the Cooperative Research Program of the Office of Education, U.S. Department of Health, Education and Welfare. Additional support was given by the Board of Education of the City of New York and by the Division of Teacher Education of The City University of New York.

187

disadvantaged pupils at the secondary school level produce better results than not making such efforts, it is obvious that the secondary school attempt is too late to eliminate the massive retardation found among pupils from disadvantaged backgrounds. For this reason, attention has been turned increasingly to the preschool and beginning school levels.

A search of the recent literature on teaching the disadvantaged to read indicates that many different ideas have been tried out and are being tried at present, but research that provides a basis for objective evaluation is conspicuously meagre. This paucity of published research is inevitable, considering the recency of concern with the problem. Nevertheless, it is striking that in two books on teaching the disadvantaged published in 1966, one (Crow, Murray, and Smythe, 1966) does not discuss beginning reading methodology at all, while the other (Loretan and Umans, 1966) covers "Reading and Listening Skills in the Early Grades" in a chapter of eight pages, in which only subjective forms of evaluation are employed.

The need for concentrated attention to the beginning stages of school learning was demonstrated by Martin Deutsch (1965). A wide variety of tests were given to Negro and white children of varying socioeconomic status at first-grade and fifth-grade levels.

> Significant correlations with race were found in eight comparisons for the first graders, and in 18 for the fifth grade sample. The number of significant comparisons on SES for each group was 22.

The findings indicated that inadequate patterns of linguistic behavior, somewhat related to race but more to low socioeconomic status, became intensified between Grade 1 and Grade 5. These results point clearly to the need for compensatory education efforts beginning in the preschool period.

The Head Start Program, initiated in a great many communities with financial support from the Office of Economic Opportunity, is a large-scale effort to improve the school readiness of preschool disadvantaged. Since at this writing it has operated for only one summer, it is premature to attempt to judge the extent to which Head Start may be able to achieve its objectives. To describe and evaluate the many Head Start programs is not within the scope of this paper. However, it may be pertinent to quote from one Head Start report:

> The convictions of the educational staff are enthusiastic and positive, but the scientific questions cannot be really answered at this time. We are certain that Head Start can be evaluated only in accordance with the aims of a specific curriculum, a specific community, and a specific pupil population. It is our conviction that any program undertaken should contain a built-in program of continuing evaluation. Surely as to whether this program accom-

plished its aim awaits the outcome of objective evaluations now under way. (Silberstein, 1966)

Reading Readiness for Disadvantaged Children

The assumption that preschool attendance in itself guarantees that the child will become more ready to read is open to question. In a current doctoral dissertation, Serwer (1966) studied the performance of disadvantaged urban Negro children at the beginning of the first grade. Girls and boys did about equally well — or poorly — on a battery of readiness tests. Four tests favored boys, four favored girls, and none of the differences were statistically significant. In addition, those who had had kindergarten experience scored significantly higher than those with no kindergarten background on only three of the measures. The kindergarten group was higher in visual-motor coordination and auditory discrimination, but not in word meaning, listening, knowledge of letter names, or visual discrimination of geometric designs.

Hillerich (1965) has recently reported on the value of two kinds of kindergarten procedure in developing readiness for reading. Classes in which a specific readiness workbook was used were compared with classes in which the readiness program did not use any specified materials. The children who used the workbook showed significantly better scores both on readiness tests and on a reading test at the end of the first grade. While this study was not done with a disadvantaged population, it confirms the Serwer findings in suggesting that prereading skills are not an automatic outcome of kindergarten, but develop best when there is a carefully planned instructional program. Its results cannot, of course, be generalized to workbooks other than the one employed in the study.

Readiness in the First Grade

A pioneer study of the long-range effects of a first-grade readiness program was conducted by Bradley (1956). In the experimental group, formal systematic instruction in reading was not given any child until he was considered ready. The first group received instruction in reading after five months of readiness work, the second group, after eight months, and the third, after ten months. The control group started reading instruction in the first month. Early in the second grade, the control group was well ahead. By the end of the second grade the two groups were equal, and by the end of the third grade the differences, although not statistically significant, favored the readiness group.

During the year 1964–65, there were twenty-seven research studies in first-grade reading that were supported by the Cooperative Research Branch of the U. S. Office of Education. A coordinating center was established at the University of Minnesota (Bond and Dykstra, 1966), and several meetings of project directors were held to decide on uniform test procedures and other common agreements that would facilitate compari-

189

sons between studies. Summaries of twenty of the studies have been published in *The Reading Teacher* (Chall and Feldmann, 1966); the other seven summaries will probably appear in the October, 1966 issue.

Of the twenty published reports, one deals specifically with the value of a readiness program for disadvantaged children. Spache and his co-workers tested the effects of readiness programs in eight Florida counties, in parallel white and Negro schools. Readiness tests were administered four times during the year and reading achievement tests were given in May. Pupils in the top quarter were inducted into reading in September. The second quarter started reading in November, the third quarter in January, and the bottom quarter in March. Specific materials to develop visual and auditory perception skills were used in the readiness groups.

> The program seemed to have an insignificant effect upon those pupils who were mature enough to read early in the school year, who hence participated in it only to a limited extent. The effectiveness of the program appeared to increase as the ability levels of the pupils decreased . . . For the Negro sample, the experimental treatment was significant for criterion achievement for the two lower quartiles only, but the nonsignificant differences favored the experimental treatment at all levels of ability . . . The Negro experimentals exceeded the white experimentals in reading achievement by a significant amount at the next to lowest quartile and by nonsignificant amounts at all other levels.

The clear implication of this study is that intensified and extended readiness programs deserve further tryout, particularly for the lower half of disadvantaged pupils.

Another of the studies, conducted by Thomas Horn (1966) of the University of Texas, compared ways of developing readiness for reading among Spanish-speaking children in the schools of Austin, Texas. In a preliminary report delivered to the International Reading Association in May, 1966, Horn said that his analysis was not yet completed, but seemed to indicate that a readiness program that was at first conducted entirely in Spanish seemed to have done better than one which attempted to build up competence in English as quickly as possible.

Beginning Reading Instruction for the Disadvantaged

Teaching the Disadvantaged in Israel

Feitelson (1965) has summarized the characteristic problems of disadvantaged school entrants in Israel and from each problem has drawn an implication for teaching them to read. Her suggestions may be summarized as follows:

190

Problem: Lack of adequate motor skills. Implication: Introduce writing in slow, easily manageable stages, with sufficient time and practice so that any possibility of experiencing failure is automatically prevented.

Problem: Lack of practice in visual discrimination. Implications: Make sure that differences are pointed out and elaborated upon at each stage in learning. Introduce new symbols slowly and in a carefully arranged sequence.

Problem: Linguistic deficiencies. Implication: Not only vocabulary, but also story content, length and complexity of sentence structure, and usage of special language forms need to be controlled.

Problem: Short attention span. Implication: Use short periods of concentrated effort rather than prolonged learning periods.

Problem: Inability to defer gratification. Implication: It is desirable to give pupils material in small units of single pages or a few pages rather than in book form.

Problem: Self-doubt, low self-confidence, and low frustration tolerance. Implication: In beginning stages, conduct group instruction at the pace of the slowest.

Problem: Unavailability of help at home. Implication: Make sure that teaching in school is as complete and all-encompassing as possible.

These implications, reported by Feitelson to have produced good results in Israel, have not been tested specifically in the United States. A method of reading instruction designed to incorporate her suggestions would seem to this writer to be worth developing and testing.

Recent First-Grade Studies in the United States

Most educators would agree that if one could decrease class size, provide experienced teachers, place more nearly adequate instructional materials in the classroom, and arrange for on-the-spot consultant help for the teachers, the achievement of first-grade pupils should benefit. A study demonstrating that such actions really do result in improved pupil performance in reading has been reported by Johnson and Kress (1965). The Educational Improvement Program was concentrated in the first-grade classes of the sixty-one elementary schools in Philadelphia that had the lowest averages on standardized achievement and intelligence tests. Average class size was reduced to not more than thirty children, part-time classes were eliminated, experienced teachers were drawn from other grades when no experienced first-grade teachers were available,

191

funds for purchase of materials were increased, and consultants were assigned.

The results were evaluated by comparing reading scores at the end of 1963–64 with scores obtained in the same schools in 1962–63, before the program began. According to pretest results the pupil populations did not differ significantly. Results of reading tests at the end of each year showed a superiority for the 1963–64 population that was highly significant.

The implications of this study are that general measures taken to reduce class size, provide a full school day, strengthen materials, and improve the qualifications of the teachers, are likely to benefit pupil learning, regardless of the method of instruction employed.

Among the twenty-seven cooperative studies of first-grade reading there were three that focused on disadvantaged children, in comparing teaching methods.

In Colorado, Roy McCanne (1966) carried out a study in which Spanish-speaking children were taught by three methods: a conventional English readiness and basal reader approach; a modified "Teaching English as a Second Language" approach; and a language-experience approach. The teachers were all experienced and rated as excellent. The main conclusion was that the basal reader method was ahead on most of the tests given near the end of the first grade. The author speculated that "certain culturally determined thinking and behavior patterns, such as an unwillingness to initiate original expression in a formal school setting, may have been partly responsible for the superiority of the basal reader approach in developing reading skills." He also pointed out that the second-language approach and language arts approach were strong in developing oral vocabulary and writing fluency, and could be recommended as supplementary approaches for the development of language skills other than reading with Spanish-speaking first graders.

The other two first-grade studies on the disadvantaged were located in New York City in schools with almost completely Negro populations.

Jeanne Chall and Shirley Feldmann (1966) carried on an observational study in twelve classrooms. All of the teachers used basal readers, but they differed markedly in the amount of emphasis they claimed to give to sound-symbol relationships. No effort was made to influence teacher behavior. Each teacher was observed on a regular schedule, and pretests and final tests were given. Four teacher characteristics had significant positive relationships with reading achievement. These were: general teacher competence, a thinking approach to learning, appropriateness of the level of difficulty of reading lessons, and a sound-symbol approach.

The CRAFT Project

The other New York City study was the CRAFT Project (Harris and Serwer, 1966), of which this writer was the director. In this project two main approaches were compared, and there were two variations of each approach, making four teaching methods in all. The project operated in twelve schools in Negro neighborhoods in central Harlem, Bedford-Stuyvesant, and South Jamaica. All schools were known to have had low averages on recent city-wide reading tests.

Methods

The main comparison was between a skills-centered approach and a language-experience approach. The skills-centered approach emphasized the need for order, structure, and built-in repetition. Skills were introduced in specific sequences, the vocabulary was carefully controlled, and the teacher followed a manual that gave detailed lesson plans. Two skills-centered methods were used. The first was a basal reader method, in which the teachers used the full materials supplied by the publisher and followed the printed lesson plans as fully and faithfully as they could. The second combined intensive phonics program (the phonovisual method) with basal readers. Each day the teacher taught a phonics lesson, and at a different time used the basal readers for oral and silent reading.

The language-experience approach emphasized the need for self-expression through the use of the child's oral language as a basis for beginning reading materials. His experiences provided a basis for concept-building, language enrichment, and vocabulary development. Out of the discussion of these experiences, chart stories were developed and used for reading and writing, for skills instruction, and for drill. The transition to book reading was gradual and individualized.

Two language-experience methods were used. These differed in the amount of audio-visual equipment provided the teachers. Half of the language-experience teachers used the method with only the amount of audio-visual equipment normally available to them, while the other half were provided with a variety of audio-visual devices such as overhead projectors, cameras, tape recorders, and earphones.

The four methods, then, were as follows: I. Basal Reader; II. Phonovisual; III. Language-Experience; IV. Language-Experience–Audio-Visual. Each of the twelve schools had four experimental classes, two using one of the skills-centered methods and two using one of the language-experience methods. Each method was employed in six schools, and each possible combination of a skills-centered method with a language-experience method was present in three schools.

Pupils

The pupils in each school were assigned at random to the two methods, with care taken to balance those with kindergarten experience and those without such experience. At the opening of school there were about 1700 children in the 48 classes, with a mean of 35 children per class. The number who completed the long pretesting program was 1,378. By the time the final tests were completed, early in June, a further loss of 17.2 per cent took place, leaving 1,141 pupils for whom both pretest and final test scores were available. These comprised the experimental population. As pupils transferred from the experimental classes to other schools they were replaced by new entrants, keeping class size fairly constant and equal to the size of nonexperimental first-grade classes in the same school. These new entrants were not treated differently from the experimental pupils in the classrooms, but were excluded from the statistical analysis.

Teachers

The teachers volunteered to take part in the project, knowing that they would get paid for the required after-school work such as attending workshop sessions and filling out research forms. They had to be willing to accept whatever teaching method was allotted to them. The school principals drew lots for the methods assigned to the schools, and within each school the four teachers drew lots for the two methods. The teachers were quite varied in education and experience. Most of them had bachelor's degrees with some postgraduate work short of an M.A. Total experience ranged from 0 to 40 years, and first-grade teaching experience ranged from 0 to 29 years. However, there was a mode of 1 year and a median of 2 years.

An intensive teacher-training program was carried out, which involved the part-time services of four reading consultants, an early childhood consultant, and an audio-visual consultant, all provided by the Board of Education. A workshop for each of the four methods began with two sessions before school opened, continued with weekly after-school meetings for three months, and then met every two weeks. The teachers were visited regularly by the assistant director of the project and by one of the reading consultants; these class visits were followed by evaluative discussions intended to improve teacher efficiency and increase closeness of adherence to the experimental method. The audio-visual consultant worked only with the twelve teachers in the language-experience–audio-visual classes. The early childhood consultant was especially helpful in structuring the plans for the reading readiness period of five weeks, uniform for all methods, during which the pretests were administered and teaching plans were developed in the workshop.

Time

The skills-centered teachers were instructed to spend 90 minutes a day on reading instruction, 30 minutes on other language arts, and 30 minutes each on social studies and science, totalling 180 minutes a day. The language-experience teachers, who attempted to integrate reading closely with other language arts and to use social science and science experiences in their reading programs, were given flexibility in allocating their 180 minutes a day. In three schools in which the experimental classes were placed on a split-session, four-hour school day because of overcrowding, the total time for reading and related activities was set at 150 minutes. The instructional time was considerably more than the amount recommended in the official syllabi of the Board of Education. Teachers kept a detailed log of their use of time for five consecutive days each month. The instructional period extended for 140 school days, following which the final tests were given to all classes within one week.

Tests

The pretest battery included the *Murphy-Durrell Diagnostic Reading Readiness Test, Thurstone Pattern Copying* and *Identical Forms,* and *Metropolitan Readiness Test,* word meaning and listening subtests. Of these, the *Murphy-Durrell* learning rate subtest, the two *Metropolitan* subtests, and the *Pattern Copying* test were used as covariates.

Five subtests of the *Stanford Primary I Battery,* Form X were given to all of the children as the main post-test measures. In addition, several oral reading tests were given individually to a randomly selected sample of four children from each class: the *Gilmore Oral Reading Test,* the *Gates Word Pronunciation Test,* and two tests of phonetically regular words constructed for the cooperative projects, one by Fry and one by Karlsen. Two samples of written composition were also obtained, and were scored for the children given the individual reading tests.

Pretest Results

On the seven pretests for which percentile norms were available, the mean score for the CRAFT population ranged from the first percentile to the 44th percentile. The lowest performance was on the *Murphy-Durrell* phonemes subtest, which is a measure of auditory discrimination in which the task is to compare the initial consonant sounds in spoken words, or final consonant sounds. The children found this task very difficult and frustrating, and there were many zero scores. The mean score on this test ranked at only the first percentile according to the test norms. On the *Metropolitan* word meaning subtest the mean score was at the 14th percentile, indicating a serious deficiency in listening vocabulary as compared to first-grade entrants in general. On the *Murphy-Durrell* letter-identification subtests and on the *Metropolitan* Listening subtest the group centered between the 23rd and 26th percentile. However, on the *Murphy-Durrell* Learning Rate subtest their mean score was at the 44th percentile. The latter test is a kind of standardized lesson in which words are taught by a "look and say" procedure, followed by a recognition test.

If it can be assumed that the Learning Rate Test is a measure of aptitude for learning to recognize words by a sight method, while the Phonemes test measures one of the abilities necessary for phonics instruction, the group would seem to have a far greater proportion of children

195

who were ready for a sight approach than for a phonic approach. It would seem, also, that the group's potential for learning was well ahead of their attained status on several measures of reading readiness.

Post-Test Results

A comparison of the means and standard deviations of the pretests showed sufficient differences among methods to make it necessary to adjust the post-test measures so as to eliminate the influence of initial differences in readiness. This was done by a covariance analysis. Of the nine available pretest scores, four were chosen on which usable results were available from all 48 classes. A special computer program was written to perform a multivariate analysis of covariance with unequal N's. With this program the class means were adjusted on the five subtests of the *Stanford Primary I*, the *Gilmore Accuracy* score, and the *Gates Word Pronunciation Test*.

Using the adjusted class means for the post-tests, an intercorrelation analysis was done by computer in which each of 54 variables was correlated with the other 53 variables—a total of 1,431 correlations. This table of intercorrelations was carefully inspected for variables other than the teaching methods that might show significant correlations with the post-test results.

The most conspicuous finding of the correlational analysis was that the teacher's use of time was a significant factor. The daily logs kept by teachers for five consecutive months provided scores for total time, reading time, and supportive activities time. Of these, only reading time was significantly related to outcomes; its correlation with the corrected post-test scores ranged from .40 to .61. Correlations for supportive activities time and total time with post-tests were generally not significant.

With the amount of time spent in the direct teaching of reading identified as an important influence, the two approaches were compared to see how the teachers used their time. Total instructional time per day was quite similar: 170 minutes for skills-centered teachers, 175 minutes for language-experience teachers. However, the skills-centered teachers spent 55 per cent of their time on reading; the language-experience teacher spent only 39 per cent of their time on reading, and 61 per cent on supportive activities.

The fact that three of the schools had been on a four-hour split-session schedule while the other nine schools had a full five-hour school day was next investigated. Three of the four teaching methods (basal reader, phonovisual, and language-experience–audio-visual) had been present in the three split-session schools. Of fifteen comparisons, eleven showed significant differences favoring the full-session schools. The language-experience-audio-visual method was more severely impaired in the split-session schools than either of the skills-centered methods.

The most valid comparison, then, is in terms of adjusted mean scores using only the classes that had full five-hour days. The results of such an analysis may be summarized as follows: (1) Within the skills-centered approach, the only significant difference was in favor of the basal reader method over the phonovisual method on paragraph meaning; the other six measures did not show significant differences. (2) Within the language-experience approach, the audio-visual method was ahead of the regular language-experience method on all seven measures, and four of the differences were statistically significant. (3) The language-experience–audio-visual method was on a par with the total skills-centered results. (4) The regular language-experience method had the poorest results, lowering the means for the language-experience approach so that it was surpassed by the skills-centered approach on six measures, with significant differences on four of them.

Many of the apparently significant differences were washed out when the raw score means were translated into grade equivalents. The adjusted grade score means are shown in Table I. An inspection of this table shows that most of the differences are of the order of one-tenth of a year, and even when such differences are statistically significant, they are not of much practical consequence.

TABLE I
Adjusted Grade Score Means for Full-Session Classes

Test	Skills-Centered Approach			Language-Experience Approach		
	Basal Reader	Phonovisual	Total	Language-Experience	Language-Experience and Audio-Visual	Total
Stanford						
Word Reading	1.5	1.6	1.5	1.4	1.5	1.5
Paragraph Meaning	1.6	1.5	1.5	1.5	1.5	1.5
Vocabulary	1.5	1.5	1.5	1.5	1.5	1.5
Spelling	1.7	1.7	1.7	1.6	1.7	1.6
Word Study Skills	1.5	1.5	1.5	1.4	1.5	1.4
Gilmore Oral, Accuracy	2.0	1.8	1.9	1.7	2.0	1.8
Gates Word Pronun. ·	2.4	2.3	2.3	2.3	2.3	2.3

In Table I one can see that there is a substantial difference between the mean grade scores on the *Stanford,* which was given to the entire experimental population, and the *Gilmore* and *Gates* tests, which were given to a random sampling of 48 children for each of the four methods, a total of 196 children in all. On the two oral tests the group means tend to equal or exceed the grade placement of 1.9 at the time of testing; on the *Stanford* the means for the two range from 1.4 to 1.7 and have a median of 1.5.

The *Gilmore* and *Gates* tests have norms based on standardization procedures carried out in the 1940's. The *Stanford,* Form X, was at the time of use an experimental form, norms for which became available in 1965. In the opinion of this writer, who has checked with the directors of other projects in which the *Stanford* Form X was used, the norms of this test are about four-tenths of a year more severe than the norms of comparable test batteries such as the *Metropolitan.* Since the *Metropolitan* has for years been used in city-wide testing in New York, the present *Stanford* results are judged to underestimate what the pupils would have done on the *Metropolitan* by about four months. In terms of those standards, the CRAFT pupils are judged to have equalled the norms and to have greatly surpassed expectations based on their low pretest scores.

An alternative explanation is that reading instruction has been improving in many parts of the country, and that the more difficult *Stanford* norms represent a genuine national improvement in the teaching of beginning reading. If this is correct—and it seems plausible—the teaching of the disadvantaged will have to be substantially improved if they are not to fall farther and farther behind middle-class children in reading achievement.

In addition to measures of reading ability, a measure of pupil attitudes toward reading was employed. This was the *San Diego Inventory of Pupil Attitude,* prescribed for the cooperating first-grade studies. The items are intended to disclose the pupil's degree of interest in reading and attitude toward reading. This attitude test was given as a group test during the posttest period. The examiner read each statement, then the pupils marked the "yes" or the "no" on their answer sheets. The score is the number of answers indicating favorable attitude.

On this instrument the means for the four methods were as follows: Basal Reader, 17.20; Language-Experience, 15.87; Language-Experience–Audio-Visual, 15.58; Phonovisual, 14.98. The basal reader mean was significantly higher than each of the other three, and the phonovisual was lowest; the language-experience methods did not significantly differ.

These results round out the picture of outcomes as of near the end of the first year of a three-year project. The basal reader method not only was slightly superior in developing reading comprehension, but also achieved significantly highest scores in attitude toward reading.

Since it was evident that there were much greater differences in results within each of the four methods than there were between any two methods, the data was studied to see if they could cast any light on the reasons why some teachers achieved so much better results than other teachers who were using presumably the same methodology.

The assistant director of the project had visited every teacher, and she was sure that she could distinguish levels of teaching competence.

When her unquantified impressions were compared with obtained re-- sults, there were many surprises. The teacher with the very best results, for example, had not given the impression of outstanding superiority. Donald M. Medley constructed a special observational instrument for use in the CRAFT Project, that he called OScAR-R (Observational Scale and Rating – Reading). It was designed to be used by research assist- ants with little knowledge about the teaching of reading. This instrument required two observer activities. One called for three minutes of obser- vation during which the observer catalogued the kinds of materials being used. The other required the observer to spend seven minutes in tallying the various kinds of statements made by the teacher to pupils. Three ten- minute cycles, lasting a total of thirty minutes, were completed in each observation. Each of the forty eight teachers was observed in this way a total of eight times, twice by each of four observers.

OScAR-R resulted in a total of thirteen measures. Eight of these were intended to verify the differences among the four teaching methods, and showed highly significant differences among the methods in the directions expected. The other five scores were measures of aspects of teaching style: number of disciplinary statements, positive motivation, negative motivation, total number of teacher pupil interchanges, and per cent of meaningful interchanges. None of these thirteen scores had a significant correlation with any of the corrected post-test measures.

Conclusions

A number of conclusions can be drawn from the first year of the study. These may be quoted from the official report (Harris, 1966, p. 102) as follows:

1. The results of the CRAFT Project as a whole show that most disadvantaged first-grade Negro children can make substantial progress in learning how to read. The pupils as a group had done quite poorly on the reading readiness tests. Their achievement was well ahead of expectations based on their pretest scores.

2. Disadvantaged urban Negro children can learn to read by the same methods that work with middle-class white children. They begin with extremely poor auditory perception skills, limited vocabularies, and other readiness handicaps, but they can re- spond to superior teaching with good learning. When books and stories are within their comprehension, they respond well to many of the same books that are favorites with middle-class children. Their new integrated favorites with multi-ethnic characters are probably gaining popularity among middle-class children also.

3. The basal reader method, employed as in the CRAFT Project, held a slight lead among the four methods at the first-grade meas- uring point. It achieved slightly but significantly highest results in meaningful silent reading comprehension. It was significantly highest also on the San Diego Inventory of Pupil Attitude. It was

relatively less impaired in the split-session schools than the audio-visual method, which was the only language-experience method with split-session classes.

4. The phonovisual method, although liked by its teachers, did not demonstrate any superiority. It was inferior to the basal reader method in paragraph meaning, and its slightly higher scores on word recognition tests were not statistically significant. It was the lowest of the four methods on the San Diego Inventory of Reading Attitudes.

5. The language-experience approach with audio-visual supplementation (L.E.-A.V.) obtained significantly higher scores on several tests than did the language-experience method without audio-visual supplementation. In grade-level scores the A-V method matched the means of the skills-centered approach on most of the reading tests and was slightly higher on one test. The L.E.-A.V. method requires expensive equipment and intensive training of teachers. Also, it did poorly in split-session classes. But present results fully justify continued explorations of the ways in which the use of audio-visual procedures can enrich reading instruction. Considering how long it took to get this method operative, its results are very encouraging.

6. The slight but statistically significant lead of the skills-centered approach over the language-experience approach is due to the language-experience method's relatively poor showing; the L.E.-A.V. method matched the skills-centered results. The differences, even when statistically significant, were not large and might disappear or be reversed during the second grade.

7. In the schools in which the CRAFT classes were on split-session schedules, achievement in both approaches was considerably lower than in the full-session schools. The implication is clear that split-session schedules for first-grade classes should be abolished as soon as possible.

8. Adequate control of instructional time is essential if controlled research on methods of instruction is to have any validity. Despite strenuous effort in the training program, there were both wide differences in instructional time within each method, and significant differences between the approaches. The skills-centered teacher spent 55.5 per cent of their language arts time in direct reading activities. The language-experience teachers spent only 39 per cent of their language arts time in direct reading activities. Furthermore, the amount of time spent in direct reading activities was one of the few control variables positively correlated with outcome measures. The teacher log (which is now available in a version that can be automatically scored and punched into data cards by an I.B.M. 1230 Visual Scanner) demonstrated its usefulness as a research tool.

9. When a new way of teaching reading is to be tried, an intensive, continuing inservice training program is necessary. With a workshop that met once a week during the early months and every two

weeks afterward, and with each group of four teachers receiving a half-day per week of reading consultant help, the CRAFT teachers learned to teach according to the methods assigned to them. The four methods were clearly distinct according to the logs, OScAR-R, and the San Diego Inventory of Approaches to the Teaching of Reading.

10. After the post-test results had been corrected for initial differences in readiness, the post-test means in some CRAFT classes surpassed the national norms, while the means in other classes were very low. This was true within each of the four methods. The implied need for further study of what makes some teachers more effective than others is clear.

11. The CRAFT Project has been extended, with federal funds provided for following children through the third grade. In addition, thirty of the first-grade teachers have repeated the use of the four methods with a new first-grade population, and these children will be followed through the second grade. It is hoped that these additional studies will show both the long-time effects of the teaching methods and the effects of teacher experience in using the specific method.

Some Final Comments on the Cooperative Studies

Although the results of both the McCanne project and the CRAFT Project must be considered inconclusive at the first-grade measuring point, and both projects are following the pupils through the second grade, the statistically significant, if small, superiority for the basal reader method in both studies is worthy of comment and speculation.

One possible explanation is that the teachers using the basal reader method were more familiar with the procedures and hence made fewer mistakes. In reading research, however, many studies have shown that almost any new experimental method will surpass the results obtained with basal readers in a control group. There is widespread suspicion that many of these alleged superiorities of method are attributable to the well-known Hawthorn effect—the effect of the teacher's knowledge that she is using an experimental method and that results are going to be carefully measured. In both the McCanne and CRAFT projects the basal reader teachers were treated, not as a control group, but as a group of experimental teachers, and were given workshop training and classroom supervision comparable to that given the teachers using other methods.

Another possible explanation is that the detailed lesson plans that come with basal readers provide security and structure for both teacher and child, which are helpful to both. It may be that freedom and flexibility of the language-experience method provide a great opportunity for creative teaching to some teachers, but insufficient guidance to others.

A third line of speculation leads to the hypothesis that children learn best what teachers emphasize most. If some teachers stress reading and reading skills, while others stress oral and written language expression, the immediate results would favor the reading achievement of the former group. This may possibly have been the major reason for the slight advantage of the basal reader approach. Since general language mastery and cognitive background become increasingly important in reading as children move up the grades, the methods stressing these factors may have delayed but important values that will show up later.

Still another possibility is that the tests used are based to a greater extent on the vocabulary used in basal readers than on the vocabulary used in experience charts and stories. If this gives the skills-centered approach an unfair advantage in the first-grade comparisons, it should disappear by the time of the second-grade testing, since the pupils in the language-experience approach will have had ample practice in reading by that time.

Since controversy over the phonics issue has been rife for many years, the bearing of the CRAFT results on this issue deserves some discussion. The particular phonic method chosen for the project had been selected because of reports of satisfaction with it in Washington, D. C., a city which has a preponderance of Negro pupils in its public schools. In the CRAFT results the basal reader method surpassed the phonovisual method in paragraph comprehension and reading interest, while the phonic method did not show a statistically significant advantage on any measure.

This may possibly be due to the extremely low state of phonic readiness in this population at the beginning of the first grade; their mean score on a test of auditory discrimination was at the first percentile of the national norms. One possibility is that these children may have developed phonic readiness by second grade and may show increased benefit from phonic instruction in the second year results.

In this paper, attention has been given to the small number of research studies that have been recently reported on teaching beginning reading to the disadvantaged. The studies are few in number, and the particular teaching methods included in them form a small sampling from the many approaches now being advocated for beginning reading instruction. It is not safe to assume that a method that works well with middle-class children will necessarily work well with disadvantaged children. Each new method that claims superiority will have to be tried out under carefully controlled conditions, and studied for both its immediate results and its delayed results, before its value with disadvantaged children can be properly judged.

References

Bond, Guy L. and Robert Dykstra. "The Role of the Coordinating Center in the Cooperative Research Program," *The Reading Teacher*, 19, (May 1966), 565–68.

Bradley, Beatrice E. "An Experimental Study of the Reading Approach to Reading," *Elementary School Journal*, 56 (February, 1956), 262–67.

Chall, Jeanne and Shirley Feldmann. "First Grade Reading: An Analysis of the Interactions of Professed Methods, Teacher Implementation and Child Background," *The Reading Teacher*, 19 (May 1966), 569–75.

Crow, Lester D., Walter I. Murray and Hugh H. Smythe. *Educating the Culturally Disadvantaged Child.* New York: David McKay Company, Inc., 1966.

Deutsch, Martin, "The Role of Social Class in Language Development and Cognition," *Amer. J. of Orthopsychiatry.* 35 (January 1965), 78–88.

Downing, Gertrude L., et al., *The Preparation of Teachers for Schools in Culturally Deprived Neighborhoods (The BRIDGE Project)*, Cooperative Research Project No. 935. New York: Queens College of the City of New York, 1965.

Feitelson, Dina. *On the Teaching of Reading to Culturally Disadvantaged School Entrants.* Jerusalem: School of Education, The Hebrew University, December, 1965. Mimeographed, 21 pp.

Harris, Albert J. and Blanche L. Serwer. "Comparing Reading Approaches in First-Grade Teaching with Disadvantaged Children," *The Reading Teacher*, 19 (May 1966), 631–35.

——. *Comparison of Reading Approaches in First-Grade Teaching with Disadvantaged Children (The CRAFT Project).* Cooperative Research Project No. 2677. New York: Division of Teacher Education, The City University of New York, 1966.

Hillerich, Robert L. "Prereading Skills in Kindergarten: A Second Report," *Elementary School Journal*, 65 (March 1965), 312–17.

Johnson, Marjorie S. and Roy A. Kress. "Philadelphia's Educational Improvement Program," *The Reading Teacher*, 18 (March, 1965), 488–92.

Loretan, Joseph O. and Shelley Umans. *Teaching the Disadvantaged.* New York: Teachers College Press, Columbia University, 1966.

McCanne, Roy. "Approaches to First Grade English Reading Instruction for Children from Spanish-Speaking Homes," *The Reading Teacher*, 19 (May 1966), 670–76.

Serwer, Blanche L. *The Relation Between Selected Reading Readiness Measures and Acquisition of Sight Vocabulary in Low Socioeconomic Urban First Grade Negro Children.* New York: New York University, 1966, unpublished dissertation.

Silberstein, Richard M., et al. "Can Head Start Help Children Learn?" *Reading Teacher*, 19 (February, 1966), 347–51.

Virginia F. Allen explores techniques and procedures for teaching of standard English as a second language. Defining standard English as "what the majority of educated speakers habitually use," Dr. Allen points out that, undemocratic and unfair though it may be, standard English is "front door" English. It is the responsibility of the school to enable every citizen to open this door, if he wishes.

She feels that time invested in discussing standard English is well spent, since it reminds both teachers and students that a person's speech is neither a moral nor an ethical issue. The speaker of standard English may not even distinguish ideas or communicate more clearly or forcefully. The terms "right" and "wrong" with respect to the dialect one uses have little meaning, except as applying to language appropriate or inappropriate to a particular situation.

TEACHING STANDARD ENGLISH AS A SECOND DIALECT

Virginia F. Allen

Dr. Allen argues the case for teaching standard English as a second dialect if need be. She then discusses suitable instructional strategies, many of which are used by teachers of foreign languages. The essential step is identifying the smallest possible number of significant items — and "teaching each of them hard!" The teacher has the student use the standard patterns as often as possible without criticizing the child for improper use. Drill, disguised as conversation, has considerable merit as a classroom practice.

The Claflin College Project provides a good model. Here, in a rural-based small Negro college, drill procedures and materials were developed to lead students toward mastery of standard patterns, while avoiding "teaching down," which they would have resisted. Role playing emerged as a useful technique. Interestingly, the stress on standard English as a dialect had some spill-over into the language development and reading achievement of the college students.

Dr. Allen cautions teachers against treating the student's home dialect as inferior. Instead, they must concede that the first (home) dialect may be the important and appropriate one for vital interpersonal relationships. At the same time, the teachers must help the student achieve fluency in standard English by adapting drill, exercises, and materials which have been shown to work in second-language teaching. To neglect this vital function in English teaching is to close a door for a large number of students for good.

TEACHING STANDARD ENGLISH AS A SECOND DIALECT

Virginia F. Allen

Few people today need to be told that standard English is virtually a "second language" for millions. Almost every teacher knows students who cannot speak, read, or write the sort of English that educated persons consider standard, even though some variety of English may be the students' mother tongue. Not only is the problem prevalent, of course, it is also old. It dates back past Huck Finn and Topsy to the eighteenth century, and beyond.

Yet two facts do appear to come as news—good news.[1] One is that some teachers are developing a fresh and clearer view of what is involved in learning a standard dialect of English in school when some other dialect is spoken in the home. A second newsworthy fact, and an even more cheering one, is that these fresh insights have suggested some practical classroom procedures which are being tried with encouraging results. Some of those promising procedures will be described in this paper.

First, however, it would be wise to show what the term "standard English" will mean in the context of this discussion. For our present purposes, standard American English is the kind of English *habitually* used by most of the *educated* English-speaking persons in the United States.

Thus "He doesn't want any" would qualify as a sample of standard English—not because some "authority" has certified it as being "correct," but because evidence suggests that educated speakers habitually *say* "He doesn't want any" in situations where less educated speakers might say "He don't want none."

It is important to note the emphasis on *habitually* and *educated* in this definition of standard English. A teacher who undertakes to familiarize her students with the standard dialect of English as here defined is careful to focus attention upon grammatical forms which educated speakers are in the *habit* of using. For instance, even though some grammar books decree that the comparative form *more* "should" be used in place of the superlative form *most* when only two are being compared, an enlightened teacher today would be undismayed if a student said, "Both Pete and Bill get good grades in school, but I think Pete really has the most sense." Habitual usage among educated speakers is what counts—whether or not that usage obeys some grammarian's rule.

---

[1] For front page news in the literal sense, see **The Wall Street Journal** for January 19, 1966, which featured an account of several current programs and approaches in standard English as a second dialect.

On the other hand, the stress on the word *educated* in this definition is significant, too. What is being advocated here is emphatically not an "anything goes" approach to English usage. Standard English, as defined here, is the variety of English generally used by the educated members of the American speech community. Statistically speaking, one has reason to suspect that the number of Americans who say "you was" exceeds the number who say "you were." This fact does not establish "you was" as standard usage, however. Standard English is what the majority of educated speakers habitually use.[2]

Teachers who start with this definition then go on to link it up with their student's experience and observation. They point out that the kind of English they have in mind is the sort used on radio and television by announcers, sportscasters, civil rights leaders, and news commentators, as well as by practically all TV heroes, including Batman, Superman, and Flash Gordon. It is the English heard in the public statements of astronauts, bankers, congressmen, and movie stars. It has been called "the language of educated ease," because it is used by people who *know* they sound "educated" and so do not have to think about their use of language.

When the target language is defined in these terms, even young children know what the teacher means by "standard English." Martin Joos (1964) who has made a special study of attitudes toward language, says:

> Long before any teacher began to correct his English, the child has learned all he needs to know, at his age, about people and their places; he has developed considerable skill in judging adults by their speech. . . .

Standard English in Perspective

Class time invested in discussing standard English along such lines is time well spent. For one thing, such discussions remind both teachers and students that the presence or absence of standard forms in a person's speech is not a moral or ethical issue. Among announcers, congressmen and movie stars there are some who are moral, honest, and upright and some who are not; yet both kinds are speakers of standard English.

Then, too, such discussions give the teacher an opportunity to grant that people who speak standard English do not always and invariably communicate any more clearly or forcefully than speakers of nonstandard dialects do. Since the students themselves will doubtless have observed this fact, they will appreciate the candor of teachers who acknowledge that a person's grammatical usage has little effect—for better or for worse—upon the clarity and vigor of his message. Too often, teachers try to convey the opposite impression by feigning incomprehension when a student says something like "I don't have no pencil"—a statement whose

---

[2]The term "a standard dialect" would be more accurate here since there are actually several varieties of English used by educated speakers in different regions.

import is perfectly clear, as the student well knows. The reason for learning to say "I don't have any pencil" has little to do with comprehensibility; when teachers imply that the standard English way is better because it is clearer, students can hardly be blamed for regarding English teachers as phonies or, more charitably, as living in an unreal world.

There is a further advantage to be gained from discussing standard English in terms of professional groups who characteristically use it. Such discussions help to dispel the impression that what the class is being urged to learn is a language spoken chiefly by teachers, by *English* teachers, at that. As a motivating force, such an impression has very low potential.

Moreover, a definition that identifies the target of instruction as "the kind of English habitually used by educated speakers" gives teachers a useful scale for weighing the relative importance of various items found on English tests and in English textbooks. Textbook "rules" that would teach the class usages no longer habitual among most educated Americans can be passed over lightly or omitted altogether, and time thus saved can be more profitably spent in a study of usages that actually do distinguish the standard dialect from other varieties.

Thus far we have been concerned with identifying the kind of English that teachers should be helping their students learn to use. We have stressed the need for frankness and realism. It is good strategy to acknowledge that this standard dialect, this variety of language habitually spoken by educated Americans, has no inherent virtue of its own, unpossessed by other dialects. It was not divinely bequeathed to some Moses on tablets of stone. Furthermore, language problems are very different from arithmetic problems, though for centuries this difference has traditionally been ignored. Standard English is not a set of "right" answers, like the answers found at the back of an arithmetic textbook. (The right answer to "two plus two" is "four"; any other is, has always been, and doubtless always will be, wrong. Yet one cannot in the same sense assert that it would be "wrong" for a slum child in a rat-ridden flat to say to his mother, "That landlord, he *mean*. Ain't nobody no meaner'n him.") Hence, in good programs for students of standard English as a second dialect, the terms "right" and "wrong" are not often used. When they are, "right" means "appropriate to the situation," and "wrong" means "likely to put the speaker at a disadvantage," much as one might say it is "wrong" to chew gum while being interviewed for a job.

Standard versus Nonstandard Dialects

There is another truth that teachers in modern programs publicly acknowledge. Students whose families speak some variety of English other than the standard dialect appreciate being told that several features of their home language were once characteristic of standard speech. In seventeenth-century England there would have been nothing nonstandard about a sentence like "My brother and his family, they live in Atlanta."

After all, the authors of the King James version of the Bible wrote: "Thy rod and Thy staff, they comfort me." Double negatives, too, were features of standard English for hundreds of years: Chaucer and Shakespeare often used them. For that matter, double negatives are regularly used in Spanish to this day.

Teachers who share this sort of information with their students earn a reputation for honesty and reasonableness that stands them in good stead when the hard work of learning the standard dialect begins. For of course the standard dialect must be taught, and it should be learned. Even though there is nothing inherently "wrong" or "bad" about using a nonstandard dialect, there are times when it can harm the person who uses it. No matter how tastefully he may dress, no matter how impeccable his grooming may be, the applicant for white collar employment does not enhance his chances by saying, "I come because I seen your ad."

"Front Door English"

Undemocratic and unfair as it may seem, the fact is that standard English is "front door" English. And American schools are committed to the task of making it possible for every citizen to enter by the front door if he wishes to do so.

Just as candor and a clear view of the facts are essential in defining what standard English is, so also one needs to be factual and frank in saying why the standard dialect ought to be learned. The student needs to understand that a command of standard English is vital to any American (particularly any "minority-group" American) who aims to associate with speakers of the standard dialect on anything like an equal footing.

Note the phrase "a *command* of standard English." To command something is not merely to have a vague notion of it, but rather to be able to *summon it up at will*. The student must be given the ability to summon up the standard dialect whenever he himself wants to use it, in any situation where fluency in that dialect would be to his advantage.[4]

Often, in the development of such fluency, the school can count on little help from the environment outside. In urban "gray areas," for example, and in the rural South, a nonstandard dialect is generally the medium of communication for most members of the student's immediate community, standard English being used only by members of the school staff. It is then entirely up to the school to teach young people how to use the standard dialect with ease and self-confidence when occasions demand.

Teachers are well aware of this responsibility, and they have worked at the task, year in and year out, but often with little success. Why? Partly because many a teacher antagonizes the very people she is trying to help.

---

[4] Of course there are other reasons for teaching standard English — reasons more palatable to those who dislike treating language as a status symbol (which, in America, it is). Quite apart from the fact that nonstandard English makes a poor impression, there is the obvious fact that the standard dialect is the medium for imparting information and ideas in print and on the air.

She makes her students feel that their natural way of talking is a shameful thing, marred by "errors" that need to be rooted out. She seems determined to wrest the students' familiar dialect from them, leaving in its place a language that may well estrange them from homefolks and lifelong friends. Small wonder that many students resist!

Linguistic Versatility the Goal

Nowadays, luckily, there *are* teachers who recognize that other varieties of English have validity for many communication situations profoundly important to their students. Such teachers offer standard English as a second—or additional—dialect without demanding that it *supplant* the student's home language.

In Europe, such a view of the standard dialect would be taken as a matter of course. In France, for example, it is taken for granted that a citizen will learn to use a standard dialect of the national language for communication in relatively formal situations involving educated speakers, and in conversations with persons from regions other than his own. It is not expected, however, that the standard dialect will replace for all time and for all occasions the dialect the individual learned at home. He retains his local dialect and uses it when he goes back to his home community, switching from one language track to the other as he moves from scene to scene. This two-track versatility in language usage seems to be characteristic of most societies, especially the older ones. It is unfortunate that the possibility of achieving such versatility has been given so little systematic attention in the United States. To the traditional teacher in America, any and all nonstandard utterances have seemed like evil tendencies, to be stamped out with Calvinistic zeal.

In earlier times, this may have been because so many teachers in American public schools were themselves members of immigrant families, to whom the learning of English had meant an unremitting struggle. Frequently, by dint of prodigious effort and some pain, these teachers had cut their ties with families whose "broken English" posed a threat to the teachers' own hard-won status as new members of an American middle class. One can understand how the experience could have accounted for a teacher's inability to tolerate the thought that a nonstandard dialect might have a right to live on in some of the relationships her students held dear.

One of the new things to be said about the teaching of standard English is that some teachers now feel secure enough in their own middle-class status to view the school's language-teaching responsibility in a somewhat different light. Such teachers try not to treat nonstandard forms with abhorrence and disdain. At the same time, they press vigorously toward the goal of developing in every student the *ability* to use the standard dialect in any situation that *requires* its use. When this is the teacher's policy, many students eventually do stop using nonstandard varieties of English altogether. They find themselves moving over to the

211

standard dialect in a widening range of situations as they develop fluency and confidence in handling the standard modes. In time, many are willing to risk speaking standard English with family and friends. But even if a student continues to use the home dialect with his family and peer-group associates, the teacher need not feel that the language program has failed. The test of success is the student's readiness to "turn on" the standard dialect in situations where his standing as a person will be judged in part by his speech.

Instructional Strategy

Sometimes, however, even when the teacher has managed to avoid arousing hostility through her attitude toward the home dialect, results have fallen short of success. A realistic, understanding attitude is not enough: one must also take stock of tactics and techniques.

Just what must be done by anyone who tries to become fluent in standard English when his home dialect is something else? His problem is much like that of someone learning a foreign language in school. Of course there are differences, too. On the debit side, the learning of a second dialect is harder to motivate than the learning of a language entirely foreign and new. And on the other hand, the nonstandard dialect speaker has at least the advantage of knowing far more of the *meanings* of the target language than the foreign learner knows.

Still, despite these differences, the needs of second-dialect students and second-language students are alike in one important respect: in both cases the learner needs to develop a new set of language *habits*. He needs new habits that will enable him to utter appropriate responses instantaneously, whenever the need arises, without having to stop and think.

A student who has to stop and think whether to say "I done it" or "I did it" in a standard English speech situation has not *mastered* the target dialect. A person who has mastered a language or a dialect is no more conscious of making such decisions than he is conscious of deciding how to tie his shoes. The problem for teachers, then, is how to lead students to develop a repertoire of routine habits in connection with the forms and arrangements that make up the grammar of the standard dialect.

Teachers of foreign languages give much thought to this matter of "automatic control over the patterns of the language" as it is often called. Hence some of the foreign language teacher's procedures will suggest useful strategy to teachers of English as a second dialect.

The first element in the foreign language teacher's strategy is *selection*. Even the most skillful teacher cannot give a student a thorough mastery of every individual linguistic feature. The teacher (or the textbook writer) tries to select the smallest possible number of really essential items to be learned. The students concentrate on these, item by item, until they are able to "produce" each essential type of utterance without hesitation. After that, if time remains, attention is turned to finer points, minor patterns, alternate forms of expression. And once the student has

212

been given a substantial start through the development of control over the major patterns of the language, he is able to fill in the remaining gaps on his own, through observation and analogy.

What does this mean for teaching English as a second dialect? It suggests that teachers and students need to concentrate their energies on features that truly do distinguish standard English from non-standard usage. These need to be taught before items that do not conspicuously characterize one dialect or the other—items that are prescribed or proscribed by some grammar books, but that are used in much the same way by speakers of both standard and nonstandard dialects.

Some concrete illustrations may be needed in order to clarify this point. In the list below, certain sentences contain obvious examples of nonstandard usage. Any novelist who put these sentences into the mouths of his bankers, stock brokers, optometrists, head nurses, or airline hostesses would be accused of having a poor ear for talk. Other sentences in the list would seem quite at home in the discourse of educated Americans. Let us sort out the fifteen sentences, noting which ones would sound out of place in the "language of educated ease"—and which ones would not.

1. Cartwright don't want nobody to help him.
2. They give the burglar five dollar, which was all they had.
3. The man die after he had drank the poison.
4. This author explain why everything cost more now.
5. They always trying to get rich, no matter how it hurt others.
6. Their children has went to spend six week with Mary sister.
7. I hope Ed and his family, they going to be more happier now.
8. In my opinion, neither Adams nor Reeves are really qualified.
9. In each of these novels, the hero has to choose between riches, fame and happiness.
10. Somehow this hotel looks different than it did the last time.
11. Both Detroit and Denver have possibilities, but I believe Denver would be the best for our conference.
12. But who could Patty stay with if we went abroad without her?
13. Even though I try not to be overprotective, I can't help but worry every time the children are away from home.
14. Carson is efficient, but Peters is the one I'd rather work with.
15. Don't look so startled, Janice; it's only me!

Every one of the fifteen sentences contains something that violates some "rule" in grammar books still extant in American schools, but that fact is beside the point here. What has significance to the teacher of standard English as a second dialect is that only seven of the fifteen sentences would sound out of place in conversations among educated Americans. Those are sentences one through seven. The patterns represented by those sentences are the ones that need to be given intensive study by students who are trying to master the standard dialect. If the class has not yet learned to use these high-priority features of standard English, it will

213

be pointless to spend valuable time on grammar-book rules which are "violated" by sentences like the last eight above—rules that condemn usages like "different than" and "neither are." It will be futile and foolish to dwell upon rules governing *between* and *among* and *who* and *whom*. It is sad to think how much precious energy is being squandered on such esoteric distinctions in courses for students who need all the help they can get in mastering the basic hallmarks of standard speech.

In essence, then, the strategy of teaching a second dialect (as in teaching a foreign language) amounts to teaching the smallest possible number of vitally significant items — and *teaching each of them hard.*

Teaching versus Scolding

What does a teacher do about a language pattern when she really wants students to learn it? Above all, she gets the students to *use* the pattern, to say sentences illustrating the pattern, again and again, until that mode of speech begins to sound natural to the students themselves. The skillful teacher of a second dialect does not simply remark in class, "Stanley should have said 'I saw it," not 'I seen it.' You remember that, Stanley, don't you? All right then, let's go on."

Yet this is the sort of "teaching" that often takes place, and it has not been of much help to children from nonstandard dialect homes. Year after year they have brushed briefly up against the same features of standard English: from grade to grade, they have been "corrected" for the same "mistakes," and they have been corrected in the same reproachful but off-hand way.

Now to get back to Stanley, a hypothetical child in perhaps the fourth grade. Supposing he has just said, "I seen it on my way to school this morning." Supposing the teacher has murmured, "You *saw* it, Stanley. You know that, don't you?" and Stanley has mumbled, "Yeah."

As a matter of fact, Stanley probably does "know it" — in a way. That is, he has heard something about *I seen* as opposed to *I saw* a number of times before. The trouble is, no one has ever made him settle down on this bit of the standard dialect long enough to learn to use it. He has never been given a chance to command the form "I saw." Naturally, then, even in situations where he would be willing to use standard English — if only to mollify the teacher — that form is just not *in* him to be summoned up.

If the teacher wants Stanley to focus on this bit of language, the very least she can do is ask him to repeat the sentence after her: "I saw it on my way to school this morning." (And she waits while Stanley repeats the sentence.)

If several of the students share Stanley's problem, and she wants the class to master this use of *saw*, something like this has to take place:

TEACHER: Let's practice using *saw* in some standard English sentences. Let's start by saying Stanley's sentence: I saw it on my way to school this morning. Class!

CLASS: (in unison): I saw it on my way to school this morning.
TEACHER: (to Thomas): Thomas, *when* did Stanley see it? Use *saw* in your answer.
THOMAS: He saw it on his way to school this morning.
TEACHER: Right! Gloria, *who* saw it on his way to school? Use *saw* in your answer.
GLORIA: *Stanley* saw it.
TEACHER: Yes! Now let's all mention things we saw on our way to school this morning. *I* saw a fire engine. What about you, Paul?
PAUL: I saw a garbage truck on my way to school.
TEACHER: Good! Laura, tell us what Paul saw, and then tell us something *you* saw.
LAURA: Paul saw a garbage truck on his way to school. I saw a . . . I saw a black kitten in front of the supermarket.
TEACHER: Fine! Anthony, what did Laura see?
ANTHONY: She seen . . .
TEACHER: She *saw*. Please say, "She saw . . ."
ANTHONY: She saw a kitten.
TEACHER: Yes. And what did *you* see?
ANTHONY: I seen . . . I *saw* a . . . a motorcycle.
TEACHER: Good. Class, what did Anthony say he saw? Use *saw* in your answer.
CLASS: He saw a motorcycle.
TEACHER: Right! Now, then, let's play the game in a different way. Did anyone see a taxi or a jeep on the way to school today? Gregory, did you see a taxi or a jeep?
GREGORY: I didn't see a jeep, but I saw a taxi.
TEACHER: Good. Daphne, did you see any dogs or horses?
DAPHNE: I seen — *saw* some dogs, but I didn't see no horses.
TEACHER: I didn't see *any* horses. That's the standard English way to say it. Say: "I didn't see any horses."
DAPHNE: I didn't see any horses.
TEACHER: Fine! George, what did Daphne see, and what didn't she see?
GEORGE: She . . . she . . . (silence)
TEACHER: Daphne, tell George what you saw and what you didn't see.
DAPHNE: I saw some dogs, but I didn't see no . . . I didn't see *any* horses.
TEACHER: Good for you, Daphne! You did it the standard English way without any help. Say it again.
DAPHNE: I saw some dogs, but I didn't see any horses.
TEACHER: Fine! George, what did she tell us?
GEORGE: She saw some dogs, but she didn't see any horses.

(And so on, with contributions from all who need to gain command over this feature of the standard dialect. The last to speak is Stanley, who is asked to say what various classmates saw on their way to school.)

215

This is the kind of drill—disguised as a conversation—that has become important in foreign language teaching. Its aim is to make a language pattern begin to sound natural, feel right, through repeated uses of the pattern in sentences that have some interest and meaning for the speaker and his listeners. It belongs, in fact, to the species of drill that is often called "pattern practice" or "substitution practice." For several years it has been widely used in courses for students of English as a Foreign Language (or Second Language); and it is used when people teach foreign languages along "audio-lingual" lines today.

True, it takes time to teach patterns of speech in this way. The easier way is merely to mention the student's "error"—or to give him a workbook exercise that he can do at home—though he probably won't. But to deal thus with a language habit is not to deal with it at all. Next year Stanley and the rest will still be using the same nonstandard forms on occasions that call for the standard dialect, and next year's teacher will still deplore and nag, rather than teach. True, too, the list of items to be learned is long (particularly if the student's home dialect differs greatly from the standard), but the number of really crucial items is finite: these *could* be mastered during the many years English teachers are given for the task. In no other subject do teachers in all grades try to work on everything at once. Why can't English teachers divide up the list of linguistic habits to be learned? If the fourth-grade teacher could make her students fluent with regard to a specified few of the items on the list, the fifth-grade teacher could go on from there, and so on up through the grades.[5]

Some Sources of Help

As yet little has been written about the possibilities of this kind of "fluency practice" for students of standard English as a second dialect, but three helpful studies will be mentioned here. One is Majorie Barrow's *Good English Through Practice* (1956), which shows how to use a set of cleverly devised games for getting junior-high-school students to use many troublesome standard English forms over and over again while taking part in entertaining, creative language activities.

A second helpful text is Ruth Golden's *Improving Patterns of Language Usage* (1960), in which the problems and attitudes of students learning the standard dialect are analyzed and many language-learning activities are suggested, including games, stories and role-playing skits.

There is irony in the fact that both *Good English Through Practice* and *Improving Patterns of Language Usage* perpetuate in their titles the

---

[5] Below grade four, the teacher's most essential task is to help children learn how to read and write the English they already know. They need to learn how letters and combinations of letters are used for representing sounds and combinations of sounds that are already familiar. They need to hear stories of the sort the children of educated Americans hear their parents read aloud. They need games that call their attention to rhymes, games that make them notice words. Above all they need to be listened to, and they need help in learning to use their minds. Activities directed toward these ends should be central to the language curriculum for grades one through three.

older, unhelpful policy of condemning nonstandard dialects as intrinsically "worse" than the standard dialect and needing to be "improved." Fortunately, however, the attitudes reflected in the texts themselves are more harmonious with the spirit of modern courses in this field.

A third, and particularly fruitful, source of help for teachers is San-su C. Lin's report (1965) on a three-year research project financed by the U.S. Office of Education, in which Dr. Lin and her associates experimented with pattern-practice techniques as a means of helping students in South Carolina master standard English.

The Claflin Project

The setting for the Lin program was Claflin College, a small, church-supported school serving mainly Southern Negroes from rural communities. The speech of many freshmen at Claflin included patterns like these: *three apple; nine childrens; I arrive here last week; Claflin have a new dormitory; They looks after theirselves; He don't want nothing; She's more prettier; She sang beautiful; I had wrote it; My uncle, he work in Richmond.* It was evident that the efforts of students and staff would need to be concentrated upon the mastery of basic grammar patterns distinguishing the standard dialect (in writing and in speech) from nonstandard varieties. Consequently, problems of pronunciation were not permitted to occupy the center of attention in the Claflin project. However a few pronunciation problems (such as difficulties in adding the -s and -ed endings) did come within the scope of the project because these interfered with the mastery of grammatical forms.

Early in 1961, when the Claflin Project was conceived, there were few guidelines for teachers of a second dialect. Dr. Lin's 1965 report tells an absorbing story of trials, false starts, frustrations, accomplishments, and—above all—cumulative learnings on the part of both students and staff. The report tells of questions to which answers were found. First there was the need to understand why the problem existed:

What makes a college freshman from a culturally deprived Negro community persist in the use of a nonstandard dialect in spite of many years of English instruction through high school and elementary school? The dialect, no matter how other people may judge it, has evidently proved socially and psychologically satisfactory to the individual who uses it. It is the language of his family—a symbol of security and love. It is the language of his initiation into life—from the dawn of awareness through successive steps in which he learned to adjust to different groups and to establish rapport with the world around him. (Lin, 1965, p. 2)

Next came the questions of approach, growing out of the staff's analysis of the human aspects of the problem. Certain fundamentals had to be established.

First of all, the teacher must become aware, and help the student become aware, of the infinite variations that exist in the

217

many dialects of American English, both regional and social. Both teacher and student must also understand the social implications of these variations. If any change is desirable, the decision to change must come from the individual himself. The teacher, with sympathetic understanding, can help speed the process of change by supplying the necessary methods and materials. (Lin, 1965, p. 3)

In their search for procedures that could help these students achieve proficiency in the use of standard English, the Claflin staff turned to the field of foreign language teaching, particularly to the teaching of English as a foreign language, in which Dr. Lin had had training and experience. As the report points out:

> . . . there has been little recognition among English teachers of the need for a program basically different from the English program catering to those who speak standard English at home. Not only are these linguistically different young people more sensitive to intolerance and tactless criticism, they also differ from standard speakers in being faced with the task of establishing a new set of language habits. In other words, if they are learning a second language to be added to their indigenous dialect, they must be taught with methods and procedures that are used in learning a second language. (Lin, 1965, p. 5)

However, after a few weeks' experience with the "repeat-after-me" type of practice material found in most language-learning laboratories, the Claflin staff realized that major adaptations had to be made, since English was, after all, not a foreign language to these American students. Quite apart from the psychological resistance to having one's national language treated like a foreign tongue, there were difficulties arising from the fact that standard English and a nonstandard dialect of English are so closely related that "the socially significant differences may be overshadowed by the similarities and fail to present a real challenge to the students (Lin, 1965, p. 8). Moreover, much as the students themselves wished to acquire skill in using standard English, they naturally resented having their entire freshman English course devoted to drill on grammar patterns: They wanted to learn about literature, composition, stylistics, and other matters that they considered appropriate to a college course.

Thus the Claflin staff was faced with the task of devising procedures and materials that would give the students the kind and amount of drill they needed for mastery of the standard patterns, while at the same time satisfying the students' natural desire for "college level" instruction. Since much this same task is faced everywhere by teachers whose students are already fluent in some variety of English, Dr. Lin's report on solutions to the problem offers much practical advice. The Claflin staff learned to avoid the use of example sentences and drill sentences that merely illustrated a grammar pattern without offering information or ideas. They learned to construct practice exercises that gave these students information about science, etiquette and job-hunting techniques. They learned to design drills that increased a student's vocabulary, or improved his spelling and punctuation, while simultaneously strengthening his control over standard grammar forms.

For example, noting that the students needed to acquire the habit of using the -s ending for the third person singular form of verbs, the staff prepared an exercise which required each student to use third-person singular forms again and again while discussing "college level" vocabulary words that he knew he needed to learn to pronounce and spell.

The exercise was conducted about as follows: The teacher mentioned a polysyllabic word, such as *curriculum*. A student was then directed to analyze the word, using this sequence of sentences: "The word *curriculum* begins with the letter c. It ends with the letter m. It contains two r's. It has four syllables. The accent falls on the second syllable." A second student would then analyze another word: "The word *accommodation* begins with the latter a. It ends with the letter n. It contains two c's and two m's. It has five syllables. The accent falls on the fourth syllable."

The exercise would continue in the same way, until most members of the class had had an opportunity to construct sentences in this mold, each sentence containing at least one word with an -s ending. If any student said, "It *end* with . . . ," or "The accent *fall* . . ." he was asked to repeat the sentence, using the -s ending appropriately. In this way, for the first time, the -s ending began to "sound natural" and "feel right" to these students, because they had said and heard it over and over again. Moreover, they had accepted the drill as being appropriate to their level of educational maturity because it sounded like "college English."

The Art of Conducting Meaningful Drills

Exercises of this sort are not nearly as easy to construct as they may seem. First the teacher must know precisely what grammatical point it is that the students need to have illustrated and repeated again and again; and then the teacher must elicit many repetitions of the pattern from the students in the course of a discussion that is more than a mechanical drill.

In the Claflin project, the staff realized that just one drill on the -s ending would not be enough, and other drills were invented. On one occasion the class discussed reading techniques, within the framework of "Five Things a Good Reader Does." Each student offered his own five sentences, based on a discussion of the reading. Sentences included:

A good reader keeps his mind on his work.
A good reader looks for answers to certain questions in his mind.
A good reader distinguishes between main ideas and details.
A good reader summarizes the writer's ideas from time to time.

(Note that this exercise would have lost its effectiveness so far as practice on the third-person -s ending was concerned if the students had

219

been permitted to alternate between "a good reader" and "good readers." What they needed was to say and to hear a singular subject plus the -s form of the verb again and again, in order to forge a link between the idea of a singular subject and the -s form of the verb.)

In similar fashion, the Claflin project students practiced the -ed ending for verbs within the context of a discussion of a chapel program, in which, they said, "The president introduced the guest speaker. The speaker talked for twenty minutes. He described . . . and, explained that . . ., etc." Once again the strategy called for an oral account, with contributions from all members of the class, carefully elicited by the teacher so as to ensure many repetitions of the standard English form (in this case, the -ed ending) over which the students needed to develop control.

Role Playing

In addition to these "structured discussions" or "fluency drills," the Claflin staff experimented with skits and other role-playing activities. The most successful skits were those that simulated life situations in which standard English would obviously be the appropriate dialect to use. Some dialogues illustrated forms of etiquette relevant to job interviews, employer-secretary conferences, and the like. After the students had taken part in skits written by the project staff, the students themselves — working in small groups — wrote a number of role-playing exercises. Each student practiced his part with the aid of a taped standard English recording of it in the language laboratory. The best skit in each class was chosen for performance in a chapel program. The students found the experience interesting and helpful: for some, speech patterns changed dramatically as a result.

Although the Claflin project extended from 1961 to 1964, a different freshman class participated during each of the three years. Thus no student was enrolled in the program for more than one academic year. As the final report pointed out, it would be wrong to claim that "any method can, in nine months, give the student a full command of the standard dialect when it is psychologically and socially difficult for him to use anything but the nonstandard dialect in his daily life, even on a college campus."

Even so, some very encouraging results emerged. From the taped interviews which formed part of the evaluation data, it was evident that the students had become more self-confident and more determined to develop dialectal versatility. Their enunciation had become clearer, they found it easier to communicate, and they appeared more ready to correct themselves after using nonstandard forms. On the locally prepared grammar test, the project students proved to be more successful than the control group in identifying nonstandard patterns and "translating" them into standard modes. In addition to items that were indisputably nonstandard, the test also included items like "Everyone was supposed to bring their lunch," and "This color is different than that" — usages decried by grammar books but often heard in the speech of educated persons. Since such items had been given little attention in the experimental program, most of them were "missed" by project students on the final test. However, in terms of the conspicuous hallmarks of standard English (as contrasted with the nonstandard dialect), the experimental students demonstrated significant improvement.

Reading and Writing

Nor were the gains at Claflin limited to matters of speech and social dialect. Somewhat to the surprise of the staff, scores on the Cooperative English Test revealed that the experimental group made greater gains in *reading* after a year of grammar pattern practice than did the members of the control group (who had engaged in free conversation in place of the structured grammar drills). What made this result the more striking was that the control group (the group not employing the experimental techniques) had given more attention to reading, as such, and to discussions of the material read. The Lin report points out that apparently

> . . . the use of pattern practice techniques can sharpen students' awareness of structural matters in such a way as to improve their comprehension of material that they read. After a year of working systematically and intensively with various patterns of English, the experimental students were apparently better equipped to read passages which required an alert attention to structural signals. (Lin, 1965, p. 142)

Another skill which benefited from the application of second-language teaching techniques in the Claflin projects was *writing*. At the end of the second year of the program, the director reported (Lin, 1963) that the compositions written by students in the project were "not only more free of errors, but more purposeful and more interesting" than any she had previously read during seven years' experience at the same institution.

Above all, what has been proved by the Claflin project (and by similar programs) is that speakers of nonstandard dialects can make significant progress toward the mastery of standard English, even in a program of very short duration. (It should be remembered that no Claflin student was involved in the project for more than nine months.) How much could be accomplished if teachers at all levels of the instructional ladder were to apply the lessons learned from such experiments!

In Summary

Fortunately, more and more teachers are coming to realize that attitudes, approaches, and procedures germane to the teaching of foreign languages have relevance to the teaching of standard English as a second dialect. More and more teachers are defining the target language as "the kind of English habitually spoken by most of the educated members of the American speech community." Guided by this definition, classes for nonstandard speakers are concentrating upon language usages which indisputably characterize "the language of educated ease." Teachers are thus freeing class time for practice upon these crucial features of the target dialect by passing lightly over esoteric distinctions that carry little or no weight outside some grammar textbooks.

In their classrooms, these teachers guard against treating the students' home dialect as something faulty, flawed, and inferior. They are willing to grant that the home dialect may even be the "right" one for a student to use in some interpersonal relationships deeply important to him. At the same time, they help their students achieve fluency in standard English by patiently guiding the class through practice exercises based on second-language teaching techniques, but adapted to second-dialect purposes with artistry and tact.

In programs conducted along these lines, there is much hope for students striving to command the dialect that is required for advancement in our national life—for entering fully into American affairs, through the front door.

References

Allen, Robert L.; Virginia F. Allen and Margaret Shute. *English Sounds and Their Spellings*. New York: Thomas Y. Crowell Company, 1966.

Bailey, Beryl. *Brown-Tougaloo Language Project: Preliminary Report on Syntax*. Mimeographed, 1966.

Barrows, Marjorie Westcott. *Good English Through Practice*. New York: Holt, Rinehart, Winston, 1956.

Dacanay, Fe. *Techniques and Procedures of Second Language Teaching*. Quezon City, Philippines: Phoenix Publishing Company, 1960.

Davis, Alva L. "Communication Barriers to the Culturally Deprived." U.S. Office of Education Cooperative Research Project 2107, 1965.

———, "English for Foreigner and Native." *College English*, 26 (January 1965), 273–276.

Evans, Bergen and Cornelia Evans, *A Dictionary of Contemporary Usage*. New York: Random House, 1957.

Fries, Charles Carpenter. *American English Grammar*. New York: Appleton-Century-Crofts, 1940.

Gleason, H. A. *Linguistics and English Grammar*. New York: Holt, Rinehart and Winston, Inc., 1965.

Golden, Ruth I. *Effectiveness of Instructional Tapes for Changing Regional Dialects*. Detroit, Mich.: Board of Education, 1962.

———. *Improving Patterns of Language Usage*. Detroit: Wayne State University Press, 1960.

Jewett, Arno (ed.). *Improving English Skills of Culturally Different Youth in Large Cities*. Washington: U.S. Office of Education, 1962.

Joos, Martin. "Language and the School Child," *Word Study*, 7 (December 1964).

Kitchin, Aileen T., *et al. Readers Digest Readings.* Books I–VI. Pleasantville, N.Y.: Readers Digest Services, 1964.

Laird, Charlton and Robert M. Gorrell. *English as Language: Background, Development, Usage.* New York: Harcourt, Brace and World, Inc., 1961.

Lin, San-su C. *Pattern Practice in the Teaching of Standard English to Students with a Nonstandard Dialect.* New York: Teachers College Press, Columbia University, 1965.

————. "An Experiment in Changing Dialect Patterns: The Claflin Project," *College English* (May 1963, 644–647.)

Musgrave, Marianne E. "Teaching English as a Foreign Language to Students with Substandard Dialects." *CLA Journal*, 7 (September 1963), 84–91.

National Council of Teachers of English, *Basic Issues in the Teaching of English.* Champaign, Ill.: National Council of Teachers of English, 1959.

————. *On Teaching English to Speakers of Other Languages.* Books I & II. Champaign, Ill.: National Council of Teachers of English, 1964, 1965.

O'Connor, Patricia. *Modern Foreign Languages in High School.* Washington: U.S. Government Printing Office, 1961.

Praninskas, Jean. *Rapid Review of English Grammar.* Englewood Cliffs, N. J.: Prentice-Hall, Inc. 1961.

Roberts, Paul. *Understanding Grammar.* New York: Harper and Row, 1954.

Shuy, Roger W. (ed.). *Social Dialects and Language Learning.* Champaign, Ill.: National Council of Teachers of English, 1964.

Smith, Alfred G. (ed.). *Communication and Culture: Readings in the Codes of Human Interaction.* New York: Holt, Rinehart and Winston, 1966.

Stack, Edward M. *The Language Laboratory and Modern Language Teaching.* New York: Oxford University Press, 1960.

Stewart, William A. (ed.). *Non-Standard Speech and the Teaching of English.* Washington: Center for Applied Linguistics, 1964.

Stone, George Winchester, Jr. (ed.). *Issues, Problems and Approaches in the Teaching of English.* New York: Holt, Rinehart and Winston, 1961.

Suloway, Irwin J. and Michael Shugrue. *Promising Practices in the Teaching of English.* Champaign, Ill.: National Council of Teachers of English, 1963.

United States Information Agency. *Oral English: Planning and Conducting Conversation Classes and Discussion Groups.* Washington, D.C.: United States Information Agency Information Center Service, 1966.

Whitten, Mary E. *Creative Pattern Practice: A New Approach to Writing.* New York: Harcourt, Brace and World, Inc., 1966.

Elizabeth Eddy has borrowed concepts from anthropology to report on the beginning teacher's induction into the inner-city school. Basing her analysis on what anthropologists call "induction theory," Dr. Eddy examines beginning teachers' experiences. She points out that for 16 or more years, the beginning teacher, as pupil, has been in formal schooling situations where he can observe and absorb the behavior of teachers. This lengthy socialization process is seldom taken into account in terms of the important role it plays in formulating the future teacher's beliefs about teaching, about educational policies and practices, and about valid interpersonal relationships to the young. At the end of this period, the young teacher participates in what Dr. Eddy calls "a ceremonial rite of passage known as student teaching." It is during this transitional period that the preservice teacher maps out new relationships that he may eventually assume as a full-fledged teacher. However, while student teaching provides a means for a ritual expression and leads to changes in human relationships, the experience is really only a prelude to the serious induction of the teacher when he faces his first class on his own as a beginning professional.

THE BEGINNING TEACHER'S INDUCTION INTO THE INNER-CITY SCHOOL

Elizabeth Eddy

The new teacher has problems under any circumstances, but in the inner-city school, problems multiply because of the clash between the school's attitudes toward academic achievement and discipline and the needs of the pupils. Youngsters often are in process of urbanization and find it hard to adapt to the school's demands. At the same time, the student-teaching experience tends to be in a setting where the students' values and orientation echo those of the student teachers.

The formal administration-conducted orientation sessions before school opens strike Dr. Eddy as informal teacher induction. The sessions center around the sharing and exchange of materials and plans, plus advice on what supervisors look for when they observe the teacher's class. In addition, the more experienced teachers mull over the handling of discipline problems. Discipline (whose model is rigid propriety) places a severe psychological strain on the new teacher, especially since he usually draws a lower-ability or more difficult class.

Dr. Eddy recommends major changes both in the preparation of teachers for inner-city schools and in the organization of the schools themselves to equip the beginners to understand their role vis-á-vis *their pupils. The teacher education process also must not overlook the social context in which the formal education of the child takes place. This context includes the family and the community and is the total environment in which personal attributes flower as a result of human interaction. Thus Dr. Eddy is arguing for changes not only in the teacher training program but in the "traditional patterns of interaction between those within the schools and between them and the communities they serve." If teachers are to be more than bureaucratic functionaries, they need the insight and the social-psychological support for carrying on the essential task.*

THE BEGINNING TEACHER'S INDUCTION INTO THE INNER-CITY SCHOOL

Elizabeth M. Eddy*

The recent years have witnessed a growing concern with the preparation of teachers for schools located in the slum neighborhood. Popular books such as *The Blackboard Jungle, Up the Down Staircase,* and *The Schoolchildren* have called nationwide attention to the deterioration of teacher-pupil relationships in these schools.[1] The less popular but more careful analyses by scholars have begun to lay a foundation for theoretical speculations and action proposals which attempt to remedy the situation. While the interest in the problem is perhaps at an all-time high, there has been very little empirical study of beginning teachers in these schools, nor has there been much attempt to formulate a theoretical framework which would enable both scholars and practitioners to look at more than the middle-class attributes of teachers, the lower-class attributes of children, and the attributes of what are perceived as more desirable educational techniques and practices.

In this paper, an attempt is made to provide a different orientation to our understanding of beginning teachers' interaction with their pupils from slum neighborhoods from that provided by an approach which is focused solely on attributes. Essentially this theoretical position is derived from what anthropologists refer to as induction theory. Following a brief presentation of the theory itself, its application to the problem under discussion will be illustrated by referring to data collected in a study of beginning teachers' experiences in inner-city schools in a large Northern city and to data that were not collected in this study but are nevertheless important additional aspects that need to be taken into account in future studies of this kind.[2]

*The author wishes to express appreciation to Dr. Solon T. Kimball for his comments and suggestions on an earlier draft of this paper.

[1] Evan Hunter, **The Blackboard Jungle,** New York: Simon and Schuster, 1954; Bel Kaufman, **Up the Down Staircase,** Englewood Cliffs, N.J.: Prentice-Hall, 1964; Mary Frances Greene and Orletta Ryan, **The Schoolchildren: Growing Up in the Slums,** New York: Pantheon Books, 1965.

[2] The author is presently engaged in the analysis of data gathered from twenty-two elementary and junior-high-school teachers whose first teaching experiences were in inner-city schools. These data were collected as a part of activities supported by the Office of Juvenile Delinquency and Youth Development. They were gathered on

Induction Theory

Anthropologists and others are indebted to the work of Gennep, a French scholar writing in the early 1900's, for an analysis of ritual observances that occur at critical points in the lives of individuals.[3] Referring to these as "rites of passage," Gennep noted that ceremonies associated with birth, becoming an adult in a society, marriage, and death provided a vehicle for the ritual expression of the movements of a person from one status or position to another within a society and the concomitant changes in relationships with others that this entailed. In his comparative cross-cultural analysis of these types of rites, Gennep discovered that they were composed of three components: separation, transition, and incorporation.

The major aspect of the ritual concerned with separation is that in which there is a symbolic acting out of an individual's separation from former associates. In this phase, there is a marked reduction or even cessation of interaction between the individual and the groups with which he has been interacting heretofore. For example, the act of a father giving his daughter away in a wedding ceremony is a ritual expression of her decreased interaction within her own family as a result of engagement and marriage.

During the transition phase of ritual observance, the individual passing through a crisis is removed from former relationships with others, but he is not yet part of the new group into which he is going to move, nor has he returned to his former associates in his new status. At this time, the individual acts out the new relationships he is to assume and goes

---

a weekly basis during the first semester of teaching. Each teacher was asked to respond individually to a series of questions about such matters as the most important thing that had happened during the week, their most successful and least successful lessons, their most difficult and least difficult children, their interaction with administrators, specialists, teachers, and so on.

Since analysis of the data is still in progress, a detailed report of it cannot be given here. The reader should understand, however, that in a general way these data constitute the background material upon which this paper is based. More than half of the teachers had done student teaching or substitute teaching in the same schools to which they were assigned for their first year, and nearly all of the teachers had had at least some experience in working with children from slum areas prior to the first year of teaching. All of the teachers were assigned to classes designated as "slow," although some of the junior-high-school teachers taught one or more sections composed of "average" children. After the first year of teaching, only two of the teachers stopped teaching in inner-city schools because of unsatisfactory experiences. However, an additional six teachers left inner-city schools as a result of marriage and moving to new communities and/or pregnancy. Among elementary teachers remaining in inner-city schools, the majority taught children who were on grade level or more nearly on it than those they taught during the

The junior-high-school teachers taught more classes in their subject field and were also more apt to be assigned to somewhat "better" classes in the second year.

[3] This work was recently published, in a new edition, by the University of Chicago Press (Gennep, 1960). For further discussion of rites of passage, see Chapple and Coon (1942, pp. 484–506).

through a period of learning about his new role. To cite the wedding ceremony again, it is the period during which the couple pledge their troth to each other and repeat the mutual responsibilities involved in marriage.

The third stage, the period of incorporation, involves a ceremonial acting out in which the person begins to interact again with the members of his community, but in his new position. Often he is actually reintroduced to his former community, as when the officiating clergyman pronounces a couple man and wife and acts on behalf of both the church and the state in officially announcing the couple as married and having a new position in society and a changed relationship with others.

From the insights of Gennep and others who have subsequently con-concerned themselves with rites of passage, it is clear that they have a profound meaning in terms of individual and social identification. Of the three phases, that of transition is the time most laden with insecurity and anxiety for the individual. Separated from former meaningful relationships, these are the moments, weeks, months or even years when the individual is most in danger of losing all significant relations as a result of his own actions or that of others. Consider, for example, the loss of individual and social identity for the bride who is left at the altar, or for the bridegroom who leaves her there.

To successfully pass through a period of transition after separation from others, a person must be incorporated by others into his new group. In primitive societies, this often meant a reincorporation into a community from whence one came but with a change of status, activities, and often associates. In modern societies, it would appear that it increasingly means an incorporation by others who are far removed from former family, friends, and associates. The young couple who, after marriage and honeymoon, shortly leave to establish their family in the husband's new work location furnish but one illustration of the greater complexity of incorporat ing individuals into society than that found in primitive societies or even small town America. It is important also to note that while persons may struggle for individual and social identification, there must be others who reach out and accept them into the new groups if they are to be incorporated into these groups.

While historically most rites of passage have been associated with individual crises as they affect the individual's relationships with the family, similar rites occur when individuals are inducted into religious groups, fraternal organizations, political offices, or occupational groups. In the remainder of this paper, consideration will be given to the induction of teachers into their occupational group in the slum neighborhood school. The theoretical perspective given above will be used to provide an understanding of these teachers' transition from roles as students in the educational system into new roles as adult workers who are to teach others. First, however, brief consideration will be given to one aspect of the teacher training program as background for what will follow.

Separation from the Student Role

Like teachers elsewhere, beginning teachers in schools primarily attended by the children of the urban poor have spent a large portion of their lives in school. This time has been spent in a subordinate role as a pupil. First, there have been the elementary and high-school years, the selection for the academic classes, and the preparation for the college years. More recently, there have been college classes, the choice to prepare for teaching, and, together with courses in other fields, the formal training in the specialized education courses designed to prepare teachers in training to remain within the school system rather than leaving it, as will their peers who pursue other occupations.

Throughout the sixteen or more years of formal schooling, teachers in training have extensively observed and interacted with those now occupying positions to which they aspire. They have had ample opportunity to observe how teachers actually act, talk, and think. In some of our large cities, the majority who prepare to teach today's generation of children are taught by teachers of teachers who, more often than not, have themselves attended the city's schools and are currently capping a long successful career in the city school system by teaching those who will now take their places at the lower rungs of the educational hierarchy. For many in the urban educational structure, for whom teaching is becoming or has been the means of upward social mobility into the middle class, the extended ties of family and kin, inherited from a lower social class level, make geographical relocation undesirable so that the way the local school system is operated becomes the only known and experienced way to do things. Local educational folklore and tradition is passed from one generation to the next. The educational system becomes the domain of those who are local in outlook rather than cosmopolitan, and invasion by outsiders is guarded against.

The long socialization of teachers into their role makes the preparation of teachers unique in length and extent in comparison with the preparation for other occupations. Although this silent, hidden dimension of the teacher-training process is seldom recognized, there can be little doubt that it plays an important role in the formulation and crystallization of the student's beliefs about educational policies and practices and provides a deep source for the perpetuation of conservative traditional approaches to the training of the young, even though these may no longer be functional in the modern world.

As a culmination of both the informal induction of the student into the teaching role and the formal induction provided by academic courses in education and other subjects, the student participates in a ceremonial rite of passage known as student teaching. The function of this ceremonial activity is to facilitate the transition of students from those who think and act like students into those who think and act like teachers. Student teaching is a cooperative venture, undertaken by the teacher-training institution and conveniently located school systems. The students are physically separated from their associates in the training institution and placed in a particular school or schools, usually on a part-time basis. There they work under the direction of one or more cooperating teachers, with occasional supervisory visits and observations from a faculty member in the training institution. During the period of student teaching, students are usually also completing course work requirements for their degree.

During this transitional period of student teaching, the students act out the new relationships which they are eventually to assume as teachers. Clerical work, lesson planning, practice teaching, classroom management, and other tasks which teachers perform may be assigned to them in varying degrees. Observations of the students' teaching performance are made, written evaluations of them are recorded, and suggestions for improvement of teaching techniques are given to them in supervisory conferences. Ideally, and nearly always, the students do well enough so that the teaching-training institution officially states that they are prepared to teach, thereby incorporating them into the occupation of teaching and declaring publicly their new status in the educational community.

It is important to note that while the student teaching experience, together with the graduation ceremony, serves to separate the teachers from a role as students (at least until they return for graduate study), it does not serve to separate them from a role as subordinates. While they now have a position superior to that of students, they are only one status position above the student level and are subject to supervision by a variety of supervisory personnel. The successful completion of student teaching and the prerequisite course work results in the former students' being claimed as teachers by the faculty who has trained them, but they must now undergo a probationary period before final licensing by the state and tenure are awarded.

Although they are prepared to work, they may not accept a job, though frequently the student teaching experience, especially in areas where teacher turnover is high, serves to introduce them to school personnel who offer them one.[4] In conclusion, it may be said that while student teaching has provided a means for the ritual expression of the movement of individuals from their position as students to their new position as teachers, and while the changes in human relationships have been symbolically acted out, this is but a prelude to the more prolonged induction of teachers that is to occur when they return to the school system and teach their first class.

---

[4] In some inner-city areas, an attempt is being made to have students do their student teaching in schools populated by a large number of the children of the urban poor and, by special arrangements with the Board of Education, to allow them to remain there as teachers if they so desire (Haubrich, 1963).

Induction into the Teaching Role

When beginning teachers embark upon their teaching careers in their first formal teaching positions, several different groups attempt to incorporate them into their new role and to claim them as professional teachers. Among these are groups composed of school administrators, fellow teachers, and pupils. Located at different points in the social system of the school, one or more of these groups may be in conflict with each other, may fully or partially incorporate the new teacher, or may reject the new teacher entirely.

In the inner-city school, special problems occur as a result of the school's orientation towards norms of scholastic achievement, academic progress, and pupil behavior that may not be congruent with the needs of many pupils who are still in the process of urbanization and who may be unfamiliar or unable to cope with the demands of the school as these are currently presented.[5] In addition, the professional training of administrators and teachers has usually prepared them primarily for the teaching of pupils who respond sufficiently well to the formal educational system to do at least average work and to behave in ways acceptable to the school. Seldom, however, has the formal training of teachers and other staff in the inner-city school prepared them for a student population comprised for the most part of pupils who have a history of school failure or underachievement and, in some instances, a history of disruptive classroom behavior. As a consequence, the successful induction of teachers into these schools is especially difficult and often does not occur at all. An examination in detail of some of the salient features of beginning teachers' induction into inner-city schools will serve to elaborate the special difficulties now encountered by those who begin their teaching in these schools. It will also serve to suggest needed changes if teachers are to be fully claimed as teachers in these schools. In the discussion to follow, attention will be given (1) to the formal induction of the beginning teacher on the part of school administrators and (2) to the informal induction of the teacher on the part of other teachers and students.

The Formal Administrative Induction

The formal induction of beginning teachers into the inner-city school begins with an orientation conference lasting for a period of several days. During most of this time, the new teachers meet together with school administrators and specialists. On the last day or two, those who have taught in the school in previous years join the new teachers for a series of formal meetings. Held during the week prior to the opening of school, the

---

[5] A description of some of the problems presented to inner-city school pupils by the present organizational structure of schools in slum areas is presented in Elizabeth M. Eddy, **Walk the White Line: A Profile of Urban Education,** Doubleday Anchor Series (1967).

orientation conference is a ritual observance of the transitional stage that the new teachers are in now that they are graduates of the teacher-training institution but not yet incorporated into the group of persons comprising the school.

During orientation, the new teachers undergo a period of learning about their new role and acting out the appropriate relationships with others that it entails. A detailed description of a typical orientation from a junior-high-school teacher licensed in social studies will provide illustrative material as background for a greater understanding of formal induction procedures. Though licensed to teach social studies, this teacher had accepted her job in June with the understanding that she would be teaching health education.[6]

At the first formal meeting on Wednesday, I found out that I would be teaching English and not Health Education. At the time I was delighted because I felt that English would be at least a classroom situation, and I would have fewer problems with the discipline in an English classroom than I would in gym where a hundred people would be staring at me at once.

The first formal meeting was an orientation conference where the principal addressed us and introduced the new staff members to each other and the four assistant principals. . . . The new teachers' orientation manual was distributed where a fictitious Miss Smith was featured. She was wondering about whether she would be able to cope with the school and the classes and what she should do now and what she should do next. I found it somewhat helpful in setting up routines, but reading something is easier than putting it into practice.

The teacher class programs were distributed, and I found out the classes I would be teaching. . . . We then went on a tour of the building. I was in Mr. Silver's group, and we picked up our keys in the main office and went up to our classrooms for a break. We were then instructed by the school secretary on punching in and out, where our mail boxes would be and where our keys would be. We were told to phone in at 7:20 in the morning if we were going to be absent and to give all personal data forms about employment to the head secretary.

At 11:00, we came downstairs again and had a lecture from Mr. Silver (an assistant principal) on building discipline and on disciplinary procedures. We were told that we could use the dean, if necessary, or a neighboring teacher to control the class, but we would be better off if we tried to gain control of a class ourselves and did not rely on outside sources. . . .

---

[6]Quotations from beginning teachers that occur in this paper have been edited so as to preserve the anonymity of all persons concerned.

At 1:00 we came back to school, and Mr. Lanzo (an assistant principal) and the school custodian gave us a lecture on precautions against fire. From there we went to pick up our basic supplies, which were given to us in a wastepaper basket by Mr. Silver. We returned to our classrooms to check pupil records against the roll book, make out the section sheet which goes to all classes and a conduct book which is to be kept on each person in the class to keep record of their charges and commendations throughout the day, our attendance card and some papers to put up, and start decorating our room.

The second day of orientation, we came in again at 9:00. . . . At 9:00, we were discussing schoolwide routines, with Mr. Silver doing the talking. He talked about hall passing, which staircases were up, which were down, the line of march, entrances and dismissals, the procedures to be used, the duties of teachers other than classroom such as patrolling, reception committee, auditorium duty, and meeting classes on time. We discussed fire drills and assemblies also, the procedures to be used for entering the cafeteria and the assembly, and the staircases and everything to be used during the fire drill.

At 10:00 we went to our classrooms to continue working on the records and setting up our rooms. At 10:45 we had meetings with the different subject supervisors, and since I was teaching English classes and have taught social studies before or at least student-taught it and was more familiar with the curriculum, I went to the English meeting. [Note: This teacher's program included teaching English to three classes and social studies to her official class.] Mrs. White (an assistant principal) and the principal addressed us for a while, telling us that some of us would have English classes more than five periods a week and that some of us would be part of a remedial reading program being conducted by the city now—a crash program. . . . We wouldn't know until next week which classes would be engaged in this special remedial program. At this meeting we were told that we would have to have approximately one grammar lesson a week, approximately one for spelling, two for reading and one for literature. Anything over five periods a week was to be devoted to reading.

In the instructional manual and the orientation schedule, there were five model lesson plans for social studies classes and five for English classes. I found that out of the English lesson plans, since I have a limited knowledge of grammar, I could only use one of them without any further preparation for a class. That was a spelling lesson.

From this meeting we went to another conference where Mr. Johnson (an assistant principal) addressed us, and he continued speaking on what to do before the first day of school, how to equip ourselves to meet with the classes. This is just that we make an outline of the routines that we expect to be followed in our official classes so that we can address them and tell them this when they come in, and it would give us something in front of us to do.

After lunch, we came back and discussed schoolwide routines such as lunch procedures, health and safety procedures. Mr. Lanzo did the talking now, and we were told where to get our supplies and books, the attendance and lateness routines to tell our children. . . . Then from 2:15, we were in our classrooms.

On Friday the full faculty was back, and the principal again addressed us in the auditorium. He welcomed back the old faculty, and he welcomed the new faculty. . . . At that point, the superintendent of schools spoke. . . . And he welcomed all the teachers back to school. . . . We were also given our buddy teachers, the old staff member who would be closest to our rooms. My buddy teacher is Mr. Panetta, and he is right next door. He is a social studies teacher who is now chairman of the math department. He's teaching out of license and has been teaching exactly one year. I spoke to him for a while, he gave me a list of places that I could write to get audio-visual aids to put in my room, and he seems like a very nice person. . . . At 11:00 we went back up to our classrooms and at 1:00 Mrs. White continued with the routines that I am supposed to teach on the first day of school. At 3:00 we went home.

In the preceding account of one formal orientation of new teachers into an inner-city school several points are noteworthy. First is the emphasis on the role of teachers as bureaucratic functionaries who are subordinate to those in supervisory positions above them. Second is the stress on the official functions to be performed by the incumbents of different educational positions and the rules that bind them together, so that the solution of problems may be standardized and persons may be treated equally. Spheres of competence and authority are delineated so that teachers may become aware of the division of labor in the school, the specialized work performed by others, and their own duties, obligations, and authority. The supervisory hierarchy is clarified so that teachers meet and know who has direct control over their activities. The fact that teachers cannot monopolize a particular position is underscored by demands on them for flexibility and a willingness to be allocated or reallocated according to organizational needs, even if this results in the assignment of teachers to work programs for which they have no special training or competence. The importance of written records of administrative acts, decisions, and rules is made plain both by the written materials received by teachers and those they are expected to keep.

In addition to the initial orientation sessions, such as those described, the formal induction of beginning teachers into the inner-city school occurs on a number of other specific occasions. These include formal observations by principals, assistant principals, district curriculum coordinators, specialists and others, formal meetings for all new teachers, official faculty meetings, grade level or subject area conferences, written administrative directives, personal conferences with school superiors, and so on. While space does not permit a detailed consideration of these events, it is important to note that they are nearly always planned and initiated by supervisory personnel and have as their function the training of the teacher in behavioral patterns appropriate to the maintenance of a vast educational bureaucracy.

When the bureaucratic behavior expected of teachers is not sensitive to the special needs of pupils in inner-city schools, beginning teachers, as well as more experienced ones, are confronted with a special dilemma in the attempt to meet both the educational needs of their students and the educational requirements of administrators and other supervisory personnel, who are found not only in the local school but also in high positions far removed from the school. In the inner-city school many examples of the discontinuity between the needs of pupils and administrative requirements may be cited. One of the more common is the pressure on the teacher to teach an established curriculum designed for the grade she is teaching when the children in her particular class are not reading on grade level, and she is not provided with textbooks appropriate to the situation (nor with other teaching materials and the pedagogical techniques so that the children may have a meaningful relationship to the formal curriculum). Similarly, the strong administrative emphasis in the inner-city school on "routinizing the class" and establishing firm discipline before teaching occurs may and frequently does result in beginning teachers' being asked to undertake what they consider to be "police" work and only seldom having the experience of "teaching." This is particularly a problem when the children, either as a class or as individuals, have been assigned to the beginning teacher because administrators do not feel they can ask more experienced teachers to take them — or fear that the more experienced teachers will leave unless they have the attraction of receiving a class with children in it who share the norms of the school and do reasonably well in school work.

In the events that constitute the formal induction of new teachers into the school system, they act out the new relationships they are to assume in that unit of the system of which they are now a part. They are the recipients of organizational activities and directives that those above them initiate. When these administrative activities are primarily concentrated on teachers as bureaucratic functionaries and custodians of children, beginning teachers often feel rejected as teachers. Finding little or no administrative support for their work of teaching, they may and sometimes do resign themselves to being caretakers of children who they now begin to define as "unteachable," an opinion sometimes shared by administrators and more experienced teachers in the school. In these cases, the formal administrative induction fails to claim the beginning teachers for a meaningful social and personal identity as teachers, and the burden on other groups becomes greater if these teachers are not to feel totally rejected.

The Informal Teacher Induction

At the same time that the formal induction of beginning teachers is occurring the beginning teachers receive an informal induction in ways of coping with the problem of performing their role adequately. In the school in the inner city, a great deal of the informal induction of the beginning teachers centers around two major foci. The sharing and exchange of supplies, lesson plans, rexographed materials, and information about what supervisors look for when they observe teachers and their classrooms represent one type. These are designed to help beginning teachers manage their work load more readily and to conform to work expectations deemed important by the administrative personnel. During her fourth week of teaching, for example, the junior high teacher cited earlier reports the following:

> As far as the teachers are concerned, I see mostly Don Panetta who is next door. Don Panetta, Joe Rubin, Bill Smythe. We've become very friendly. Don is next door to me. We talk to each other out in the halls all the time. It's mutual. . . . He's given me some materials for my bulletin boards, in case I haven't had enough, because I first started decorating them this week.
>
> I see Joe Rubin — he's on the second floor — quite often during my free periods when I patrol, and I have taken home his lesson plan books from last year for the seventh grade. He teaches social studies, and I wanted to see how he broke down the curriculum. So I've taken his lesson plans home to use as models and to help me see how to break it down because as I said before, I am without textbooks. And Bill Smythe is another member of that crowd, so I talk to him in the halls occasionally when I run into him and in the cafeteria. . . .

The second major area in which the more experienced teachers in inner-city schools induct beginners is that of handling discipline problems.[7] Children and youth who become defined as discipline problems are those who, for one reason or another, act in ways which disturb the orderly relationships of the classroom and upset the model of the quiet classroom comprised of children doing their assigned work and initiating actions toward the teacher only in prescribed ways. Children who are discipline problems are found primarily in classes for those defined as

---

[7] Significantly also, discipline is a major focus of some of the formal induction procedures, nearly all of the contacts with guidance personnel and parents of children, and a substantial proportion of the teacher-initiated contacts with administrators.

being "below average in ability." The common policy of assigning the
most experienced teachers to the "better" classes usually means that
beginning teachers encounter those classes in which the children are
described as "slow" and in which there may be discipline problems.[8]

The psychological strain on beginning teachers as a result of their
class assignment has many roots, of which several are particularly important. The rigidity of the model of what constitutes proper pupil behavior allows little, if any, room for flexibility in coping with a recently
displaced rural population or with pupils who, for other social reasons, come
to the school unknowledgeable about the appropriate behavioral patterns
demanded. The teachers' own success experience in school has limited
their exposure to the problems of the unsuccessful student, as has their
student teaching experience which, even though it has been in an inner-
city school, has frequently been under the direction of the better teachers
in the more academic classes. The rigidity of the curriculum assigned, the
lack of adequate textbooks and supplies, the comparatively low prestige
of both the "slow" children in the school and those who teach them, and
the lack of teacher preparation for the realities of the inner-city school are
additional factors that enhance the difficulties of beginning teachers, who
often are under pressure from supervisors to control their classes and keep
the pupils quiet. Some of the kinds of help given by other teachers is
shown in these excerpts from the diary of a beginning teacher who was
assigned the bottom class in the seventh grade as her official class in the
junior high school from which she herself had graduated.

> The other teachers have all stopped and given me little clues
> as to how to control the class. For instance, the kids were rather
> noisy at dismissal time, and they weren't going down the same
> staircase. Some were jumping over the bannisters, and they were
> not going down like human beings. So one of the teachers whom
> I had worked with last year told me the best way to control them
> is to stop after each landing and just wait for silence. And if I
> don't get it say, "John is holding up the class. As soon as he's quiet,
> we'll go down." This way there will be pressure from the rest of
> the group, and the kids don't like this. They don't like to be in
> bad, as the saying goes, with the rest of their classmates. . . . This
> was a very good hint and just applying it once really showed me
> that it was a valuable hint. As I say, I'm really very grateful to
> those teachers. Most of them have been teaching between five
> and two years, so they still remember the experience of just
> starting, at being faced with thirty kids and just dying there in
> front of the room not knowing what to do.
>
> . . . my former teachers come over and give me helpful hints

---

[8] For an understanding of model pupil behavior as presented in one large city, the
interested reader is referred to Guide for Newly-Appointed Teachers in the New York
City Elementary Schools, New York: Board of Education of the City of New York,
1964.

238

as to who is afraid of whose father, and if I want to control that child, "Speak to the father . . ."

I never realized I could be so mean, nasty, and rotten. As one of the teachers said, "It's either you or them, and you make sure that you make up your mind that it's going to be you."

At the beginning of the term when I had a lot of difficulty with Robert, I had discussed this with a lot of the other teachers, and they had given me suggestions such as making him the leader or the monitor and letting him set an example for the others.

Although space has only permitted a brief glimpse into this induction on the part of the other teachers, its importance for the on-the-job training of beginning teachers should not be underestimated, for it is through this induction that the beginners become those who are claimed by other teachers into their occupational group. If the older, more experienced teachers in the inner-city school are successful in really helping the beginner to teach the children in her class and to establish a relationship of mutual respect with them, the beginner may be claimed for a role as teacher in these schools. If, on the other hand, the older teachers have themselves failed to develop ways of teaching the student population and can only offer techniques to the beginners that alienate them from pupils, the beginning teachers are not only left unclaimed as teachers by the other teachers, but are also likely to be unclaimed by their students.

The Informal Student Induction

Although little is known about it empirically, a consideration of teachers' induction into the inner-city school would be incomplete without recognition of the important role played by students in the induction process. Just like their counterparts elsewhere, students in inner-city schools have opinions about teachers, compare them with one another, and respond to different teachers in different ways. Further, in very special and sometimes dramatic ways, students in schools in slum areas demonstrate that the authority of teachers is not inherent in them, but rather rests on their ability to carry their class with them and on the willingness of pupils to accept their authority.

They came in like a bunch of screaming animals. In this class, it wasn't one or two troublemakers. It was the whole class. I couldn't control them. I couldn't get them into their seats. I lined them up on the side of the room, and I alternated boy, girl with the seating so they wouldn't be sitting next to a friend. It took me the whole period to get them seated and to fill out Delaney cards, and at that time I was just grateful to get the Delaney cards cards from them. . . .

I came home Monday night, and I started to cry that this is

239

pure hell. . . . I expected a little bit of a behavior problem, but I expected to be able to control the class. What I had done the year when I student taught, even when I was in the room alone . . . if I stood in front of the room and had the children standing and didn't say a word and just told them that I wasn't going to speak while anybody else was, they would just calm down. . . . This is something that did not happen with these people, and I was shocked. I was shocked with the vulgarity of their language . . . and I didn't know quite how to cope with this. . . . They just wouldn't cooperate with me in any way.

The above experience is but one of many examples that might be cited. A substitute's experience illustrates what may happen to teachers, depending on students' acceptance or rejection of them:

> On Wednesday, I was asked by the assistant principal to cover 7-13 because their teacher had left. When he said this, I didn't realize that she left for good, but I was given a hint by the class when they came up to me and said that they had run her away . . . .
>
> I took over 7-13 in the morning. I took the attendance and sent them out, and that afternoon the class came back. Four little girls came up to me and said would I be their official teacher— that they would like me to be their official teacher from now on. I was very thrilled about having been asked. I covered 7-13 before for English, but I had never seen them again. It was a big thrill being asked to be someone's official teacher, and they knew that their teacher had left which I did not. So this was one of the most important things that ever happened to me. I was overwhelmed by it, to have a class of students come up to me and ask me to be their official teacher because they like you and they want you.

The examples quoted above from the experiences of beginning teachers in inner-city schools, while different in content, are alike in indicating the importance of the interaction between teachers and pupils in the classroom if the teacher is to feel a sense of being fully incorporated into her role. This aspect of the induction process is further illuminated by a consideration of the characteristics of pupils whom teachers consider to be their least difficult. For the most part, these are children who are making progress in school work, have good work habits, and come to school prepared and anxious to work. In addition they are those who don't get into trouble, get along well with others, help the teacher with classroom chores, and are generally quiet and well behaved. Not only do these children live up to the teacher's expectations of how pupils should behave, but, even more importantly, they enable her to do what her professional training and her own long experience as a student have led her to believe is what teachers *should do* and thus they make her feel that her profession is worthwhile and that she has something to offer that is well received.

The special problem of beginning teachers in the inner-city school arises because they are confronted with some children, sometimes many, who do not respond in ways supportive of their role as teachers. If beginning teachers are also rejected by administrative policies and procedures that do not provide them with the necessary help to adapt to the particular needs of children in inner-city schools or by other teachers who provide them only with techniques that further alienate them from pupils, the first year of teaching can be a dismal experience indeed, often alleviated only by a forthcoming marriage which will enable escape to a suburban school system or an administrative promise that next year one will be assigned to a class where one can "really teach." In either event, the human cost is high not only for the teacher who has been unable to teach but also for the pupils who have not been taught.

Together with the beginning teacher, the student in the inner-city school has a need to be inducted into the school and to find meaningful personal and social identity within it. For the child of the slum, who is ill prepared for the separation from family and peers that schooling entails, the period of transition into the school is particularly fraught with danger. In many instances, what may be viewed by teachers as his "animalistic," "emotionally disturbed," or just plain "ornery" behavior results in a sufficient degree of rejection so that he is a social casualty in the educational system and eventually in the adult role of work in our society. From another viewpoint, it is clear that the failure of many of the pupils in inner-city schools to claim and incorporate their teachers results in a number of teachers becoming casualties either to the occupation of teaching as a whole, or at least to the pursuit of it in the inner-city school.

The Preparation of Teachers for the Inner-City School: A New Look

In the foregoing discussion, an attempt has been made to outline briefly the implications of induction theory for an understanding of beginning teachers' experiences in inner-city schools. Beginning teachers in these schools have been viewed as persons in a transitional phase of their careers. Now separated from a role as a student and claimed by the teacher-training institution as professional teachers, these teachers have yet to be fully incorporated into the local urban school system and their newly earned position.

As newcomers to the profession, beginning teachers encounter a formal administrative induction that attempts to incorporate them into comparatively low positions as bureaucratic functionaries in an educational system where the road to professional advancement is paved with the teaching of the "academic" and "gifted" child or entering the ranks of administration and specialization. In addition to this formal induction, beginning teachers are also informally inducted into their role by other teachers and students. All three groups, administrators, teachers, and

241

students, must reach out and claim the beginning teachers, if they are to successfully make the transition into teaching in the inner-city school and establish a meaningful personal and social identity as teachers of the children of the contemporary urban poor—even when these children are not only poor but also slow in doing school work and disruptive of the traditional model of classroom decorum.

Two major implications of induction theory for the preparation of teachers for inner-city schools may be noted. The first is, that in order to be more than a passing experimental program, changes in the preparation of teachers for these schools must be accompanied by changes within these schools themselves. The formal and informal induction of the teacher must be modified so that teachers are claimed as teachers and given the necessary help that will enable them to develop new understandings about their role in relationship to pupils in the urban slums of our times. It will do little good, for example, to train new teachers in the special educational problems of rural migrants in the process of urbanization and then send them into schools where class size, curriculum materials, and administrative policies and procedures have not been oriented toward reaching out and incorporating the urban newcomers into a meaningful participation in the educational system. Indeed, it is likely that unless significant changes *are* made in the schools in the inner city, even the most helpful array of courses and experiences concerned with the preparation of teachers for these schools will be finally judged by teachers themselves as not applicable to the realities of the situation they face when they begin to teach in these schools.

There is a second and related major implication. For teacher education programs to focus solely or even primarily on changing teachers' attributes and techniques so that the attributes of children in inner-city schools may be changed is to overlook the social context within which the formal education of the child occurs. Including both the family and community from which the child comes to the school as well as the social relationships within the school itself, this social environment provides the setting within which the attributes of persons find their meaning as they interact with each other. Thus the fact that a given teacher may have the attribute of being white and a given group of children may have the attribute of being Negro is not in and of itself significant. It only becomes so as teacher and pupils interact. These ways either enable the children to feel they are being claimed for significant roles in the educational system and the occupational system or cause the children to feel that they are being rejected from participation in the educational system and relegated to a permanent status as outsiders in our society.

It is beyond the scope of this paper to present a more detailed examination of the above points. It is, however, the final purpose of this paper to suggest that if the induction of both teachers and pupils into the inner-city school is to be an induction into a human organization where educational rather than custodial goals are primary, changes will have to occur not only in the formal training of the teacher but also in the traditional patterns of interaction between those within the schools and between them and the communities they serve. In most cases, the needed changes would appear to be vast and far-reaching. However, they are necessary if teachers are to be claimed as more than bureaucratic functionaries, if they are to be given a true understanding of their sociocultural role in the induction of the children of the urban poor into modern society, and if they are to be provided with the social-psychological support necessary for the educational task to be accomplished.

References

Chapple, Eliot D. and Carleton S. Coon, *Principles of Anthropology*. New York: Holt, Rinehart and Winston, 1942.

Eddy, Elizabeth M. *Walk the White Line: A Profile of Urban Education*. New York: Doubleday Anchor Books, in press, 1967.

Gennep, Arnold van. *Rites of Passage*. Chicago: University of Chicago Press, 1960.

Haubrich, Vernon F. "Teachers for Big-City Schools" in *Education in Depressed Areas*, ed. A. Harry Passow. New York: Teachers College Press, Columbia University, 1963.

New York City Board of Education. *Guide for Newly Appointed Teachers in the New York City Elementary Schools*. New York: The Board, 1964.

Edward J. Meade, Jr. is disenchanted with much of what he sees passing for vocational and technical education, especially in those areas where the disadvantaged American resides. These children challenge educators to face and to resolve basic issues they have tended to sidestep. The disadvantaged child enters school without the tools required "to beat the system."

For the author, vocational and technical education represents an important part of general education, rather than specific job training for youngsters with a restricted academic future. He questions the assumption that certain youngsters must have modest aspirations or that educators have the right to limit their performance. Educators have the responsibility, he argues, to present opportunities in such ways that the learner, and not the program, fixes the limits.

The traditional vocational school tends to shut out the disadvantaged youngster. That those who do get in receive a relatively decent education does not imply advantages of the program over similar offerings to youngsters in comprehensive schools. However, in many cases, the vocational schools are providing instruction in processes that are obsolete or are rapidly becoming so.

VOCATIONAL AND TECHNICAL EDUCATION FOR DISADVANTAGED YOUTH: A CRITICAL LOOK

Edward J. Meade, Jr.

Examining the work-study program, Meade finds that too few programs are structured to allow work and study to reinforce one another. Instead, work-study programs have become "bribes," wherein the student is permitted to hold his job only as long as he has "passing" school work. The tragedy is that the job is probably many times more relevant than the so-called general curriculum offered the disadvantaged student. Cooperative plans in which work and study are related and reinforce one another may "zero in" on better general education, as well as better career prospects.

Another alternative is to transfer the student into one of the new programs, such as one supported by the Manpower Development and Training Act or the Economic

Opportunity Act. The most visible alternative is the Job Corps, which recruits youngsters who have turned away from traditional schooling. Such programs, Meade comments, represent society's way of enlarging opportunities for youngsters with whom the schools have failed.

The real problem at the secondary level appears to be the so-called general curriculum — the alternative if traditional academic and vocational programs fall flat. Youngsters are offered a grab-bag of "watered down" courses which have no organic relation to one another. Dr. Meade proposes a prevocational sequence of courses which could be categorized as "general education in career fields" and all of which could lead either to employment, to continued education, or to some kind of training opportunity. The curriculum needs to be one that makes sense to the disadvantaged pupil. Meade argues that the separate systems of education as we know them — academic, general, vocational, for example — necessarily deny a pupil resources. Making all resources freely accessible would be a welcome change.

VOCATIONAL AND TECHNICAL EDUCATION FOR DISADVANTAGED YOUTH: A CRITICAL LOOK

Edward J. Meade, Jr.

This assignment to concern myself about vocational and technical educa tion for disadvantaged children is welcome and disturbing. It is welcome, for it presents an opportunity to take a hard look at what is passing for vocational and technical education, particularly in the densely populated urban center and the remote rural community where most of the so-called disadvantaged Americans reside.

The assignment is also disturbing, for I cannot believe there should be separate education categories such as vocational and technical education, nor can I truly believe that we can separate out entirely the so-called disadvantaged child.

Before analyzing what is going on and making a few suggestions for improvement, let me point out that by singling out particular programs identified as vocational and technical education and by singling out particular youngsters identified as disadvantaged, we run the risk of hardening categories, at the least, or of developing separate cults, at the worst. While these categories have been useful in drawing attention and funds to some major problems of the school, I am disturbed by the growing specialization in a field labeled vocational and technical education and in dealing with certain youngsters labeled "disadvantaged."

To my way of thinking, vocational and technical education represents a part of general education—and an important part. As for the disadvantaged youngster, he presents an opportunity for all of us in education. Being disadvantaged, however described—economically, culturally, socially, geographically—this learner brings fundamental problems to the school and to the teacher. Due in part to his lack of advantage this child presents educators with an unusual opportunity to see basic issues and problems confronting the school.

To put it another way, the disadvantaged child comes to the school lacking the social and cultural tools that enable him either to adjust to the school program or to overcome it. He lacks the equipment to "beat the system." To a large extent many persons who succeed in school do so be-cause they have the ability to beat the system. The disadvantaged child, however, is almost wholly dependent on the school—its program, its teachers, its facilities, its resources—if he is to learn at all. As a result of his dependency, attempts to educate him bring to the surface many flaws and mistakes in the current systems of instruction in school. Teachers, administrators, and the public cannot depend on this youngster to compensate for the tragic curriculum situations existing in many schools; nor can he be expected to outrun poor teachers. The home and the neighborhood from which this youngster comes cannot be depended on to supply much of the necessary basic education which anyone needs in order to cope with modern society. The school must do it.

Vocational and technical education presents us with another kind of opportunity. One of the claimed virtues of the vocational system is that it presents reality to the learner. It offers the opportunity for the reinforcement of learning at a practical level and presents tangible evidence to the learner about how well he has learned. Vocational education also can show the value of piling knowledge upon knowledge until a product results. Done well, it offers jobs and careers as well as an education.

With this brief introduction, I hope that it can be seen that this topic deals with a variation on the theme of education. It does not represent any new tunes at all. The problems presented by the disadvantaged child are those that face all learners, and the opportunities which are presented by vocational and technical education are those which can be useful to all children.

The following is what many educators consider to be vocational and technical education, particularly when they are dealing with youngsters who might be described as disadvantaged. To these educators—and I am afraid it means most educators—this form of education is simply one of offering specific job training to youngsters who, in the opinion of many, have a limited future, particularly academically. I don't question the importance of training for a specific job or training for jobs in general. The schools have done too little job training. Still, I question the assumption that these youngsters, or indeed any youngster, have a limited future, or that we have the right to prescribe the bounds within which they can perform.

Certainly not all youngsters have equal ability, nor can they show it in the same way or to the same degree. Still, we seem to be engaged in making such assumptions with many disadvantaged youngsters. We assume that since their reading level is poor, since their personal habits might leave something to be desired, and since they generally belong to minority groups, their life chances are severely limited. In some instances this assumption might prove to be true. However, no educator has the right or privilege to make such an assumption. As educators, it is our responsibility to present opportunities in such ways that any limits are set by the learner and not by the program.

The Traditional Vocational School Program

It was just about fifty years ago when the Congress of the United States passed the Vocational Act of 1917, or the Smith-Hughes Act, as we have come to call it. This act provided federal funds for the support of vocational and technical education at the secondary school level. Now, fifty years later, the programs begun under the Smith-Hughes Act have become a way of life. Most of what we now call vocational education resulted from this legislation, which was based on the industries and trades existing at the time it was passed. While there have been some additions to the kind of training for which funds are available, the programs remain almost as designed back in 1917.

In 1963, however, after a review by a presidential commission, Congress passed the Vocational Education Act of 1963. This act provided for many changes from the way in which vocational education had been presented. For example, it is now possible to divert funds from farm-based occupations into service-based occupations. The new act also provided for home economics as a career, not merely as a way to help young women become better housewives. To a degree, the Vocational Education Act of 1963 represents a breakthrough. Still, some three years later, the legislation exists, but the changes in the field are few. Characteristically, our culture shows once again that it is easier to change its laws than it is to change its traditions.

In most instances where there are traditional vocational schools, the disadvantaged youngster, particularly the most disadvantaged youngster, is shut out. Most vocational schools, like many schools, prefer to teach those who need the least help rather than those who need the most. In some ways, it is easier to get a candidate into some of the more prestigious colleges than it is to get certain kinds of youngsters into vocational schools in some of our cities. In New York City, for example, vocational schools are not the haven for the disadvantaged that they once were. The masses of the disadvantaged are now in the comprehensive high school and study the so-called general curriculum.

For those disadvantaged youngsters who do get into vocational schools, chances are they will receive a decent education. They will be placed in jobs. A recent study by the American Institutes of Research revealed that programs in the traditional vocational schools offered about the same kind of career advantages as those which were offered to similar youngsters from comprehensive high schools. The report did not address itself to what might have been for these youngsters. It only reported what were the results of existing programs.

Generally these schools prepare carpenters, plumbers, masons, cooks, bakers, machine operators, and so on. In some cases, techniques that are, or are in the process of becoming, obsolete in today's technological age still are being taught. For example, in a vocational school in New England, the staff was proud of the placement record of its graduates in printing. To maintain a high placement record, the staff would go to the most remote community in Northern New England to place a boy rather than to change the system of teaching printing, which presented processes and techniques that had long since been abandoned by many of the more modern printing firms in this country. Rather than trying to keep pace with progress, this program was dedicated to keeping the status quo. In another vocational school, this time in the Midwest, youngsters were being trained in the shoe trade industry, employing techniques and practices that were abandoned by the industry some ten years ago.

Why are these schools out of touch? In the former instance, it was a case of a staff gone stale. In the latter instance, it was a case of continuing to make use of equipment already obsolete in the industry at which the training was aimed. Certainly these cases are extreme. Unfortunately, however, these cases are not as rare as they ought to be.

Despite my criticisms of the traditional vocational school, I must say that the chances of a youngster from a disadvantaged background getting an education are better in the vocational school than they are in most comprehensive high schools, particularly the large urban ones. While many vocational schools have too many ties with past technology and are rigid in their instructional and scheduling practices, they do promise the enrollee a job, and they generally deliver. On the other hand, the present general curriculum in the comprehensive school is a course of study aimed at nothing, and its production in terms of job placements generally proves its point.

The Work-Study Program

A second and increasingly popular form of vocational experience used by schools — particularly where large numbers of disadvantaged youngsters are involved — is the "work-study" program. The idea is simple and sensible. Work-study is an attempt to give a youngster the opportunity to engage in real work while he is still studying. Unfortunately, too few of these programs take advantage of ways and means that work and study can be made to reinforce each other and help the youngster.

Many work-study programs are nothing more than bribes. Too often they exist because the school does not know what to do with youngsters we label as "dropouts," "disadvantaged," or "troublemakers." Have you noticed how many work-study programs are being initiated in the comprehensive high schools, where youngsters have not "cut the mustard" in the academic curriculum or been able to make much of the general curriculum — not that anyone can anyway?

At any rate, for many schools, the solution to failure with some youngsters seems to be to put them out to work for part of the day. Certainly it is not a new notion; certainly it is not a solution—at least not the way most work-study programs are operating. As I said before, I think most of the present programs are bribes. At its most corrupt, the work-study program merely excuses youngsters to work part of the time when they would normally be in school. A youngster is encouraged to find a job. Often he gets assistance in finding a job or he is placed in a job by the school. His school makes an arrangement so that he can study in the morning and work in the afternoon or makes a similar arrangement.

In many cases the student is allowed to hold onto his job as long as he is "passing" his school work, or at least as long as his school attendance is steady. The tragic element is that all too often the job, however menial, poor-paying or pedestrian, is a thousand times more relevant and more real than the clutter of courses we offer as the general high school curriculum.

In most high-school work-study programs the jobs to which youngsters are assigned, particularly disadvantaged youngsters, are low-order occupations—limited in terms of career opportunities and reward. When the school decides to use its curriculum to reinforce the job, there is the danger that such a move may be locking the youngster into such a job for the rest of his working life. I have seen in schools work-study programs that do little more than help the enrollee perform better on his specific job. If he is a checker at a supermarket, the school trains him to work the cash register more effectively. If the enrollee is working as a general aide in a playground, he or she is trained to supervise specific games.

This may be all well and good but where is the opportunity for the youngster to move up the ladder in a career or to acquire a base for more education? A curriculum that is too immediate and oriented specifically to a present job is as much a dead end as one that is not related at all. As I stated earlier, neither educators nor anyone else has the right to set the limits for any learner. By addressing themselves to the needs of a specific job and by doing no more than that, the curriculum may result in closing opportunities, not in expanding them.

Of course there are desirable forms of work-study programs. The so-called cooperative plans are good examples. In these cases, work and study are related and do reinforce one another, and the focus is on a better general education for the pupil and a career—not a job.

The Out-of-School Program

When faced with the lack of a vocational school or a traditional vocational program, where work-study programs do not seen possible, schools tend to continue as they now do, trying to educate in a narrow sense of the word and letting the disadvantaged youngster stay in the program. Whether he passes or fails is of little or no consequence. If he is persistent enough and quiet enough we allow him to stay in school until be becomes

251

a "graduate." Have you ever thought of how many certificates of attendance have been awarded under the guise of diplomas? Neither the school nor the student is satisfied with what that piece of paper represents. Still, this is one way of dealing with disadvantaged youngsters, regardless of how useful it is.

A second alternative allows the student to escape as soon as he is legally permitted to do so. Once a student has dropped out, he is no longer a problem of the school; he is now a problem of society at large. What alternatives are open for him? Years ago it was possible for a youngster to drop out of school and immediately be absorbed into the labor market. There should be no need for me to elaborate on the present state of the labor market. You know that job opportunities for dropouts are severely limited. The least likely person to be employed is the one who comes in with the fewest skills and the lowest order of education. Since we cannot depend on the general economy to absorb the disadvantaged dropout, to whom can we turn?

Modern society has developed some new alternatives. Through such legislation as the Manpower Development and Training Act and the Economic Opportunity Act, a number of training programs have been established for disadvantaged youth which take on the responsibility of doing something about training the dropout.

Perhaps the most visible of these alternatives is the Job Corps. The Job Corps intends to provide both basic and vocational education to students who have failed in traditional school programs. Much has been said and written about the Job Corps and its success, its failures, its problems and its possibilities. While I am not one who prefers to attack problems at their edges, the Job Corps does just that by spending millions of dollars trying to undo what has been done wrong by schools. Still, there is no question in my mind that given the present set of circumstances the Job Corps is an important alternative for school dropouts and unemployed youth in this country. It may be said that if the Job Corps succeeds, not only will it rehabilitate many youngsters who have heretofore had limited opportunities, but also it will represent an indictment against what schools now do for disadvantaged youth. If the Job Corps can succeed with youngsters who have been turned out by the schools, what does this say for the traditional school program and its relevance to this kind of youngster?

Why should the Job Corps succeed? Perhaps because of an improved motivation on the part of the enrollees who, after all, are volunteers. They are volunteers with few alternatives. They found that after dropping out of school is was not possible to get a job; they were even rejected by the Army. Theoretically, then, enrollees enter the Job Corps with a greater motivation than they brought to the school. In addition, the Job Corps puts its emphasis on vocational training even if in a limited sense in many instances. The Corps is interested in producing men and women who can hold jobs. If by way of his own motivation to learn to work and through the

Job Corps' program of training him, the youngster also improves his basic skills in reading, writing, communications, numbers, and the like, so much the better.

Fortunately the Job Corps has an ingredient that we don't find in the schools—that of American industry. As many of you know, most of the Job Corps centers, particularly the larger ones, are being operated by industry. The talents and resources of some of America's greatest technological organizations are now being applied to the problem of the school dropout and the disadvantaged youngster. Concepts such as "cost benefit analysis systems," "self-contained educational systems," "components of work," and the like are creeping into education. If the effectiveness and efficiency of industry can be useful in education, that is all to the good.

I shall not belabor the point about out-of-school programs except to say that when schools fail, society then has to find other ways and means to cope with the problems of opportunities for the disadvantaged youngster. Whereas years ago it was possible for schools to turn out these youngsters, either as less-than-satisfactory graduates or directly as dropouts, and then have them absorbed directly into the economy, this is no longer the case. Now society has to set up extra schools, if you will, to do what the regular schools have not been able to do. Somehow society must give these people an education on their own terms, commensurate with their interests, aspirations, and abilities. To the extent that society has to set up these alternative programs, it is fair to conclude that schools, as we know them, are not living up to their goal of giving an education to everyone.

What can schools do? Well, for one thing, educators can start earlier in the system to get at the problems of the disadvantaged. This is an obvious alternative. Fortunately there are signs of promise along these lines—Head Start programs, drastic revisions in beginning reading programs, improved diagnostic services in primary schools, and so forth.

What use do we make of simple tools and primitive manufacturing processes to help children "see" abstractions? For example, is it possible to help a pupil learn to read symbols by having him learn to set printing type? Could manipulative means be found that would measure learning as we now use verbal or written expression? The early years of schooling may represent a fertile area for the use of vocational experiences to reinforce instruction. Now that we are beginning to realize the inadequacy of much of what is elementary school education, we ought not to exclude the possible use of other than traditional ways of presenting knowledge and reinforcing and evaluating learning.

Rather than devote more attention to this possibility, for the sake of brevity I will concentrate on more familiar ground for vocational and technical education—the high school. Unlike some educators, I still believe that there is usefulness, perhaps more than ever, in providing vocational experiences at the high-school level. I do not share the opinion of those who claim that all vocational education—or, as they limit it, job training—should be deferred until after high school.

Currently, the majority of high school pupils who are considered to be disadvantaged are neither in vocational schools nor in work-study programs, regardless of kind or quality. Rather, they are to be found in the general or comprehensive high school and usually mired down in the so-called general curriculum. They are there because traditional academic and vocational programs are denied to them. They are denied these programs because there is too much risk involved; that is, the likelihood of their being able to pass successfully through one of these programs is remote—an indictment of education if I ever heard one.

What is the "general" high-school curriculum? For the life of me I don't know what it is supposed to be. I assume it is expected to give a high school pupil a firm foundation of general or basic information. As it is offered in most schools, however, this curriculum resembles a "grab bag" of courses, many of them watered down or thinned out. In all but a handful of instances does this curriculum represent systematic development or a relationship of course to course? Some might argue that it is truly the "cafeteria" curriculum so symbolic of the elective system of American education. If it is, it represents a rather poor bill of fare.

Why face this pupil with a loose collection of such anomalies as "commercial geography," "business arithmetic," "basic English," and "boys' cooking"? This porridge of courses represents our worst attempt to build a program of studies that is useful for work, for further study, or, for that matter, life. It should come as no surprise to anyone that the greatest share of school dropouts were enrolled in this curriculum. Perhaps dropouts show more wisdom than we realize.

Of course there are alternatives; there must be. Since no one seems satisfied with the "general" curriculum and since the present-day vocational programs offer limited opportunities, why not replace the general curriculum with something more realistic and relevant to pupils, particularly to the disadvantaged pupil?

Should such a program be looked on as a remedial effort? Given the present state of affairs, there are numbers of pupils in high schools who are years behind in their education. The school must accept the pupil and deal with him as he is—not as the school hopes he will be. However, to see this program as a salvage operation would be less than satisfactory. The program I am proposing must offer basic and useful content in ways that these youngsters can cope with it and use it. In addition, it must be an educational program, not merely job training.

Instead of the present general high-school curriculum, I propose a prevocational sequence of courses that prepare pupils for work, vocational and technical training, and for more education as well. Generally, vocational courses have been seen as the hub of the wheel, with other courses relating to them, such as "shop-related English" or "shop mathematics."

In many ways, vocational education has resembled the "core curriculum" —everything revolving around and relating to it. Often as not, as in the case of the core curriculum, this has led to a prostitution of fundamental education in order to serve a narrowly defined set of job skills in vocational education or some irrelevant "problem" in the core curriculum. Why not turn the coin over and design shop or laboratory courses that relate to English and mathematics? It seems to me that genuine general education, not what is presently offered, is necessary for all pupils. If so, we need to find ways to help pupils acquire it.

In education, we make much of the need to reinforce and test what has been taught and, hopefully, learned. Where can we better test learning than in the shop or the laboratory? Are not these the places where one's knowledge of mathematics, science, communications, and the like can be reinforced by the attempt to apply such knowledge?

Disadvantaged youngsters are generally reality-bound. They live at the "gut level." No phony world will satisfy them, for they see more reality in a year's time than many of us see in a decade. Most of them want to know—and know right away—the utility of matters taught to them. Generally these youngsters do not have the capacity to defer rewards in learning. Many of them live on a day-by-day basis with little promise of tomorrow's being any better. If you expect them to learn something, they must understand—almost tangibly—the relevance of that learning. It must be valid in their terms. It can be done by setting up ways and means to apply knowledge soon after it has been taught. Perhaps after accomplishing a more rapid and effective set of reinforcement techniques—tangible and workable—this youngster may begin to trust the school and be more patient about the "payoff" in learning.

Think of the many ways a shop experience could reinforce what a pupil learned elsewhere. Building a piece of test equipment—or even a muffler for an automobile—can reinforce physics, drafting, mathematics, and even English. Preparing a meal can reinforce chemistry, general science, mathematics, reading, and writing. Shops, laboratories, yes, and even kitchens can be used as the loci for reinforcing general education.

But what about the preparation for work? If shops are used merely as testing and synthesizing arenas for general education, how can we prepare people for jobs? Vocational competence can be achieved this way as well. The design of the reinforcement experiences in the shops can be vocationally oriented. Classes in foods or home economics can reinforce other subjects and also can prepare the student for jobs in the ever-growing field of food preparation, handling, and management.

There are examples of these kinds of programs in comprehensive or general high schools. For instance, in New York City, a few high schools will be testing out programs in pre-engineering technology, food technology, business technology, and medical technology. These high schools will be using existing shops and cafeterias as the technology laboratories.

255

In each of the schools, these places will be where matters learned in other parts of the program will be tested. Teams of teachers from a relevant range of disciplines — English, mathematics, science, shop, and so forth — will be assigned to work through an entire program in food technology, for example, in sequence for a large group of pupils. These teachers will plan and evaluate the work as a team. The shop teachers will be responsible for developing exercises — rooted in reality — that test what has been taught elsewhere. In addition, each teacher will know what is going on in each of the other parts of the program, and, whenever possible, the natural relationship and relevance of each particular course to the others will be emphasized. Pupils will get a consistent view, reinforced by actual experiences of their own in the school's closest approximation of the work world. Of course, if real work experiences could be fashioned, these would be superior. However, at this stage of the game, shops are better than sterile classrooms.

These pre-employment programs will be defined by the needs of general education and career fields. If this works, the comprehensive high school, as we know it, will demonstrate that it can provide some form of vocational education. In all cases, any follow-up or continuation programs in the community colleges and technical institute would be dependent on this form of secondary school program.

This kind of program demands another kind of integration, that of the academic educator with the vocational educator. It seems to me that if academicians truly believe that their disciplines have a relevance to life — as I am sure is the case — they should welcome the chance to get involved with the vocational educators who profess to be constantly dealing with reality. The merger of various disciplines should bring about situations for the consideration of theory, actual practice, and for the reinforcement of both.

The disadvantaged pupil, more than most, wants to know — and has a right to know — the relevance of what he is taught and what he has learned. This youngster cannot wait until he is older or until he is an adult to see the usefulness of what he has learned. He needs to know that sooner; he needs to see — tangibly — that education makes sense in his world as well as in that of others.

As usual, the disadvantaged child presents us with an opportunity rather than a problem. He offers us a chance to bring about a change we have needed since vocational education got started. The separate systems of education as we know them now — academic, general, scientific, vocational, technical, or what have you — deny all pupils the resources of each system. We must bring these systems into one or in combination where access to each by all is possible: not one system so rigidly defined that pupils must fit its mold, but rather one that offers the widest possible range of resources and alternate ways to attain the same general ends.

Prior to World War I, John Dewey foresaw the dangers of the development of a separate system of vocational education. At that time he urged that vocational education be integrated into the general school program, emphasizing that it would benefit both forms of education. Note that he saw benefit for *both* programs. As he perceived it, there would be benefit for workers, citizens, industry, and for democracy. Interesting, isn't it, that John Dewey identified this problem so long ago—and he never claimed to be an expert in dealing with either the disadvantaged child or in vocational education?

Abraham J. Tannenbaum takes a fresh look at some of our traditional notions about early school withdrawal. He marks down some of the recent research on school dropouts for failing to include as independent variables the social and/or emotional incompetences that underlie the educational failure.

Basically, the dropout is a complex of multiple handicaps and requires relatively expensive programs of social rehabilitation. The psychological and social correlates of early school withdrawal are discussed in some detail. The school's retention power has continued to increase over the years. Our high schools are tending to become absorbing rather than selecting institutions. The value of a high school diploma has been diminishing as more and more adolescents stay in school. In the past forty or fifty years, the retention rate has shifted: while 80 per cent of youngsters failed to complete twelfth grade in 1920, 75 per cent now complete it, removing "involuntary withdrawals" of youngsters who are handicapped or have severe emotional problems.

THE SCHOOL DROPOUT TODAY

Abraham J. Tannenbaum

The author traces the dropout problem as it is related to limited employment opportunities for members of minority groups and to the current civil rights activities. Despite improvements, the nonwhite's chances for employment are far smaller than those of his white counterpart. Jobs are limited to the less skilled or service occupations. His unemployment rate continues to be at least twice that of the white. Antidropout efforts by school personnel have followed several patterns: increased counseling, curriculum adaptations and modifications, and vocational and prevocational experiences. The author concludes his survey by summarizing a proposal by Cervantes, who advocates a large-scale coordinated attack by community groups, government, business, labor, and educators. The family is the ultimate back-up force for reducing and alleviating the pressures to drop out.

259

In the past, withdrawal from school has tended to cut the individual off from any supportive services. However, new legislation makes it possible to provide many services even though the student has withdrawn from school. The author concludes that the school dropout problem should concern not only educators. The current multifaceted attack on premature school-leaving may put the educational problem into proper perspective and dramatize the responsibility of other groups in society for the school dropout.

THE SCHOOL
DROPOUT TODAY
Abraham J. Tannenbaum

In the social and behavioral sciences, a correlate often masquerades as a consequence. Human conditions that tend to go together are frequently placed in a cause-and-effect relationship that is rationalized with more wishful thinking than logic or evidence. Such is the case in popular discussions of early school withdrawal. Usually, the gambit is to show that high-school dropouts are not as employable and law-abiding as their graduating peers, and then to slip into the convenient conclusion that the dropout is at a disadvantage because he has no diploma. This leads to some clear and simple caveats for high-school students. To those who are able and stable enough to earn a diploma, the message is, "Stay in school, or your future will be ruined." To the marginal students who are inclined to withdraw early, the message is, "Stay in school and your future will probably be saved." The first piece of advice is gratuitous, since it is beamed at a group that will probably finish school anyway. The second is little better than a placebo, since its audience is handicapped in so many other ways that it needs far more than a diploma to face the future successfully.

A high-school diploma can be valuable in two ways. It can symbolize achievement in academic or vocational studies, and it can have credential value in a society that places a high premium on school attendance regardless of how much is accomplished there. For many young people, it has served as a ticket to employment, even when the job has not demanded the kind and level of skills acquired in high school. But the certificate loses its glitter as a prize to be coveted and honored when schools dilute their learning demands in order to improve their retention rates. Today, the diploma is not necessarily a mark of distinction, as it once was. In the early 1920's, when nearly 80 per cent of fifth-grade pupils never finished secondary school, the median I.Q. of public high school seniors in general was equivalent to the median I.Q. of today's seniors *in honors classes only* (Hollingworth, 1926). It stands to reason, therefore, that a high-school education was stiffer and more prestigeful at that time than it is today, when closer to two-thirds of all fifth graders eventually complete high school.

The credential value of the diploma is also diminishing as more and more adolescents are persuaded to stay on until graduation. Not much stock can be placed in a "union card" if it is within reach of the vast majority of young people. Its mere accessibility makes it the kind of possession (not unlike the elementary-school diploma) that one can't do much with and can't do much without. It will not open doors to privilege for anyone who has it; but on the other hand, these doors will not open *unless* one has it. Diploma devaluation already exists in the job world as evidenced by the fact that the educational attainment of the unemployed is increasing more rapidly than that of the employed (U.S. Department of Labor, 1965B). The net effect of reducing dropout rates is to add more graduates to the army of unemployed rather than to guarantee jobs for those young people who have to be persuaded to graduate.

For the dwindling few who are unable or unwilling to earn the diploma, dropping out becomes a more terrible stigma than it ever has been, partly because it is seen as failure at an easy task, and partly because failure classifies them as extreme nonconformists. But obviously, incomplete schooling is not their only handicap. The kind of person who drops out of school today, when the diploma is a minimum essential, is quite different from the kind of person who dropped out of school some fifty years ago, when the diploma was a valuable credential. He is likely to be beset by many other deterrents to life success that would probably linger on even if he finished school. The chances are that he comes from a poor, low-prestige family, or a disenfranchised minority group. More often than not, he is failing at school or suffering any number of physical and emotional handicaps. To dub him a "school dropout" and suggest by that label the cause and cure of his subsequent problems requires a good deal more evidence than we now have.

Since the law obligates children to remain in school usually until the age of sixteen, only two years of attendance separate most dropouts from high-school graduates who do not go on to college. Keeping today's dropout-prone in school for the two years so that they can graduate with their classmates is not going to help much in doing away with the factors that caused them to consider leaving school in the first place. Whatever derailed them from their journey through the grades will probably prevent them also from becoming attractive choices as employees, marriage partners, community workers, or members of the armed forces. Surprisingly, reports of research on school dropouts fail to include the social and emotional concomitants of early school withdrawal as independent variables. In most studies, the importance of a diploma for occupational success is "proven" by comparisons between the job histories of dropouts and of *unselected* graduates without regard for the fact that the two groups differ in many other ways that are perhaps even more critical to employability.

A close look at research on education and employment shows that a high-school diploma can be relatively useless to some people. It has been noted, for example, that in 1964 about 25 per cent of the unemployed Negro males 18 years old and over had high school diplomas, as against 32 per cent of the employed—a difference of only 7 per cent. Comparable figures among white males, on the other hand, were 38 per cent and 57 per cent, respectively—a difference of as much as 19 per cent (U.S. Department of Labor, 1965B). This finding suggests that, assuming the diploma *alone* accounts for these discrepancies, it is a more precious credential in the hands of a white adolescent than in the hands of a Negro. It also lends some credence to the hypothesis that at the lower skill levels, color of skin is more important to success in landing a job than is a high-school education.

With so many other factors complicating the life of the school dropout, why is so much attention given to his finishing school? Why, indeed, is he called a "school dropout" rather than a Negro who has left school, or a slum dweller who has left school, or a scholastic failure who has left school, or an emotionally disturbed adolescent who has left school? The answer can only be a matter of conjecture. Part of it may lie in the fact that it is easier to manipulate a person's educational history than to change his social status, his academic aptitude, his mental health, or the color of his skin. It is like the well-known folk tale about the person searching for his wife's lost diamond brooch under a lamp post, and when asked whether that is where it had been lost, answering "No, but the light is better here."

Emphasis on the value of a high-school diploma may also reflect wide-spread faith and vested interest in universal, free, compulsory education. The school rivals the church in the public's image of an institution that can have a powerful social impact among the masses. Many are convinced that it can cure social ills and personal defects if a proper dosage of school-ing is administered with enough skill and patience. In our society, educa-tion is above criticism, despite the fact that educators are fair game for attack. Its alleged bounty so dazzles public imagination that hardly any-body ever bothers to find out what it *cannot* do even under the best of circumstances. Who would dare argue that achieving 100 per cent school retention is *not* a desirable goal? Certainly not industry and the labor unions, since they want to keep unskilled young people in school — and out of the glutted job market — for as long as possible. Certainly not the school administrator whose school subsidies are computed on a per capita attendance formula. Therefore, by emphasizing the importance of finish-ing school, the public champions a noncontroversial cause that is in the best interests of everybody concerned, and thus relieves itself of the responsibility for cataloging the dropout's *multiple* handicaps and planning complex, expensive programs of social rehabilitation. This is not to suggest that education is something of an opiate and should be exposed as such. It is, in fact, as indispensible to personal fulfillment as basic nutrition is to physical subsistence. However, it cannot guarantee good fortune any more than basic nutrition can guarantee good health.

The prime targets for "Stay in School" campaigns are the impov-erished, lower-class groups — with their disproportionately high nonwhite membership — who are vastly over-represented in the nation's dropout population. Such pleas often create the impression that a high school diploma can go a long way toward reversing the deprivation effects of their *total* environment and upbringing. This is purely euphoric. Perfecting school retention rates in depressed areas won't do much by way of combating poverty and alienation. However, there isn't a comprehensive plan that stands a chance of success without a strong educational component. No matter how ingenious and costly are the social engineering strategies for bringing privilege to the slum youth who drops out of school, this youth will become increasingly conspicuous as one of the near-vanishing few in his age group who could not or would not graduate. He needs the credential to show for his years of schooling, even if his achievement is mininal, because the spirit of the times demands it. What is more, he needs to show satisfactory scholastic achievement because the criterion for minimum essentials in education is rising. We are fast approaching the time when a child from an underprivileged environment will be doomed to a life of economic dependency and status depression unless he can master even more academic skills than are necessary to earn the high school diploma.

The Schools' Retention Power

How serious is the dropout problem in American schools? Not serious at all, by international standards. It is said that proportionately more Negroes in the South finish college than do Englishmen in Great Britain. The difference probably lies in the cultural traditions of the New and Old Worlds. Schools in this country tend to be *absorbing* institutions following the principle that there ought to be a place and program for all children, while European schools are more inclined to be *filtering* institutions with programs restricted to those capable of measuring up to preset standards. This may be one reason why the rate of college attendance among 18-year-olds in this country is at least twice that of any other country in the world.

The degree to which early school withdrawal is a problem is not easy to assess with precision. One method is to estimate the numbers dropping out each year, and these range anywhere from 650,000 to about one million. Another commonly used method is to trace a high-school graduating class back to the fifth grade and calculate the rate of attendance shrinkage over the seven-year period. This figure is declining each year, and by all odds the present graduating class has decreased by no more than a third of its size since it was in the fifth grade. Dentler (1964) has examined the steady improvement in the schools' retention power, and he notes that at this rate 70 per cent of the 1967–68 fifth-graders will graduate in 1975 and 80 per cent of the 1992–93 fifth-graders will finish high school by the end of the century. This reflects a change from 80 per cent dropping out in 1920 to 80 per cent graduating in the year 2000.

Impressive as these figures are, they are on the conservative side. Many students disappear from school for any number of involuntary reasons, such as severe physical disabilities, emotional disturbance, trouble with the law, and impending marriage or parenthood. Kohler (1962) estimated that in a large city school system, as many as 5 per cent of the total high school population are enrolled in special programs for the handicapped, and another 5 per cent show signs of delinquent behavior or serious emotional disorders. If the involuntary withdrawals were removed from dropout inventories, the retention rates from fifth grade through high-school graduation would be closer to 75 per cent in 1960 (Dentler and Warshauer, 1965) rather than the 62 per cent reported in government surveys (National Education Association, 1963B). Even these figures fail to take into account the sizable numbers of students who do not graduate with their age peers but are enrolled in school anyway. Saleem and Miller (1963) report that as many as 10 per cent of the 1959–60 high-school dropouts in Syracuse returned to school within two years of their withdrawal, and another 15 per cent were engaged in other kinds of study at the same time.

A dropout is generally defined arbitrarily as a student who withdraws prior to finishing high school. With retention rates improving and the credential value of the diploma declining, it may be necessary to redefine the term on the basis of college attendance. The college diploma seems to be a more hard-won prize for students entering college than is the high school diploma for those entering high school, as evidenced by the fact that the current college dropout rate exceeds 50 per cent, which is much higher than the attrition rate for high schools. Moreover, the difference in lifetime earnings is much greater between college graduates and dropouts than between high school graduates and dropouts. There is already talk of persuading high school graduates to continue on to college and thus improve its image as an absorbing institution rather than a filtering one. The slogan of "everybody passes" has moved from the elementary to the high school and may continue on to college with the result that for an increasing number of students earning a diploma will one day be more of a ritual and a sign of patience and conformity than that of accomplishment.

Employment, Civil Rights, and the Dropout

The social barriers facing the school dropout have not received balanced coverage in popular and professional journals. Most of what is known and reported about his post-dropout history deals with how he fares in finding a job. Much is made, for example, of the fact that employment opportunities are becoming increasingly inaccessible to the uneducated. His problems on the labor market are continuously in the public eye because of the constant monitoring of labor conditions in this country by the U.S. Department of Labor. Much less is known about his other hardships in the social world. There is some evidence to show that he is overrepresented among delinquent and criminal groups (Schreiber, 1963). However, virtually nothing is known about the manner and degree to

265

which he exercises his citizenship rights and responsibilities at the polls, in community affairs, and in the armed forces. Nor is much known about his problems in making a happy marital choice and building a wholesome family life. The chances are that if his post-dropout experiences were thoroughly researched, he would be depicted as a multiple failure, not only in the job world but in other important social domains as well. The current literature, however, deals mainly with his history of employment, possibly because so much more is known about this aspect of his life than about any other. It may also reflect a popular feeling that the major function of the school in society is to prepare youth for vocational success.

Some basic statistics regarding youth and the job market offer important insight into the plight of the dropout. In 1964, there were approximately 15 million persons aged 16 to 21, half of whom were employed, generally in the lower-paying, less stable jobs. Some 1.2 million were jobless, and their rate of unemployment was 14 per cent — more than 3.5 times that of persons aged 25 and over. This age group constituted approximately 12 per cent of the total labor force in 1964, but its unemployed accounted for 31 per cent of all out-of-work persons. Joblessness declines with increased age for men in their teens and twenties, the 16- and 17-year-olds showing an unemployment rate of 17 per cent as against 11 per cent for the 20 and 21-year-olds during 1964. In October 1964, a special survey was made of unemployment rates among youth, and the results showed that about 7 out of 10 unemployed youths aged 16 to 21 were no longer attending school and that half of this group had dropped out before graduating from high school. The unemployment rate for dropouts was 1.5 times as high for those who had at least a high school education (U.S. Department of Labor, 1965E).

Unemployment is generally much higher among youthful job seekers than among older ones, especially those who are married. A young person is not prepared enough to choose from a wide range of job alternatives on the job market, even if he has earned a high school diploma. He must rely on work shortages in the unskilled and semiskilled occupations, which have limited openings. The dropout fares even worse despite the fact that in many instances he is as equipped with work skills as the high school graduate in the jobs open to them. While unemployment rates generally decline from lower to higher age groups, the downward trend is steeper for graduates than for dropouts. In 1964, for example, the rate of unemployment among graduates was about 82 per cent that of dropouts at age 16–17, some 75 per cent at age 18–19, about 70 per cent at age 20–21, and only a bit more than 50 per cent at age 22–24. It seems, therefore, that although the dropout stands to improve his job status with the passage of time, age and experience do less for him than they do for his age mate who has finished school.

In October 1959, 60 per cent of unemployed out-of-school youth aged 16–21 were dropouts, but by October 1964 the situation had become reversed, with a majority of these jobless youths holding high school diplomas. During that period, the proportion of dropouts in the out-of-school population aged 16–24 fell from 43 per cent to 36 per cent (U.S. Department of Labor, 1965C). This means that while a smaller fraction of young people were dropping out of school, those who would have withdrawn but were persuaded to stay on until graduation probably continued to find it hard to locate a job. The diploma by itself was apparently not a ticket to job success for these students.

Teenagers and young adults are over represented on the unemployment lists primarily because they are the most poorly trained and least experienced job seekers. There are simply too many of them, and there are too few opportunities for the kind of work they are capable of doing. Moreover, the discrepancy threatens to widen sharply for the next decade and beyond. By 1970, half of the nation's population will be under 26 as the bumper crop of postwar babies comes of age (Bienstock, 1964). What these vast numbers of young people will probably face is a declining need for unskilled blue-collar workers and a sharp increase in opportunities for professionals and technicians as well as for workers in the service industries (U.S. Department of Labor, 1965A). Technological change will force an upward swing in the minimum education requirements in those occupations for which a rise in job openings is anticipated (U.S. Department of Labor, 1965G). With the occupations that have the lowest educational prerequisites showing actual decreases in employment opportunities, the uneducated don't stand a chance, and that includes those who hold a high school diploma. What constitutes basic literacy in today's world will be inadequate for the world of the future. One of the most serious questions of our time, therefore, is whether the schools are capable of responding to the increasing educational demands made upon them. They have done a commendable job in providing education for the masses, and they are raising the general achievement levels steadily; but the rate of improvement is not rapid enough to keep pace with society's requirements in an age when knowledge is multiplying more rapidly than ever and the unskilled labor force is becoming obsolete.

Against the background of shrinking opportunity for young people with limited scholastic achievement stands the Negro's demand for social justice and economic well-being. In his battle for civil rights, he is caught in the crossfire of two conflicting realities. On the one hand, he must elevate his educational horizons in order to neutralize the depressing effects of racial bigotry; otherwise, racial equality will remain but a dream no matter how much civil rights legislation is passed. On the other hand, there is the painful reality that racial bigotry neutralizes the elevating effects of his education unless he is able to advance far beyond the high-school level.

It is twelve years since the Supreme Court ordered racial integration in the schools, and if anything, the nation is straying farther from this goal in its largest municipalities as the in-migration of Negroes from the rural South increases and the whites speed up their exodus to the suburbs. In New York City, the nonwhite public school population is now 50 per cent, as compared to 32 per cent only ten years ago. In Chicago, the nonwhite public school population has also grown to 50 per cent, and in the nation's capital it now hovers around 93 per cent. The educational problems of these schools are so enormous that one highly placed urban school official was quoted as stating that there is a whole generation of children who seem incapable of being taught enough to hold a job in their entire lifetime (Alexander, 1966).

Dropout figures among Negroes are much higher than among white students. In October 1964, for example, fully one half of the nonwhite boys aged 16 to 21 were not in school, as compared with only one-third of the white boys in that age group—a difference largely attributable to disproportionate college enrollment rates (U.S. Department of Labor, 1965D). The Negro dropout rates at the elementary and high-school levels are also relatively high. Although Negroes constitute less than 11 per cent of the total population in this country, their 18- to 26-year-olds have contributed more than 26 per cent of the dropouts in that age group and less than 10 per cent of the high-school graduates (National Education Association, 1963A). However, there is some question as to whether dropping out of school, *per se*, is a major contributor to Negro unemployment. Studies show that even among high-school graduates, nonwhites find it harder to locate jobs than whites. In October 1964, twice as many nonwhite high-school graduates no longer in school were looking for work than were their white counterparts (U.S. Department of Labor, 1965E). Even more startling is the fact that unemployment rates for nonwhite high school graduates in the 16–24 age group *exceeded* that of white dropouts and just about equaled that of nonwhite dropouts (U.S. Department of Labor, 1965C). It is apparent, therefore, that in a climate of racial prejudice, a high-school diploma is virtually powerless to combat unemployment among Negro youth. Without the privilege to use the credential as a self-help tool, the Negro also faces a bleak economic future. The low-skill jobs traditionally open to him are becoming scarcer, and the high-level occupations in industry and the professions which are opening for him as never before are finding that there are not enough Negroes with the perseverance to continue on to advanced schooling and qualify for these openings. This leaves the vast area of middle-status positions in the job world—mostly the white collar and semi-skilled service occupations—where the white job seeker has traditionally been a preferred choice, even when his Negro competitor has had comparable educational qualifications.

Fortunately, recent reports show that the job picture is beginning to become somewhat brighter for the Negro. Since 1955, employment of Negroes and other nonwhites increased from 6,400,000 to 7,700,000, a much faster rate of growth than that of employment among whites (U.S.

Department of Labor, 1966A). This brought the ratio of nonwhite workers to total employment from 10.2 in 1955 to 10.7 in 1965. Another study of Negro employment trends conducted by the National Industrial Conference Board showed a recent increase of job opportunities in industry and attributed the breakthrough to the Civil Rights Act of 1964 (New York Times, June 13, 1966). Progress toward racial equality may also explain a change in job opportunities for Negro high-school graduates. Whereas Negro dropouts and graduates found it equally difficult to gain employment as recently as in 1964, a sharp discrepancy had already developed by late 1965. The jobless rate for nonwhite dropouts remained unchanged at 16.5 per cent from October 1964 to October 1965, as against a decline from 13.6 per cent to 11.8 per cent for dropouts in general; however, the rate for nonwhite graduates did show a drop of 6 percentage points over that period (U.S. Department of Labor, 1966B). Once again it is apparent that in the job world a high school diploma is useless without racial equality, and *vice versa*.

Despite improvements in the educated nonwhite's chances for employment, there is still a relatively high concentration of Negroes in less skilled blue collar jobs and in service occupations. Only one out of five nonwhite employees held white collar jobs in the past ten years, as against one out of two whites. The extent to which Negro unemployment remains a serious problem is reflected in the finding that in 1965 nonwhites constituted 11 per cent of the labor force, 21 per cent of those out of work 15 weeks or longer, and 27 per cent of those jobless more than 6 months. These proportions have remained fairly constant over the past eight years (U.S. Department of Labor, 1965F).

Some Correlates of Early School Withdrawal

There are many studies of the social and economic milieu in which the dropout problem flourishes. There are also large numbers of investigations into the behavioral characteristics of those who do not finish school. Surveys of community conditions associated with dropout rates provide a fairly clear picture of the critical factors involved. Young (1963) found an inverse relationship between early school withdrawal and such indices as average income in the community, rental rates, teachers' salaries, the amount of schooling completed by adults, the proportion of professionals residing in the area, and the per capita student expenditure. Positively related were the incidence of overcrowdedness in dwelling units and pupils and teacher turnover in the local schools.

A more recent study by Dentler and Warshauer (1965) dealt with demographic correlates in 131 large cities across the nation. They found a cluster of social and economic variables correlating .87 with dropout rates among white students and accounting for 76 per cent of the variance for this subpopulation. More than half of the variance could be explained by

269

such factors as per cent of population in white collar occupation, per cent of white families with annual incomes under $1000, and the white adult illiteracy rate. From the data presented, it is evident that in communities where income is low, population growth stable, and where the very young constitute a large proportion of the population, there would be a high incidence of early school withdrawal among white residents.

Also identified were several social and economic variables that correlated .67 with nonwhite dropout rates and accounted for some 45 per cent of the variance. By far the most important factor was the white dropout rate, followed by the per cent of nonwhite male operatives, the nonwhite illiteracy rate, and the per cent of nonwhite, non-Negroes residing in the communities. Interestingly enough, economic impoverishment was *not* associated with high dropout rates among the nonwhite groups.

Dentler and Warshauer did separate analyses of cities where dropout rates were higher or lower than expectation according to their prediction formula. They found that in those communities where there was a low incidence of illiteracy, low population density, few male operatives, little public expenditure on health and hospitals, and high payments for aid to families with dependent children (AFDC), there tended to be lower-than-expected dropout rates among the white population. For the nonwhite population, the critical variables were per pupil expenditure and average payment per family of AFDC.

Studies of community conditions as they relate to dropout rates show that the problem is severest among the poverty stricken and socially disadvantaged, especially the nonwhites in these groups. These are the slum dwellers, many of whom gravitate to the big city in search of employment primarily in the unskilled labor force. As their influx increases, the middle-class families flee to the suburbs, leaving behind large ghettoes ridden with poverty, social pathology, and educational failure. Thus Schreiber (1964A) found that the holding power of the 1963 graduating high school class in 128 large cities was more than 5 per cent less than the national average, based on grade ten enrollment. The loss in New York City from tenth grade in 1960–61 to high school graduation in 1962–63 was as great as the dropout rate from the fifth grade in 1952–53 to high school graduation in 1960 for the nation as a whole (National Education Association, 1963B). In Philadelphia, nearly half of the 1960 tenth graders failed to complete twelve grades by 1963.

The crisis environment in the lower-class home makes it difficult for the child to see much need or much possibility of finishing school. He lives in a dingy, overcrowded home where there is no privacy for schoolwork, no calm and quiet in which to concentrate on ideas, no model of success to emulate. The family is large and the siblings can often distract a student from serious work. Sometimes he is denied a good night's sleep because his sleeping quarters are uncomfortable and someone in the

270

family is invariably demanding attention during the night. When he awakens in the morning, his breakfast is rationed according to food supply, and he is sent off to school hungry and unprepared to compete against national achievement norms. Too often there is no father in the home to help make ends meet, and all able-bodied members of the family must lend a hand as soon as they reach employment age. The family must live for the present because subsistence is at stake. It cannot afford the luxury of allowing its members to defer entrance into the job world by prolonging schooling, even if the time investment in education means a better job in the future. Today's need cannot be satisfied with the promise of tomorrow.

Poverty and poor living conditions are not the only deterrents to success at school among the socially disadvantaged. Children coming from these homes grow up in an environment that is virtually barren of educational interests. Although parents pay lip-service to education, they rarely have the desire or reserve wherewithal to make sacrifices for it. Schreiber (1964B) found that approximately two-thirds of the parents of dropouts are either hostile or indifferent toward school, and more than 70 per cent of them have failed to complete twelve grades. Thus, children who withdraw from school are often merely following in the footsteps of their parents. They learn to hate school almost from the day they enroll. The classroom teacher punishes them for behaviors that seem acceptable at home and holds them to academic standards that their home environment has never prepared them to meet. They take a cynical view of the teacher who constantly preaches that hard work inevitably leads to success because they see how futile has been the hard work of their own parents. Small wonder that more than 85 per cent of the nation's dropouts come from the lower classes (Bowman and Matthews, 1960).

Studies of personal characteristics of dropouts also provide clues as to why they withdraw from school. Voss, Wendling, and Elliott (1966) reviewed a sampling of studies of students who leave school early and found that they could be separated into three categories: (1) the involuntary dropout who withdraws because of personal illness or accident; (2) the retarded dropout who is unable to handle the required work at school; and (3) the capable dropout, who could finish school if he were motivated to do so, but who is discouraged by peer and parental attitudes toward education.

Dropout inventories do not take a close account of those who leave school involuntarily, but much is known about the retarded and capable students who fail to earn a high-school diploma. As might be expected, studies of scholastic aptitudes among school dropouts generally show lower-than-average scores on intelligence tests, and the discrepancies are greater between high-school graduates and those who never enter high school than between the graduates and those who enter and drop out. A survey conducted by the U.S. Department of Labor (1960) showed that some 31 per cent of students never reaching or completing high school

271

had I.Q.'s of 85 and under, as against only 10 per cent of the high-school graduates, and that a mere 6 per cent of those failing to finish school had I.Q.'s of 110 and above, as compared to 16 per cent of the diploma recipients. On the other hand, a study by McCreary and Kitch (1953), dealing only with sophomore withdrawals from high school matched with attending classmates on the basis of school attended, sex, socioeconomic status, and rate of promotion showed no difference in I.Q. Research in New York City schools (Board of Education of the City of New York, 1956) also showed far more overlap than discrepancy in I.Q. scores when high-school dropouts were compared with graduates. However, the picture is much different for those who leave school in the pre-high-school grades. Dillon (1949) found that about 36 per cent of his sample of more than 1,000 dropouts in grades 7 through 12 had I.Q. scores below 85, while some 75 per cent of the dropouts who had left school in the seventh grade scored below this level.

Deficiency in verbal skills and in school achievement are more closely related to early school withdrawal than is I.Q. A Labor Department survey found that whereas 75 per cent of the school dropouts tested below average in intelligence, 84 per cent of the dropouts were in classes at least one year below the grade levels they should have reached at the time of withdrawal. As many as 30 per cent never went as far as the tenth grade (U.S. Department of Labor, 1960). A more recent study in Rochester showed that while the median I.Q. for male dropouts was at the 41st percentile, their reading scores were only at the 31st percentile (New York State Division for Youth, 1962). These data suggest that a serious problem of scholastic underachievement can be an important factor in precipitating early school withdrawal. Many of the so-called underachievers who are likely to drop out show signs of failure as early as the fourth grade, and the rest of their school experience is merely a matter of marking time before they are legally able to withdraw (Lichter, 1962). Their school attendance becomes irregular, they refuse to participate in extracurricular activities, they frequently change schools, and their records show a long list of disciplinary problems (Cervantes, 1965).

There are also many adolescents with sufficient ability to succeed at school but who are inhibited by any number of intrapsychic and interpersonal problems. One study estimated that fully 80 per cent of those discharged from the armed services for personality disorders do not complete ten grades of schooling (Rohrer, 1964). These young people do not seek psychotherapeutic help, nor does much behavior change result when they do obtain help. They are particularly resentful of all kinds of authority at home, at school, on the job, in church, and with the police. Their self-image is weak, and they find it difficult to defer the gratification of immediate needs and desires. They come from homes where the parents have difficulty in controlling their offspring, where the relationships among members of the family is not warm and supportive, where the father figure

272

is either weak or absent, and where there is little evidence of a clear and consistent code of behavior (Cervantes, 1965; Rohrer, 1964).

The many emotional disorders and intellectual deficits that inhibit school completion attack children of all ethnic groups at all class levels. They are particularly devastating among the lower socioeconomic subpopulations. Where the general life circumstances are depressing, young people do not have the necessary resilience to resist personal problems and maintain a steady course toward long-range goals. The middle-class child—even the one with serious personal problems—somehow finds enough supportiveness in his milieu to encourage him to stay in school. His lower-class counterpart receives no such help. Yet, the tragic irony is that the lower-class child is the one who can least afford to enter adulthood without sufficient education.

Dropouts are frequently viewed by educators as students who elect to shorten their education because of pressures originating outside of school. The dropouts view themselves quite differently. The reasons they give most often for leaving school have to do with discouragements and dissatisfactions relating to the school program. One study reports that 38 per cent of male dropouts and 32 per cent of female dropouts listed "adverse school experience" as their reason for withdrawing (Sofokodis and Sullivan, 1964). This response was given more often than any other, which suggests that dropouts frequently see themselves as having been pushed out of school rather than having left under their own power. Many report that they received no encouragement or inspiration from their teachers, nor did they enjoy good relationships with their fellow students. Staying in school would have meant continuing on a treadmill without much hope for accomplishment. The only solution for them was to cut loose, get out into the world, and earn some money.

How the Dropout Problem is Attacked

Many programs have been developed in the recent past to make young people education-conscious or employable, or both. Schools have assumed the bulk of the responsibility, but they are being assisted in growing measure through special projects sponsored by community organizations and by industry, as part of the nation's war against poverty. Strategies range all the way from preventive programs beginning at the preschool level to "return to school" campaigns and job training for those who have withdrawn. One of the widest-scale, most publicized efforts took place in the summer of 1963 at the request of the late President Kennedy, who allocated a quarter of a million dollars to 23 states and the District of Columbia to persuade would-be dropouts to return to school in September. Other agencies and organizations at the national, state, and local levels joined in the campaign in order to mobilize efforts in as many municipalities as possible. So many participating sponsors contributed efforts to the crash program that it is impossible to determine exactly how many children were contacted. However, the 63 communities receiving allocations from the President's Emergency Fund reported: (1) 1,375 counselors and other professional workers whose salaries were paid from the special fund participated in the campaign; (2) 59,300 young people identified by these workers as dropouts and prospective dropouts were contacted during the campaign; (3) somewhat more than half of the target group returned to school in September; and (4) more than 90 per cent of the youths returning to school in September were still enrolled at the end of October. Needless to say, the program had enormous public relations value. However, there is no information available as to how many would have come back to school anyway, how many were compelled to return by law because they were underage, and how many stayed on to graduate.

Aside from the nation-wide crash programs aimed at discouraging would-be dropouts from going through with their plans, there have been many ongoing guidance projects at the local school levels designed also to exercise preventive measures. Counselors generally agree that their work has little value after the pupil has made up his mind to leave school. Potential dropouts can be spotted as early as the elementary grades, provided that the school has a well-designed testing program. Given a clear picture of the pupil's personal development and an opportunity to reach him long before his is legally able to withdraw, the guidance counselor can succeed in persuading him to stay in school. Moore (1963) reports some evidence to show the success of intensive guidance programs in reducing dropout rates. These programs were effective where potential dropouts were identified early, where total faculties contributed their efforts in coordinated fashion, where schedules allowed for additional counseling time, where the dropout-prone could receive work readiness, and where close contact with parents could be achieved. In most schools, however, especially those in depressed areas where the dropout problem is severest, such coordinated, intensive efforts are difficult to achieve. It is perhaps for this reason that counseling programs have not been dramatically successful in depressed areas.

One special program in New York City (Board of Education of the City of New York, 1956) illustrates how difficult it is to make a dent in dropout rates in slum schools. In this project, the school officials considered themselves fortunate to be assigned one counselor per 125 students. But even though these services were considered lavish by city-wide standards, there were simply not enough counselors to establish frequent, prolonged contact with the pupils showing signs of early withdrawal from school. Nor was there enough time to teach the parents and solicit their close support. Instead, the counselors were involved mostly in collecting test data, making programmatic adaptations to fit the ability and interest levels of the dropout-prone, finding part-time work for them, and exchanging correspondence with local social agencies. As might be expected, little of substance was accomplished.

274

The need for large-scale, well-coordinated counseling services in order to achieve success in slum schools was dramatically illustrated by the contrasting results obtained in the P.S. 43 demonstration program in New York City and in its derivative Higher Horizons Program. The essential difference in services between the two programs was quantitative rather than qualitative. At P.S. 43, the counseling and remedial education staffs were sharply augmented to provide a high concentration of supplementary help to pupils in a single depressed-area school. Added services were also available to these pupils when they continued on to the local high school. The staff had no magical formula for obtaining results; they effected better school performance and better retention rates purely by hard compensatory work over a long period of time. The eventual payoff was highly dramatic. Of the 105 children tested at the beginning of the project and three years later, 78 of them showed an increase in I.Q., 40 of them gained more than 10 points, and 13 gained more than 20 points. The dropout rate from high school for these children prior to the project was around 40 per cent; the rate for the project children was less than 20 per cent.

The Higher Horizons Program, on the other hand, provided relatively token special services to large numbers of schools in the hope that the success of P.S. 43 could be replicated on a large scale at minimum extra cost. The result was failure, perhaps because the amount of services was no match for the magnitude of the problem.

Some dropout prevention programs are designed to keep the dropout-prone in school by modifying its requirements to fit the ambitions and tastes of every student. In effect, they say to the student, "Stay in school, and we will provide you with something to hold your interest." It may be a watered-down version of the conventional curriculum, or limited vocational training as a substitute for academic instruction, or a combination of study at school and salaried employment in the field. These programmatic modifications are often attempts at making class attendance attractive to the student, even if it means sacrificing educational standards traditionally associated with secondary schooling. Unless these programs have long-range value, they simply fill a void and constitute little more than a bribe to stay in school. On paper, they may be instrumental in improving school retention rates, but their net effect on the students' growth and development needs to be tested.

Most of the procedures for retaining potential dropouts in school are designed for the junior and senior high schools. Efforts are made to change the role of the teacher from an enforcer of preset classroom demands to one who pitches his program at the pupil's level of functioning. The course of study is designed to be of immediate practicality to the student and introduces simple vocational readiness experiences as a way of bringing him into contact with the demands of the job world. In inner-city schools, where large numbers of students lack the motivation to finish school, these special programs are designed on a school-within-a-school basis,

275

drawing the marginal students off from regular programs in order to relieve them of the competition of more highly motivated schoolmates. Curriculum designs for socially disadvantaged pupils who need special encouragement to continue their schooling vary greatly in schools across the country. However, they usually follow the kinds of curriculum guidelines set forth by Savitsky (1965), as follows:

Personalize. Bring the student into focus by making the learning content relevant to his own experiences and aspirations. What is of practical interest to the child from a disadvantaged background may be quite different from what appeals to children from favored environments.

Orient to job experience or world of work. The disadvantaged pupil is job-conscious and seeking a short-range goal that holds some promise of economic stability. Anything that helps prepare him for the world of work is meaningful to him. This basic interest may be used as a medium for improving instruction in basic skills as well as preparing him to be a successful job-seeker.

Use the present and current events as a basis for understandings. All pupils need to benefit from general education, not just the skills that are of practical, immediate value. Teachers can capitalize on the disadvantaged pupils' concern with the here-and-now world by introducing present-day problems as a springboard toward formulating more generalized concepts.

Adapt or arrange text materials to fit reading levels, interests, and needs. Most of the existing textbooks do not take into consideration the special backgrounds, vocabulary, and interests of disadvantaged children. These pupils need content that is more relevant to their everyday lives and with which they can readily identify. It may be simpler to elicit responsiveness by developing textbook content at their interest levels without overburdening them with complex language structure.

Correlate with more than one subject area. Fragmentation of instruction at the junior-high-school level and beyond may, in effect, depersonalize learning for the socially disadvantaged, and thereby discourage them from making progress. If teachers could operate as teams, pooling information, interrelating content, and planning cooperatively, the students may come to realize that their interests are not being neglected.

Oral communication. Verbal interaction is one of the key elements of socialized behavior. Teachers often discourage the development of oral communication skills among disadvantaged children when they sense the difficulties these pupils have in utilizing them. The teacher gives up prematurely, and the child is afflicted with a permanent handicap.

Work for standards. Disadvantaged pupils are capable of learning and should be required and encouraged to accept standards of accomplishment. This is necessary to build the child's self-esteem in the school world. However, these responsibilities should be the kind that are attainable by the student; otherwise, failure will become compounded, and he will be discouraged from coming to grips even with those learning tasks that he is capable of negotiating.

Organize short, achievable units. These shorter units facilitate mastery, by gradation and posit, by pupils whose attention spans are short and whose work habits are poorly organized.

Build in elements of success. Positive reinforcement of correct learning responses can be a powerful encouragement for continued concentration and learning success. The disadvantaged rarely experience success in and out of school and are therefore often unable to assess their true capabilities. Providing them with meaningful experiences of success can help counteract the debilitating effects of repeated frustration.

Provide for exploration and discovery, including learning how to think. Help these students develop their own strategies for problem-solving that they can utilize independently and with skill. Once the child has developed a method of attack, with the help of a talented teacher, he will reach out into worlds of ambiguity and know how to achieve clarity by himself.

Aside from modifying the conventional curriculum, beginning at the junior-high-school level, dropout prevention programs also stress job preparation and experience. Guidance counselors play a major role in helping would-be dropouts see the advantages of preparing adequately for employment. Academic work is supplemented by some vocational raining, often in special schools designated for that purpose. These institutions have the facilities for developing skills in woodworking, metal work, automotive trades, ship building, food service, tailoring, upholstery, and other semiskilled occupations.

Unfortunately, the work of vocational high schools has not met with universal approval among educators. Some point to the fact that the dropout rate in these schools is 60 per cent higher than it is in academic high schools. These schools therefore serve more as dumping grounds for unwanted students than as learning centers catering to special needs. Minority groups are often over represented in many of these schools, thus making the school system vulnerable to criticism as practicing *de facto* segregation. The program is characterized as rigid and obsolete, and students who complete it are said to be no better prepared for work than students who have no such training (Kohler, 1962; Public Education Association Committee on Education, Guidance, and Work, 1963). As an alternative to maintaining vocational schools, some big cities will soon offer exploratory work courses to all students in all high schools. In these programs, there will be less sacrifice of academic studies in order to accommodate vocational training, and the hoped-for goal is better mastery of basic skills with no loss of vocational preparation.

Work-study programs have also been adopted by school systems throughout the country to discourage some children from dropping out by enabling them to continue their studies and to earn money at a part-time job. Junior-high-school students are carefully groomed to meet the success demands of the job world and then placed in part-time work under close supervision, supported by intensive training at school. Some schools offer paid work experience only in the school building while others arrange for employment off campus. All programs preserve some emphasis on academic study and offer considerable guidance services during the time the student spends at school.

Most of the dropout prevention programs that focus mainly on the junior and senior high school levels are little better than stopgap measures. They concede the student's scholastic failure and try to help him live with that handicap as best he can. The more comprehensive programs, however, aim at forestalling educational retardation and provide for a large-scale coordinate attack on the problem from the home, the school, and the community. Project Head Start, with its emphasis on early intervention, remains yet to be fully evaluated, but if it enhances the school preparedness of pupils from socially disadvantaged environments, it may also reduce dropout rates, provided that improved readiness is translated into *sustained* school success. There is still a great need to determine the special readiness curricula, teaching techniques, and optimum age of intervention. One carefully controlled study (Tannenbaum and Hodell, 1966) showed that well-planned readiness experiences administered to slum neighborhood first graders, singled out as potential reading retardates, had no measurable effect on their achievement after one full year of instruction. It should therefore not be assumed that early intervention will guarantee improved school performance for the lower-class child.

Cervantes (1965) advocates a large-scale, coordinated attack on the dropout problem, bringing to bear the following forces:

Community. A citizens' group can be organized representing the schools, employment services, labor and management, social service agencies, "character building" agencies, churches, civic and fraternal groups, service clubs, foundations, and communication and government agencies. This committee can alert the community to the special problems of early school withdrawal and sensitize itself to ways of dealing with the problem. It can stimulate industry to hire more untrained young workers and call upon labor unions to liberalize its membership requirements. It can encourage summer antidropout campaigns similar to the crash program organized in 1963. It can also promote preschool programs and urge large numbers of slum-neighborhood parents to enroll their children in them.

Government. The Economic Opportunity Act of 1964 is a prototype of the kind of help the federal government can provide. Many thousands of young men with limited skills have entered into special government projects and are receiving the kind of help that would otherwise not be easily available to them. Federal intervention has also stirred many state and local communities to mount their own programs.

Business. On a much too limited scale, American businessmen are beginning to realize that rehabilitating the school dropout represents a good business investment. Some large companies are therefore hiring teenagers without high-school diplomas and providing special assistance for them to succeed on the job. Such projects have exercised some holding power on these young people thus far, and there are enough positive results to encourage large corporations to broaden the practice. In some instances, too, representatives of big business have visited local high schools regularly to persuade students to stay in school rather than allow themselves to be cast adrift in the job world without any marketable skills.

Labor. Some of the arbitrary membership restrictions in labor unions ought to be eased in order to accommodate young people from poor backgrounds and with limited schooling. Since minority groups are over represented in the dropout population, racial discrimination in some trade unions constitutes a serious barrier to economic independence. Not only should these practices be abolished, but labor ought to develop training programs and should promote apprenticeships for those who need the extra help.

Schools. Any number of curriculum modifications designed to fit the backgrounds, interests, and performance levels of potential dropouts should be introduced in schools where the problem is severe. In addition, the teacher must be especially skillful and dedicated to do one of the most difficult jobs in the profession. Finally, intensive counseling services can help convince the poorly motivated that the school is really interested in their progress and is prepared to help them make the most of their innate abilities. School systems throughout the country are responding to public pressures to improve education for the

279

socially disadvantaged. As a result, a large number of programs have been written, fewer have been implemented, and fewer still have been evaluated.

Volunteer Groups. Communities generally have enormous amounts of talent that could be marshalled to assist schools in upgrading the education of marginal students. High-school graduates, college-trained parents, widows with adequate education, and other knowledgeable laymen have the time and can develop the skill to provide a variety of educational services. In some cities, they offer tutorial help to children who need it, and in others they assist teachers on trips and with clerical chores. The enormous possibilities of out-of-school volunteer and paid services have hardly been explored by educational institutions.

The Family. Systematic efforts are needed to reduce the social distance between the potential dropout's home and the school. Most teachers working in slum areas are barely familiar with the dynamics of community life surrounding the school building and the degree of importance attached to the school by its inhabitants. They can learn much by visiting the homes of their pupils and learning about parental attitudes toward school and the neighborhood conditions that inhibit or encourage school success.

Once the student drops out of school, it is difficult to maintain contact with him in order to supply supportive services. In the past, dropouts have been written off as failures mainly because they no longer have any institutional affiliation. However, with the Economic Opportunity Act of 1964, the federal government acknowledged that school withdrawal is too serious a problem to be handled solely by the schools. The act established the Job Corps and Neighborhood Youth Corps under federal support and administration. The Job Corps is a residential training program similar to the Civilian Conservation Corps of the 1930's. In 1965, its first year of operation, it enrolled 40,000 youths in urban and rural centers and provided them with job training as well as remediation in basic skills. The Neighborhood Youth Corps provided short-term employment and some ancillary services for 100,000 youth, in and out of school, in 1965. In addition, the federal government has expanded existing agencies, especially the state employment services, which for the first time are beginning to reach out to slum youths who were formerly regarded as unemployable.

Most of the new programs for dropouts are designed to provide educational and vocational adjustment; some even attempt to stimulate upward economic mobility. It is as yet much too early to determine the success of these vigorous attempts to help undereducated and underemployed young people achieve a productive life for themselves. Research and evaluation lag far behind programing. However, these out-of-school programs make it clear that the school dropout is not simply a problem for educators. The current many-sided attack on the so-called "dropout" problem may indeed be a first step toward placing the school in proper social perspective and discrediting the popular myth that the schools *alone* have the capability to prepare the entire present-day youth population for the world of tomorrow.

References

Alexander, J. "Shift Emphasis from Integration to Comprehensive Quality Education." New York: Teachers College, Columbia University, 1966. Paper prepared for the School Administrator's Conference sponsored by the National Urban League and Teachers College, Columbia University, June 17–18, 1966. Mimeographed.

Bienstock, H. "Realities of the Job Market for the High School Dropout," in *Guidance and the School Dropout*, ed. Daniel Schreiber, Washington: National Education Association, 1964.

Board of Education of the City of New York, Bureau of Educational and Vocational Guidance. *Experiment in Guidance of Potential Early School Leavers*. New York: The Board, 1956.

Bowman, P. H. and C. V. Matthews. *Motivations of Youth for Leaving School*. U.S. Department of Health, Education and Welfare, Office of Education, Cooperative Research Program, Project No. 200. Quincy, Illinois: University of Chicago, Quincy Youth Development Project, 1960.

Cervantes, L. F. *The Dropout: Causes and Cures*. Ann Arbor: The University of Michigan Press, 1965.

Dentler, R. "Dropouts, Automation, and the Cities," *Teachers College Record*, 65 (1964), 475–483.

Dentler, R. A. and Mary Ellen Warshauer. *Big City Dropouts*. New York: Center for Urban Education, 1965.

Dillon, H. J. *Early School Leavers: A Major Educational Problem*. Publication No. 401. Washington: National Child Labor Committee, 1949.

Hollingworth, Leta S. *Gifted Children, Their Nature and Nurture*. New York: The Macmillan Company, 1926.

Kohler, Mary Conway. *Youth and Work in New York City*. New York: The Taconic Foundation, 1962.

Lichter, S. O., *et al. The Dropouts*. New York: Free Press, 1962.

McCreary, W. H. and D. E. Kitch. "Now Hear Youth." *Bulletin of the California State Department of Education*. 22 (October, 1953), 27–44.

Moore, J. W. *Reducing the School Dropout Rate — Report on the Holding Power Project*. Albany: University of the State of New York, The State Education Department, Bureau of Guidance, 1963.

National Education Association, Research Division. "Graduates and Dropouts in the Labor Force." *National Education Association Research Bulletin*. 41 (1963), 120–121.

——. *School Dropouts.* NEA Research Memo 1963-10. Washington: National Education Association, 1963.

New York State Division for Youth. *The School Dropout Problem: Rochester.* Albany: The Division, May 1962.

Public Education Association Committee on Education, Guidance, and Work. *Reorganizing Secondary Education in New York City.* New York: The Association, 1963.

Rohrer, J. H. "Psychosocial Development and Acting-Out Behavior," in *Guidance and the School Dropout,* ed. Daniel Schreiber. Washington: National Education Association, 1964.

Saleem, Betty L. and S. M. Miller. *The Neglected Dropout: The Returnee.* Syracuse, New York: Syracuse University Youth Development Center, 1963.

Savitsky, C. "Reaching the Disadvantaged," in *Mental Health and Achievement: Increasing Potential and Reducing School Dropout,* eds. V. Paul Torrance and Robert D. Strom. New York: John Wiley and Sons, 1965.

Schreiber, D. "Juvenile Delinquency and the School Dropout Problem," *Federal Probation* (September 1963).

——. *Holding Power: Large City School Systems.* Washington: National Education Association, 1964.

——. "An Introduction to the School Dropout," in *Guidance and the School Dropout,* ed. Daniel Schreiber. Washington: National Education Association, 1964.

Sofokidis, Jeanette H. and Eugenia Sullivan. *A New Look at School Dropouts.* Washington: U.S. Department of Health, Education and Welfare, 1964.

Tannenbaum, A. J. and Louise Hodell. "An Early Intervention Program That Failed." New York: Mobilization for Youth, 1966. Mimeographed.

U.S. Department of Labor. *Manpower Implications of Automation.* Washington: U.S. Printing Office, 1965.

U.S. Department of Labor, Bureau of Statistics. *School and Early Employment of Youth.* Bulletin 1277. Washington: U.S. Government Printing Office, 1960.

——. *Monthly Labor Review, April, 1965.* Washington: U.S. Government Printing Office, 1965.

——. *Monthly Labor Review, May, 1965.* Washington: U.S. Government Printing Office, 1965.

——. *Monthly Labor Review, June, 1965.* Washington: U.S. Government Printing Office, 1965.

——. *Monthly Labor Review, July, 1965.* Washington: U.S. Government Printing Office, 1965.

——. *Monthly Labor Review, August, 1965.* Washington: U.S. Government Printing Office, 1965.

————. *Monthly Labor Review, September, 1965.* Washington: U.S. Government Printing Office, 1965.

————. *Monthly Labor Review, May, 1966.* Washington: U.S. Government Printing Office, 1966.

————. *Monthly Labor Review, June, 1966.* Washington: U.S. Government Printing Office, 1966.

Voss, H. L.; A. Wendling and D. S. Elliott. "Some Types of High School Dropouts," *The Journal of Educational Research.* 59 (April, 1966), 363–368.

Young, N. *Community Predictors of School Holding Power.* New York: Yeshiva University, 1963. Unpublished doctoral dissertation.

Abraham J. Tannenbaum surveys the education-based programs of Mobilization for Youth (MFY) in its first five years of operation. The first of the large-scale demonstration projects designed to cope with juvenile delinquency, MFY predated the antipoverty programs and other federal activities designed to aid the disadvantaged.

Following a two-year planning period, MFY was funded in mid-1962, and a program was launched to help the residents of New York's Lower East Side cope with the problems of poverty and discrimination. The MFY program offered the following services: (1) youth employment and training — subsidized work experience, on-the-job training, vocational counseling, job placement, and basic education; (2) community organization and development aimed at "organizing the unaffiliated," support of neighborhood councils, and help with community coordination and planning efforts; (3) housing services, such as assistance in locating housing and training for collective protest activities; (4) legal services to the poor residents of the area; (5) storefront Neighborhood Service Centers providing concrete and immediate assistance to individuals and families; (6) services of visiting homemakers and detached group workers; (7) the support of a mental hygiene clinic and narcotics program; (8) a program to reintegrate the juvenile parolee; and (9) an Adventure Corps for preadolescents.

This incomplete listing of MFY programs indicates the scope of their activities, aimed at helping youth and upgrading the community and its impoverished, powerless inhabitants. The author describes the educational programs as they operated until mid-1966. The programs are grouped under five headings: curriculum planning and development, teacher education, early intervention, correction and remediation, and pupil personnel services. The author is analytical as well as descriptive. MFY and its counterparts in most large cities have served to stimulate many school systems to develop their own programs for the disadvantaged.

MOBILIZATION FOR YOUTH IN NEW YORK CITY

Abraham J. Tannenbaum

285

MOBILIZATION FOR YOUTH IN NEW YORK CITY

Abraham J. Tannenbaum

Mobilization For Youth in New York City is a large-scale community project designed to combat delinquency and poverty by opening opportunities for low-income, minority groups in a slum area. The neighborhood it serves is old and famous as the place where immigrants have traditionally settled after stepping off the boats at the nearby docks, strangers in the New World and often ill-equipped to "make it" in these unfamiliar surroundings. Today, the majority of residents are impoverished Puerto Rican in-migrants, with a smaller sprinkling of low-income Negro, Chinese, Jewish, Italian, and Polish groups. In order to help these low-status people cope with their debilitating life conditions, Mobilization has since September, 1962 provided job training and placement for unemployed youth, group social work, organization of the unaffiliated for community action, social services to individuals and families, and special educational programs for children and youth. A saturation plan of such wide scope facilitates coordinated and mutually supportive action on behalf of clients in need. Multiproblem families can benefit from multifaceted services, thus strengthening the impact of the Mobilization program upon the community. These cooperative efforts can also be viewed as separate entities, each carefully designed to do a special job.

Among the vital offerings of Mobilization For Youth are its education programs, planned by its own staff and financed by public and private funds. Some are mounted in local public schools, with the prior consent of school officials, while others serve out-of-school youth in need of compensatory education. Despite its heavy emphasis on extra instructional and pupil personnel services, the primary objective of the program is not to fill gaps in the child's educational experience or to provide more of the same kinds of help offered at school. Instead, the emphasis is on educational innovation. Mobilization is mainly concerned with demonstrating new ways to improve the education of pupils in depressed areas by seeking greater understanding of their unique learning deficits, the unique strategies and materials needed, and the unique administrative logistics required to reach their vast numbers more efficiently and effectively.

Although Mobilization concentrates heavily on formulating programmatic alternatives, it does not equate innovation with improvement. One of its major tasks is to design and field its offerings in such a manner as to allow for objective evaluation. Operationally, however, two major steps

287

have to be taken before a fully blueprinted experimental program can be field tested: Mobilization must gain access to the testing ground, which in most instances is in the public schools, and it must recruit staff capable of carrying out the plan. Thus far, Mobilization has succeeded in moving only a small proportion of its designs for program research intact from the drawing board to the testing ground. It has had even less success in moving its adequately demonstrated and evaluated programs from the testing ground into the mainstream of educational practice in New York City.

Several impediments probably account for Mobilization's inability to actualize many of its experimental projects. From the beginning of its operation, it has committed itself to influencing educational policy in the public schools by designing educational strategies to be tested and (if proven effective) adopted in an ever-widening circle of depressed-area schools. However, as an independent agency, it has no status in the school system nor even a commitment from the city's Board of Education allowing it to bypass any of the established procedures for gaining clearances to conduct program research in public school classrooms. The school system has appointed a liaison officer to facilitate activating Mobilization's programs, but he has no special authority to help the agency carry out that function. In effect, Mobilization has had no easier access to classrooms than any other private agency (or individual) seeking to test a new educational idea and willing to pay the extra expense required to give the idea a fair evaluation. All programmatic proposals have had to be turned over to the liaison officer, who in turn presents it for approval to a number of school officials up and down the institutional hierarchy who have direct or tangential interest in the problem area attacked by the proposed program. As a rule, innovative plans—especially those originating outside of the school system—are reviewed with utmost caution by officials below the top level of the bureaucratic strata, since approval implies confidence in the program and some measure of accountability if it should eventually attract criticism from colleagues, parents, or the community. With so many school authorities scrutinizing each Mobilization blueprint, its chances of approval often depend on the consent of its most skeptical reviewer, regardless of his position of authority and regardless of its support from other reviewers. The time spent in obtaining reactions from reviewers has postponed the introduction of many programs for as long as a year and forced the cancellation of others.

Approval to mount the programs could be facilitated by backing from local school officials, especially school principals and coordinators of instruction. Unfortunately, no such grass-roots support has been kindled. Local teachers, supervisors, and administrators all concede that educational failure is a serious problem in the area served by Mobilization. But there is a wide gap between acknowledging the existence of a problem and a readiness to determine whether the best solutions are presently being applied. Some school principals interpret proposals for experimenting with new educational strategies as implying criticism of current practices. There are those who feel it improper to use school children as "guinea pigs" to test untried and unproven programs. In many instances, the organizational structure of the school — its grouping of pupils, its scheduling of instruction, and its space facilities — has made it impossible to conduct experimentation even though the principals are willing to allow it.

Most of the local school officials have felt that Mobilization could serve the children best by underwriting an increase in existing personnel services. This would mean augmenting remedial reading, guidance, attendance, teacher training, and curriculum development staffs in an effort to improve the implementation of current school programs, the assumption being that schools have the know-how to solve the community's educational problems, given enough practitioners to do the job. Mobilization, on the other hand, has perceived its role as that of designing and testing new educational strategies rather than bolstering staffs for old ones, and, as a result of this disagreement with the schools, it has fallen short of implementing its plan of experimentation, and the schools have fallen short of benefiting from the full array of innovative educational practices it could derive from the Mobilization project.

Another problem facing Mobilization has been that of staffing its programs. It is not enough for personnel at the supervisory level to be conversant with the specialized field to which they are assigned; they must also have the imagination and desire to explore new territory in that field. There are many practitioners who meet the first set of qualifications but relatively few who meet the second. Moreover, the source of supply of qualified personnel at all levels is primarily the school system, which has granted Mobilization the privilege of obtaining transfers of professional staff members to its project without jeopardizing their rights and status in the school system. But few have the experience of engaging in experimentation, much less conducting it. Those who have the background are subject to the same cautionary attitudes toward innovation as are others in the school system, since they continue as employees in the system under the supervision of its liaison officer even while serving on the staffs of Mobilization programs with the support of Mobilization funds.

Some of the above-mentioned obstacles faced by Mobilization are generic to projects of this kind in urban areas throughout the country; others relate to the particular dynamics of interinstitutional relationships (formal and informal) between Mobilization and the school system. In describing its programs, therefore, it would be misleading to create the impression that all of them have reached the full-scale operational stage and have been objectively evaluated. In fact, most of them have not. Some are fully developed only on the drawing board, but remain there. The majority have been fielded in one form or another, but only a few of these have had the benefit of careful assessment. All contain some promising ideas for improving the quality of education in depressed areas, and because of their possible usefulness to educators planning compensatory programs for inner-city schools, the remainder of this paper is devoted to brief descriptions of them and of the objectives they serve.

Curriculum Planning and Development

Teachers in depressed areas habitually plead for new instructional ideas and help in implementing them. They need materials and techniques particularly appropriate for doing an effective job in slum schools. For this reason, Mobilization has established a curriculum center, staffed by educators with considerable experience in depressed areas, and serving both the local schools and the internal curriculum needs of the Mobilization agency. The staff creates, assembles, systematizes, and disseminates curriculum ideas and materials for experimental use with slum children and youth. The Center serves also as a sounding board and communications agency for the best ideas developed in the local classrooms.

The Materials Development Unit is an important part of the Center staff. Its major, though by no means exclusive, area of concern is the language arts. Reading, writing, listening, and speaking take priority because they are necessary skills for success in the modern curriculum, and they are often poorly mastered by slum children. Developed thus far at the Center are various kinds of reading matter for Spanish-speaking pupils, skill exercises for reading retardates, science lessons containing the same verbal content at different reading levels, a new preschool language readiness program, special mathematics drill problems for supplementary review, and a social studies unit on life in the local community.

A group of curriculum specialists go into the local schools to implement the use of materials developed and assembled at the Center. They work with the teachers to help put curriculum ideas into practice. As such, their role in bringing about changes in teacher style, technique, and the use of materials is a crucial one. To further improve classroom instruction, the Center has inaugurated summer workshops for teachers interested in developing new instructional aids that are then tested and disseminated. It has maintained contact with school staffs also by issuing a professional newsletter that brings together new ideas and materials in the field and encourages their use in classrooms. Its professional library and consultative service are always available for use at the Center after school hours.

Generally, the Curriculum Center is endeavoring to experiment with teaching styles and materials to which lower-status pupils can be more responsive. It operates with the understanding that responsiveness is a two-way street, that it is necessary not only to adapt curriculum materials to the life styles of slum pupils, but teaching methods as well.

Preschool and Early Childhood Programs

Early intervention with enriched educational experiences is recognized as an important way of possibly forestalling later retardation and school failure among socially disadvantaged children. Mobilization sponsors several programs designed to test this hypothesis, all under the direction of the supervisor of early childhood programs. The emphasis of these programs is on early language readiness and beginning reading.

Recent developments in educational research, curriculum theory, and instructional techniques make it possible to design school readiness programs in several distinctive ways, each emerging from a separate rationale with regard to human growth and learning. Differences in reading instruction are most marked in the early stages of the child's schooling. These differences may be associated more closely with variations in school success among low-status children than among those from advantaged environments. The latter pupils can compensate for deficiences in instructional methods through incidental learning at home, in the community, and even at school. They can learn much that is useful at school from an environment rich in language material and highly supportive of verbal development. The low-status child, on the other hand, may depend more heavily on the quality of formal instruction for his success at school. Moreover, methods that are most appropriate for him may be different from those proven most appropriate for the child from a more advantaged background. Mobilization is therefore investigating more closely the effects of early intervention on later pupil development. It is also intensifying its intervention efforts not only to provide greater service but to help determine the relative effectiveness of various special services.

Since several distinctive approaches to reading readiness and beginning reading are now available, some of the more promising programs are being introduced in local classrooms in an effort to compare their effects on growth in the language arts.

Sensory-Motor Training

It is by now well known that children from socially disadvantaged environments show deficiencies in motor development, visual perception, and auditory discrimination. These factors may be related not only to each other but to language growth as well. It is not known what antecedent factors in the slum environment account for these deficiencies. To some extent there may be a congenital basis for sensory-motor dysfunction. However, if preschool and early grade experience can reverse these deficits, a systematic training program may prove profitable. Mobilization is testing this hypothesis at the earliest level of schooling with general practice in physical coordination and balance, eye movement exercises, guided experiences in form perception, and developmental activities to sharpen visual memory. Visual perception exercises include matching, identification, classification, sequence recognition, and fine differentiation. Auditory discrimination exercises are sequentially designed, focusing on memory and recall, sound matching and discrimination, and perceiving sound detail. These experiences provide a basis for moving into the more advanced stages both of language readiness and of concept formation.

Designed for easy guided growth in language, the program builds from simple, almost primitive sensory-motor tasks to the more complex. Some of these exercises are so simple that they may offer no real challenge to socially disadvantaged preschool children. However, careful diagnosis would reveal that their mastery of the developmental steps is erratic, since they are able to perform relatively complex tasks while failing to negotiate simpler ones. The Mobilization program is designed to take them back to the earliest steps and watch their progress in a sequence of activities that become progressively more difficult. The content of this program is a carefully structured combination of exercises developed by Kephart (1960), Getman and Kane (1964), and some Mobilization adaptations of material developed by Frostig (1964), and Stern (1963).

Culturally Relevant Basal Readers

Many educators have made note of the fact that until quite recently, no basal reading series contained material that is as meaningful to children from low-status homes as it is to children from more advantaged environments. A study by the author (1954) revealed that the illustrations in primary grade reading texts rarely depicted urban life, particularly life in slum areas. Nor were disadvantaged ethnic or minority groups represented in illustrated stories. The implication derived from these findings was that if slum neighborhood children could relate more intimately to story content and illustrations in basal readers they would be motivated to achieve better. This would, in turn, be reflected in improved scores on achievement tests. Today, publishers are producing more and more basal reading series with content that touches on the everyday life experiences of children from disadvantaged environments. These materials may not be flawless in conceptualization and design, but they represent enough of a sampling of "culture fair" readers for Mobilization to test the hypothesis that beginning reading material depicting situations familiar to low-status children will produce better progress in their reading growth.

A Part-Synthetic Approach to Beginning Reading

Reducing emphasis on the whole word, look-say method in beginning reading and increasing emphasis on code-breaking may prove effective

292

with the low-status population. Success in building sight vocabulary may depend not only on visual-perceptual training but also on the kinds of experience in the home and neighborhood that fill the child's memory bank with a rich variety of verbal symbols. The low-status child who has no comparable readiness for sight recognition may therefore succeed better in a reading program that requires learning letter sounds and diagnosing letter blends through a step-by-step approach. The Fries program developed in Philadelphia (Fries, 1963) seems to show promise with low-status groups there. Some classrooms in the Mobilization area are planning a Fries reading program, while others may replicate experimentation with the Catherine Stern program which has already received preliminary testing in one of the Mobilization schools. Both rely heavily on a part-synthetic approach although the content is markedly dissimilar. Still another program being tested is Cecelia Pollack's *Inter-Sensory Reading Methods* (unpublished), a highly structured readiness and beginning reading sequence offering a multisensory approach to reading and making use of linguistic methods. It is worked out so carefully from simple to advanced levels that it enjoys the advantage of easy-step progress found in programed instruction.

Spanish Language Readiness for Bilinguals

More than half of the elementary school children in the Mobilization For Youth area are Puerto Rican, many of them non-English-speaking when they come to school. In addition to their sociocultural handicap, they suffer a language deficit unique even in depressed areas. Early readiness experiences in a non-native tongue may, by their very nature, be early stumbling blocks that lead later to reinforced failure at school. Many local Spanish-speaking children don't have enough of a listening vocabulary in English to function successfully in the conventional reading readiness program, yet, they may have the capacity to respond well to exercises involving visual and auditory perception in the language that is most familiar to them.

Once the child experiences success with beginning reading in Spanish, it may be easier for him to make the transfer to English than to progress step-by-step in the English language alone. There is enough similarity in the verbal symbols in the two languages to facilitate the transition, especially if early success with Spanish helps enhance the child's self-concept as a learner. The objective of such an experiment as conceived by Mobilization, is to achieve better reading results in English, not to help children become proficient readers in two languages. The method of instruction is a conventional one. Readiness exercises in the Spanish language are designed to be handled by specially trained Spanish-speaking teaching assistants working exclusively with Puerto Rican first graders. Once having reached a predetermined level in the readiness sequence, the children make the transfer to English, using their newly acquired skills to break the English code.

Ungraded Preprimary Unit

Mobilization has planned an experiment with ungraded preprimary instruction in which five-year-olds having had prekindergarten experience will be combined with a newly admitted four-year-old group. This class will remain together for two years with another group of four-year-olds admitted for the second year. At the end of the two years, some six-year-olds will go into the first grade, while others will remain with the group for another year before entering the first grade. The objective is to establish a pattern of grouping 4-, 5-, and 6-year-olds in an ungraded unit, with each child spending as few as two and as many as three years in it, progressing at his own rate without promotion or retardation. It is preferable, but not necessary, for a single teacher to remain with the unit group for the entire period to give the educational experience greater stability. Grouping within the unit is based on the achievement and maturation patterns of the individual child.

The ungraded preprimary unit will help insure continued progress during the crucial readiness period, while reducing the threat of failure which tends to lead to further retardation of the child who gets off to a slow start at school. During the two- or three-year period, the child will be preparing for formal school at a pace commensurate with his abilities and early experience. Admission to the various grades will be based on performance demonstrated over a period of time that is long enough to enable the child to form good preparatory experiences.

Parent-Child Readiness

The advantage of orienting parents as well as children from disadvantaged areas to school life is being explored at Mobilization. One study (Brazziel and Terrell, 1962) reports the effects of a six-week readiness program for 26 Negro children in the first grade. The program included parent meetings once a week, 30 minutes of educational TV watched in the home, and a series of reading readiness experiences. As a result, the children showed unusual gains not only in reading readiness but in IQ as well.

Part of the program's success is due to parental involvement. Indeed, if orientation of parents to school life can be helpful in the early stages of the child's education, efforts ought to be made to concentrate such services in depressed areas, where the social distance between school and home is so great. Accordingly, some of the teachers involved in Mobilization's early childhood program plan to visit the homes regularly and conduct meetings at school. Efforts will be made to assess the differential effects of early schooling combined with parental orientation as against early schooling without it. This program should lead to new insights into the value of parental involvement. It should also produce appropriate curriculum material for a parent orientation program that parallels the child's experience at the preschool level.

Corrective Reading

School and community lay heavy stress on language development, and it is a fact that children in the Mobilization community are seriously handicapped by reading retardation, as are children in urban depressed areas throughout the country. Attempts to overcome these deficiencies have not yet met with success, despite a sharp increase in helping services and despite the best-intentioned efforts of highly skilled and dedicated teachers. One reason for the failure thus far may be that there is no clarity as to which approaches to reading instruction are uniquely suitable for socially depressed pupils. Mobilization, therefore, operates on the premise that alternative strategies and instruments designed to upgrade reading achievement in general should be assessed separately for their differential effectiveness in the classroom and in the reading clinics.

Although the role of reading teachers in Mobilization for Youth has been roughly comparable to that of reading specialists in elementary schools, there are some important differences. Mobilization personnel carry a lighter pupil load in order to allow for more time to demonstrate new techniques and materials in the regular classrooms. There has also been a greater emphasis on acquiring diagnostic skills and on organizing remedial materials to attack specific perceptual weaknesses associated with reading retardation. Mobilization's *Diagnostic Test of Word Attack Skills* was field tested and found to be an efficient instrument for quickly assessing performance in ten reading skill areas: initial consonants, final consonants, initial consonant blends, final consonant blends, short vowel sounds, visual discrimination of vowel sounds, auditory syllabication, visual syllabication, visual memory of known demons, and structural analysis. The Mobilization reading teachers are able to make good use of the instrument as a basis for testing tailor-made reading programs for retardates. They have also developed and assembled remedial material to fit each of the ten aforementioned categories of skill deficiency. These sets of ten remedial kits are placed in elementary classrooms, with Mobilization reading teachers demonstrating them to classroom teachers.

Another plan for experimentation involves some simple team teaching to reduce reading retardation in the regular classrooms. Three teachers at a given grade level set up fully equipped skill stations, one classroom emphasizing study skills, the second comprehension skills, and the third word attack skills. Children from the three classrooms are directed to the appropriate stations depending on the nature of specific remediation planned for them.

It is interesting to note that a much earlier design of the skill-station technique was introduced and evaluated in Mobilization's homework helper program, in which high school students used these materials to tutor elementary school pupils after school. Although it produced positive, but no better, results than general tutorial methods at that time, it has since been felt that the experiment ought to be replicated with newly developed material that currently fits that program. Adolescent tutors can be trained to operate skill stations, and the program may produce better results now than it has in the past. Those who observed the program and assessed it objectively are confident that a skill-station approach is most promising in an after-school tutorial project.

Services in the Reading Clinics

Reading clinics in depressed areas are faced with two basic problems. First, they must develop or locate instructional techniques and materials that can be used successfully with low-status children. Secondly, unlike clinics in favored communities, they must design appropriate logistics for distributing their services widely in order to accommodate the great number of children who need special help.

For the past three years, the Mobilization Reading Clinic has been working with first-graders identified by their kindergarten teachers and by objective predictive measures as potential severe retardates in reading. The children come to the clinic in groups of four and receive three half-hour instructional sessions each week. A matched control group is also being followed in order to assess the effects of clinic intervention. Thus far, the program has met with enthusiastic acceptance on the part of the school teachers and supervisors involved, but objective tests have not yet shown salutary effects on pupils. Nevertheless, it seems promising enough to merit continued refinement and expansion. The intention is not only to evaluate the effects of clinic services at an early grade level, but to assess the predictive validity of informal teacher evaluations and of formal measures at the preschool level.

In order to explore the usefulness of selected new instructional materials in working with severely retarded low-status children in the middle and upper grades, nonreaders at these levels have become subjects of intensive treatment. Programed techniques designed for wider application in the classroom are being used to facilitate learning. Experience in the clinic has shown that a great need exists for intensive work with potential holdovers in the upper elementary grades in order to prepare them for entrance into junior high school. For this reason, most referrals from the middle grades are those children who are in danger of being forced to repeat a grade.

Pupil Personnel Services

One of the important services for children in slum schools is rendered by guidance counselors. Their work in the elementary and junior high schools is designed to help provide the necessary ego support for those who are having difficulty in class. The service usually takes on many forms, different for each school, with the counselor ranging wide in her contacts on behalf of the child. She may work with parents, local social agencies, and other pupil personnel services at school as a catalyst coordinating many helping efforts with her own.

In order to test new guidance functions in the school, the counselors have been involved in various instructional programs and experimenting with several counseling techniques. Primary-grade children showing signs of early school failure are targets for intensive service to help strengthen their motivation and their ability to achieve better in class. The extra encouragement and skill training can be crucial at these beginning stages of the child's schooling. Furthermore, by bringing parents into the picture at this time, the guidance counselor is in a good position to forestall later problems between home and school. Group guidance is also being tried.

Counselors are concentrating on problems of scholastic underachievement in the early and middle grades. They feel that many children have the ability to do outstanding work if they are given extra attention outside the classroom. Relatively little experimental work has been done with underachievers in the elementary grades, despite the fact that adolescent underachievers seem to benefit little from special counseling or remediation. Perhaps the efforts with younger children will prove more effective.

One common denominator for the various experimental guidance programs is an effort to broaden the counselor's perspectives, so that services are not restricted to "hard core" groups in the schools.

To lend needed support to the guidance counselor's work in the junior high school, Mobilization has assigned an attendance teacher to each of the five junior high schools in the area. Theirs is the responsibility of identifying children who are habitually truant and those exhibiting a variety of absence patterns that reflect the early symptoms of truancy. They work directly with the pupils and parents, as well as with the teachers and guidance counselors, in an effort to minimize various problems that contribute to truancy. They have also developed an educational program in each school to increase "attendance consciousness."

Teacher Education

Educators often point to the need for teachers to identify themselves closely with the values and behaviors of low-status subcultures. It is assumed that by learning more about family life in slum areas, teachers will be able to bridge the gap between their middle-class orientations and their pupils' lower-class backgrounds, and thus improve the learning atmosphere in the classroom. Such an assumption is difficult to test, partly

297

because it is not easy to bridge the cultural gap. Teacher-training programs conventionally do not familiarize students with the sights and smells of slum life, much less the so-called cultural positives of that environment. Mobilization is attempting to make up for this deficiency in teacher preparation by offering special services to teachers in training and in service.

Through a special arrangement with cooperating local colleges, selected student teachers assigned to Mobilization schools and planning on careers in depressed areas, receive expanded and guided learning opportunities. In addition to student teaching, they visit the local neighborhood, meet various representatives of minority groups, attend meetings of local organizations, and generally try to learn first-hand the dynamics of community life. By spending time with the various Mobilization projects, they are exposed to a variety of experimental education and social work projects in action. To further augment their student teaching experiences, they attend after-school workshops run by master teachers of the areas. Finally, the various social work programs at Mobilization involve them as observers and participants, in order that they may view family and community life from perspectives other than the classroom.

The training of inservice teachers is likewise rich and varied. One of the serious problems to be dealt with is the high rate of teacher turnover, which reduces the quality of education in the local community and has a demoralizing effect on the schools. To help offset this, Mobilization has offered special help to beginning teachers, helping them overcome serious difficulties and stay on.

The more seasoned teachers also need many new insights and experiences to reduce the social distance between home and school. A course called *Home and Family* is designed to do just that. Under the guidance of trained social workers, teachers visit the homes of each pupil in their classes and meet in a series of seminar sessions to analyze and draw educational implications from these visits. They are trained by the social workers to interpret what they see. From such face-to-face encounters, there emerge new ideas about how to reach the child more successfully in the educative process. For their part, parents will perhaps feel freer to participate in school activity more regularly, not just during stress periods.

A companion course to *Home and Family* is one entitled *The Lower East Side Community*. As the title implies, it was designed to provide teachers with a first-hand encounter with the many subcultures, languages, and traditions of the community served by Mobilization. A series of lectures, seminars, and field trips are coordinated toward this end. Teachers visit with minority groups and agencies and examine various community organizations. One cannot overestimate the extent to which teachers are isolated from life in the home and neighborhood that exerts such a powerful influence on the development of their pupils. There is much to be learned from a systematic investigation of the child's environment outside of school, and this ought to be part of every teacher's training experience.

Since Mobilization has developed new instructional techniques and materials through its various programs, it has recently incorporated this know-how into its inservice programs. Staff members involved in various projects train teachers and other professional personnel in seminar groups on classroom applications. Thus Mobilization's early childhood, reading, and curriculum specialists work with inservice personnel to disseminate the insights they have derived from trying out untested ideas.

Out-of-School Education

It is not cynical to assert (with apologies to George Bernard Shaw) that education is becoming much too big and important to be confined to our schools. Society keeps demanding an ever better-educated citizenry in order to maintain its present course of growth, and the schools are staggering under these mounting pressures. The storehouse of human knowledge is expanding at such a dazzling rate that schools are able to transmit an ever shrinking proportion of that treasure to its pupils. One can foresee the time when a college graduate will have to continue on to graduate school in order to complete his basic education (if, indeed "complete" and "basic education" have any meaning at all any more). There was a time, not so long ago, when the educator's dream was that every man, woman, and child in this country possess at least the basic literacy skills. Today, literacy skills are no more adequate as minimum essentials than is the once sought-after fifty-cents-an-hour minimum wage. The barely literate are rapidly becoming obsolete in our modern industrial society, but thanks (to some extent) to our schools, illiteracy is not becoming extinct.

One oft-repeated solution to the educational problems of the under-privileged is to improve the schools. There is, of course, always room for such improvement. But if the schools are to be judged by their success in educating the underprivileged to function adequately in the modern world, the odds against their being judged favorably within the foreseeable future are prohibitive. The magnitude of the problem is so great and its rate of aggravation so rapid that the schools as we know them may *never* find the solution. One must therefore conclude that with the cards stacked so heavily against the schools today, formal education cannot be restricted to the formal classroom but it must also break out of the school and reach into centers of work, worship, and social activity.

Right now little out-of-school education has been provided for the underprivileged. To appreciate how primitive these services are, one need only look at the spotty efforts made thus far by private industry and the labor unions to rehabilitate school failures and thereby improve their employability. Social service agencies working with the underprivileged have also been slow in incorporating education into their rehabilitation services. Even when the worlds of business and social work try their hand at education, they often do it without seeking help from school people. It

299

seems as if they have written off the school as a failure and must therefore "go it alone" in making up the educational deficits.

Homework Helper Program

The Homework Helper Program is designed to serve two populations: high-school youth and elementary school pupils. The high-school students provide after-school tutorial help to elementary school children under the training and supervision of master teachers. The program enables adolescents to engage in highly purposeful, constructive activity on behalf of children who can benefit from the extra assistance. It offers individual assistance to elementary school pupils in need of help with basic skills, especially reading, and brings them into association with useful adolescent models who might enhance their aspirations for success at school. At the same time, it is designed to encourage and help underprivileged high-school students to remain in school by paying them for their services, motivating them toward improved academic achievement, and providing an experience that might even lead to the choice of teaching as a career.

Currently, the program operates in thirteen centers housed in ten elementary schools, two junior high schools, and one senior high school, each center under the supervision of a master teacher. The master teachers, each of whom is a regular staff member in a local school, are responsible for program operations and for training and supervising tutors assigned to their centers. The master teachers work in the centers four afternoons a week and attend staff conferences with the overall program coordinator on alternate Friday afternoons. Centers are supplied with appropriate materials, including books, educational games, reading laboratories, audiovisual materials, puppets, and art supplies.

The 250 student tutors are tenth-, eleventh-, and twelfth-graders representative of the ethnic and social groups in the depressed area in which they live. They spend two weeks in preservice training and continue to meet once a week with their master teachers for continued inservice training throughout the year. Tutoring is on a one-to-one basis, with pupils receiving help twice a week in two-hour sessions. The elementary school pupils are escorted to their homes by the tutors after the sessions. The student tutors are paid for the eight hours of tutoring as well as for their own training sessions.

There was some objective evaluation of this program, and the results have been encouraging. Pupils tutored two afternoons a week (for a total of four hours) made significant gains in reading as against a matched group that did not receive any tutoring. It was also found that this salutary effect was most pronounced for those pupils who were initially the most retarded in reading. There is also some evidence that the student tutors likewise showed remarkable growth in basic skills as a result of this experience.

Since the program has demonstrated that high-school students in a depressed area can contribute significantly to the educational progress of younger disadvantaged children, the possibilities for intensifying such a program and varying the approach to treatment are vast. Mobilization has therefore engaged in several experiments that derive from its initial success. There was also experimentation with several variations on the tutoring arrangement. One experiment tested the effects of prolonged minimal instruction (a single day per week over a long period of time) as against shorter term concentrated help (two or three days per week for a few months). Another experiment dealt with the effects of training tutors to be specialists in specific remedial skills. A third experiment substituted small-group instruction in a team-learning situation for the previous one-to-one structure. In all instances, the plan is to follow up the program to see whether the accelerated growth of pupils is sustained.

Projecting into the future, if these successes continue, Mobilization will be in a position to prepare administrative and curriculum guides that school systems can use in mounting similar programs in other depressed areas. Plans call for producing an administrative manual aimed at providing guidance for individuals responsible for the initiation and operation of such a tutoring program. It will include instruction for master teachers responsible for training and supervising the tutors. Mobilization will also design an instructional manual for tutors to help orient them to the general objectives of the program and offer specific suggestions on how to work effectively with younger children. It will be accompanied by a loose-leaf manual of instructional materials which have been found helpful by tutors and master teachers in the past. The loose-leaf format will facilitate adding and deleting materials as new publications become available.

The possible derivatives of such a program are indeed vast. High-school students (and even dropouts) might be trained to assume a paraprofessional role in the day-school classroom. Mobilization has found, for example, that high school students fit excellently into a preschool program when they are given a highly structured language readiness task to perform. Some of the adolescents placed in such classrooms were functional illiterates, and their work with very young children has spurred them to sharpen their own literacy skills.

Supplementary Teaching Assistance in Reading

Supplementary Teaching Assistance in Reading (STAR) is a program designed to provide parents in a depressed area with the tools and techniques to tutor their children in reading at home. Trained reading specialists with considerable experience in offering direct service to children have developed at Mobilization the strategies for training parents to assume this responsibility. But like the Homework Helper program, this kind of out-of-school service depends largely on nonprofessionals — housewives, indigenous to the culture of the slum community, who are trained to go into the home to help parents help their children.

There are some basic reasons for developing such a program. It is

301

well known that schools in depressed areas face a Herculean task in developing techniques and materials to combat reading retardation. Methods that are effective with more favored populations are not necessarily appropriate with socially disadvantaged children. But even if schools could find ways of providing equally effective services to pupils from all backgrounds, their style of treatment for reading retardates in the slum would have to be modified considerably. Remedial reading teachers are usually trained to work with individuals and small groups, and therefore reach out directly to relatively few children. This poses no problem in communities where severe reading disability is rare. In slum neighborhoods, however, failure is so widespread that the reading specialist can accommodate only a small proportion of those who need his help..The cost of augmenting remedial services to handle the required case load would be prohibitive. It is therefore obvious that there is a serious logistic problem in delivering compensatory services to the growing masses who need them.

Deputizing parents to assume tutorial responsibilities is one approach that seems promising. The parent has far more contact with the child than a remedial teacher could possibly have. Schools can capitalize on this daily parent-child contact by placing in the parents' hands some simple, carefully structured activities designed to improve reading skills. If such a program proved successful, it would enable reading specialists to concentrate more heavily on parent training than on direct service to children. Mobilization's experience has shown that it is possible to reach more parents more easily and more often by training indigenous teacher aides to carry the message and the skills into the home.

Many more parents than children can be accommodated, since the indigenous teacher aides require relatively short training periods and have the ability to range widely into the community. The parents, in turn, spend a good deal of time in making use of their newly acquired know-how in tutoring at home each day. Aside from the hopeful benefits in reading growth, this instructional relationship between parent and child may also help improve the climate of the home. In short, the STAR program is not simply an experiment with new methodology, but an effort to better adapt school services to the realities of a disadvantaged area.

Education of Out-of-School Youth

Mobilization is testing the hypothesis that high-school graduates who fail to qualify for admission to college under existing standards can be successful in pursuing college courses if they receive academic, financial, and emotional support. The academic assistance of these students consists of a summer of remedial instruction in reading, English composition, and mathematics, and twenty hours of tutoring per week while they attend college classes in the fall. The tutoring stresses the application of specific study skills in doing the assignments for each course. Graduate students tutor the target group in one-to-one arrangements for a minimum of twelve hours a week. For this the latter receive stipends and the textbooks they need for their courses. Guidance is provided through individual conferences with the head of the program every week, group conferences every week, and the services of the social worker as individual and family needs arise.

The program has not been in existence long enough to suggest outcomes. Plans are to expand offerings in order to provide a wide range of educational opportunities for residents in the area served by Mobilization. High-school students, school dropouts who may need help in obtaining high-school equivalency diplomas, and adults in the community who wish to receive further education will be served. There are plans to use closed-circuit and open-circuit television to enhance learning opportunities.

Mobilization For Youth is operating in the hope that alternatives for improving education in slum areas can yet be demonstrated. It is groping for answers to long-standing unsolved problems by emphasizing innovation and research wherever possible. What started out as educated guesswork may turn out to be an exercise in futility in some Mobilization programs and demonstrated success in others. There has been so much failure in slum schools that it is unrealistic to expect appreciable improvement by providing *more* of the same services currently available in these schools. There does not seem to be much more value in mining the same educational lode. New explorations are needed desperately, or else schools will have to admit ineptitude for the present and promise nothing better for the future. So much is at stake in the education of children in depressed areas that any salutary outcomes of the Mobilization experiment will be well worth its public support.

References

Brazziel, F. F. and Mary Terrell. "An Experiment in the Development of Readiness in a Culturally Disadvantaged Group of First-Grade Children," *Journal of Negro Education*, 31 (1962), 4–7.

Fries, Charles C. *et al. My Reader* (series of eight booklets). Philadelphia, Pa.: The authors, 1963.

Frostig, Marianne *et al. Program for the Development of Visual Perception*. Chicago: Follett, 1964.

Getman, G. N. *et al. Physiological Readiness*. Minneapolis: The author, 1964.

Kephart, N. *The Slow Learner in the Classroom*. New York: The Merrill Publishing Company, 1960.

Stern, Catherine. *Structural Reading Series*. Syracuse: L. W. Singer Company, 1963.

Tannenbaum, Abraham. "Family Living in Textbook Town," *Progressive Education* (March, 1964).

John H. Fischer examines the issues related to racial balance in the schools. The tasks that the schools now face as a result of the 1954 Supreme Court Decision, Fischer contends, are far more complex than those that preceded the decision. The job is now "not only to end segregation but to correct the effects it has generated." There is little merit in debating whether de jure or de facto segregation is more of an evil, since both represent practices which cannot be condoned. Too many school authorities have not only failed to desegregate their schools but have been unwilling to accept integration as a desirable goal.

There is no completely satisfactory measure of segregation or racial imbalance, but it is suggested that if a school is perceived as a "Negro school" or is assumed "to belong to a Negro neighborhood" then the usual consequences of segregation can probably be found in it. Various guidelines for achieving racial balance are weighed as potential solutions; there are estimates as well of their inherent shortcomings. Reconsidering the notion of the neighborhood school, Dr. Fischer proposes that when such a school no longer assures all of the children of the district equal educational opportunity and equal access, then it may no longer be defensible as a valid institution. In the last several years, city and suburban schools have steadily become more segregated not only by race but by socioeconomic level as well. In fact, there is some evidence to suggest that this socioeconomic segregation has effects that are at least as harmful as racial segregation.

RACE AND RECONCILIATION: THE ROLE OF THE SCHOOL

John H. Fischer

Dr. Fischer examines the problems the city develops when it is surrounded by a sort of "white noose." He raises the question of whether existing political jurisdictions should not be altered if racial segregation in the schools is to be reduced or eliminated. Finally, he addresses himself to the problem of providing quality education in the ghettoized inner-city. Conditions there may make correction of racial balance difficult if not impossible. Under *those circumstances, it is a fair question whether or not the ghetto schools can be improved to a point where the education offered to racially isolated children is of high quality. This, of course, has been the basis of the efforts of so-called compensatory programs found across the nation. Dr. Fischer maintains that "the evidence is now irrefutable that until each American has full access to the means to develop his capacities, every other American's chances and attainments will continue to be diminished." If the moral question is faced head-on by the educational and political leadership of the country, there are grounds for optimism that solutions will be found to this vexing problem.*

RACE AND RECONCILIATION: THE ROLE OF THE SCHOOL

John H. Fischer*

I

When George Counts asked in 1932, "Dare the schools build a new social order?" the response could hardly have been called resounding. A frightened few took the query for a Marxist threat, the Progressive Education Association spent a year reaching a split decision, but the majority even of those who gave it any attention at all dismissed the challenge as educationist hyperbole. Whatever it was the country needed, not many expected to find it in the schools. Two wars, a technological revolution, and a massive social upheaval have put a different face upon the matter. No longer is education the optional affair it was a generation ago. The easy rhetoric about the nation's reliance on its schools has become an uneasy reality.

President Johnson reflected the discovery when he said that "One great truth" he had learned is that "the answer for all of our national problems, the answer for all the problems of the world comes down, when you really analyze it, to one simple word — education."[1] Mr. Johnson is not the first President to speak well of learning. The dependence of democracy on popular education has been a continuing theme in our history. But it was not until the end of World War II that the country began seriously to consider the full implications of that relationship, and later still that it officially acknowledged the corollary proposition that to limit a man's education is to limit his freedom.

The rationale for improving the Negro American's chance to be educated derives from basic principles and well-established practice, but merely to proclaim a new policy of equality is not enough. Steps to equalize the Negro's educational opportunities must be accompanied by prompt and vigorous action to improve his access to those opportunities and to increase the inducement for him to use them. Until, in all three respects, he is brought to full parity with his white neighbor, the Negro citizen will continue to depress the composite level of American society, and the society to diminish his standing as a man.

As the struggle to secure the Negro's proper place in that society gains headway and success, it becomes steadily more clear that the two great

*Reprinted from Daedalus, 95 (Winter 1966) by permission.
[1] Lyndon B. Johnson, address delivered at the 200th Anniversary Convocation, Brown University, September 28, 1964.

307

educational handicaps he has suffered—segregated schools and inferior instruction—are so closely interrelated that they can be attacked successfully only when they are attacked simultaneously.

This is not to argue that segregation is the sole deficiency Negro children suffer in school or that only Negro pupils receive inferior education. Nor is it true that every Negro child is being poorly taught or that effective learning is possible only in the presence of white children. It is important to set the facts, the probabilities, and the proposals straight. Not every Negro child lives in deprivation: each year more Negro families join the middle class. Nor is every white child raised in a good home. Slums are often ghettos, but the two are not always the same. Poverty of purse and poverty of spirit often go together, but the exceptions are numerous and important. Yet when all the differences have been explained and all the exceptions admitted, the hard facts of racial discrimination remain to be faced.

Until the present generation, almost every action affecting Negroes as a group in this country, whether taken by the government or by private agencies, has been to some degree discriminatory and quite often hypocritical. The Negro's just cause for pride in the fortitude of his ancestors in no way alters the fact that from the moment of his birth he becomes the product and the victim of his people's history. The scars he carries are difficult to hide and slow to heal.

Assuring the Negro his proper place in American society involves more than opening a few doors, giving everybody his choice, and waiting for what is certain to come naturally. Many of the trends that have influenced the Negro individually and collectively have carried him not toward but away from the main currents of American life. The momentum that has been built up suggests a sociological analogue on Newton's first law of motion. Unless the course that the Negro race has followed for three centuries is altered by the application of external energy, its direction cannot be expected to change. The heart of the integration question is to determine what forms of energy are most appropriate and how they may be applied to bring the separate courses together. For some Negroes the process is already under way, but for many more significant change awaits intervention on a scale commensurate with the forces that must be checked and redirected. To serve this purpose no agency offers greater promise than the school.

We can begin on the educational task by considering some facts. One is that a school enrolling largely Negro students is almost universally considered of lower status and less desirable than one attended wholly or mainly by white students. Regardless of the quality of the building, the competence of the staff, or the size of classes, a school composed of three-fourths Negro children and one-fourth white children is viewed by members of both races, virtually without exception, as inferior to one in which the proportions are reversed. Whether all such appraisals are valid remains, at least for the time being, beside the point. So often are "Negro" schools inferior and so long have Negro students been assigned the hand-me-downs that unhappy memories and generalized impressions must be expected to persist despite the occasional presence of really good schools in Negro neighborhoods.

The contention that no school of Negro pupils can under any circumstances be satisfactory unless white students enter it is absurd. The argument insults every Negro child and credits white children with virtues they do not possess. But the effort to establish genuinely first-rate schools in Negro communities has been so long delayed that anyone undertaking to demonstrate that an institution known as a "Negro" school can produce first-rate results must be prepared to accept a substantial burden of proof.

A second impressive fact, closely related to the first, is the unfortunate psychological effect upon a child of membership in a school where every pupil knows that, regardless of his personal attainments, the group with which he is identified is viewed as less able, less successful, and less acceptable than the majority of the community. The impact upon the self-image and motivation of children of this most tragic outcome of segregated education emphasizes the dual need for immediate steps to achieve a more favorable balance of races in the schools and for every possible effort to upgrade to full respectability and status every school in which enrollment cannot soon be balanced.

The destruction of the legal basis of segregation by the *Brown* decision in 1954 marked the climax of an obviously necessary first campaign, but the new problems to which *Brown* gives rise are even more complex than those which preceded it. The task now is not only to end segregation but to correct the effects it has generated. There is little profit in debating whether *de jure* or *de facto* segregation is the greater evil. It was the consequences of the fact of segregation that convinced the Supreme Court that "separate schools are inherently unequal" and led the Court to strike down the laws supporting such schools. Only by a curious twist of logic could it be argued that segregation statutes having been declared unjust, the practice itself may now be condoned.

This is not to deny significant differences between segregation established by law and that resulting from other causes. As the Court itself pointed out, "The impact is greater when it has the sanction of the law." But underlying this greater impact is the Court's finding that "Segregation of white and colored children in public schools has a detrimental effect upon the colored children."

Imperative as the need for prompt desegregation is, it would be irresponsible to attempt to deal with a condition so deeply rooted in practice and custom, and so often due to causes lying beyond the school, without taking account of its complexity. The need for intelligence, imagination, and wisdom in effecting fair and workable reforms can hardly be overstated. Yet, however complicated the situation or the final solutions may be, a firm and forthright confrontation of the problem is essential and is everywhere possible.

Some of the most bitter attacks on school authorities have been occasioned not by their failure to integrate every school, but by their unwillingness even to accept integration as a desirable goal. Among the reasons offered in support of this position, two are especially prominent. One is that the only acceptable basis for school policy is simple and complete nondiscrimination. Unless the school is color-blind, this argument runs, the spirit of the *Brown* decision and the 14th Amendment is violated. What this approach overlooks or attempts to evade is that the consequences of earlier discrimination cannot be corrected merely by ending the practices that produced them, that without corrective action the effects inevitably persist. To teach anyone in a way that influences his further development it is invariably useful and usually necessary to take account of the background he brings to the classroom. So often are the disabilities of the Negro students directly traceable to racial factors that a refusal on grounds of equality to recognize such factors in the school is not only unjust; it is also illogical. A physician reasoning in the same way would deliberately disregard his patients' histories in order to assure them all equal treatment.

A second justification commonly offered for not taking positive action to integrate schools is the lack of evidence that better racial balance leads to better learning, and it must be conceded that solid, objective evidence on this question is difficult if not impossible to find. The number of Negro children from deprived circumstances who have attended schools that were both integrated and educationally sound is still so small and the period of integration so brief that neither provides more than a limited basis for study. Because the Negro children with the longest experience in good integrated institutions have more often come from relatively fortunate and upwardly mobile families, their performance, although interesting, is only partly relevant to the task of equalizing opportunities for those who are both segregated and otherwise disadvantaged.

Moreover, even when better statistical data become available, it should not be expected that they will furnish, *per se*, a firm basis for policy. The purpose of school integration is not merely, or even primarily, to raise the quantitative indices of scholastic achievement among Negro children, although such gains are obviously to be valued and sought. The main objective is rather to alter the character and quality of their opportunities, to provide the incentive to succeed, and to foster a sense of intergroup acceptance in ways that are impossible where schools or students are racially, socially, and culturally isolated. The simplest statement of the situation to which school policy must respond is that few if any American Negro children can now grow up under conditions comparable to those of white children and that of all the means of improvement subject to public control the most powerful is the school. The Negro child must have a chance to be educated in a school where it is clear to him and to everybody else that he is not segregated and where his undisputed right to membership is acknowledged, publicly and privately, by his peers and his elders of both races. Although his acceptance and his progress may at first be delayed, not even a decent beginning toward comparable circumstances can be made until an integrated setting is actually established.

Some important gains may come rather quickly in newly integrated schools, but lasting changes in the deep-seated behavior patterns of children and parents of both races cannot realistically be expected to take place overnight. The effects of fourteen generations of discrimination, deprivation, and separation are not likely to disappear quickly. What a school has to boast about at the end of the next grading period is somewhat less crucial than what happens to the quality of living in America during the next generation. School integration will, of course, be more productive when parallel improvements are made in housing, economic opportunities, and the general social condition of Negro Americans; but the absence of adequate effort elsewhere only increases the urgency that prompt and energetic action be taken by the school.

The effort to identify and define *de facto* segregation, particularly where school enrollment is predominantly if not wholly of a single race, has led to the concept of racial "balance." While no single ratio of races can be established as universally "right," there is no doubt that when the number or proportion of Negro children in a school exceeds a certain level the school becomes less acceptable to both white and Negro parents. The point at which that shift begins is not clear, nor are the reasons for the variation adequately understood, but the results that typically follow are all too familiar: an accelerated exodus of white families; an influx of Negroes; increased enrollment, frequently to the point of overcrowding; growing dissatisfaction among teachers and the replacement of veterans by inexperienced or unqualified junior instructors.

Although there are no completely satisfactory measures of segregation or imbalance, several tests are applicable. The simplest is to ask whether a particular school is viewed by the community as a "Negro" school. Whether the school is assumed to "belong" to a Negro neighborhood or merely to be the one that Negroes "just happen" to attend, whether it has been provided expressly *for* a Negro population, or has gradually acquired a student body disproportionately composed of Negroes, the typical consequences of segregation can be predicted.

In gauging the degree of segregation or imbalance, the percentage or number of Negro students in a given building is usually less important than the relationship of the school to the entire system of which it is a part. As Robert Carter (1965) has so cogently argued, it is the substantial isolation of Negro and white students from each other rather than the numbers

311

involved that produces the implication of differential status and prevents the association that is the indispensable basis for mutual understanding and acceptance.

One set of guidelines for correcting such situations has been proposed by the New York State Education Commissioner's Advisory Committee on Human Relations and Community Tensions:

> In establishing school attendance areas one of the objectives should be to create in each school a student body that will represent as nearly as possible the cross section of the population of the entire school district but with due consideration also for other important educational criteria including such practical matters as the distance children must travel from home to school. (New New York State Department of Education, 1963)

Although it would be impossible in a sizable district to create or maintain in every school a student body that reflects precisely the racial composition of the total district, the cross-section criterion offers an appropriate yardstick.

Most of the proposals for dealing with the issue attempt to strike workable compromises between desirable ideals and practical possibilities. The same Committee (1964, p. 2) defined a school in New York City as segregated when any single racial group comprised more than 90 per cent of the enrollment.

A more flexible criterion was used by Robert Dentler (1964, p. 1). Using the borough as the reference point, he proposed that a school be considered segregated if the proportion of any racial group in its student body is less than half or more than twice the proportion that group represents in the total population. Thus, in Brooklyn, where Negroes comprise 15 per cent of the population, a school would be classified as "Negro segregated" when Negro enrollment reached 30 per cent. Since Puerto Ricans form about 8 per cent of the borough population, a school would be "Puerto Rican" segregated if it enrolled 16 per cent or more pupils of that background. Conversely, a school enrolling fewer than 6 per cent Negro students or 2 per cent Puerto Rican students would be designated as "white segregated." Dealing with the issue in Chicago, Robert Havighurst (1964) defines an integrated school as one enrolling at least 60 per cent white students.

II

The dilemma of definition cannot be entirely avoided, but far more important is the creation and retention of student bodies that will be considered acceptably integrated by the largest possible number of persons in both races. As the New York City report pointed out, an essential test of any plan for desegregation

312

. . . must be its mutual acceptance by both minority group and whites. It should be obvious, but does not always appear to be, that integration is impossible without white pupils. No plan can be acceptable, therefore, which increases the movement of white pupils out of the public schools. Neither is it acceptable, however, unless it contributes to desegregation. (New York State Education Commissioner's Advisory Committee, 1964, p. 14)

Of the administrative schemes for bringing children of both races together the most widely used is "open enrollment," under which pupils are allowed to transfer from schools that are segregated or overcrowded to others in the district. The receiving school may be one with a better degree of racial balance, or its enrollment may simply be smaller than its capacity. While open enrollment reduces congestion in the sending schools, allows parents wider choice, and improves integration in the receiving schools, its usefulness, especially for poor children, is sharply reduced unless transportation is furnished at public expense. Freedom of choice is also more effective when it is supplemented by special counseling services and by the careful preparation of pupils, teachers, and parents of the receiving school.

In large cities, open-enrollment plans have uniformly been found to affect only a small percentage of Negro students. In Baltimore, where relatively free choice of schools (subject to legal segregation) was standard practice before 1954, open enrollment became the sole basis for desegregation following the *Brown* decision. In the school year 1954–55 only about 3 per cent of the Negro students transferred to formerly white schools (Maryland Commission, 1956, p. 10). In subsequent years the number of integrated schools and the percentage of pupils enrolled in them steadily rose, but much of the change was due to the continued expansion of the Negro residential areas.

For readily understandable reasons, the free choice policy affects younger and older pupils differently. Most parents, and especially those in restricted circumstances, prefer to send elementary-age children to the nearest school, regardless of its condition. Families in more affluent circumstances are ordinarily willing to accept the added inconvenience of transportation to get their children into better schools, but the regrettable fact is that if opportunity is to be equalized by traveling it is invariably the slum children who must accept the inconvenience of going to where the more fortunate already are.

At the secondary level, distance is less of an obstacle. This is one of the reasons that in New York City in 1963, when 22 per cent of the elementary schools and 19 per cent of the junior high schools were found to be segregated, by the same criteria only one of the eighty-six senior high schools was segregated (New York State Education Commissioner's Advisory Committee, 1964).

The most tightly structured approach to desegregation, the Princeton Plan, achieves racial balance by pairing adjacent imbalanced schools, the combined attendance areas being treated as a single unit and the pupils being divided between the schools by grade rather than by residence. The advantages are clear: Both schools are integrated, and each is enabled to concentrate upon a narrower span of grades. There are also disadvantages. Travel time is increased for approximately half the children and transportation may be required, each school's established identity and its relations with its neighborhood are altered, and large-scale faculty transfers may be required. In addition, the possibility that white families will choose to leave the community becomes an uncertain hazard in every such situation.

Early and largely impressionistic evaluations of pairing suggest that the device may be more appropriate in smaller communities with only a few elementary schools than in larger places where neighborhood patterns and rates of residential change are more complex. One analysis of the probable result of pairing twenty-one sets of elementary schools in New York City showed that, at most, the proportion of segregated schools would have been reduced from 22 to 21 per cent (New York State Education Commissioner's Advisory Committee, 1964, p. 40).

A more comprehensive method of correcting imbalance is the re-zoning of all the attendance areas of a school system in order to obtain simultaneously a viable racial balance and reasonable travel time for all pupils. Rezoning and the related practice of revising the "feeder" patterns by which graduates of lower schools move on to junior or senior high schools are usually more practicable in closely populated communities than in less compact suburbs where travel distances are greater.

Among the more recent innovations is the "educational complex" proposed for the New York City schools (New York State Education Commissioner's Advisory Committee, 1964, pp. 18–20). The term denotes a group of schools serving differing racial constituencies and consisting typically of one or two junior high schools and their feeding elementary units. The attendance areas of the individual schools are not changed, but within the complex a variety of joint activities may be undertaken to bring the pupils, teachers, and parents into closer association. Programs and services that cannot be offered uniformly in all of the schools may be centered in one or two of the buildings and pupils transported to them as necessary. Faculty specialists may be shared by more than one building and common problems met cooperatively. Parents of two or more of the schools working together may bridge over old neighborhood lines that inhibit communication and joint action. The "complex" offers unusual possibilities for countering the effect of segregated housing. By retaining the advantages of neighborhood schools while introducing the social opportunities of a more diversified community, it offers children and parents a chance to try new experiences without totally abandoning the security of their familiar attachments.

Of all the schemes proposed for desegregating urban schools, the boldest and most imaginative is the educational park (Jacobson, 1964).[2] The rationale of the park rests on the hypothesis that the effect on the school of pockets of segregated housing will be offset if an attendance area can be made large enough to include white and Negro populations in balanced proportions. Thus, all the pupils of a greatly enlarged zone, perhaps 10,000 or more (in a medium-sized city, the entire school population), would be accommodated on a single site or park. Within the park, which could range all the way from a 100 acre campus with many separate buildings to a single high-rise structure covering a city block, students would be assigned to relatively small units, each maintained as a separate school in which teachers and pupils would work closely and continuously together. The distribution of students among the smaller units would be made without regard to the location of their homes but with the purpose of making each school as well integrated as possible.

Beyond these general outlines, there is little agreement on what an educational park should be. One view is that the full grade range should be included, from nursery school to community college. Others propose that a park serve one or two levels, perhaps elementary and junior high schools, or a comprehensive secondary program of three, four, or six years. New York City has examined the feasibility of using middle-school parks for grades five to eight, retaining small neighborhood schools for prekindergarten, kindergarten, and primary programs.

With such a combination, children and parents would be introduced to the public schools first in their own neighborhoods, where familiar relationships, short distances, and close home-school ties would be at their maximum. In these primary centers each child, depending on his age at entry, would spend four to seven years, and some children a longer period, receiving fundamental preparation that primary education at its best should provide. Remedial services, compensatory curricula, and enriched programs would be available to all who need them. At the fifth grade, each pupils would move on to the middle-school park where for the first time his classmates, now drawn from a much wider area, would reflect the diversity of a truly common school and, hopefully, a genuinely integrated one. All high schools, under this proposal, would operate under a city-wide policy of free choice for all students, subject only to such restrictions as were needed to prevent overcrowding and to respect requirements for admission to specialized programs.

One criticism of the educational park is the excessively high costs that

---

[2] The papers included in the report edited by Jacobson contain the most perceptive appraisals of the educational park concept currently available.

some associate with it. A single site and the construction required to house 10,000 pupils need be no greater, however, than the combined cost of ten sites and buildings for a thousand pupils each. Indeed, a larger site located on relatively open and cheaper land might well be less costly to assemble than comparable acreage in congested sections. The total operating costs for a single, well-managed park should be lower than those for several separate units. In almost every case, however, a large proportion of the pupils would have to be transported and the cost of that service financed as a new expense. As in any other new venture, the increased outlay required must be set against the anticipated return. In a well-conceived educational park the better education and the improved social situation that may be expected offer future assets of substantial value.

Beside the possibilities for accomplishing school integration must be set the deterrents that currently retard the process, of which the most visible and powerful is the concept of the neighborhood school. Although the close identification of a school with its immediate community produces results beneficial to both, the battles now being fought in the name of that relationship, and sometimes for virtual possession of particular schools, obscure fundamental principles. The public school is the property not of its neighborhood but of the school district. Since the district itself is created by the state, it is quite reasonable to argue that both title and control rest ultimately with the people of the state as a whole. However commendable the interest of a neighborhood in its school may be, concern is not to be confused with proprietary control. Subject to the state's supervision, the school board alone is legally empowered to determine for any school whose children shall be admitted and whose excluded.

The neighborhood school is essentially an administrative device designed to assure all the children of a district equal educational opportunity and equal access to it. When the device ceases to serve those functions, and especially when its use is so distorted that it frustrates rather than furthers the primary purpose, it is the device rather than the purpose that must give way.

It is a curious coincidence that during the very period that city and suburban neighborhood schools have been gaining an almost sacrosanct status, the rural sections in which such schools were first established have been abandoning them. The neighborhood school in its original and most authentic form, the one-room schoolhouse, has been disappearing from the United States at the rate of 3,000 a year for the last half century. Despite understandable misgivings about school consolidation, rural parents by the millions have exchanged their nearby schools and the intensely local form of control many of them embody for the superior instruction and broader educational experiences more comprehensive institutions offer. They have learned that, despite its relative remoteness from the neighborhood, the consolidated school not only provides a broader curriculum, better books and equipment, and abler teachers, but, by drawing its pupils from a wider and more varied attendance area, also furnishes them an out-look upon the world that is impossible in the more homogeneous society of the local school.

City and suburban schools meanwhile have gone in quite the opposite direction, becoming steadily more segregated not only by race but also by social and economic level. The momentum of this movement creates one of the principal forces opposing integration in schools and communities. Combined with more common forms of racial prejudice, segregated hous-ing, and repressive economic practices, the growing social stratification of the public school carries the most serious implications for the future of American society.

Despite the generous lip service that the common school has tra-ditionally received, it is a clear fact that, in many parts of the country, substantial minorities of American children at both extremes of the social scale have not been educated in schools that could, by any reasonable criteria, be called inclusive. Yet the complementary truth is that the vast majority of our citizens, the white ones, at any rate, have been brought up in schools that "everybody" was expected to attend. Whether the connec-tion between such childhood experiences and the health of a democratic society is still or ever was as close as Horace Mann held it to be, is beyond explicit demonstration. But whether an open society can be maintained and, even more to the present point, whether a hitherto excluded group can be brought into the full enjoyment of citizenship without the instru-mentality of the common school, are questions this country cannot much longer evade. On so complex a matter, clear causal relationships are difficult to establish, but the correlation between the rise of the common school and the development of an open society in the United States is, to say the least, impressive. Before we accept by default or support by intent the trend toward stratified public education it would be well at least to project and appraise the probable consequences.

A second force impeding integration, in certain respects the first writ large, is generated by the growth of solidly white suburban communities around the heavily congested urban centers into which the Negro popula-tion finds itself channeled and confined. The "white noose" not only prevents the outward dispersion of Negroes but equally, if less directly, discourages white families from remaining in the city. As population density and neighborhood depression worsen, larger numbers of families with the freedom to choose and the power to act abandon both the city and its schools.

The steady increase of urban segregation, the growing ghettos, and the declining attractiveness of the city for all groups produce problems whose magnitude and complexity carry them beyond the control of separate localities. Every day the deteriorating situation emphasizes more strongly the need for a total reappraisal of city-suburban relationships. If the present trend is allowed to continue, the difficulties that now plague the central city can be expected inevitably—and soon—to trouble entire metropolitan areas. The almost total segregation of the incorporated area, the political entity officially called the city, is hardly an acceptable alternative to the systematic desegregation of the total social and economic network that is in fact the city. It becomes constantly more evident that, unless steps are taken to bring about a better dispersion and integration of Negro citizens throughout metropolitan areas, direct action will be required to equalize educational opportunities and the process of school integration between the cities and their suburbs. This responsibility for re-examining urban-suburban racial imbalance and its locus is implied by a sentence in the *Brown* decision: "Such an opportunity [to secure an education] where the state has undertaken to provide it is a right which must be made available to all on equal terms." If the right to equal treatment in the schools, including freedom from racial segregation, overrides, as it does, statutes placing children in particular schools, the question naturally arises whether that right is to be restricted indefinitely by statutes that fix lines between local jurisdictions.

III

Imaginative and forthright action to bring as many children as possible into integrated schools as rapidly as possible is an urgent necessity, but it would be grossly unrealistic to assume that integration can be accomplished everywhere in the foreseeable future. In the borough of Manhattan 78 per cent of the public elementary-school pupils are Negro and Puerto Rican. Immediate and total integration could be accomplished there only by closing most of the schools in Manhattan and distributing their pupils among the remaining boroughs or by setting up a vast "exchange" system to move hundreds of thousands of children daily in both directions between Manhattan and other parts of the city. Quite aside from the sheer administrative and teaching problems such an operation would pose, little imagination is needed to predict the virtually unanimous objection of parents.

Important progress can be made, however, on the periphery of segregated communities, through the procedures described earlier and by energetic efforts to concentrate on the possible instead of deploring the impossible. When all the possibilities are exploited and new ones ingeniously devised, there will still remain many ghetto schools in which integration is simply not feasible. In those places, the only reasonable action is the massive improvement of schools to educate children where they are.

It is unhappily true, as Kenneth Clark points out, that to ask for good schools in the ghetto is to risk the charge that one acquiesces in segregation (Clark, 1965, p. 117). Yet, even though supporting better schools in ghettos has become a favorite ploy of the advocates of separate equality, that fact does not justify neglecting ghetto children. Indeed, many of these children are already so badly victimized by deprivation and neglect that, if integration were instantly possible, strong remedial and compensatory programs would still be necessary to give them any reasonable chance to compete or succeed.

In designing educational strategies to meet the special needs of Negro ghetto children the public schools are undertaking tasks they have never really faced up to before. The curricula of slum schools have almost invariably been no more than adapted versions of those designed for middle-class pupils. Even now, a number of the changes being introduced into slum schools involve little more than efforts to apply to the ghetto, although somewhat more effectively and more intensively, the character-istic practices of middle-class schools: smaller classes to teach traditional subjects; more time for reading, using standard readers; increased guidance service employing the customary techniques.

Such projects to multiply and intensify established procedures are by no means wholly wasteful or necessarily wrong. Kenneth Clark (1965, p. 117) insists with considerable justification that the change most needed in slum schools is an elevation of the teachers' expectations of the children. The main reason, he argues, that Negro students rank low academically is that too many teachers and the "system" as a whole consider them un-educable.

However much ghetto children could gain from proper motivation and a decent respect for their potentiality, strong encouragement and high expectation are not enough. No teacher can hope to teach effectively or fairly unless he differentiates between the child whose environment re-enforces the school's influence and the one whose out-of-school world is rarely even so good as neutral and more often is severely damaging. While much can be said for holding both children to the same level of expecta-tion, it is hardly realistic to assume that both will reach it with equal personal effort and the same assistance from the school. The child suffering unusual deprivation would appear obviously to require — and to deserve — unusual attention. The extent to which the special help should be compen-satory, or remedial, or unusually stimulating is, of course, a suitable sub-ject of investigation and debate; but that it must be particularly adapted to the child who is victimized by his environment would seem self-evident.

A growing volume of research not only documents the relationship between a child's cultural environment and his school success but also illuminates with increasing clarity the crucial importance of the early years. Benjamin Bloom (1964, pp. 68–76) has examined many of the pertinent studies in the field and estimates that the difference between a culturally deprived and a culturally abundant environment can affect a child's IQ by an average of twenty points, half of the difference being attributable to the influences of the first four years and as much as six points to the next four. After another comprehensive survey, J. McVicker Hunt (1964) concludes that while the notion of cultural deprivation is still gross and undifferentiated, the concept holds much promise. He considers it entirely possible to arrange institutional settings in which culturally handicapped children can encounter experiences that will compensate for what they may have missed. Martin Deutsch, whose work has included extended experimentation with such children, has found that those with some preschool experience attain significantly higher intelligence-test scores at the fifth grade than do children of the same background who did not have the experience (Deutsch, 1962).

Opinions differ as to the type of preschool program that offers the most fruitful compensation to slum children. One approach assumes that ordinary home-supplementing nursery schools designed for middle-class children will also help the deprived youngster. A second concentrates on preparing the culturally deprived child for school by teaching him to follow directions and to use such things as toys, pencils, crayons, and books. A third approach begins with the view that the culturally deprived child differs fundamentally from others in self-concept, language values, and perceptual processes and offers specialized programs to compensate for the deleterious effects of his lean environment.

While there are still no systematic comparisons of the relative effectiveness of these different programs, two generalizations can be stated with some assurance. One is that preschool programs do appear to be effective in raising intelligence-test scores, vocabulary level, expressive ability, arithmetic reasoning, and reading readiness.

The second is that the results do not run uniformly in one direction. A study made in the Racine public schools reports that

> Potentially the most useful conclusion which can be drawn . . . is that "one shot" compensatory programs would seem to be a waste of time and money. The fact that differences between groups disappeared and that in several areas the rate of growth of both groups regressed during the traditional first grade years supports this contention.

> If these implications are supported by future research, it would seem that curriculum revision over the entire twelve year school curriculum is a necessary part of any lasting solution to the basic problem of urban public school education. (Larson and Olson, 1965)

The Racine finding bears out what anyone experienced in slum schools would probably have predicted. Any such teacher knows that the moment the child steps outside, at whatever age, he is caught again in the cultural downdraft of the street and all too often of the home itself. Efforts to compensate within the school must, therefore, begin at the earliest possible age and continue with steady and strong consistency throughout the whole length of the child's school career.

One outstanding example of what may be done in the upper grades was the Demonstration Guidance Project, initiated in 1956 in New York's Junior High School 43 located on the edge of Harlem (New York City Board of Education, 1959–60, pp. 2–15). The principal aim of the project was to identify and stimulate potentially able pupils and to help them reach levels of performance more nearly consistent with their capacities. The project students, all selected because they were thought to possess latent academic aptitude and most of them from disadvantaged backgrounds, were placed in small classes, given double periods daily in English, and tutored in small groups. Intensive counseling, clinical services, and social work were provided, and regular contact was maintained with the parents. Scholastic achievement was stressed and special efforts made to prepare the students for college or jobs. Visits were conducted to museums, theaters, concerts, the ballet, and places of special interest in New York and elsewhere. The program was continued into the George Washington Senior High School and the last experimental group graduated in 1960. After three and a half years of this special attention, these students, most of whom would ordinarily have been considered poor academic risks, showed substantial gains over their own earlier records, and over the usual performance of students from the same school. Of 105 in one group, 78 showed an increase in IQ, 64 gaining ten points or more. The median for the entire group rose in the three-year period from 92.9 to 102.2. Against a previous average for their school of 47 per cent, 64 per cent earned high-school diplomas. Three students ranked first, fourth, and sixth in their class; two and one-half times as many as in previous classes went to college, and three and one-half times as many to some form of further education.

On a modified and reduced scale, the Demonstration Guidance Project was subsequently introduced as the Higher Horizons Program to other schools in New York City with results that have been comparably positive if somewhat less spectacular.

IV

Special programs to meet the needs of deprived children have been undertaken in a number of school systems. A project in the Banneker Group of the St. Louis school system has stressed the teaching of reading, English, and arithmetic. Particular attention was directed to the motivation of the pupils, to setting standards of performance. The support of parents was solicited, and their pride in their children's accomplishments was stimulated. By the end of the third year of the project the achievement of Banneker eighth graders equalled or exceeded national norms in reading and language and fell only one month short in arithmetic. In the years immediately preceding, the comparable scores had ranged from one to two years below the national norms. The theme of the Banneker project is

321

expressed by Samuel Shephard, the administrator who conceived it, in his instructions to teachers: "Quit teaching by IQ and the neighborhood where the child lives. Teach the child all you can teach him." (Wynant, 1962)

Detroit set up a new effort during the 1960–61 academic year with some 10,000 elementary and secondary pupils, mainly in the Negro residential areas, concentrating not only on the children but also on work with parents and teachers. A principal aim was to modify teachers' perceptions of children with limited backgrounds. The program included curriculum revision, reorganized teaching schedules, tutoring, home visiting, and supplementary activities for pupils during after-school hours and summer months.

A Pittsburgh project centered in the "Hill" district employed team teaching to improve instruction in reading and the language arts.

Virtually every large school system in the country and many of the smaller ones are now attacking the problem of the culturally deprived child, but the volume of well-intentioned activity still substantially exceeds the amount of imaginative and well-designed research that is being done to analyze and appraise the innovations. Until the quality of experimental design and research matches the quantity of sheer energy being devoted to the task, much of the energy is certain to be wasted and potentially valuable information and insights to be lost.

A field in which further study and fresh thinking are badly needed is vocational education, where the long-standing practice of separating vocational students from those in academic programs has more recently been compounded by the effects of racial imbalance. The result has been to render vocational programs in some schools all but useless. The field has suffered also because many schools have adhered too long and too closely to the concepts of curriculum and organization developed forty years ago. The tragically high rate of unemployment among Negro youth is only one of urgent reasons for the early and thorough reform of this essential part of American education.

In higher education impressive progress in some institutions has diverted attention from the massive obstacles that remain to be overcome. While a detailed discussion of this situation is beyond the scope of this paper it is relevant to emphasize the reciprocal relationship between accomplishments by Negroes in colleges and universities and the improvement of elementary and secondary schools, a prominent element in this relationship being the supply of well-prepared Negro teachers. Hard facts on the relative competence of white graduates and Negro graduates of teacher education programs are not easy to secure, but such evidence as has come to light, most of it subjective, suggests that much remains to be done to equalize the quality of programs and the availability of places in first-rate schools. Despite the fact that thousands of Negro teachers have attained high levels of professional competence and status, many others who hold teaching certificates are unable to obtain employment even in schools that want Negro teachers, because of their inability to compete with other applicants. A largely similar situation prevails in graduate-school admissions.

McGrath's study of Negro colleges (McGrath, 1965, pp. 21 ff.) provides part of the explanation and suggests directions in which some of the answers must be sought: the prompt and substantial upgrading of faculties, curricula, libraries, laboratories, and physical facilities of the colleges that serve predominantly Negro student bodies and enroll more than half the Negro college students of the country.

Another important part of the solution must be found in programs in high school and between high school and college to furnish the supplemental instruction that many Negro students require in order to qualify for first-rate institutions. The encouraging reports of such programs as those conducted by the National Scholarship Service and Fund for Negro Students (Clark and Plotkin, 1963, pp. 7 ff.), as well as by a number of the institutions themselves, indicate what special effort and thoughtful planning toward that end can accomplish.

"A grand mental and moral experiment," Horace Mann once called free schools, "whose effects could not be developed and made manifest in a single generation" (Mann, 1891, p. 246).

For the Negro American, the development of those effects has taken a good deal longer — far too much longer — than was required to make them manifest for his white countrymen. The knowledge that the Negro's right to education has been restricted is no new discovery, but what is new is the growing consciousness that what has been withheld from him has impoverished the whole people.

The argument for enlarging the opportunities and enhancing the status of the Negro minority goes far beyond extending a modicum more of charity to the poor. The appeal to equity and to the humane principles that undergird the democratic enterprise is the heart of the matter, to be sure, but the evidence is now irrefutable that until each American has full access to the means to develop his capacities every other American's chances and attainments will continue to be diminished.

That this relationship should become so critically significant in a time characterized by technological progress may seem paradoxical; yet it is that progress and the insatiable demand it generates for intellectual competence that now re-enforces our long-standing moral obligation to re-examine the standards by which we live as a society.

The detailed problems of procedure which flow from this obligation impose a complex array of tasks upon the network of the arts, the sciences, the humanities, and the professional specialities that contribute knowledge and skill to the educational establishment. But here, too — here especially — the prior question and the transcendent issue are moral: What ought we to be doing?

323

If the educational and political leadership of the country can muster the strength of conscience to face that query forthrightly and honestly, there are abundant grounds for optimism that the subsidiary tasks will become both more clearly visible and more readily feasible.

References

Bloom, Benjamin S. *Stability and Change in Human Characteristics.* New York: John Wiley and Sons, Inc., 1964.

Carter, Robert L. "De Facto School Segregation: An Examination of the Legal and Constitutional Questions Presented," *Western Reserve Law Review,* 16 (May 1965), 527.

Clark, Kenneth B. *Dark Ghetto.* New York: Harper and Row, 1965.

—— and Lawrence Plotkin. *The Negro Student at Integrated Colleges.* New York: National Scholarship Service and Fund for Negro Students, 1963.

Dentler, Robert A. *A Basis for Classifying the Ethnic Composition of Schools.* New York: Teachers College, Columbia University Institute for Urban Studies, December 1964. Unpublished memorandum.

Deutsch, Martin. "The Influence of Early Social Environments on School Adaptation," presented at the Symposium on School Dropouts, Washington, D. C., December 1962.

Havighurst, Robert J. *The Public Schools of Chicago.* Chicago: University of Chicago Press, 1964.

Hunt, J. McVicker. "The Psychological Basis for Using Preschool Enrichment as an Antidote for Cultural Deprivation," *Merrill-Palmer Quarterly,* 10 (July, 1964), 236.

Jacobson, Nathan (ed.). *An Exploration of the Educational Park Concept.* New York: Board of Education of the City of New York, 1964.

Larson, R. G. and J. L. Olson. *Final Report: A Pilot Project for Culturally Deprived Kindergarten Children.* Racine, Wisconsin: Unified School District No. 1, April 1965. Mimeographed.

Mann, Horace. "Intellectual Education as a Means of Removing Poverty and Securing Abundance," Twelfth Annual Report of the Board of Education of Massachusetts, 1848.

Maryland Commission on Interracial Problems and Relations. *The Report of a Study on Desegregation in the Baltimore City Schools.* Baltimore, Md.: The Commission, 1956.

McGrath, Earl J. *The Predominantly Negro College and Universities in Transition.* New York: Teachers College Press, Columbia University, 1965.

New York City Board of Education. *The Demonstration Guidance Project, Fourth Annual Report.* New York: The Board, 1960.

New York State Education Commissioner's Advisory Committee on

Human Relations and Community Tensions. *Desegregating the Public Schools of New York City.* Albany, N.Y.: The Committee, 1964.

New York State Department of Education. *Guiding Principles for Securing Racial Balance in Public Schools.* Albany, N.Y.: The Department, 1963.

Wynant, William K., Jr. "Reading: A Way Upward" in *Civil Rights USA, Public Schools, Cities in the North and West.* Washington, D.C.: U.S. Civil Rights Commission, 1962.

Dan W. Dodson examines the crisis for school systems implied by powerlessness as the state of the Negro minority. The schools must recognize this crisis and act on this power hypothesis—that the youth who is a member of a disrespected social group cannot mature without traumatic damage to his self-perception. It is not enough, says this author, to "siphon off" bright Negro youths and integrate them into the mainstream of American culture, alienating the brighter youth from his heritage. Power to strengthen the minority group cannot be given to it by another group in society; in the last analysis, the minority group itself must take power.

The author discusses the implications of this hypothesis for a number of problems, including racial balance in the schools. He treats the neighborhood school—with its resulting racial imbalance, its apathy, and its low esteem for Negro culture as a crucial issue in the education of children of the powerless. The author contends that the professional leadership —in education and in the social sciences—simply contributes to a rationalization which has become a modern version of infant damnation. The depressed area child has to overcome the hurdle of his own poor self-image, compounded by the mythology draped about him by those who are there supposedly to educate him. The whole bureaucracy of the large-system city shares in the guilt by failing to keep creative persons from leaving the system.

EDUCATION AND THE POWERLESS

Dan W. Dodson

The educator is urged to consider how the school can impart meanings and values that help orient and direct inner-city children. It is suggested that classroom climate and environment be altered to teach minority youth techniques for gaining political, economic, and social power. The author argues that "every classroom should be a laboratory in how to take power, how to shield the group from power which is abused, how it will work through shared relationships." This, he says, is the task of the curriculum maker, the teacher, and the entire educational structure.

EDUCATION
AND THE
POWERLESS

Dan W. Dodson

In the large cities of America, education is in crisis. The revolution in agriculture has driven out those who marginally subsist. Over one million more agricultural workers now live in slums of the large cities than live on all the farms — there are one and one half million more to come. The major portion of these migrants from the rural heritage are Negroes. They bring, not only a heritage of poor education, but as well a trauma of servitude that is historical. The school systems of the cities are called upon to close the gap between them and the sophisticated population *in one generation.* What is more, the problem cannot be hidden as it has been with other groups. The Negro migrants speak the same language (approximately) as the remainder of the community, and their residence in America is of the oldest, so the failure cannot be laid to bilingualism in the same kind of rationalization that explained away lack of ability to deal with newcomers of past generations.

In addition, the public school has full responsibility for this task of social leadership. Except for the Jewish group, which was composed of people accustomed to living in urban communities, the past mass migrations of peoples with rural heritages relied on parochial schools for the training of a part of their children, so that public education was excused from the total task of closing the gap for these groups. There are still vestiges of Italian-American and Polish-American neighborhoods in many cities where the public school was a sort of an annex to the parochial school, and in the name of cultural autonomy these children of the marginal members of the society were neglected by public education, for to have made their education commensurate with their need would have made public schools too competitive with the parochial. A leader from one of these communities was amazed when he found that the achievement levels of schools in his Italian-American neighborhood were below those of some of the Negro schools. He said "Thank God! At least one thing we will get out of this (study of racial imbalance) is good education for all the children." He was amazed to find the gap that still existed between the children of his heritage and the remainder of the white community.

As a result of this historical situation, the school systems have little to offer in intervening on behalf of the rural child in modern-day slums. Vast foundation grants have been made, innumerable conferences have been held, projects named using almost every letter of the alphabet have been set up, in the hope of finding ways of making these children "malleable to the forges" of the educational system. To date there is precious little accretion from these experiences to guide program development. Studies, demonstrations, and "experiments" rarely fail to demonstrate the validity of what their designers set out to prove, but rarely do they give hope that they have found the key closing this gap for educationally disadvantaged children within a generation. Some despair that it can be done. They would make acculturation a matter of time. Others would even blame the human potential (Shuy, Garrett) indicating that race itself is a factor. Most try to use the family and the community as scapegoats for lack of effective education (for example, Conant, who says essentially that unless the family and the community are good there is little one can do in the school). Others are now saying that unless there is stimulation in the early years it is impossible to do much later. "This early deprivation amounts to irreparable loss of ability to deal with abstract symbols," they say. This tends to be a modern version of a stereotype from East Texas fifty years ago when I was a boy. They contended that something closed in a Negro child's head when he was about six. Hence it was impossible to teach him anything beyond that point. Efforts to educate him were a waste of money. This current theory amounts to about the same thing. Whatever the rationalizations, suffice it to say there is no panacea in modern American education for the children of the Negro slum. The evidence has largely been one of deteriorating morale and standards of accomplishment, both for the students and for those who purport to teach them. Clearly business as usual in American education is not enough, if this generation of children is to be salvaged. Neither is business as usual plus a few extra grants from the federal government and the large foundations going to bolster the current approaches to the problem, in this writer's estimation.

The Power Hypothesis

During the past few years the power hypothesis has seemed to loom significant in the consideration of this problem. It is not contended here that there is a single simple pattern of causality; it is rather to invite examination of an alternate hypothesis. *It is probably impossible for a youth who is a member of a group that is powerless to grow to maturity without some traumatic effect in the perception of himself because of the compromised position of his group in the community.* This trauma is expressed in various ways. Adler, in his psychology, contended that one who felt inferior tended to overcompensate for his sense of impotence. There are some who do. These we refer to as having a "chip on the shoulder." On the other hand, the vast majority of those who feel extremely powerless resign in apathy. The mass apathy of the slums, it is here contended, results from the pervading sense of powerlessness.

It may be pointed out that this is not restricted to the minority. We all tend to become apathetic about those things we feel powerless about. Witness the apathy in the large city about the bad government, or the apathy over the threat of atomic destruction. To understand the weakness of the school in dealing with such concentrations of impotent populations, it is necessary to review the role of the school as a part of the power order. They must teach some that they are "brahmins" and are the academic elite. It teaches 30 to 40 per cent of the students that the rewards and recognitions of the schools are not for them; hence they drop out of high school before they finish. The schools must teach all the children the mythologies of the "American Way" in such fashion that all will understand that their failures are their own, rather than those of the system. Otherwise they would rebel and blow the system apart. They must offer hope to the bright ones of the minority that if they meet the demands of the order they will be recognized. On the other hand they cannot offer this incentive to too many, for they will be accused of not having standards.

As with all institutions of the power order, the school tries desperately to work through integrative processes rather than through conflict. This means working through involvement, process, participation, earned leadership roles, and growth through discipline *to the rules that operate the social order.*

The characteristic approach to the powerless is to get the bright ones involved, get them to take stock in the mythologies of the American Way (which say that all will be recognized according to their ability and initiative), alienate them in their sentiments and sympathies from the group of which they are a part, make them ashamed of their heritage (every minority group has wrestled with the phenomena of group-self hate among its second-generation youths), shape them to the dimensions of the order that is, and ultimately transmute them into "ideal Americans." Hence, we have never solved the problem of the slum. We have siphoned off the bright youths and left the group itself to its own devices. The bright ones, after being transmuted, rarely ever return to the community to give leadership in solution of problems. With the Negro group this process does not work so well. One reason is that color stands as a barrier. When the bright one has been alienated and made ashamed of his heritage and is "transmuted" there is no place for him to go. His transmutation is into limbo. Furthermore, the Negro has never been a part of this "American dream." It is hard to sell the mythologies to youths who perceive on every side that they are not for him.

The alternative to this process is motivation that stems from different sources. There is not time for this alienating, "siphoning-off," transmuting process—even if it were desirable. The alternative must be for the group to take power and move under self-direction. It must be possessed by group goals requiring that the youths learn what the schools have to teach in order to prepare themselves to make a worthy group contribution to the autonomous goals of the group itself. The two great issues are related to this process: Will the power order that is allow such an approach? Is it possible to help such groups take power?

A significant dimension of the problem is that power has to be taken. It cannot be given. Moe Chusid said it best when discussing the Puerto Ricans in Chelsea, on Manhattan's West Side. He said they were the majority group. He gave them every opportunity possible to take leadership. But in the last analysis they had to take power. He couldn't give it to them.

Some Methodological Implications

One of the first implications of the hypothesis advanced above relates to school assignment policies. The all-Negro school in today's world stands as a symbol of the Negro's powerlessness. It represents to the Negro child his rejection by the majority group. It puts him outside the circumference of power and leaves him an alienated soul. Such schools are impossible to maintain as first-rate educational enterprises because morale is impossible to achieve, expectations are lowered, standards fall, and most of the time such schools are discriminated against in services. The HARYOU study indicated that such children fall back steadily relative to the national achievement norms.

Concerning Racial Imbalance

The most basic curriculum decision a board of education makes is the determination of who is going to school with whom. It is the determination whether children are to learn the skills of citizenship in a pluralistic world, or on the other hand, whether the minority group is to be left segregated in its impotence. The acid test of whether a group has power is its capacity to require the total community to share whatever facilities as exist equally among all the children.

In this context it is doubtful that the neighborhood school can maintain its integrity as an educational entity in the years ahead. It is impossible for a community to keep all its schools at the same educational level. In most communities, one may as well rate the schools as to their popularity or status in the community as to rate them on the collective achievement of the youths to determine their academic standing. The less good schools are harder to staff. The teachers assigned to them are considered less fortunate. The children have less expected of them. They are, as a consequence, traumatized by being required to attend them.

Another aspect of the issue also is pertinent. In such a situation, the neighborhood school became a turf on which those who have power shield themselves from meaningful encounters with those who are powerless. They are able to attract for the education of their children what cannot be provided for the entire community. Such unshared privilege tends to corrupt both the powerful and the powerless. The proposition is hereby submitted that it is impossible to teach *community* in a neighborhood school—the Parents and Taxpayers Groups to the contrary notwithstanding. The neighborhood school teaches the child far more about his worth and the potency of himself and his group than do all the citizenship courses.

In the *New York Times* for Sunday, June 7, 1964, nine out of fourteen houses listed "For Sale" in Mt. Vernon, New York indicated the name of the school zone in which the property was located. Three others indicated they were also north of the New Haven Railroad. So important did seven of them consider the school to which the property was attached that they put the name of the school next to the name of the town in which the property was located, and before any description of the property itself. Needless to say, none of the advertisements of properties on the south side mentioned their location with regard to schools. They have the heavy concentration of Negroes. The children really learn the neighborhood social arrangements.

Children study about citizenship in the books. They pass examinations on what the books say, and perhaps, on what the teachers teach. They live what the community teaches. The neighborhood school is the outstanding mentor. Thus racial imbalance becomes a crucial issue in education of the children of the powerless. It cannot be separated from the general sense of apathy and low esteem which the whole culture purveys.

Professional Leadership

Closely related to the problem of racial imbalance is the role of the professionals. The power order or bureaucracy that is the school system is programed to teach what the established order thinks is relevant. It scarcely knows anything else. In showing the children their place in the order, the teaching profession must do two things. First, it must help the children learn their place in the power order in such a fashion that they and their parents come to believe the reasons for failure are those of their group and not the system. Hence there is a variety of myth and ritual involved in this assorting task. Grades are given. It is better if they are based on objective tests; then they can be better defended. Grouping assigns some to higher status than others. The school purports to offer the same opportunity for all to make the first or the fastest group. Intelligence scores become the *alpha* and *omega* of the educative process. It is understandable that the professional leadership of the schools identify with and provide the rationalizations for the status position of the power order that is. The major responsibility of the historian is to provide the historical rationalization for the power position. When the country was dominantly Protestant, the history was Protestant. When the Catholics came to power also, the history was enlarged to include the Christian heritage. As the Jews came into the power stream, the history is gradually merging into a common Judeo-Christian heritage. When labor was powerless in New York State, it

333

was necessary for them to write history books themselves that depicted labor's role in building the state. As labor has come into the power order, the histories have become more cognizant of the common contributions. So it is with the Negro, who tends to be powerless. As he takes power, the histories and the literature anthologies will come to recognize his contribution to the common heritage, and will ignore it until he so arrives.

On this point, one must also complain as to the impact of the learned studies of my own colleagues in the behavioral sciences. When one is through reading the proceedings of any one of the many conferences held on this problem, he is impressed with their relation to the power order. One wades through such jargon as "low I.Q.," "low social class," "weak ego strength," "lack of a father image with which to relate," "inability to forego immediate pleasures for long-range goals," and "cultural deprivation." If a teacher ever had any hope of working creatively with these children of the ghettos, he would be handicapped if he took us seriously, for the pictures we build in the back of his head would determine what he saw in the human potential rather than what was reality. What does it all mean? Does it not mean that we, too, are the soothsayers for the order which is? Ours is the task of providing the rationalizations for the power order that is, and the explanations as to why it operates as it does.

In the middle of the last century the learned divines afforded the rationalizations for the conditions of the deviants. It was infant damnation. God had damned some before birth, hence the social order could not get creativeness out of them. By the end of the century the psychologists had supplied a "scientific," secular version of the phenomena. It was the low "I.Q." Today the sociologists are coming up very rapidly with their version. It is "low social class." When one is through reading our "verified hypotheses," he feels like saying "For God's sake, if this is all we see in the human potential with which we work, we had better turn them over to the Black Muslims and resign from the business." Somehow, when youths get a dose of that ideology, and take power, they show considerable imaginativeness, intelligence, and ability. Their "low I.Q.'s," their "low social class," their "weak ego strengths," their inability to "forego immediate pleasures for long range goals," "their lack of the father image with which to relate," and even the demonstrable fact that they perceive differently in the preschool years does not seem to deter them too much. If the first great hurdle of the depressed-area child is the trauma to his image occasioned by his sense of impotence, the second hurdle is that of overcoming the mythology built about him by those who purport to serve him.

Another dimension of professional leadership relates to its quality. As school systems have grown larger, they have become increasingly bureaucratic. This means that people are assigned to increasingly specialized roles, so that the teacher of today is the instructor of the common branches of the advanced section of the seventh grade, of a homogeneous neighborhood. She is responsible for developing neither her curriculum (a specialized bureau does that for her) nor her schedule. Someone else specializes in the child's recreation, his creativity, his psyche, his family, and his guidance. The teacher is an interchangeable part in a vast bureaucratic machine.

As a result of this trend, teaching is rapidly passing from an art in which teacher related to child, to a science in which teacher is increasingly preoccupied with matters of "what and how" in instruction, rather than "who." Very rapidly, the educator as an idea man in the community is being replaced with the operator: the charismatic leader with the bureaucratic leader; the prophet with the priest; the man of vision with the caretaker of the bureaucracy. Unless the educationist can "quicken the spirit" of those he leads, it does not matter much what else he does. In no small measure this aspect of education has been downgraded in American life.

In the past decade there have been millions of dollars spent on the experimentation and demonstration of this and that nostrum designed to test this or that hypothesis on the culturally deprived. Of all the efforts, the most outstanding job I know about is being done by Sam Shephard in St. Louis, Missouri. Here, a district superintendent took over a traditional slum district several years ago. Within six years he brought the children to slightly above national norms in reading, and almost to comparable advances in mathematics. Although the Ford Foundation made him a grant to assist with testing after he was under way, he had no great resources of outside help to operate a deluxe program. When one tries to examine how he did it, the most that can be gotten is the charismatic quality of his leadership.

He had the vision to see the human potential of those he served. He had the wisdom not to believe the clichés the scholars had provided as to why these children were as they were. He had the courage to challenge the stereotypes about their abilities, and he had the quality of leadership to persuade his principals and staff to likewise forget these things they had been taught and to bear down and hold these youths to the same high standards of expectations as other children were held to.

Now you will ask me how we train people to have charismatic leadership. I frankly do not know. However, it suggests that more attention must be paid to selection of educational staff to make sure bureaucratic requirements, qualifications increasingly written out in job specifications which usually are related to objective tests, do not drive from the schools the last vestiges of uniqueness, which is at the core of creativeness.

Concerning Ideology

Another aspect of the slum situation relates to the role of ideology. Since the second world war there has been a downgrading of this dimension of the human estate. Man, however, cannot escape the issue of values in human personality.

For this speaker, there is serious doubt as to whether much can be done for these children who are victims of slum shock until some ideology takes hold of life to give it meaning and structure and purpose. Granted that the Black Muslim is considered antisocial, he does stand as testimony to the regenerative power of ideology.

There is enough evidence in the examination of such problems to raise the issue as to whether the major threat the depressed areas present to us may be our inability to interpret the ideologies of "our way of life" sufficiently that such youths have an attraction to them. In fact, is not the major threat of our times to all of us the problem that increasingly the motivation is away from inner direction and self-purpose to outer direction that stems from the mass culture? Youths study and make grades so their parents won't be ashamed of them, rather than to achieve inner purposes. Motivation is not from inner drives and purposes, but outside mass culture pressure.

Mannheim indicated several years ago that the scholar did not have the privilege of standing outside some value system. Neither does the student. Educators would do well to reexamine their own ideological orientation as they work with such youths. Unless they can inspire hope and faith, there is little reason for the slum student to work. In order to do that the educator must be able to impart meanings and values which give orientation and direction to those who sit at his feet.

Methodologies

There are several issues relating to methodology which are puzzling. They will be raised as questions rather than as positions.

Classroom climates. One of the most pervasive problems of working in culturally deviant schools is the climate of the group or classroom. More teachers fail, by far, because they cannot deal effectively with the class as a group than because of their limitations in subject matter. Most educators would contend that classroom climates that are permissive and warm, which unite children in working toward common goals, are more desirable than those which are rigid and formal. How different these can be is illustrated by two schools involved in our evaluation of the Open Enrollment Program of six elementary schools of New York City. Here, Negro children were brought to the host school in the outer part of the city from overcrowded inner city by bus. They were distributed proportionately throughout the sections of each grade. They were ethnically identifiable. We studied them in May, after a scholastic year of association. In one of these schools whose students were highly motivated, middle-class whites had 44 majority background boys in the fifth grade. Each was asked to make ten sociometric choices—five related to work committees in the classroom and five on the playground. Of the 440 choices these youths made, only one single choice of a Negro child by a white child was made. In other words there seemed to be coracial education in the school. In another situation where the host and Open Enrollment children were more nearly peers, 84 white boys with 840 choices made 118 of their choices from among the Open Enrollment youths. This was about the proportion of Negro youth to the total group. Yet the minority children in the situation where the acceptance was almost nonexistent made better progress in their reading than did those where they were well accepted.

Whyte in his *Street Corner Society* study of an Italo-American group indicated that the youth from such a background who wishes to really go ahead and make something of himself must become an isolate from his group. The question then arises as to whether these permissive classrooms with their methodologies geared to social acceptance, their concern for the isolate—that he be brought into social participation—may be middle-class educational methodologies that we have adapted to children of lower social class without effect. It may be a technique utilized to make "baby sitting" with them palatable without its contributing educational merit.

The role of tension. It is doubtful that any learning of consequence is achieved without some tension and anxiety. In some middle-class neighborhoods, the school's role is more to shield the child from anxiety so overpowering that it interferes with learning. In the deviant cultural situations, however, reversal of these roles may be needed. How to induce a certain amount of anxiety without being considered rejecting of the children is not easy. Again, one wonders if the methodologies validated on middle-class children are useful for the disadvantaged.

The Alternatives

In conclusion, it appears that education in the inner cities is faced with two possibilities in dealing with the powerless. They are not necessarily exclusive, but they are different. The first is the traditional way. They can get the bright ones involved, alienating them in their sentiments and sympathies from the group of which they are a part. They can make them ashamed of their heritage, and hold out the hope to them that if they will meet the standards of the dominant group they will be recognized. The schools can take them on trips and show them the few of their kind who have made it and hold good jobs. They can persuade some of them to become alienated from their groups and try to aspire to the horizons which the dominant group holds out to them. It will be especially helpful if the teachers will tell them about good jobs they can get. This is a materialistic culture, and it can be figured on the average, at least, how much it is worth per day to stay in school.

In this context the power order will follow the path of the British as they dealt with colonial possessions—when tension arises, squirt a little more welfare on the powerless. This will keep them sufficiently tranquilized in Egypt that they will not seek out the promised land. This will be costly, but it will mean that the power order is not threatened. Those who are transmuted through these processes will not provide leadership in creating dysfunction in the system. Frazier has described them in the *Black Bourgeoisie*. This group will sit on the sidelines as long as possible when tension occurs and will come into action only when maneuvered by the mass. Each grant made to provide ever more costly services will give high visibility to those who give it and those who receive it. Each such largesse will further push down the masses of the Negro community, for each grant further reinforces the sterotype that the problem is really the human potential, the children and their parents, and not the society itself. Ultimately, however, under these circumstances the group can be dissolved into the mainstream — if there is time enough.

The alternative to this so-called integration approach resides in the Negro group itself taking power and moving under self-direction. In this situation the youth are challenged to learn what the schools have to offer because they need it to prepare themselves to make their maximum contribution to the group's efforts. This approach calls for conflict, that is, the ability to bring to bear the pressures necessary to make one's interests felt in communal decision-making. This does not necessarily mean violence. It means inducing dysfunction into *the system* until the social order comes to recognize the interdependency of the whole to its parts.

This taking of power is the hope of the present revolution. It provides a new faith, a new hope, it gives the powerless a sense of potency that he has not had before. Educators identified with the power structure that is, become frustrated and confused when the school boycotts come. They fume about these parents and leaders teaching children to disobey the law. They do not understand that this "taking of power" is the antidote to apathy. They should use the opportunity it affords to assist children to identify with the fight. They should point out the great contribution being made by such leaders as Martin Luther King. His letter from the Birmingham jail should be among the most prized literary compositions of Americans.

In this identification with the revolution should also come the interpretation of the need to study to make oneself capable of "carrying responsibility for" his share in the undertaking. In the community, the school should also identify with this upreach of the human spirit. There should be encouragement to grapple with the issues, so that growth is made in functioning as a citizen. The infusion of such hope should be a powerful stimulus to learning. Immediately after emancipation, the Negroes had great hopes of participating worthily with the white in making the new destiny of the South. They tied their Bibles between the plow handles so they could study as they farmed. Then came the abdication of federal power and the era of violence in which this light of hope was blown out. Today is is rekindled. This time there will not be abandonment of rights by the federal government. What was then a mirage must now become a reality. Negroes must learn the art and skill of taking power — as they rapidly are doing. They must learn the responsibilities which go with it—which they rapidly are doing. Out of this process with a little help, will come a sense that there are no footnotes to this American creed. It includes Negroes, too.

Every classroom should be a laboratory in how to take power, how to shield the group from power which is abused, how to work through shared relationships.

You asked about curriculum. Curriculum is the composite of the confrontations that the school provides the youth in his search for self-hood.

The great documents of history have been produced by those who were outside the power order, as they attempted to interpret the upreach and outreach of the human spirit chafing under oppression's yoke. They have not come from those in the power stream who were defending their entrenched positions. Teachers who are handmaidens of the power order should not sell these children of the ghetto short. Out of their protestations is coming the fulfillment of the greatest faith we have—that all men love freedom and that all men have the capacity to participate worthily in the collective direction of their own destiny. Will we as educators see this upreach as goodness and encourage it, or will we stand in the middle of it, be frustrated by it, and let history pass us by? This is a moral issue and not a racial one. We are threatened when the Negro psychologically disengages himself from interracial efforts, because he does not trust us. Whether white teachers can lead these students of the depressed areas out of their apathy depends on whether we can sufficiently identify with them that we together lose sense of who is Negro and who is white, but rather see ourselves enlisted together in a common moral encounter. Consequently, it is not for the Negro's sake alone that we are involved in these conferences. It is for the sake of the souls of us all as well.

BIBLIOGRAPHY
AND INDEX

Selected Bibliography *

Books

Allen, Robert L.; Virginia F. Allen and Margaret Shute. *English Sounds and Their Spellings.* New York: Thomas Y. Crowell Company, 1966.

Almy, Millie; Edward Chittenden and Paula Miller. *Young Children's Thinking: Studies of Some Aspects of Piaget's Thinking.* New York: Teachers College Press, Columbia University, 1966.

Ausubel, David P. *The Psychology of Meaningful Verbal Learning.* New York: Grune and Stratton, 1963.

Beck, John M. and Richard W. Saxe (eds.). *Teaching the Culturally Disadvantaged Pupil.* Springfield, Ill.: Charles C. Thomas, 1965.

Bereiter, Carl and S. Engelmann. *Teaching Disadvantaged Children in the Preschool.* Englewood Cliffs, N.J.: Prentice-Hall, 1966.

Bernstein, Abraham. *The Education of Urban Populations.* New York: Random House, 1967.

Bloom, Benjamin S. *Stability and Change in Human Characteristics.* New York: John Wiley and Sons, 1964.

———; Alison Davis and Robert Hess. *Compensatory Education for Cultural Deprivation.* New York: Holt, Rinehart and Winston, 1965.

Booth, Robert E., et al. *Culturally Disadvantaged: A Keyword-in-Context Index.* Detroit: Wayne State Press, 1966.

Brady, Elizabeth H. (ed.). *Seminar Selections on the Disadvantaged Child.* New York: Selected Academic Readings, no date.

Cervantes, L. F. *The Dropout: Causes and Cures.* Ann Arbor: The University of Michigan Press, 1965.

Cheyney, Arnold B. *Teaching Culturally Disadvantaged in the Elementary School.* Columbus, Ohio: Charles E. Merrill Books, Inc., 1967.

Cicourel, Aaron V. and John I. Kitsuse. *The Educational Decision-Makers.* New York: Bobbs-Merrill Co., 1965.

Clark, Kenneth B. *Dark Ghetto: Dilemmas of Social Power.* New York: Harper and Row, 1965.

---

*This selected bibliography includes only materials published since **Education in Depressed Areas** was published in 1963. In this volume, there are no listings of school reports and bulletins. Information about unpublished materials and journal articles is now available from the Educational Research and Information Center (ERIC) on the Disadvantaged. For further details, write to: Information Retrieval Center on the Disadvantaged, Ferkhauf Graduate School of Yeshiva University, 55 Fifth Avenue, New York, New York 10003. See also: U.S. Office of Education, Educational Research Information Center, **Catalog of Selected Documents on the Disadvantaged, Number and Author Index** (OE-37001) and **Subject Index** (OE-37002). Washington: U.S. Government Printing Office, 1966.

────── and Lawrence Plotkin. *The Negro Student at Integrated Colleges.* New York: National Scholarship Service and Fund for Negroes, 1963.

Crosby, Muriel. *An Adventure in Human Relations.* Chicago: Follett Publishing Co., 1965.

Crow, Lester D.; Walter I. Murray and Hugh M. Smythe. *Educating the Culturally Disadvantaged Child: Principles and Programs.* New York: David McKay Company, 1966.

Dacanay, Fe. *Techniques and Procedures of Second Language Teaching.* Quezon City, Philippines: Phoenix Publishing Co., 1960.

Dentler, R. A., and Mary Ellen Warshauer. *Big City Dropouts.* New York: Center for Urban Education, 1965.

Eddy, Elizabeth M. *Walk the White Line: A Profile of Urban Education.* New York: Doubleday Anchor Books, 1967.

Elkins, Deborah. *Reading Improvement in the Junior High School.* New York: Teachers College Press, Columbia University, 1963.

Educational Policies Commission. *American Education and the Search for Equal Opportunity.* Washington: National Education Association, 1965.

Ferman, Louis; Joyce L. Kornbluh and Alan Huber (eds.). *Poverty in America: A Book of Readings.* Ann Arbor, Mich.: The University of Michigan Press, 1965.

Frost, Joe L. and Glenn R. Hawkes (eds.). *The Disadvantaged Child: Issues and Innovations.* Boston: Houghton Mifflin Co., 1966.

Fuchs, Estelle. *Pickets at the Gates.* New York: The Free Press, 1966.

Fusco, Gene C. *School-Home Partnership in Depressed Urban Neighborhoods.* Washington: U.S. Government Printing Office, 1964.

Gittell, Marilyn. *Participants and Participation: A Study of School Policy in New York City.* New York: Center for Urban Education, 1966.

────── (ed.). *Educating an Urban Population: Implications for Public Policy.* Beverly Hills, Calif.: Sage Publications, 1967.

Gleason, H. A. *Linguistics and English Grammar.* New York: Holt, Rinehart and Winston, 1965.

Gordon, Margaret S. (ed.). *Poverty in America.* San Francisco: Chandler Publishing Co., 1965.

Gowan, John C. and George D. Demos (eds.). *The Disadvantaged and Potential Dropout: Compensatory Educational Programs, a Book of Readings.* Springfield, Ill.: Charles C. Thomas, 1966.

Gray, Susan W.; Rupert A. Klaus, James O. Miller and Bettye J. Forrester. *Before First Grade: The Early Training Project for Culturally Disadvantaged Children.* New York: Teachers College Press, 1966.

Greene, Mary F. and Orletta Ryan. *The School Children: Growing Up in the Slums.* New York: Pantheon, 1965.

Havighurst, Robert J. *Education in Metropolitan Areas.* Boston: Allyn and Bacon, 1966.

————. *The Public Schools of Chicago.* Chicago: The Board of Education of the City of Chicago, 1964.

Hechinger, Fred M. (ed.). *Pre-School Education Today.* Garden City, N.Y.: Doubleday and Co., 1966.

Heller, Celia S. *Mexican American Youth: Forgotten Youth at the Crossroads.* New York: Random House, 1966.

Hentoff, Nat. *Our Children Are Dying.* New York: Viking Press, 1966.

Herman, Melvin and Stanley Sadofsky. *Youth-Work Programs: Problems of Planning and Operation.* New York: New York University Press, 1967.

Hickerson, Nathaniel. *Education for Alienation.* Englewood Cliffs, N.J.: Prentice-Hall, 1966.

Humphrey, Hubert H. (ed.). *Integration vs. Segregation.* New York: Thomas Y. Crowell Co., 1964.

Hunnicutt, C. W. (ed.). *Urban Education and Cultural Deprivation.* Syracuse, N.Y.: Syracuse University Press, 1964.

Janowitz, Gayle. *Helping Hands: Volunteer Work in Education.* Chicago: University of Chicago Press, 1965.

Jewett, Arno; Joseph Mersand and Doris V. Gunderson (eds.). *Improving English Skills of Culturally Different Youth in Large Cities.* Washington: U.S. Government Printing Office, 1964.

Kendall, Robert. *White Teacher in a Black School.* New York: Devin-Adair, 1964.

Keniston, Kenneth. *The Uncommitted: Alienated Youth in American Society.* New York: Harcourt, Brace and World, 1965.

Kerber, August and Barbara Bommarito (eds.). *The Schools and the Urban Crisis.* New York: Holt, Rinehart and Winston, 1965.

Klopf, Gordon and Garda W. Bowman. *Teacher Education in a Social Context: A Study of the Preparation of School Personnel for Working with Disadvantaged Children and Youth.* New York: Mental Health Materials Center, 1966.

Klopf, Gordon and Israel Laster (eds.). *Integrating the Urban Schools.* New York: Teachers College Press, 1963.

Kvaraceus, William C. *et al. Negro Self-Concept: Implications for School and Citizenship.* New York: McGraw-Hill Company, 1965.

Lanning, Frank W. and Wesley A. Many. *Basic Education for the Disadvantaged Adult: Theory and Practice.* Boston: Houghton Mifflin Co., 1966.

Lin, San-su C. *Pattern Practice in the Teaching of Standard English to Students with a Nonstandard Dialect.* New York: Teachers College Press, Columbia University, 1965.

Loretan, Joseph O. and Shelley Umans. *Teaching the Disadvantaged.* New York: Teachers College Press, Columbia University, 1966.

Manuel, Herschel T. *Spanish-Speaking Children of the Southwest.* Austin: University of Texas Press, 1965.

Mayerson, Charlotte L. (ed.). *Two Blocks Apart: Juan Gonzales and Peter Quinn*. New York: Holt, Rinehart and Winston, 1965.

McGeoch, Dorothy *et al*. *Learning to Teach in Urban Schools*. New York: Teachers Collège Press, 1965.

McGrath, Earl J. *The Predominantly Negro Colleges and Universities in Transition*. New York: Teachers College Press, Columbia University, 1965.

Miller, Elizabeth W. (ed.). *The Negro in America: A Bibliography*. Cambridge, Mass.: Harvard University Press, 1966.

Miller, Harry L. (ed.). *Education for the Disadvantaged: Current Issues and Research*. New York: The Free Press, 1967.

—— and Marjorie B. Smiley. *Education in the Metropolis*. New York: The Free Press, 1967.

Moore, G. Alexander, Jr. *Realities of the Urban Classroom: Observations in Elementary Schools*. Garden City, N.Y.: Doubleday and Company, 1967.

National Council of Teachers of English. *Language Programs for the Disadvantaged*. Champaign, Ill.: The Council, 1965.

Noar, Gertrude. *The Teacher and Integration*. Washington: National Education Association, 1966.

Panel of Consultants on Vocational Education. *Education for a Changing World of Work*. Washington: U.S. Government Printing Office, 1963.

Panel on Educational Research and Development, The President's Science Advisory Committee. *Innovation and Experiment in Education*. Washington: U.S. Government Printing Office, 1964.

Passow, A. Harry; Miriam Goldberg and Abraham J. Tannenbaum. *Education of the Disadvantaged: A Book of Readings*. New York: Holt, Rinehart and Winston, 1967.

Pearl, Arthur and Frank Riessman. *New Careers for the Poor: The Nonprofessional in Human Service*. New York: The Free Press, 1965.

Pettigrew, Thomas F. *A Profile of the Negro American*. Princeton, N.J.: D. Van Nostrand Company, Inc., 1964.

Rainwater, Lee and William L. Yancey (eds.). *The Moynihan Report and the Politics of Controversy*. Cambridge, Mass.: The M.I.T. Press, 1967.

Reiss, Albert J., Jr. *Schools in a Changing Society*. New York: The Free Press, 1965.

Riessman, Frank. *Helping the Disadvantaged Pupil to Learn More Easily*. Englewood Cliffs, N.J.: Prentice-Hall, Inc., 1966.

Roberts, Joan I. (ed.). *School Children in the Urban Slum: Readings in Social Science Research*. New York: The Free Press, 1967.

Schlesinger, Benjamin. *Poverty in Canada and the United States: Overview and Annotated Bibliography*. Toronto: University of Toronto Press, 1966.

Schreiber, Daniel (ed.). *The School Dropout*. Washington: National Education Association, 1964.

———— and Bernard A. Kaplan. *Guidance and the School Dropout.* Washington: American Personnel and Guidance Association, 1964.

———— and Robert D. Strom. *Dropout Studies: Design and Conduct.* Washington: National Education Association, 1963.

Sexton, Patricia C. *Spanish Harlem: Anatomy of Poverty.* New York: Harper and Row, 1965.

Sheldon, Eleanor B. and Raymond A. Glazier. *Pupils and Schools in New York City: A Fact Book.* New York: Russell Sage Foundation, 1965.

Shuy, Roger W. (ed.). *Social Dialects and Language Learning.* Champaign, Ill.: National Council of Teachers of English, 1964.

Silberman, Charles E. *Crisis in Black and White.* New York: Random House, 1964.

Smith, Alfred G. (ed.). *Communication and Culture: Readings in the Codes of Human Interaction.* New York: Holt, Rinehart and Winston, 1966.

Stewart, William A. (ed.). *Non-Standard Speech and the Teaching of English.* Washington: Center for Applied Linguistics, 1964.

Strom, Robert D. *Teaching the Slum Child.* Columbus, Ohio: Charles E. Merrill, 1965.

Sullivan, Neil V.; Thomas L. Maynard and Carol L. Yellin. *Bound for Freedom: An Educator's Adventures in Prince Edward County, Virginia.* Boston: Little, Brown and Co., 1965.

Swanson, Bert E. *The Struggle for Equality.* New York: Hobbs, Dorman and Co., 1966.

Taba, Hilda and Deborah Elkins. *Teaching Strategies for the Culturally Disadvantaged.* Chicago: Rand McNally and Co., 1966.

Thomas, R. Murray. *Social Differences in the Classroom: Social-Class, Ethnic and Religious Problems.* New York: David McKay Co., 1965.

Torrance, E. Paul and Robert D. Strom (eds.). *Mental Health and Achievement: Increasing Potential and Reducing School Dropout.* New York: John Wiley and Sons, 1965.

U.S. Office of Education. *Programs for the Educationally Disadvantaged.* Bulletin 1963, No. 17. Washington: U.S. Government Printing Office, 1963.

Usdan, Michael and Frederick Bertolaet (eds.). *Teachers for the Disadvantaged.* Chicago: Follett Publishing Co., 1966.

Washington, Bennetta B. *Youth in Conflict: Helping Behavior-Problem Youth in a School Setting.* Chicago: Science Research Associates, Inc., 1963.

Wattenberg, William W. (ed.). *Social Deviancy Among Youth.* Sixty-Fifth Yearbook, Part I of the National Society for the Study of Education. Chicago: University of Chicago Press, 1966.

Webster, Staten W. (ed.). *The Disadvantaged Learner: Knowing, Understanding, Educating.* San Francisco, Calif.: The Chandler Publishing Company, 1966.

Weinberg, Meyer (ed.). *Learning Together: A Book on Integrated Education.* Chicago: Integrated Education Associates, 1964.

Witty, Paul A. (ed.). *The Educationally Retarded and Disadvantaged.* Sixty-sixth Yearbook, Part I of the National Society for the Study of Education. Chicago: University of Chicago Press, 1967.

Articles

Ausubel, David P. "A Teaching Strategy for Culturally Deprived Pupils: Cognitive and Motivational Considerations," *School Review,* 71 (Winter 1963), 454–463.

————. "Some Psychological and Educational Limitations of Learning by Discovery," *Arithmetic Teacher,* 11 (1964), 290–302.

————. "How Reversible Are the Cognitive and Motivational Effects of Cultural Deprivation? Implications for Teaching the Culturally Deprived Child," *Urban Education,* 1 (Summer 1964), 16–38.

———— and Pearl Ausubel. "Ego Development among Segregated Negro Children," in *Education in Depressed Areas,* ed. A. Harry Passow. New York: Teachers College Press, Columbia University, 1963.

Beilin, H. "Perceptual Cognitive Conflict in the Development of an Invariant Area Concept," *J. of Experimental Child Psychology,* 1 (1964), 208–226.

————. "Learning and Operational Convergence in Logical Thought Development," *J. of Experimental Child Psychology,* 2 (1965), 317–339.

————. "Feedback and Infralogical Strategies in Invariant Area Conceptualization," *J. of Experimental Child Psychology,* 3 (1966), 267–278.

————; J. Kagan and R. Rabinowitz. "Effects of Verbal and Perceptual Training on Water Level Representation," *Child Development,* 37 (1966), 317–329.

Bienstock, H. "Realities of the Job Market for the High School Dropout," in *Guidance and the School Dropout,* ed. Daniel Schreiber. Washington: National Education Association, 1964.

Bond, Guy L., and Robert Dykstra. "The Role of the Coordinating Center in the Cooperative Research Program," *The Reading Teacher,* 19 (May 1966), 565–568.

Braun, Jean S. "Relationship between Concept Formation Ability and Reading Achievement at Three Developmental Levels," *Child Development,* 34 (September 1963), 675–682.

Brookover, Wilbur B. and Thomas Shiler. "Self-Concept of Ability and School Achievement," *Sociology of Education,* 37 (1964), 271–278.

Bruner, Jerome S. "The Course of Cognitive Growth," *American Psychologist,* 9 (January 1964), 1–15.

————. "Some Theorems of Instruction Illustrated with Reference to

Mathematics," in *Theories of Learning and Instruction*, ed. E. P. Hilgard. Sixty-third Yearbook, N.S.S.E., Part 1, Chicago, Ill.: University of Chicago Press, 1964.

————. "Learning and Thinking," in *Readings in the Psychology of Cognition*, eds. Richard C. Anderson and David P. Ausubel. New York: Holt, Rinehart and Winston, 1965.

Clark, Kenneth B. "The Cult of Cultural Deprivation: A Complex Social Psychological Phenomenon," in *Environmental Deprivation and Enrichment*. New York: Ferkhauf Graduate School of Education, Yeshiva University, 1965.

Carter, Robert L. "De Facto School Segregation: An Examination of the Legal and Constitutional Questions Presented," *Western Reserve Law Review*, 16 (May 1965), 527.

Chall, Jeanne and Shirley Feldmann. "First Grade Reading: An Analysis of the Interactions of Professed Methods. Teacher Implementation and Child Background," *The Reading Teacher*, 19 (May 1966), 569–575.

Cronbach, L. J. "Issues Current in Educational Psychology," in *Mathematical Learning*, eds. L. N. Morrisett and J. Vinsonhaler. *Monographs of the Society for Research in Child Development*, 30 (1965), 109–125.

Dale, Edgar. "Life Management Curriculum," *The Newsletter*, 29 (November 1963), 1–4.

Davis, Alva L. "Communication Barriers to the Culturally Deprived," Washington, D.C.: U.S. Office of Education Cooperative Research Project 2107, 1965.

————. "English for Foreigner and Native," *College English*, 26 (January 1965), 273–276.

Dentler, R. "Dropouts, Automation, and the Cities," *Teachers College Record*, 65 (1964), 475–483.

Deutsch, Cynthia P. "Auditory Discrimination and Learning: Social Factors," *Merrill-Palmer Quarterly*, 10 (July 1964), 277–296.

Deutsch, Martin P. "The Disadvantaged Child and the Learning Process," in *Education in Depressed Areas*, ed. A. Harry Passow. New York: Teachers College Press, Columbia University, 1963.

————. "The Role of Social Class in Language Development and Cognition," *American Journal of Orthopsychiatry*, 35 (January 1965), 78–88.

Duncan, Carl P. "Transfer after Training with Single versus Multiple Tasks," in *Readings in the Psychology of Cognition*, eds. Richard C. Anderson and David P. Ausubel. New York: Holt, Rinehart and Winston, 1965.

Eisenberg, Leon. "Strengths of the Inner-City Child," *Baltimore Bulletin of Education*, 41 (1963–64), 10–16.

Friedlander, Bernard Z. "A Psychologist's Second Thoughts on Concepts,

Curiosity, and Discovery in Teaching and Learning," *Harvard Educational Review*, 35 (Winter 1965), 18–38.

Goldberg, Miriam. "Adapting Teacher Style to Pupil Difference," *Merrill Palmer Quarterly*, 10 (April 1964), 161–178.

Gray, Susan and Rupert A. Klaus, "An Experimental Preschool Program for Culturally Deprived Children," *Child Development*, 36 (1965), 887–898.

Harmin, Merrill and Sidney B. Simon. "The Year the Schools Began Teaching the Telephone Directory," *Harvard Educational Review*, (Summer 1965), 326–331.

Harris, Albert J. and Blanche L. Server. "Comparing Reading Approaches in First-Grade Teaching with Disadvantaged Children," *The Reading Teacher*, 19 (May 1966), 631–635.

Haubrich, Vernon F. "Teachers for Big-City Schools," in *Education in Depressed Areas*, ed. A. Harry Passow. New York: Teachers College Press, Columbia University, 1963.

Hess, R. D. and D. J. Jackson. "Some New Dimensions in Providing Equal Educational Opportunity," *Journal of Negro Education*, 34 (1965), 220–231.

Hess, R. D. and Virginia Shipman. "Early Experience and the Socialization of Cognitive Modes in Children," *Child Development*, 36 (1965), 869–886.

Hillerich, Robert L. "Pre-Reading Skills in Kindergarten: A Second Report," *Elementary School Journal*, 65 (March 1965), 312–317.

Holland, John L. and James M. Richards, Jr. "Academic and Nonacademic Accomplishment: Correlated or Uncorrelated?" *ACT Research Reports*, 2 (April 1965), 20.

Hunt, J. McVicker. "How Children Develop Intellectually," *Children*, 11 (May–June 1964), 83–91.

———. "The Psychological Basis for Using Preschool Enrichment as an Antidote for Cultural Deprivation," *Merrill-Palmer Quarterly*, 10 (July 1964), 209–248.

Inhelder, B. *et al.* "Comment: On Cognitive Development." *American Psychologist*, 21 (1966), 160–164.

John, Vera P. and Leo S. Goldstein. "The Social Context of Language Acquisition," *Merrill-Palmer Quarterly*, 10 (July 1964), 265–276.

Johnson, Marjorie S. and Roy A. Kress. "Philadelphia's Educational Improvement Program," *The Reading Teacher*, 18 (March 1965), 488–492.

Katz, Irwin. "Review of Evidence Relating to the Effects of Desegregation on the Intellectual Performance of Negroes," *American Psychologist*, 19 (June 1964), 381–399.

Klineberg, Otto, "Life is Fun in a Smiling, Fair-Skinned World," *Saturday Review* (February 16, 1963), 77.

Lafferty, J. Clayton. "Values That Defeat Learning," in *Proceedings, Eighth Interinstitutional Seminar in Child Development*, 1962.

Dearborn, Mich.: The Edison Institute, 1963.

Leiderman, Gloria. "Mental Development and Learning of Mathematics in Slow-Learning Children," in *Conference on Mathematics Education for Below-Average Achievers.* Stanford, Palo Alto, Calif.: School Mathematics Study Group, 1964.

Lin, San-su C. "An Experiment in Changing Dialect Patterns: The Claflin Project," *College English*, 24 (May 1963), 644–647.

Lowry, W. C. "Structure and the Algorisms of Arithmetic," *The Arithmetic Teacher*, 12 (1965), 146–150.

Mastain, R. K. and B. C. Nossoff. "Mathematics in the Kindergarten," *The Arithmetic Teacher*, 13 (1966), 32–36.

McCanne, Roy. "Approaches to First Grade English Reading Instruction for Children from Spanish-Speaking Homes," *The Reading Teacher*, 19 (May 1966), 670–676.

Musgrave, Marianne E. "Teaching English as a Foreign Language to Students with Substandard Dialects," *CIA Journal*, 7 (September 1963), 84–91.

Reese, H. W. "Verbal Mediation as a Function of Age Level," *Psychological Bulletin*, 59 (1962), 502–509.

Riessman, Frank. "The Culturally Deprived Child: A New View," in *Programs for the Educationally Disadvantaged.* Washington, D.C.: U.S. Government Printing Office, 1963.

Robinson, G. E. "The Role of Geometry in Elementary School Mathematics," *The Arithmetic Teacher*, 13 (1966), 3–10.

Rohrer, J. H. "Psychosocial Development and Acting-Out Behavior," ed. Daniel Schreiber, *Guidance and the School Dropout.* Washington: National Education Association, 1964.

Savitsky, C. "Reaching the Disadvantaged," in *Mental Health and Achievement: Increasing Potential and Reducing School Dropout,* eds. V. Paul Torrance and Robert D. Strom. New York: John Wiley and Sons, 1965.

Schreiber, D. "Juvenile Delinquency and the School Dropout Problem," *Federal Probation*, 27 (September 1963), 15–19.

———. "An Introduction to the School Dropout," in *Guidance and the School Dropout.* Washington: National Education Association, 1964.

Silberstein, Richard M., *et al.* "Can Head Start Help Children Learn?" *Reading Teacher*, 19 (February 1966), 347–351.

Strodtbeck, Fred L. "The Hidden Curriculum of the Middle-Class Home," in *Urban Education and Cultural Deprivation*, ed. C. W. Hunnicutt. Syracuse: Syracuse University Press, 1964.

Taba, Hilda. "Cultural Deprivation as a Factor in School Learning," *Merrill-Palmer Quarterly*, 10 (April 1964), 147–159.

Voss, H. L.; A. Wendling and D. S. Elliott. "Some Types of High School Dropouts," *The Journal of Educational Research*, 59 (April 1966), 363–368.

Wallach, L. and R. L. Sprott. "Inducing Number Conservation in Children," *Child Development,* 35 (1964), 1057–1071.

Whiteman, Martin. "Developmental Theory and Enrichment Programs," in *Environmental Deprivation and Enrichment.* New York: Ferkhauf Graduate School of Education, Yeshiva University, 1965.

———. "Intelligence and Learning," *Merrill-Palmer Quarterly,* 10 (July 1964), 297–309.

Wolf, Richard M. "The Measurement of Environments," in *Proceedings of the 1964 Invitational Conference on Testing Problems.* Princeton, N. J.: Educational Testing Service, 1965.

Index

acculturation of disadvantaged, 111 ff.
action style of disadvantaged, 9–10;
65–70
ADLER, A., 328
adults, as mediators in cognitive development, 161–163; as models, 70;
as motivation, 162–163; as sources of
information, 163; see also mothers;
parents
AFDC, 270
affect, as linked to cognition, 21, 25 ff.;
defined, 25, 27–28; as instructional
content, 28 ff.; as sacrificed in conventional programs, 27 ff.; school's
assumptions about, 29
affective concerns, cues to, 37 ff.; of
disadvantaged, 38; and instruction,
35 ff.; integrated with outcomes of
learning, 39–40; vs. interests, 29,
36–37
affective development, importance for
cognitive development, 25–26
aid to families with dependent children
(AFDC), 270
ALEXANDER, J., 268, 281
algorithmic method, arguments
against, 141–142; defense of, 142–143
All-Day Neighborhood School Program, 54
ALLEN, R. L., 222, 341
ALLEN, VIRGINIA F., 205–206, 222,
341
ALMY, MILLIE, 13, 17, 145, 153, 341
ALPERN, G. D., 55 n., 57
ANDERSON, R. C., 183, 347
APEX, see Project APEX
ASHT, W., 73
ASHTON-WARNER, SYLVIA, 69, 73
ASTIN, 27
AUSUBEL, D. P., 6, 7, 11, 12, 13, 17,
128, 141, 143, 145, 149, 153, 161,
162, 167, 183, 341, 346, 347
AUSUBEL, PEARL, 7, 13, 17, 346

BAILEY, BERYL, 223
Baltimore Area Health and Welfare
Council, 3
Bank Street College, 70
Banneker Group, 321

BARROWS, MARJORIE, 216, 223
basal reader in programs for disadvantaged, 70, 100, 193 ff., 201–202,
292
BEAR, ROBERTA M., 127, 128
BECK, J. M., 341
beginning teaching in inner-city
schools, 238–239; see also teacher
induction
BEILIN, H., xv, 131–132, 137, 144, 145,
150, 153, 154, 346
belonging as motivation, 168–169
BEREITER, C., 57, 341
BERNSTEIN, B., 8, 13, 17, 114 n., 128,
135, 151, 154, 161, 162, 183
BERTOLAET, F., 345
BIENSTOCK, H., 267, 280, 346
bilingualism, see standard English as
second language; language; dis-
advantaged groups in U.S. popula-
tion
Biological Sciences Curriculum Study,
24
BLOOM, B. S., 11, 13, 17, 319, 324, 341
BOND, G. L., 189, 203, 324, 346
BOWMAN, P. H., 271, 281
BRAZZIEL, F. F., 294, 303
BRADLEY, BEATRICE E., 189, 203
BRAIN, G., 71
BRAUN, JEAN S., 13, 17, 346
BREEN, JOSEPH M., 54 n.
BRIDGE Project, The, 163 ff., 183
BRINK, CAROL R., 179
BROOKOVER, W. B., 183, 346
BROPHY, J., 114, 128
Brown vs. Board of Education (1954),
309–310, 313, 318; see also U.S.
Supreme Court
BRUNER, J. S., 13, 17, 144, 145, 147,
154, 183, 346, 347
Bureau of Elementary and Secondary
Education, 78, 85
business, role in dropout prevention
programs, 279

CARTER, R. L., 309, 322, 345
CERVANTES, L. F., 259, 272, 273, 278,
281, 341
CHALL, JEANNE, 189, 192, 203, 346

353

concept, definition, 139; in learning, 139; relation to syntactical rules, 139
concrete material, role in developing abstractions, 161–162
conservation, acquisition of, 144–145; necessary conditions, 145–146; Piaget's conflict theory about, 145; training, formal vs. informal, 136
consumer education, in high school programs, 83
COON, C. S., 228 n., 243
COUNTS, G., 307
CRONBACH, L. J., 141, 154, 347
CROW, L. D., 188, 203, 342
cultural deprivation, concept questioned, xiii; see also disadvantaged
cultural gap, between teacher and community, 297–298; efforts to bridge it, 297–298
curriculum for disadvantaged, 13 ff., 21–43, 133–145, 276–278; see also disadvantaged, high-school dropout prevention, instructional model, language, learning sequences, Mobilization for Youth, reading instruction, schools for disadvan-